Blessed Are the Peacemakers

Blessed Are the Peacemakers

Pacifism, Just War, and Peacebuilding

LISA SOWLE CAHILL

FORTRESS PRESS
MINNEAPOLIS

BLESSED ARE THE PEACEMAKERS

Pacifism, Just War, and Peacebuilding

Scripture texts in this work are taken from the New Revised Standard Version Bible © 1989, Division of Christian Education of the National Council of the Churches of Christ in the United States of America. Used by permission. All rights reserved.

Cover image: Medallion with bird and three olive branches. From Tunisia. Late Roman mosaic, 48 x 43 cm. Inv. Cl.17505. Caroline Rose. © RMN-Grand Palais / Art Resource, NY

Cover design: Laurie Ingram

Print ISBN: 978-1-5064-3165-9

eBook ISBN: 978-1-5064-5779-6

The paper used in this publication meets the minimum requirements of American National Standard for Information Sciences — Permanence of Paper for Printed Library Materials, ANSI Z329.48-1984.

Manufactured in the U.S.A.

Contents

Preface

I believe that the most important challenge facing Christian ethicists in the twenty-first century is not so much to figure out what is the normative content of a Christian, biblical ethical-political theory but how to make the content that is already more than obvious (to love God and neighbor, including the "enemy" and prioritizing "the poor") practical and transformative in the real world. The "real world" today is one in which human connections are intensified and magnified, thanks to economic globalization and to the rapid, globe-spanning development of new communication and transportation technologies. It is also a world in which economic inequality rages, violence kills hundreds of thousands a day, and women and racial-ethnic minorities are trapped in subhuman lives. In other words, to use a phrase from Augustine, the *libido dominandi* (lust to dominate) still controls much of human motivation and behavior. Centuries of Christian theology, ethics, and political analysis have done little to reduce its power. Where is our sense of shared humanity and respect? Where are Christ's resurrection and the Holy Spirit? Where is the renewal of all creation? Where is the "reign of God" Jesus Christ not only promised but inaugurated? Where is the church as "body of Christ," called to share in Christ's ministry of reconciliation (2 Cor 5:11–21)?

The present work addresses an important part of the appalling picture of contemporary global society: violent political and societal conflict including but not limited to war. The work's primary aim is to make an ethical, theological, and practical argument for Christian peacebuilding as an answer to the question: "Where is the church?" I see peacebuilding as an alternative to more traditional forms of just war theory and pacifism and as an effective way to transform conditions of violence and lead to just and sustainable peace. Yet, although this book is a call to the church, it is also a call to Christian ethicists to take a new look at our theological-ethical traditions and our current frames of analysis. We should question whether the traditional categories of "just war theory" and "pacifism" suffice to capture the theoretical questions and options relevant to a Christian ethics of war and peace, and whether they represent accurately the realities to which they purportedly speak. As will be developed further in the introduction, it is in fact already the case that Christian just war theorists and pacifists are starting to converge on the practical priority of nonviolently transforming situations of armed military and societal conflict. Peacebuilders bring this commitment front and center, partnering with other religious traditions, civil society, and governmental and nongovernmental organizations to avoid and reduce violence and rebuild violence-torn societies.

I believe that traditional just war thinking and pacifism have ignored or underestimated the fact that both killing in war, and the refusal of force to defend innocent life, place agents (individual and collective) in a moral bind. Killing is never unambiguously right because, even in self-defense, killing violates the inalienable dignity of another human being. Renunciation of force is also morally ambiguous, insofar as an agent declines to rescue a fellow human from a grievous assault on his or her dignity. Decisions to use or not use force cannot always free even rightly acting agents from guilt and remorse, even when they are convinced they "did the right thing" on the whole. Just war and pacifism, therefore, must yield to the more pragmatic, realistic, and appropriately ambiguous work that is peacebuilding.

A recurring and important question throughout the whole book is whether some moral decisions engage agents in "irreducible moral dilemmas," understood as situations in which there is no available course of action that does not somehow involve the agent in wrongdoing, *even though* the action on the whole may be justified. The prospect that there are some situations in which there is no truly moral way out, for circumstances constrain us from doing everything that we are morally required to do, has been an unpopular one in Christian ethics historically. It calls into question moral freedom, the meaningfulness of justice as a moral standard, and the goodness of God and divine providence. Yet there is a significant philosophical literature on moral dilemmas opening the door to this prospect. The reality of irreducible moral dilemmas shall be brought to bear on Augustine and Aquinas particularly, then invoked in later chapters to assess twentieth-century figures like Dietrich Bonhoeffer and Reinhold Niebuhr, and finally to support the priority this book places on peacebuilding.

A related purpose of the book is to review major figures and movements in Christian tradition, analyzing critically how war and other state-sponsored armed violence has or has not been justified. It therefore can serve as a historical-theological introduction to the main proponents of just war and pacifism, as well as a point of entry to the contemporary ethics of war and peace. The book engages recent scholarly work around focal points in the Christian theological tradition, entering into constructive debates about interpretation and appropriation—e.g., of the New Testament, Augustine, Aquinas, and the Reformers. Finally, it brings forward a synthetic proposal that Christian peacebuilding best represents the Christian commitment both to nonviolence and to political responsibility. Moreover, peacebuilding is engaged and confident that, while the world is torn and suffering, it is still permeated with transformative possibilities.

A point of departure for this work is my 1994 book, *Love Your Enemies: Discipleship, Pacifism, and Just War Theory*. Yet it would not be accurate to say this book is a revision, for three of the chapters (1, 2, and 10) are entirely new, while four more are so extensively rewritten as to constitute a new argument (4–6, and especially 9). The remaining three chapters (3, 7, 8) are significantly updated, and the theses have been adapted to accommodate my new interest in moral dilemmas.

Many things have changed in the twenty-four years since that book appeared—in the geopolitical situation, in theology, and in my own engagement with these issues. On the worldwide scene, we have seen the murderous ethnic conflicts in Bosnia and Rwanda, the 2001 terrorist attacks on the United States (9/11), the deployment of US and allied military forces in Iraq and Afghanistan, the powerful spread of international terrorist organizations, and ramped-up nuclear proliferation. Related phenomena are growing wealth inequality, the 2009 global recession, the resurgence of the political right internationally, and the rebalancing of global political and economic power. In theology, there has been increasing interest in and commitment to global Christianity, interreligious dialogue, and a strengthened resolve among Christians and theologians across denominations to take practical action against global injustices such as the "diseases of the poor," racism, sexism, climate change, and violent conflict, all of which affect vulnerable populations first and most.

Personally, in 2005–10 I served as a theological consultant to the Catholic Peacebuilding Network, sponsored by Catholic Relief Services and the Kroc Institute for International Peace Studies at the University of Notre Dame. The CPN brings together activists, religious representatives, and scholars to address the needs of conflict zones around the world, especially in Mindanao, the Philippines, Colombia, and the Great

Lakes region of Africa. Even before that, I learned from scholarly and collegial interactions with the late Glen Stassen, developer of the "just peacemaking" approach in Protestant theological ethics. In 2016, I was fortunate to participate in a landmark meeting in Rome on "Nonviolence and Just Peace," sponsored by the Vatican Congregation for Justice and Peace and Pax Christi International. That meeting sparked a lively and ongoing debate online, in print, at scholarly conventions, and in person among scholars and others about the continuing viability of just war theory in a violent and unjust world, where the theory is more often used to excuse than to exclude war and where pacifist protests can seem honorable, yet naïve and ineffectual. I am convinced that whether one works out of a Christian just war or pacifist framework, all must be committed both theologically and practically to the urgency of nonviolent conflict transformation. This is a cause behind which all can and should rally—a growing conviction among many international partners.

When I wrote *Love Your Enemies* in the early 1990s, the Vietnamese-American war and the Cold War were recent memories. Many US Christians rightly protested national militarism and war crimes committed in the name of patriotism and democracy. As will be discussed further in the introduction, a powerful US Christian theology and ecclesiology emerged in which the church was called to a countercultural witness in the name of biblical discipleship. I shared (and still share) a widespread impatience with easy rationalizations of violence and the refusal of Christian theologians historically and at present to take the Sermon on the Mount and gospel nonviolence seriously. In the earlier book, even while not defending it strictly, I depicted Christian pacifism as a way of life committed existentially and ecclesially to evangelical ideals, while just war theory was presented more as a theoretical framework tenuously connected to Christian identity and frequently exploited for disordered ends.

Various critics (e.g., James T. Johnson, Joseph L. Allen, John Kelsay, and John Berkman) complained—respectfully—that just war thinking should also be associated with Christian discipleship, specifically with an evangelical call to political responsibility in a world beset by sin. I remain unconvinced that just war embodies the gospel as well as pacifism. Still, I am now more sympathetic to the idea that many occasions on which lethal force is arguably just place agents amid an "irreducible moral dilemma," where neither using nor refusing force leaves agents morally free and clear. On some of these occasions, for example humanitarian intervention, the use of force may be a morally defensible last resort, even in a Christian theological analysis. In other words, neither just war theory nor pacifism are fully satisfactory expressions of gospel identity and community, although each seeks to embody moral values endorsed by Christianity (justice and love). Peacebuilding is not quandary-free either, but it is a theological-practical approach, a creative living-out of Christian and ecclesial identity, that offers much to the avoidance of the dilemma.

The person who first called it to my attention that it might be a good idea to compare my new book to what reviewers had said of the first one was my editor, J. Andrew Edwards. Andy once studied with Douglas Ottati, with whom I shared a dissertation director, James M. Gustafson; and the aforementioned John Berkman was on Andy's dissertation committee. Andy read *Love Your Enemies* in seminary and has a better perspective on its present evolution and potential audience than I do. Thanks for your many insights, Andy.

Many colleagues over many years have provided intellectual and practical engagements that have made these new ideas possible, not least of all members of the alliances mentioned above, and those who have offered critical counterweights. The faculty and doctoral students in ethics in the Boston College Theology Department have been generous and generally amazing interlocutors. Colleagues Stephen Pope, Kenneth Himes, and Erik Owens are working on similar issues of war, peace, and theology, and have had much wisdom to share. Various versions of these chapters have weathered tough, amiable, and invaluable critiques in our Ethics Doctoral Seminar, where faculty and students share research. The same is true of colleagues giving me their precious time in our departmental faculty lunches. I have been privileged to work with many doctoral students writing on questions related to this book and whom I count among my teachers. They include Maureen O'Connell developing a concept of political compassion; Anna Floerke Scheid studying just revolution; Joshua Snyder, David Kwon, and Joseph McCrave writing on aspects of political violence and reconciliation; Elisée Rutagambwa and Marcel Uwineza working on Catholicism and the Rwandan genocide; Stephanie Edwards studying trauma and theological ethics; Joseph Mben, Leocadie Lushombo, and Marianne Tierney, respectively theologizing against gender-based violence in Africa and Latin America; Kate Ward on moral luck; and Kate Jackson-Meyer urging Christian ethicists to confront the reality of tragic dilemmas.

My students are valued companions in the theological quest to understand both the intellectual and the practical dimensions of what we read, think, and write. For decades I have taught "Christian Ethics: Major Figures" as a graduate seminar, where smart and creative emerging theologians helped me grapple with just war as envisioned by Augustine, Aquinas, Luther, and Calvin, and as repudiated by the Radical Reformers. This was especially important in the fall of 2017, when final revisions on this manuscript were in progress. During the following term, we confronted the Christian response to radical evil in "Theology, Ethics and Politics," reading the twentieth-century political theologians who appear in chapter 9 and making the connections to contemporary racism and violence that appear in that same chapter. Fresh questions and perspectives were contributed by a wonderful class of Boston College undergraduates who studied war, peace, and peacebuilding with me in the fall of 2017.

Villanova University, committed to theology in the Augustinian tradition, has provided a hospitable and challenging environment in which to test my evolving thoughts about Augustine's "miserable necessities," war, and moral dilemmas. A 2012 lecture at Villanova entitled "Peacebuilding: A Practical Strategy of Hope" led to chapter 10 of this book. Papers on Augustine were presented on two recent occasions at Villanova, where I profited from the scrutiny of the formidable Augustine scholar, Allan T. Fitzgerald, OSA, and many of his faculty colleagues. In 2016, I was privileged to offer a lecture celebrating the inauguration of Villanova's doctoral program in theology and culture, and in 2017 I was honored to receive the Civitas Dei Award. Also in 2017, I presented another rendition of Augustine at a conference on the thought of Michael Walzer, at the US Military Academy (West Point) and cosponsored by Villanova. Collegial interaction and improvement of my argument on conflict and religious peacebuilding has been provided in many more venues over the past decade including Bellarmine University, Siena College, Fordham University, the University of Notre Dame, the University of Chicago Divinity School, and Arizona State University.

Among those who offered astute comments on and more resources for individual chapters are Gerald Beyer, Craig Ford, Cathleen Kaveny, James Keenan, Kenneth Himes, Richard Miller, Erik Owens, Stephen Pope, and Vanessa White. Many more than these have made up the supportive intellectual community so indispensable to productive and personally enriching scholarship. To all of you, my deep gratitude.

Throughout my theological career—now spanning four decades—my doctoral mentor, James M. Gustafson, has been a strong and unwavering support and influence, although he is a Calvinist and I find in Thomas Aquinas a much more amenable home. Jim Gustafson taught me and many others to appreciate the theological "greats" inside and outside one's own tradition. Gustafson never was interested in collecting "disciples," but taught students to form and refine our own theological positions critically, dialogically, and with appreciation for their existential significance (or lack thereof). I learned from Jim that theological claims are empty or dangerous if they fail the test of human religious experience or trivialize the scandalous reality of human suffering. While Jim might not see as much hope in peacebuilding as I place there, the idea that human beings are entangled in impossible moral situations resonates with his (and Calvin's) conviction that the divine purposes are beyond human understanding. Though now in his nineties, Jim's wide-ranging intellect, finely attuned religious affections, and perceptive readings of our human and Christian condition sustain me (and many other "former" students) through emails and occasional visits to his present home in New Mexico. As far as Jim is concerned, my gratitude is infused with the profound *pietas* owed an exemplary icon of reverence for God and of theological honesty.

1.

From Just War and Pacifism to Peacebuilding
An Introduction

The dual aim of this book is to offer a critical historical understanding of the Christian traditions of pacifism and just war and to illustrate the promise of a newer approach sometimes called "peacebuilding." While pacifists prioritize conformity to the nonviolent Jesus of the gospels, just war theorists maintain that Christians should and can take responsibility for the just ordering of social life, even if force is required to do so. Like pacifists, peacebuilders take their primary inspiration from the life and teaching of Jesus Christ, but they especially stress the fact that he inaugurates God's reign and renews all creation, making it possible to transform social injustices. Like Christian just war theorists, they are committed to social justice but seek alternatives to armed force that are constructive, bridge-building, and politically effective.

Where peacebuilders differ from just war theory is that they give almost exclusive priority to the positive and nonviolent cultivation of peace, rather than to delineating exceptional situations where violence might be justified. Where peacebuilders differ from pacifists is that peacebuilding as a movement and theology brings together partners who disagree on whether some extreme violations of human dignity might make killing to protect the innocent acceptable from a Christian point of view. However—again unlike just war theorists and pacifists—debates about whether violence is forbidden or permitted in extreme situations are not central to how most peacebuilders define their project. The main reason is that they are most concerned about practical results in immediate situations where loss of life is imminent or ongoing. An implied reason is that even when moral analysis is not up to the task of sorting out complex and ambiguous exchanges of violence, specific practical interventions can work. The primary concern of peacebuilders is to create, highlight, and implement concrete alternatives to violence, strategies that can and do transform conflict situations. They aim to do so in a comprehensive, sustainable process that goes beyond conflicts to a just and peaceful society.[1]

The longstanding contention between just war theory and pacifism is part of a deeper, enduring problem in Christian ethics: even though the gospels offer us Jesus's inauguration of God's reign, Christ as redeemer, resurrection life, and inspiration by the Spirit, it seems difficult if not impossible to change the broken conditions of history, eradicate injustice, and establish new patterns of individual and social life. The power of sin is strong. Therefore, Augustine referred to political life and government as full of "miserable necessities" that make it impossible to achieve any true peace in this world.[2] Dominant forms of just war theory and pacifism deny that Christian social action can substantially reorder the world's sinful character or the corrupt nature of government and politics. Pacifists (typically) see nonviolence as possible within the church but not as a realistic social goal. Just war theorists (typically) take for granted that force must be countered by force, conceding that Christian agents of justice will always need access to this tool—and will use it frequently. Yet contemporary theorists on both sides are moving closer together, partly because both envision longer-term social goals. Just war thinkers put renewed emphasis on peace as the motive and purpose of war.[3] "Stringent" or "restrictive" just war theory stresses the truly exceptional nature of justified force, relative to efforts to keep and sustain peace.[4] Meanwhile some pacifists believe that nonviolence can make inroads in public policy, or even that it may be possible to abolish war;[5]

1. Daniel Philpott, "Introduction: Searching for Strategy in an Age of Peacebuilding," in *Strategies of Peace: Transforming Conflict in a Violent World*, ed. Daniel Philpott and Gerard Powers (New York: Oxford University Press, 2010), 4. See also Maryann Cusimano Love, "What Kind of Peace Do We Seek? Emerging Norms of Peacebuilding in Key Political Institutions," in *Peacebuilding: Catholic Theology, Ethics, and Praxis*, ed. Robert J. Schreiter, R. Scott Appleby, and Gerard F. Powers (Maryknoll, NY: Orbis, 2010), 56–91.

2. Augustine, *City of God*, 19.13.1.

3. See Oliver O'Donovan, *The Just War Revisited* (New York: Cambridge University Press, 2003) and Joseph E. Capizzi, *Politics, Justice and War: Christian Governance and the Ethics of Warfare* (New York: Oxford University Press, 2015).

4. For an example of this position, see Gerard F. Powers, "From an Ethics of War to an Ethics of Peacebuilding," in *From Just War to Modern Peace Ethics*, ed. Heinz-Gerhard Justenhoven, William Barbieri Jr., Arbeiten zur Kirchengeschichte (Boston: De Gruyter, 2012), 275–312. Anna Floerke Scheid, while extending just war to include just revolution, links just revolution to Christian hope for justice, and believes resistance to injustice "should always involve nonviolent just peacemaking strategies" and that armed resistance should meet a high bar of justification. See Scheid, *Just Revolution: A Christian Ethic of Political Resistance and Social Transformation* (Lanham, MD: Rowman & Littlefield, 2015), 64.

5. See Arthur J. Laffin and Anne Montgomery, eds., *Swords into Plowshares: Nonviolent Direct*

while others limit the concept to show that it is contingent on historical circumstances (e.g., "nuclear pacifism")[6] or to indicate that its basic presumption of nonviolence is not exceptionlessly absolute (e.g., "realistic pacifism").[7]

Peacebuilders draw from both these camps, insofar as partners with different convictions about the ultimate justifiability of violence can work together to transform conflicts nonviolently. Peacebuilders take seriously the inbreaking power of salvation in historical communities, and do not limit this power to the church. They not only see Christians as agents of social justice but also are convinced that, despite risks and setbacks, nonviolent strategies can and will be effective in avoiding, reducing, and ending conflicts, as well as in fostering the building of just and peaceful societies.

The real prospects that Christian ethics has for moving societies toward peaceful coexistence should—at least to some degree—be measured against social-scientific assessments of the propensity of human beings to violence and of the likelihood that this propensity can be restrained and mutual respect enhanced. Sociobiology and evolutionary psychology have long shown that while competition for resources, xenophobia, and aggression are part of our evolutionary heritage, they do not completely define us. Human beings are also capable of empathy, altruism, and forming social norms and patterns of behavior so that violence is avoided.[8]

Anthropologist Douglas Fry argues, in relation to war, that war is less likely when six conditions obtain: an overarching social identity including potentially competitive groups, interconnections among subgroups, interdependence concerning basic survival needs, values that explicitly reject war and reward peaceableness, symbols and rituals that reinforce peace, and superordinate institutions that negotiate and manage conflict.[9] As illustrations, Fry offers case studies of tribes from the Upper

Action for Disarmament, Peace, Social Justice (Marion, SD: Fortkamp, 1996) and David Carroll Cochran, *Catholic Realism and the Abolition of War* (Maryknoll, NY: Orbis, 2014).

6. Both John XXIII's 1963 encyclical, *Pacem in terris*, and the US Catholic bishops' 1983 pastoral letter, *The Challenge of Peace: God's Promise and Our Response*, can be interpreted as rejecting all present or future war due to the overriding danger of nuclear weapons.

7. David Cortright proposes a "realistic pacifism," that is essentially the same as "restrictive" just war theory. "It is predicated on a presumption against armed violence, but it acknowledges that the use of force, constrained by rigorous ethical standards, may be necessary at times for self-defence and the protection of the innocent." See Cortright, *Peace: A History of Movements and Ideas* (New York: Cambridge University Press, 2008), 334.

8. See Stephen J. Pope, *The Evolution of Altruism and the Order of Love* (Washington, DC: Georgetown University Press, 2003) and *Human Evolution and Christian Ethics*, New Studies in Christian Ethics (New York: Cambridge University Press, 2003).

9. See Douglas P. Fry, "Life without War," *Science* 336 (May 18, 2012): 879–84; Douglas P.

Xingu River basin of Brazil, the Iroquois Confederacy of Upstate New York, and the European Union. Not surprisingly, Fry finds that it is easier to maintain peace within associations of interdependent groups than among those with no common history or interests. Nevertheless, the existence of social systems free of war demonstrates that it is possible for human beings to create such systems, and it begins to show what is necessary to do so.

Christian approaches to the ethics of war and peace differ on the likelihood of creating peaceful societies and relations among societies, as well as on the continuing need to use violence in the restraint of violence. But they all agree not only that peace is to some degree a human possibility but also that Christians must be committed to peace—and that the historical potential for peaceful human relations has been heightened in Jesus Christ.

All are in some way accountable to the joyful experience of Jesus Christ as the one who unites us to the mysterious, loving, and glorious God in whom we "live and move and have our being" (Acts 17:28). Eschatologically, this God renews all creation (Rom 8:21–23), affecting present existence, and entrusting to humans now "the ministry of reconciliation" in a suffering world (2 Cor 5:17–21). Renewal in Christ is not merely personal, for salvation creates a new community. Jesus announces the "gospel" with a corporate and political metaphor, "the reign of God" (Mark 1:14).

This signifies that salvation is membership in a community united in love of God and neighbor, forgiveness, reconciliation, and hospitality toward the stranger, the sinner, and the oppressed (Mark 2:13–17; 12:40–41; Matt 5:38–48; 11:19; 22:28–29; Luke 7:34; 10:27; John 13:34). "Love your enemies and pray for those who persecute you, so that you may be children of your Father in heaven; for he makes his sun rise on the evil and on the good, and sends rain on the righteous and on the unrighteous" (Matt 5:44–45). From the standpoint of the teaching and ministry of Jesus, his nonresistant and forgiving death on a cross, and the witness of his first followers, it is indisputable that peace and reconciliation are essential to the Christian way of life and definitive of Christian ethics. The following chapters will show a variety of responses to

Fry, *Beyond War: The Human Potential for Peace* (New York: Oxford University Press, 2007). See also Fry, ed., *War, Peace and Human Nature: The Convergence of Evolutionary and Cultural Views* (Oxford: Oxford University Press, 2013). Fry's argument is a reply to Steven Pinker, *The Better Angels of Our Nature: Why Violence Has Declined* (New York: Viking, 2012), who argues that the present is the least violent period of human history, succeeding millennia of pervasive war. Fry maintains that peaceful social systems have existed throughout human history, even if not universal.

the question how great an effect the Christian way of life can have on the larger society. But there is no question that the gospel establishes a peaceful community of faith. How to live out the normative commitment to peace not only within the church, but also in broader social relationships, is interpreted in a diversity of ways.[10]

In fact, the first Christians were, for the most part, *pacifists*.[11] They renounced violence, refused participation in roles that involved killing (such as military service) and accepted martyrdom as the potential cost of faithfulness to Christ. The repudiation of all violence has always been a strong strand in Christian belief and practice. Nevertheless, from the fourth century onward, Christianity also developed a tradition of "just war," in which violence and killing are seen as acceptable or even as mandated, in order to protect the innocent "neighbor," defend against unjust aggression, preserve the common good, and uphold a social order in which peace and justice may flourish. While neither early Christian pacifists nor just war thinkers had much confidence in the socially reformative role of the church, pacifists responded by saying that Christians must accept the consequences of nonconformity. Just war thinkers thought that Christians had a responsibility to use available means, including armed force, to reduce societal violence and secure as just an order as possible.

In a book debating the respective merits of these two approaches, David Clough and Brian Stiltner conclude that Christian pacifism is perennially attractive and worthy because "it points to a kind of faithful Christian discipleship that witnesses to the new ordering of the reign of God." Yet the just war tradition represents, positively, "the attempt of Christians to come to terms with what it means to love their neighbor, protect the widow and orphan, and recognize God's providential ordering of human affairs through political authority."[12]

Proponents of *peacebuilding* agree that God orders human affairs through political authority, but they have an expansive view of politics

---

10. Richard B. Miller distinguishes among different varieties of pacifism according to, for example, how they see the duty to forego violence in relation to active political engagement; in relation to nonviolent resistance or civil disobedience as tools of social change; whether they believe harmonious social relations are possible or think commitment to peace requires continual self-sacrifice and suffering; and whether they regard nonviolence as governing the life of the church only, or as applicable to all persons and societies. See Miller, *Interpretations of Conflict: Ethics, Pacifism, and the Just-War Tradition* (Chicago: University of Chicago Press, 1991), 77–78.

11. See Ronald J. Sider, *The Early Church on Killing: A Comprehensive Sourcebook on War, Abortion and Capital Punishment* (Grand Rapids, MI: Baker Academic, 2012) and further discussion in chapter 3.

12. David L. Clough and Brian Stiltner, *Faith and Force: A Christian Debate about War* (Washington, DC: Georgetown University Press, 2007), 222–24.

and authority as involving "on the ground" efforts by people in communities where the effects of war and violence are most acutely felt. They are also convinced that dignity, rights, and human security are best served by replacing cycles of violence with relations of trust. Moreover, they believe that their efforts can bring significant changes in societies beyond the church. Peacebuilders concur that disciples are faithful when they witness to a new ordering of reality; they also believe that faithfulness challenges and changes personal and structural injustice.

Pacifism, just war, and peacebuilding are not pure "types" that have existed in the same way across history. Just as in any other sphere of social ethics, the Christian vocation to build peace and defend the innocent takes practical shape within specific contexts that vary geographically and over time.[13] Historical communities and experiences shape Christian theology and ethics, even as theological proposals simultaneously enlighten and organize practical life.

The contemporary stage is set for analysis of war and peace by the two world wars of the past century, the Cold War and its nuclear threat, and the continuing realities of weapons of mass destruction (including nuclear proliferation), terrorism, revolution, ethnic and religious conflict, and the armed confrontation of nation-states around the globe. Newer developments are the emergence of intrastate conflict as an even more deadly threat than international wars; the growth of transnational terror networks; justifications of "humanitarian intervention" across national borders; and the rise of interreligious peacebuilding movements, working with nonreligious entities to end violence and stabilize societies on just and participatory terms.

Conditions specific to the beginning of the present century allowed peacebuilding to emerge as a viable alternative to traditional forms of pacifism and just war. Among these are the relative ineffectiveness of both just war and pacifism in ending conflict and securing the conditions of cooperative social living; the end of colonialism, the rise of democracies, and empowerment of previously marginal or oppressed groups; the decentralization of national and international governance; the emergence of communications networks that foster the growth of political and social movements; and the reinvigoration of religious identities with immense social power and reach.

---

13. For discussion of the historical and political settings of developments in just war theory, pacifism, and peacebuilding, see Kenneth R. Himes, *Christianity and the Political Order: Conflict, Cooptation, and Cooperation* (Maryknoll, NY: Orbis, 2013).

In the twenty-first century, religious peacebuilding is a response to the use of just war criteria to validate questionable uses of military force (2003 US-led invasion of Iraq); the failure of formal cessation of hostilities to bring actual peace and social reconstruction (Israel–Palestine); ethnic and religious conflicts and genocides (East Africa and the Balkans); the likelihood that smoldering tensions will eventually break out into cycles of insurgency and civil conflict (Syria); and the realization that lasting peace requires the transformation of attitudes and relationships, as well as the rebuilding of civil society (South Africa). A Peace Studies Institute defines peacebuilding as

> the development of constructive personal, group, and political relationships across ethnic, religious, class, national, and racial boundaries. It aims to resolve injustice in nonviolent ways and to transform the structural conditions that generate deadly conflict. Peacebuilding can include conflict prevention; conflict management; conflict resolution and transformation, and post-conflict reconciliation.[14]

Peacebuilding is a family of practices, embodied in a network of activists responding to the threat or reality of direct violence, and corroborated and supported by midlevel, national, regional, and global policies and institutions.[15] Its theological interpretation builds upon its practical successes and limits. For example, introducing a book on the theology of peacebuilding, the Nigerian Catholic bishop John Onaiyekan shares that he has long worked to overcome ethnic divisions in the church and society that lead to societal violence. He understands his ministerial role as prophet, priest, and king (servant leader) to require mediating conflicts and being a guide to peace and reconciliation. His experience has convinced him not only that "peacebuilding is the normal work of the church of Jesus Christ," but also that the church must build bridges internationally and with other social entities, for peacebuilding is "always global."[16]

In the twenty-first century, Christian just war thinkers and pacifists are achieving consensus on the urgency of avoiding and reducing political violence through practical and flexible initiatives. Christian peace-

---

14. "What Is Strategic Peacebuilding?," Kroc Institute for International Peace Studies, University of Notre Dame, accessed May 1, 2013, https://tinyurl.com/yc79hy9k.

15. See John Paul Lederach, *Building Peace: Sustainable Reconciliation in Divided Societies* (Washington, DC: United Institutes of Peace, 1997), 37–61; Cusimano Love, "What Kind of Peace Do We Seek?," 56–91.

16. John O. Onaiyekan, "Foreword," in *Peacebuilding*, ix.

builders make such initiatives their defining concern, seeing them as integral to Christian discipleship.

JUST WAR IN OUTLINE

Just war theory is often presented as a set of coherent criteria, justified on both religious and philosophical grounds, to be applied prospectively to determine the morality of a given military engagement. Just war theory aims to supply a cogent ethical framework both to justify and to limit war.[17] Historically, however, just war criteria have not represented in any direct or simple way an objective and impartial theory. Rather, just war theory has been developed from the perspectives and politics of elites within powerful empires or nations, who have the capacity to wield military violence. Christian just war thinkers envision that violence used on behalf of justice can be accommodated within a Christian way of life. Augustine and Aquinas, the primary Christian formulators of just war theory, lived in eras that offered Christians opportunities to assume political and military roles. They encouraged Christians to consider whether the customary tools of civil government could be bent to the ends of Christian ethics, especially given the depth of sin in the world.

Just war theory is most useful and effective as a guide for national and international leadership, but this very setting is also an inevitable source of bias. Government officials and their advisors propose that violence can be used proportionately and successfully to pursue political ends. Just war theory aims then to cultivate and to express a moral and political consensus among decision-makers and their publics about how to validate, restrict, and restrain war's destructive powers, harnessing them to positive outcomes. Yet just war theory is less sensitive than pacifism and peacebuilding to the partiality of its viewpoint, to the prima facie clash of violence and the way of Jesus Christ, and to the profound and lasting effects of violence on combatants and societies.

This is why John Courtney Murray, one of the foremost midcentury Catholic proponents of just war theory—whose definition of just war

---

17. In the words of John Courtney Murray, just war theory aims "to condemn war as evil, to limit the evil it entails, and to humanize its conduct as far as possible." See Murray, "Remarks on the Moral Problem of War," *Theological Studies* 20, no. 1 (1959): 57. This essay is included as chapter 11 in Murray, *We Hold These Truths: Catholic Reflections on the American Proposition* (New York: Sheed & Ward, 1960). Neither Murray nor more recent just war theorists are implying that all war is *morally* evil. Rather, war unavoidably brings with it many human evils. There is, therefore—and as shall be discussed below—a presumption against war as a tool of social change. This presumption can be overridden under certain conditions, as stipulated by the criteria of the theory.

theory as condemning, limiting, and "humanizing" war as far as possible is frequently cited—also grants that the paradox involved in trying to fit violence into the order of justice "is heightened when this effort takes place at the interior of the Christian religion of love."[18]

Augustine, one of the earliest and certainly the most influential of Christian theorists of war, makes peace the main reason to go to war and qualifies pursuit of war by saying that it must be approved by a lawful authority and guided by an intention of love. Yet he also regards punishment of offenders, as such, as a valid motivating factor.[19] Several centuries later, Thomas Aquinas—most important for the Roman Catholic tradition—reiterates this basic framework on the assumption that war is prima facie an offense against charity. Yet war can be justified in certain circumstances, under certain criteria.[20] Aquinas names these as just cause (defense of the "common weal"), right intention, and legitimate authority. In modern times, these criteria have been developed and expanded and are usually regarded as falling into two categories: *jus ad bellum* and *jus in bello* (right to go to war and right in war). *Jus ad bellum* includes defense of the common good, right intention, and legitimate authority—as well as last resort, reasonable hope of success, and proportion.[21]

18. Murray, "Remarks on the Moral Problem of War," 57.

19. See Augustine, *City of God*, 19.12; *Reply to Faustus the Manichean*, 22.71–75.

20. Thomas Aquinas, *Summa Theologiae*, II-II, q. 40: "Is it Always a Sin to Wage a War?" The relation of war to charity will be a major concern of chapter 5.

21. These criteria can be differentiated and enumerated in different ways. Some reviews of the development and formulation of just war theory, with an emphasis on religion, theology, and ethics, are Frederick H. Russell, *The Just War in the Middle Ages* (New York: Cambridge University Press, 1975); Arthur F. Holmes, ed., *War and Christian Ethics: Classic and Contemporary Readings on the Morality of War*, 2nd ed. (Grand Rapids, MI: Baker Academic, 2005); Roland H. Bainton, *Christian Attitudes toward War and Peace: A Historical Survey and Critical Re-evaluation* (Nashville: Abingdon, 1960); James Turner Johnson, *Just War Tradition and the Restraint of War* (Princeton, NJ: Princeton University Press, 1981); Miller, *Interpretations of Conflict: Ethics, Pacifism, and the Just-War Tradition* (Chicago: University of Chicago Press, 1991); Oliver F. O'Donovan, *The Just War Revisited* (New York: Cambridge University Press, 2003); Thomas A. Massaro, SJ, and Thomas A. Shannon, *Catholic Perspectives on Peace and War* (Lanham, MD: Rowman & Littlefield, 2003); Nigel Biggar, *In Defence of War* (New York: Oxford University Press, 2013); Joseph E. Capizzi, *Politics, Justice, and War: Christian Governance and the Ethics of Warfare* (New York: Oxford University Press, 2015); and Tobias Winright and Laurie Johnson, eds., *Can War Be Just in the 21st Century?: Ethicists Engage the Tradition* (Maryknoll, NY: Orbis, 2015). See also J. Bryan Hehir, "The Moral Measurement of War: A Tradition of Change and Continuity," in *The Sacred and the Sovereign: Religion and International Politics*, ed. John D. Carlson and Erik C. Owens (Washington, DC: Georgetown University Press, 2003), 41–65; Hehir, "Religion, Realism and Just Intervention," in *Liberty and Power: A Dialogue on Religion and US Foreign Policy in an Unjust World*, ed. E. J. Dionne, Jean Bethke Elshtain, and Kayla M.Drogosz, Pew Forum Dialogues on Religion and Public Life (Washington, DC: Brookings Institution Press, 2004), 11–33; Hehir, "International Politics, Ethics and the Use of Force," *Georgetown Journal of International Affairs* 3, no. 2 (Summer/Fall 2002):

Defense of the peace or common good is today read to mean self-defense or defense of an ally, and it has been extended to "humanitarian intervention" aiming to protect civilian populations across national borders.[22] In 2004, the United Nations recognized "the responsibility to protect" (R2P), an evolution of the concept of humanitarian intervention, as an international obligation.[23] R2P refers protection of innocent civilians to the international community, in cases where states are unable or unwilling to protect human rights. The recognition of R2P was prompted by international failures in Rwanda and Bosnia, thus establishing that national sovereignty is not supreme in cases of gross violations of human dignity.

Jus in bello is a category that did not receive much attention until the twentieth century, with the development of weapons of mass destruction, such as area bombing during WWII and eventually the atomic bomb. However, in the tenth and eleventh centuries, the Peace of God and the Truce of God already tried to limit means used in European infighting.[24] The Peace of God began as a late tenth-century decree of the local church in France to prohibit, under penalty of excommunication, violence toward unarmed peasants and clergy. It spread through Western Europe and lasted in some form until the thirteenth century. It provided that there should be no attacks on women; nor on men who were clergy, pilgrims, merchants, peasants, or visitors to church councils; nor on church property, shepherds and flocks, agricultural animals, wagons in fields, and olive trees. The Truce of God, which likewise began in France, then became a broader European movement expanding the traditional prohibition of fighting on Sundays. It exempted certain cat-

17–23; and Hehir, "The Just War Ethic: Protecting the Global Common Good," *Pursuing the Global Common Good: Principle and Practice in US Foreign Policy* (Washington, DC: Center for American Progress, 2007), 17–29, https://tinyurl.com/y9y8cvfv.

22. Kenneth R. Himes, "The Morality of Humanitarian Intervention," *Theological Studies* 55, no. 3 (1994): 82–105. John Courtney Murray maintains that while wars both to defend and to punish were allowed by just war tradition up to the modern period, only defensive wars are now accepted. See Murray, *We Hold These Truths*, 255–57. Nigel Biggar, however, makes the case for retributive war in *In Defence of War*, 8. James Turner Johnson claims that the punitive wars validated through the Middle Ages should be justified again today, because government has the duty to maintain justice. See Johnson, "The Idea of Defense in Historical and Contemporary Thinking about Just War," *Journal of Religious Ethics* 36, no. 4 (2008): 543–56. The question whether morally justified war must be defensive will be taken up again in the chapters on Augustine and Aquinas.

23. A resolution on the responsibility to protect was adopted by the UN General Assembly in 2005.

24. Russell, *The Just War in the Middle Ages*, 34. See also Massaro and Shannon, *Catholic Perspectives*, 16.

egories of people from attack entirely and prohibited fighting among combatants on certain feasts, liturgical seasons, and days of the week.[25]

The most important limit on means in war, a brake on the terrible progress in twentieth century weaponry, is *noncombatant immunity*. Noncombatant immunity should also exclude serious "collateral damage" that involves indirect or long-term civilian loss of life, or that affects the ability to rebuild after conflict has ended. Examples would be damage to arable land, water supply, electrical systems, and hospitals. And the final criterion of means is proportion: Is the immediate and long-term damage caused proportionate to the objective gained?

Just war theorists have tended to see wars between or among states as their primary concern; to envision a single head of state or national representative body who makes lawful and authoritative decisions on behalf of the whole—that is, on the basis of national sovereignty; to view the undertaking of violence prospectively—that is, from a standpoint of prior noninvolvement; and to claim motivations of justice and the common good, as additionally guaranteed by the provision of right intention. These assumptions about the nature of armed force and decision-making about its use are being challenged today by the adaptations of just war theory required to address humanitarian intervention, terrorism, and the proliferation of weapons of mass destruction (WMDs).[26]

The peace activist and scholar of international relations David Cortright challenges those actually applying just war criteria to be more stringent and much more concentrated on deflecting and defusing "the often predatory aims of state power" in favor of "the demands of justice."

> An honest appraisal of war through the lens of just war criteria would forbid any consideration of nuclear strikes and would rule out virtually all forms of large-scale, unilateral military intervention. It would leave only self-defense and limited, legally constrained uses of multilateral force to protect civilians to restore conditions of justice. The "responsibility to protect" principles that have recently gained international endorsement embody this perspective.[27]

---

25. Alexander Gillespie, *A History of the Laws of War*, vol. 3, *The Customs and Laws of War with Regards to Arms Control* (New York: Bloomsbury, 2011), 59–60. According to Gillespie, these restraints did not have much practical effect on customary ways of defeating an enemy, such as starvation by siege and despoilation of property. See also Thomas Head and Richard Landes, eds., *The Peace of God: Social Violence and Religious Response in France around the Year 1000* (Ithaca, NY: Cornell University Press, 1994).

26. For the problems posed by humanitarian intervention, terrorism, and WMDs, as well as a discussion of just war resources that are or are not available to resolve them, see Hehir, "Moral Measurement of War," 47–63; Hehir, "Religion, Realism, and Just Intervention," 22–32; and Himes, "Humanitarian Intervention and the Just War Tradition," in *Can War Be Just?*, 50–64.

27. Cortright, *Peace*, 16. Cortright devotes a chapter to the responsibility to protect.

In view of the longstanding and complex nature of most contemporary conflicts; the ways in which their causes are intertwined with far-reaching religious, ethnic, economic, and political factors; and the inclination of most national representatives and subnational interest groups to act on the basis of their own advantage, the shortcomings of the just war approach, at least as traditionally formulated, are numerous and obvious.

An important initiative in favor of those who are the actual victims of war and of war-torn societies is the addition to just war theory of the category of *jus post bellum* (justice after war).[28] *Jus post bellum* considers the effects that measures of war can be predicted to have on the social infrastructure (such as public utilities, education, health care, economic productivity, and environmental pollution). They also prescribe just peace accords excluding "victor's justice" and establishing human security through the rule of law, a transitional government, an effective police force, and democratic elections favoring self-government. A related category, *jus ante bellum*, is close to the condition of "last resort." Yet, like peacebuilding, it stresses diplomatic and sometimes faith-based measures that should be taken to avoid war and reduce the destructive capacity of potential war.[29] To a large extent, *jus post bellum* and *jus ante bellum* build on the implications of preexisting criteria of just war, such as right intention, proportionality, noncombatant immunity, and reasonable hope of success.

These new categories call attention to the plight and rights of the many affected by war who have neither the prerogative of deciding when war will be engaged, nor the privilege of insulation from its lasting devastations. *Jus post bellum* and *jus ante bellum* criteria are, however, like just war theory as a whole, typically developed from the perspective of those who do not share the position of relative powerlessness of the majority of war's victims. They are attempts to make influential decision-makers more responsible for the actual human consequences of the policies and strategies they pursue.

A related effort to restrain the legitimization of violence by just war theory is Gerald Schlabach's proposal that a model of "just policing" might provide a way between just war theory and pacifism. This model accepts that coercive measures may be required to protect the public order and protect human rights. Violence and killing, however, are not

28. See Mark J. Allman and Tobias L. Winright, *After the Smoke Clears: The Just War Tradition and Post War Justice* (Maryknoll, NY: Orbis, 2010) and "Growing Edges of Just War Theory: Jus ante bellum, jus post bellum, and Imperfect Justice," *Journal of the Society of Christian Ethics*, 32, no. 2 (2012): 173–91, which is an excellent overview of these developments.

29. See Maureen O'Connell, "Jus Ante Bellum: Faith-Based Diplomacy and Catholic Traditions on War and Peace," *Journal for Peace and Justice Studies* 21, no. 1 (2011): 3–30.

regarded as part of the ordinary function of police officers, and thus they are subject to the rule of law. Similarly to peacebuilding, just policing or community policing invests time and resources in building relationships between the police and the communities they serve. "It employs health and human service programs as well as more traditional law enforcement, with an emphasis on crime prevention. It represents a change from a reactive model of law enforcement to one dedicated to developing the moral structure of communities."[30]

Tobias Winright connects the model of just policing to R2P and the international order, arguing that though disagreements may remain among just war theorists and pacifists about the justifiability of lethal force to stop crimes in progress, all should be able to concur that R2P, like policing, should aim not only to stop crime, but to prevent it. Just policing strengthens communities through "practices that seek to foster a relationship of mutual trust, bonds of empathy, and a common purpose between police and people."[31] Just policing prioritizes some of the same proactive measures as *jus ante bellum*, which will reappear in chapter 10 on peacebuilding. A caution regarding the vocabulary of "just policing" is that, in many contexts, civilian populations do not see the police as their friends or protectors, and the police are not interested in mutual trust and common purpose. As connoted by the term "secret police," police officers can be not only perpetrators of unauthorized violence but also agents of illegal violence authorized by repressive states.

In sum, just war has been structured historically by categories of criteria meant both to authorize and to deter, as well as to restrain, conflicts between legal heads of government and their peoples. In recent decades, new categories within the just war rubric have been developed to avoid conditions that make violence more likely, and to foster conditions favorable to the building of long-term peace.

30. Gerald W. Schlabach, "Just Policing, Not War," *America*, July 7, 2003, accessed July 18, 2017, https://tinyurl.com/yax5meuq. See also Schlabach, ed., *Just Policing, Not War: An Alternative Response to World Violence* (Collegeville, MN: Liturgical Press, 2007) and Schlabach, "Must Christian Pacifists Reject Police Force?" in *A Faith Not Worth Fighting For: Addressing Commonly Asked Questions about Christian Nonviolence*, ed. Tripp York and Justin Bronson Barringer (Eugene, OR: Cascade, 2012), 60–84. For a critical discussion, including the "sticking point" of lethal force, see Nathaniel Grimes, "Applying Just War Theory to Community Policing," *Political Theology Today*, September 16, 2016, accessed July 18, 2017, https://tinyurl.com/y7bhm3vg.

31. Tobias Winright, "Just Policing and the Responsibility to Protect," *The Ecumenical Review* 63, no. 1 (2011): 90.

PACIFISM IN OUTLINE

Pacifists consider the enterprise of war with much greater skepticism about whether its destruction can be proportionate to goods achieved. More importantly, they are convinced that violence is inherently gravely objectionable, or even absolutely wrong.[32] Similarly to just war theory, pacifism is sometimes construed as consisting in a norm or rule, defended on either religious or humanistic grounds, that excludes any resort to violence. Yet pacifism is not most fundamentally about theoretical analysis and rules. Christian pacifism as a moral perspective on war inheres in a way of life in which forbearance, forgiveness, nonviolence, and reconciliation are embodied in concrete communal virtues and practices.[33]

More overtly and intentionally than most just war theory, Christian pacifism is part and parcel of a coherent, communal way of life informed by religious ideals. Nonviolence is the obvious connecting thread in all types of pacifism. Less noted is the fact that varieties and commitments of Christian pacifists are attuned to the situations of historical communities not derived in any simple or direct way from the Bible. Certainly, nonviolent responses to injury and aggression have a solid basis in Jesus's example. Yet differences emerge in different historical circumstances. The early church was not in a position of political power, and thus it was not presented with the realistic possibility of reordering politics and government. In fact, Christians were a minority sect within the Roman Empire and were on the whole politically marginal and sometimes persecuted. Many early Christians renounced military service not only to follow Jesus's example but also to avoid idolatrous state rituals.

Pacifism was the dominant Christian stance in the early church, and even after Augustine and "the age of Constantine"[34] it has been a constant presence in Christian thought and practice.[35] Those who followed the sixteenth-century European "radical reformation," whose great theologian Menno Simons lighted the way for the historic peace churches,

32. Cortright, *Peace*, 334, distinguishes absolute pacifism from "conditional and pragmatic" pacifism, which he also calls "realistic pacifism." The latter, which he advocates, "is predicated on a presumption against armed violence, but it acknowledges that the use of force, constrained by rigorous ethical standards, may be necessary at times for self-defense and the protection of the innocent." *Peace* is a comprehensive historical overview of peace movements from primarily the time of the two world wars onward. Cortright's focus is on Christianity, but the book addresses other religious traditions, as well as "secular" parallels.

33. See Eli Sasaran McCarthy, *Becoming Nonviolent Peacemakers: A Virtue Ethic for Catholic Social Teaching and U.S. Policy* (Eugene, OR: Wipf & Stock, 2012).

34. Constantine was the fourth-century Roman emperor who, by giving Christianity legal status, paved the way for Christians to approve of and participate in the functions of state power.

35. See Marlin E. Miller and Barbara Nelson Gingerich, eds., *The Church's Peace Witness* (Grand Rapids, MI: William B. Eerdmans, 1994).

were under persecution from virtually every other major Christian group. They had no realistic chance of avoiding injury, short of converting to other versions of Christianity. Such pacifists could not envision that society as a whole could be changed in any significant way by Christian ideals and practices. Some contemporary pacifists follow in this strand in that they see their vocation as witness against culture, not reformation of it.[36]

The US theologian Stanley Hauerwas depicts nonviolence as a requirement of the church as a community formed by the gospel, and he mounts a powerful critique of the defection of liberal Protestantism to a militaristic and morally relativist culture in the years following the Vietnam war.[37] Hauerwas's call for the church to be a prophetic "contrast society" resonated with many who not only saw US military adventures as imperialist but were also seeking a vital sense of Christian community in an increasingly secular culture.[38] His version of pacifism encourages Christians to opt out of politics in the name of faithfulness to Jesus and to opt for a countercultural witness instead. As he puts it, "Jesus did not have a social ethic," for "his story is a social ethic. . . . The truthfulness of Jesus creates and is known by the kind of community his story should form."[39] Therefore he seems close to the early church and to the Anabaptist radicals.

A clear difference, however, is that Hauerwas lives in a society that protects the basic rights of most people most of the time, making pacifism less risky and peacebuilding less urgent, at least in his immediate context. Moreover, despite his disclaimers regarding the political effectiveness of pacifism, the ecclesial isolationism seemingly implied by his writings has had a public effect by reminding members of mainline churches and US society as a whole how easy and tempting it is to ratify self-serving uses of violence in the name of religion and morality. The public notoriety of Hauerwas and his critique is attested by his appear-

36. See Peter Brock, *Freedom from Violence: Sectarian Nonresistance from the Middle Ages to the Great War* (Toronto: University of Toronto Press, 1991).

37. Representative writings of this prolific author include Stanley Hauerwas, *Vision and Virtue: Essays in Christian Ethical Reflection* (Notre Dame, IN: Fides, 1974); *A Community of Character: Toward a Constructive Christian Social Ethic* (Notre Dame, IN: University of Notre Dame Press, 1981); and *The Peaceable Kingdom: A Primer in Christian Ethics* (Notre Dame, IN: University of Notre Dame Press, 1983).

38. "Contrast society" characterizes Hauerwas's view of the church as an alternative society. Hauerwas calls the church a "political alternative" and a "contrast model." A biblical defense of such an ecclesiology is offered by Gerhard Lohfink, according to whom "the entire New Testament sees the church as a contrast-society which stands in sharp contrast to the world." See Hauerwas, *A Community of Character*, 12, 84; Gerhard Lohfink, *Jesus and Community: The Social Dimension of Christian Faith*, trans. John P. Galvin (Philadelphia: Fortress, 1984), 132.

39. Hauerwas, *A Community of Character*, 37.

ance in *Time* magazine on September 17, 2001, garnering him the label "America's Best Theologian."[40] The country's reaction to the events of the preceding week, however, shows how difficult it is for pacifist ideals to make a deep practical impact on the national culture and entrenched modes of response to threats.[41]

Hauerwas's friend and colleague (for a time) at the University of Notre Dame, the Mennonite John Howard Yoder, shared his basic view of the church and, in fact, influenced Hauerwas greatly. Yoder does not deny that Jesus was political but sees his politics as radically at odds with what the world can accept. "God's Man in this world was facing, and reject-ing, the claim that the exercise of social responsibility through the use of self-evidently necessary means is a moral duty."[42] The faithful disciple of Jesus must be "willing to accept evident defeat rather than complicity with evil," which is also "what happens to God when he works among men."[43] In his later career, however, Yoder contemplated the possibil-ity that the church can be a public witness to the world, bearing "good news" that may have political effects.[44]

A different type of contemporary pacifism is represented by the Catholic Worker houses founded by Dorothy Day. The Catholic

40. Jean Bethke Elshtain, "Theologian: Christian Contrarian," *Time* (September 17, 2011), 76–77. In this brief essay Elshtain makes the point that despite Hauerwas's ostensible disengage-ment from the world, he has had significant cultural impact.

41. Following the terrorist attacks of September 11, 2011, President George W. Bush's "war on terrorism" eventually led to invasions of Iraq and Afghanistan. These military actions turned into prolonged and ongoing engagements, and terrorist violence in the region continues after almost two decades, taking new and more virulent forms. This response has been subjected to strong criticism both in terms of justice and just war and in terms of perpetrating cycles of vio-lence that might have been avoided through other types of interventions—such as a criminal justice approach or diplomatic, cultural, and economic initiatives to reduce incentives to terror-ism. Some of these issues will be addressed in chapter 9.

42. John Howard Yoder, *The Politics of Jesus* (Grand Rapids, MI: William B. Eerdmans, 1972), 100. See also Yoder, *The Priestly Kingdom: Social Ethics as Gospel* (Notre Dame, IN: Uni-versity of Notre Dame Press, 1984) and his posthumous *The War of the Lamb: The Ethics of Non-violence and Peacemaking*, ed. Glen Stassen, Mark Thiessen Nation, and Matt Hamsher (Grand Rapids, MI: Brazos, 2009). A difficult reality that should be acknowledged when Yoder is lifted up as a theological model is that he was involved in multiple instances of sexual harassment and abuse that both Yoder and the Mennonite Church were slow to publicly acknowledge and act upon, despite many reports from the victims. See Rachel Waltner Goossen, "The Fail-ure to Bind and Loose: Responses to Yoder's Sexual Abuse," *The Mennonite Quarterly Review*, January 2, 2015, accessed July 19, 2017, https://tinyurl.com/y9vltbpd. As Goossen states, "The peace theologian's perpetration of sexual violence upon women had far-reaching consequences among families, within congregations and throughout church agencies." An assessment of Yoder's theological significance, J. Denny Weaver, ed., *John Howard Yoder: Radical Theologian* (Eugene, OR: Cascade, 2014), includes two chapters on this painful subject.

43. Yoder, *Politics of Jesus*, 245.

44. Yoder, *For the Nations: Essays Public and Evangelical* (Grand Rapids, MI: William B. Eerd-mans, 1997), 6.

Worker echoes Hauerwas's call for a biblically based countercultural community but instantiates it more intentionally and practically in the form of actual communities structured around shared religious practices and a social mission. Catholic Workers share the gospel-based activism of modern Catholic social teaching, as well as the felt responsibility of progressive US Catholics to take the part of the less privileged. The Catholic worker mission is to provide "hospitality for the homeless, exiled, hungry, and forsaken," while aiming to rid society of "injustice, war, racism, and violence of all forms."[45]

Pax Christi International is another originally Catholic pacifist organization that had its origins in World War II. In today's global environment, its 120 member groups share a proactive, constructive agenda not only to refrain from violence but to end it entirely, building civil society, national and international institutions, and human security. There are many Pax Christi associations in the Global South—for example, Colombia, the Democratic Republic of Congo, and South Korea. "Pax Christi International . . . promotes peace, respect of human rights, justice & reconciliation throughout the world. Grounded in the belief that peace is possible and that vicious cycles of violence and injustice can be broken, Pax Christi International addresses the root causes & destructive consequences of violent conflict and war."[46] This brings it under the umbrella of peacebuilding, though its condemnation of all forms of violent force is more explicit, and its hope for a permanent end to all kinds of violence more ambitious, than that of some others under the same umbrella.

Pacifism is best understood as neither an absolute duty of nonviolence or nonresistance nor a competing ethical theory to be set alongside just war. Pacifism is essentially a practice—an ongoing communal way of life that, in the Christian instance, envisions discipleship as an unwavering commitment to conversion, at the spiritual, dispositional, and practical levels. The heart and inspiration of Christian pacifism is the reality of a transformed life embodied in Christ and enabled in the church by his Spirit. Today Christian pacifism—Catholic, Protestant, or Mennonite—is often expressed in efforts to bring social change through outreach and partnerships.

45. The Catholic Worker Movement website, accessed October 5, 2016, https://tinyurl.com/yagnss2w.

46. The Pax Christi International website, accessed October 5, 2016, https://tinyurl.com/y8kjemyn.

PEACEBUILDING IN OUTLINE

A distinctive development in the present century, joining some in both the just war and the pacifist camps, has been a theological-ethical interpretation of violent military and civil conflict from the side of those who not only have been war's victims—the majority of whom are civilians in the Global South—but also live in societies in which guarantees of basic material and social goods and of human rights are precarious or nonexistent. For people in such situations, the justification of wars undertaken by major national powers is looked upon with well-founded suspicion, as are the ideologies of armed factions competing for power and resources. Yet adoption of a nonviolent witness for Christian pacifism might require acceptance of the starvation, torture, or murder of their children.

Peacebuilding is a new approach to resolving conflicts and building just societies that is recognized by the United Nations, the United States Institute for Peace (USIP), and by some policies of the United States Department of State and Department of Defense.[47] Religious actors and organizations play key roles in peacebuilding.[48] Peacebuilding as a Christian theology and ecclesial practice is sometimes called "just peace" or "just peacemaking." David Little gathers these and related approaches under the term "justpeace" and points out that they are different from the more standard approach of "liberal peace." Liberal peace tends to favor state-centered solutions, prioritizes retributive justice, and is often tied to neoliberal economic policies. Justpeace is broader; engages grassroots, international, and religious actors; puts social welfare over market economics; and prioritizes restorative justice.[49] Peacebuilding fits Little's description of justpeace.

The World Council of Churches issued an *Ecumenical Call to Just Peace* in 2011 and sponsors peace activism networks internationally.[50] Peacebuilding is represented in the work of the Catholic Peacebuilding Network supported by the University of Notre Dame and Catholic Relief Services, the Just Peace movement of the United Church of Christ, the Center for Justice and Peacebuilding at Eastern Mennonite University,

47. On the latter, see Cusimano Love, "What Kind of Peace Do We Seek?," 59–73.

48. Susan Hayward, "Religion and Peacebuilding: Reflections on Current Challenges and Future Prospects, *United States Institute of Peace Special Report* 313 (2012), accessed October 24, 2016, https://tinyurl.com/yc4tfr4g.

49. David Little, *The Oxford Handbook of Religion, Conflict and Peacebuilding* (New York: Oxford University Press, 2015), 63, 82.

50. World Council of Churches, "Promoting Just Peace," accessed August 12, 2017, https://tinyurl.com/ydemhcxt.

and the Just Peacemaking initiative of the late Baptist theologian Glen Stassen.

Peacebuilding has arisen at a specific time (the turn of the twenty-first century) to fulfill specific demands on the Christian vocation (to constructively seek peace in view of ongoing and emerging threats to human dignity worldwide) and in light of the global agency of Christians and the churches (to enhance the universal common good, the good of local communities, and the dignity of every person). Peacebuilding is the rightful heir of Christian just war and pacifism, in that it is embodied in evangelical communities of peace and reconciliation; transforms societies by upholding the rule of (just) law, democratic participation, and restorative justice; and builds alliances among the many faiths and cultures that together are marred by violence and together must overcome it.

Peacebuilding is a practical response to conditions of violence that aims to alleviate the existential situations of those affected by war; and to do so in cooperation with other advocates and activists, on a spectrum from grassroots to midlevel to national and international governments and civil society organizations. Peacebuilding addresses the many contexts in which violence is due to civil conflicts within states, or among religious and ethnic groups that span multiple states. Peacebuilders commonly work in the midst of ongoing conflicts where responsibility can be diffuse and where parties on all sides must come together for success to occur. A key characteristic of peacebuilding is that it seeks a long-term and sustainable peace that depends on addressing the root causes of conflict, pervasive global cycles of conflict, and the infrequency with which parties to conflict use violence "justly."[51]

Peacebuilding embraces the pacifist-generated conviction that Christians should take seriously the call actually to live in conformity to the gospel, but it envisions doing so in active political roles. Action for justice is crucial for communities that bear the brunt of war's destruction without having much say in the ways war is waged. Peacebuilders work nonviolently in and for such communities, whether or not they reject force in any and all situations.

Some principles of just peacebuilding are to restore the fundamental dignity of life, to create a positive peace through a participatory process involving all stakeholders, to form just social relationships vertically and horizontally, to heal the personal wounds of war, to build up the human and material infrastructure, and to develop sustainable institutions and

---

51. This is the key message of Cusimano Love, "What Kind of Peace Do We Seek?"

practices so that peace can endure over time.[52] A longtime leader in advocacy for effective nonviolent strategies (which will be taken up again in chapter 10) is peace activist Gene Sharp, who puts forward no fewer than 198 methods of tested nonviolent action. These include letter-writing campaigns, position papers and statements, "mock awards" and other kinds of humor, demonstrations and protests, boycotts, strikes, walk-outs, and non-cooperation with unjust policies.[53]

All peacebuilders agree on the preeminent importance of taking non-violent yet forceful measures to deter ongoing violence, undo social injustice, and bring opposed groups together around a negotiated vision of social coexistence and cooperation. From the standpoint of interreligious peacebuilding, Christians are called to solidarity, activism, reconciliation, and hope for social renewal.

Elias Omondi Opongo, SJ, is an African priest who has worked on peace education and mediation in conflict settings in Eastern Africa and the Horn of Africa; who has worked with refugees from Yemen, Tanzania, Kenya, and Somalia; and who has been a program officer with a Jesuit center for peace and justice in Nairobi, Kenya. He defines peace-building as the promotion of life and the well-being of the human person, and calls it "a life-time process geared towards the transformation of the unjust structures in the society and the institution of just ones as well as the facilitation of the participation of everyone in the organization of society."[54]

A parallel development, with roots in biblical, evangelical Christianity, is the "just peacemaking theory" of Glen Stassen, and colleagues, who like just war theorists, begin from the standpoint of wars between nation-states. Questioning how Jesus's love command and the Sermon on the Mount can be taken with political seriousness, Stassen proposes ten initiatives that have been demonstrated to make wars less likely. Both pacifists and those who defend war should be able to come together around these initiatives.[55] For example, at the international level, the United Nations Peacebuilding Commission lends support to the efforts of national governments, countries sending peacekeeping troops into troubled areas, international financial institutions, and international donors, while also sending representatives into targeted local

52. Cusimano Love, "What Kind of Peace Do We Seek?," 56–57.

53. Gene Sharp, *The Politics of Nonviolent Action, Part Two: The Methods of Nonviolent Action* (Boston: Porter Sargent, 1975). See also Sharp, *Waging Nonviolent Struggle: 20th Century Practice and 21st Century Potential* (Manchester, NH: Extending Horizon, 2005).

54. Elias Omondi Opongo, SJ, *Making Choices for Peace: Aid Agencies in Field Diplomacy* (Nairobi: Pauline Publications Africa, 2006), 14 n4.

55. Glen H. Stassen, *Just Peacemaking: The New Paradigm for the Ethics of Peace and War* (Cleveland: Pilgrim, 2008). Stassen will be discussed further in chapter 2.

settings to help identify gaps in the recovery strategies that could under-mine peace efforts.[56] International efforts, and frequently peacebuilding internal to nation-states or regions within nations, requires interreligious cooperation among Christians and other faiths.

The diversity and practical nature of peacebuilding testify to the fact that defeating violence requires flexibility, creativity, pragmatism, and determination. Christian peacebuilding is a way of yoking gospel non-violence to effective action for change, despite the existentially and morally ambiguous circumstances in which its mission must be em-bodied.

POLITICS AND ESCHATOLOGIES

This brief, initial review of just war, pacifism, and peacebuilding high-lights the interdependence in all three approaches of historical-political context, located experiences of church, interpretation of the practical meaning of the gospel in relation to the scourge of violence, and expec-tations regarding the effect that Christian action might have on society. An important aspect of these approaches is the degree to which their proponents believe that Christians or the churches can actually transform the cultures in which they live to be more just. Partly this is dependent on opportunity and experiences of success. But hope for social change is also interdependent with biblical and theological warrants for seeing his-tory as an arena of grace, such that creation retains an essential goodness and that worldly conditions are even now being redeemed or re-created. One key question is how seriously each approach or thinker takes the reign of God, salvation, and resurrection life as offering new possibilities not only for the church but for the world and all creation.

The term "eschatology," referring to "the last things" (*eschata*), has tra-ditionally envisioned the nature of life after death and the end of the world. An important question for biblical scholars since the rise of his-torical criticism in the nineteenth century has been how the apparent expectation of the early Christians that the Lord would return soon, even in their own lifetimes, affected their view of Christian morality and the social role of the church (e.g., 1 Cor 7:29 and Rom 13:11). If the Sec-ond Coming is soon to end history as we know it, then it might be less urgent or even a distraction to engage in the reform of institutions.

To the contrary, some scholars interpret sayings of Jesus such as "the kingdom of God is at hand" (Mark 1:15; Matt 3:2; 4:17) to mean that the

---

56. United Nations Peacebuilding Commission website, accessed May 1, 2013, https://tinyurl.com/yd9ks96m.

reign of God is not delayed until the end of history but is already present during Jesus's own lifetime, an idea that the early twentieth-century scholar C. H. Dodd popularized with the phrase "realized eschatology."[57] Such an interpretation gives more power to social reforms carried out in the name of the gospel. It can help diminish the supposedly "apocalyptic" and supernaturalistic connotations of eschatology, making it more palatable to modern readers. But dangers are that "realized eschatology" can refer to a present spiritual transformation, not a social or political one, and that hope for redemption beyond history as well as within it is abolished.

A different biblical reading, resulting in a more useful eschatological framework for ethics, holds that the completion of the reign of God is possible only by divine power at the end of or beyond human history, but the anticipatory presence of the reign of God begins now and has sociopolitical ramifications. God's reign is inaugurated in Jesus's ministry, empowered by the risen Christ and the Spirit, and it can and should inform Christian social existence today. From this perspective, renewed human relationships and greater realization of human dignity, equal respect, and social justice are temporal possibilities available to those who work for peace in the name of Jesus Christ. Peacebuilders would endorse this premise, but that is less true for some just war theorists and pacifists.

Christian just war theory often goes hand-in-hand with an insistence that since the kingdom is not yet fully present, Christian behavior cannot be expected to conform fully to it. Instead, even Christians should deal realistically with the threats to human welfare that sin presents. Christian theorists do not typically defend just war in explicitly religious terms to politicians, government leaders, military officers, or the general public. Despite the fact that the development of just war theory took place largely under Christian auspices (building on Roman sources), invoked religious and theological validation, and was and is applied by theologians and ecclesial spokespersons, it is today considered by its proponents be a public, political rubric of analysis, with applicability across cultures and eras.

Pacifism, in comparison, is typically derived from expressly religious premises and commitments; is often, if erroneously, equated with nonresistance (vs. nonviolent resistance); and is frequently assumed to be persuasive only or primarily to religious believers, evoking rejection or persecution from outsiders. Many pacifists agree with just war theorists who think that since the kingdom is not yet fully present, political soci-

57. See Wendell Willis, ed., *The Kingdom of God in 20th-Century Interpretation* (Peabody, MA: Hendrickson, 1987).

ety cannot be expected to embody its ideals. The anticipatory sphere of the reign of God is the church. Church members should confine their peacemaking activities to that sphere and stay away from the sphere of violence (i.e., politics).

Yet for progress toward justice to be a realistic goal of Christian ethics, it is necessary not only that the church be empowered, but that Christians find similarly motivated and like-minded partners. It is key to work across cultural and religious lines and to facilitate the process through some sort of shared language or the mutual recognition of values expressed in particular religious vocabularies. If Christians striving for just peace expect that their social ideals will be shared at some fundamental level with non-Christians who work for similar goals of justice, the implication is that the transforming power of God is present across traditions. But such a claim is rejected both by pacifists who see it as their vocation to be a church against the world and by Christian just war theorists who see force as justified precisely because it is the only way to achieve incremental justice in an unjust world. In fact, some would say, killing may be necessary to carry out love of neighbor when the neighbor is under attack.

Peacebuilding can be either religious in inspiration or "secular." But since the majority of the world's cultures are religious, peacebuilding activists necessarily work within and among religious communities.[58] Peacebuilders enlist diverse religious organizations and leaders to build peace interreligiously. Whether or not they use the technical term "eschatology," they work on the assumption that God's transforming power is already opening new possibilities in their societies. Peacebuilding can be public, political, and pluralistic without losing its religious character. Christian and other religious peacebuilders trust in shared goals and shared power to effect change, though they may not give this an explicit theological validation. Since religious narratives and identities not only can bring reconciliation but also can spawn or exacerbate violence,[59] it is important that religious leaders and all believers committed to peaceful coexistence can and should highlight the ways in which religious visions, values, and practices (including liturgies) can join together in the cause of peace.

---

58. For a multireligious overview, see Susan Hayward, *Religion and Peacebuilding*. A specific example of Muslim peacebuilding advocacy is Qamar-ul Huda, ed., *Crescent and Dove: Peace and Conflict Reslution in Islam* (Washington, DC: United States Institute of Peace, 2010). See also Ned Lazarus, *A Future for Israeli-Palestinian Peacebuilding* (London: Britain Israel Communications and Research Center, 2017), accessed January 11, 2018, https://tinyurl.com/ybbzuocy.

59. R. Scott Appleby, *The Ambivalence of the Sacred: Religion, Violence, and Reconciliation* (New York: Rowman & Littlefield, 2000).

Most defenses of just war theory and pacifism in the several decades after World War II took as their point of departure the historical experiences of Western Europe and North America. Many proponents of the just war saw the Second World War as a clear contest between good and evil, whose winning was worth the bloodshed and destruction unleashed. They thought that armed intervention could be a lasting force for social good, rather than holding the effect of grace in the world sufficient to make force unnecessary. Explaining that he "grew up in a country [England] haunted by the two world wars," Nigel Biggar acknowledges war's horrendous evils, but still maintains that war is necessary and justified to punish "gross and intractable wickedness."[60] Moreover, from their postwar perspective, such proponents envisioned that it will be the continuing responsibility of the world's "superpowers" (preeminently the United States) to beat back the forces of atheistic Communism and fascism under the banner of democracy, religious freedom, and of course national interests. Jean Bethke Elshtain asserts, "Despite all the clamor about U.S. power, and the resentment it engenders in some quarters, the 'we' likely to be called upon to intervene to protect the innocent from harm, the 'we' to whom a country without the means to intervene would likely make its case, is the United States."[61]

The pacifism that developed in the same era and grew in strength during the period of the Vietnamese-American war, often looked at matters from the viewpoint of the citizenry of the superpowers. Many of these pacifists shared the skepticism of just war thinkers about whether nonviolence could be a force for social justice. Yet they drew a contrasting conclusion: violence begets violence, and it flatly contradicts nonnegotiable moral obligations, especially from a gospel perspective. Thus the moral, and especially the Christian, mandate is to protest liberal-capitalist nationalism and militarism, even by opting out of politics altogether. According to Stanley Hauerwas, Christians must live in and through the Christian story, forming a community in which the cross and sacrifice are central. The narrative that gives this community its distinctive identity and virtues requires absolute nonviolence: "nonviolence is simply one of the essential practices that is intrinsic to the story of being a Christian."[62]

60. Biggar, *In Defence of War*, 1, 11.

61. Jean Bethke Elshtain, "Military Intervention and Justice as Equal Regard," in *Religion and Security: The New Nexus in International Relations*, ed. Robert A. Seiple and Dennis R. Hoover (Lanham, MD: Rowman & Littlefield, 2004), 127. See also Jean Bethke Elshtain, *Just War against Terror: The Burden of American Power in a Violent World* (New York: Basic Books, 2004).

62. Stanley Hauerwas, *Dispatches from the Front: Theological Engagements with the Secular* (Durham, NC: Duke University Press, 1994), 137.

Defenders of just war like James Turner Johnson and Nigel Biggar react against the pacifism of Hauerwas and Yoder, as well as pacifist-leaning but still socially activist Catholic teaching documents, in which they see a lack of the realism, prudence, and courage necessary to a responsible social ethics. Their pacifist contemporaries (especially Hauerwas and Yoder) react equally strongly against Christian defenses of war that they see as caving in to civil religion, the inroads of liberalism in the churches, and superpower ideology.

Many just war theorists share Augustine's conviction that redemption in Jesus Christ has very limited practical effect on the political order. Christlike love should inform every aspect of a Christian's personal life, but the political realm is inhabited mostly by people whose loves are disordered and whose idea of "peace" is distorted by vice. Especially when carrying out public roles, the Christian—even when motivated by love—is unavoidably caught up in "miserable necessities," entailing justified participation in acts of violence, including even judicial torture.[63]

Pacifists and peacebuilders are more convinced than just war theorists that it is possible to live out evangelical ideals within the frame of history, by the grace of Christ and Spirit. However, they too differ among themselves as to the effects of the reign of God on and in history and politics. While some pacifists regard redemptive peace and practical nonviolence as only possible within the church, other pacifists and most peacebuilders believe that salvation in Jesus Christ transforms all creation in a way that can enable a new politics in every society and culture, though the political order will never equate to God's kingdom.

Christian peacebuilding is internally diverse in its views of the justice and aims of governments and the acceptability of Christian cooperation with states and international bodies that employ force. Within peacebuilding, not all agree about whether, given the reality that love of neighbor and care for the common good must be enacted historically against mortal obstacles, violence is permissible in exceptional circumstances—for example, to halt war crimes or genocides. Yet all do agree both that Christ and the Spirit make it possible to extend peace historically yet nonviolently and that local, national, and international governments, civil society organizations, and NGOs should be persuaded and pressured to provide better deterrents to violence. The main focus of peacebuilding is nonviolent social action, which is seen as the most realistic, responsible, and sustainable mode of conflict transformation.

63. Augustine's example of the torturing judge appears in *City of God* book 14, while descriptions of the inevitable "miseries" of social and political life are in book 19. These will be given further consideration in chapter 4. On Augustinian political pessimism, see Jean Bethke Elshtain, *Augustine and the Limits of Politics* (Notre Dame, IN: University of Notre Dame, 1998).

Christian social ethicists today—including just war theorists, pacifists, and especially peacebuilders—are more likely than ever before to see positive changes in the balance of justice and injustice to be not only a Christian responsibility but a historical possibility. Even if it is not possible to predict with any confidence that the world as a whole is evolving toward a nonviolent future, it is still possible and mandatory to identify, address, and remedy specific injustices, and to put specific human communities and societies on a path to just peace.

A SHARED PRESUMPTION AGAINST WAR

Pacifism and just war theory seem to adopt opposite approaches to the use of violence, with peacebuilding occupying a broad middle ground closer to pacifism. Yet the fact that the Catholic Church and mainline Protestants have always been hospitable to internal pacifist subtraditions, and that theorists of just war and just peace have converged on the vital imperative of national and international reconciliation processes, already indicates that just war thinking, pacifism, and now peacebuilding share some common values and can be supported by shared scriptures and theological traditions. Common to all is the fundamental commitment to seeking and preserving peace and avoiding violence. Just war, pacifism, and peacebuilding all agree that violence is in no way a part of the eschatological unity of all things in God through the love of Christ and the power of the Spirit. All are attempts to grapple with the concrete meanings in a sin-marred world of the inbreaking reign of God and the pull of resurrection life. But all would agree nonetheless that resorting to violence is far from ideal and needs very strong justification—if justifiable at all.

Over thirty years ago, James F. Childress observed that just war theory and pacifism share an aversion to violence and a presumption that it is always morally problematic, even when ultimately justified.[64] Richard Miller takes this point of convergence as "axiomatic," and most Christian advocates of just war would agree.[65] But whereas just war theory regards nonviolence as a prima facie duty, pacifism sees that duty as absolute. Peacebuilding likewise entails a presumption against war, and for the movement as a whole that presumption is extremely stringent. Peacebuilders acknowledge more directly and integrally than standard just war theory that societal violence is frequently an ongoing condition, and

---

64. James F. Childress, "Just-War Theories: The Bases, Interrelations, Priorities and Functions of Their Criteria," *Theological Studies* 39, no. 3 (1978): 427–45.

65. Miller, *Interpretations of Conflict*, 7.

decisions about uses of force are not only *about* violence, but they are *within* it.

Most peacebuilders, as witnesses to ongoing human rights violations, appreciate the value of systems of government and law enforcement that protect human security. Thus peacebuilders may approve or accept the use of police or humanitarian military force to protect human rights. Yet peacebuilders are also likely to see lethal force as feeding into cycles of violence. Therefore, even among those who might rarely justify it, the presumption against all violent force is strong. What defines peacebuilding is positive, constructive engagement with parties on all sides of conflicts, in order to reinstate social conditions of stability and cooperation and build up civil society and government with just, participatory institutions.

In contrast, remaining just war pessimism about the possibilities of politics is well illustrated by the vociferous objections that some just war theorists have raised about the view that the theory accommodates any such thing as a "presumption" against war. James Turner Johnson is most vehement on this point. Johnson embraces an "Augustinian theology" of history in which peace movements are not only utopian and unrealistic, but also idolatrous.[66] He regards violent force as a morally neutral tool that not only can be justified for serious reasons but against which there is no moral presumption in the first place. Reacting to the 1993 assertion of the Catholic bishops to the contrary (in their nuclear-era pastoral letter, *The Challenge of Peace*),[67] Johnson maintains that the just war tradition has no "presumption against war" due to the harm it is sure to do, but rather that this tradition is based on a "presumption against *injustice*" entailing the "responsible use of force." Those who think otherwise have come under the pernicious influence of pacifists, in Johnson's view, and have no more to validate their position than a "general uneasiness" with destructive modern war and the "venality" of modern states.[68]

Following Johnson, Nigel Biggar sees the presumption against war as part of a "liberal-left" story that is "virtually pacifist," and, as exem-

---

66. James Turner Johnson, *Morality and Contemporary Warfare* (New Haven, CT: Yale University Press, 2001), 16.

67. USCCB, *The Challenge of Peace: God's Promise and Our Response*, no. iii: "Catholic teaching begins in every case with a presumption against war."

68. Johnson, *Morality and Contemporary Warfare*, 35. These points, targeting recent Catholic teaching specifically, are developed at much greater length in Johnson, "Just War, as It Was and Is," *First Things* (January 2005), accessed May 15, 2013, https://tinyurl.com/y8om7hxt. In this article, Johnson also questions the developing proposal of the Catholic *magisterium* that the legitimation of war should fall under the authority of the United Nations, rather than of individual nation-states. See also James Turner Johnson, "Just War I: The Broken Tradition," *The National Interest* 96, no. 5 (1996): 27–36.

plified in Europe today, "draws the moral that war is evil and must be renounced always and everywhere."[69] For Johnson, the "classic" just war theory does not construe force "to be a moral problem in itself," for it justifies force to right injustice. "There is, simply put, no presumption against war in it at all."[70] Daniel Bell Jr. goes so far as to argue that war is a positive good, once it meets just war criteria, and thus is even in itself a form of faithful discipleship and of following Jesus.[71]

Is this line of argument coherent? It is one thing to renounce war or violent force completely (as the Catholic bishops have *not* done[72]), and another to say it can be justified under very stringent criteria. In fact to regard war as in need of "justification"—as Johnson and Biggar surely do, for they endorse just war standards—is, in fact, to confirm a presumption against it. If there were no such presumption, there would be no need for reasons or limits. Consider someone who truly embodies the lack of a presumption against violent force: Homer's Odysseus, known by the epithets "raider of cities" and "man of war."[73] Odysseus pillages the island of the Cicones on his way home from Troy, just because he wants their valuables. It is a good thing to bring home loot, no prejudice against means used.

Christian just war theory, however, views forceful and coercive political action as necessary only because of historical evil and conflict that are actually distortions or violations of God's will for creation and that will not be part of God's reign as fully realized in the *eschaton*. These violations are the justifying reasons for war, the reasons why the prima facie duty to avoid it can or must be set aside. As Reinhold Niebuhr emphasized, just war may not be sinful, but it is a consequence of and a response to sin, and it enacts human (if not moral) evils, even if it avoids a great evil (and so is morally justified).[74] War should be limited as far as possible, within the requirements of justice. The "presumption against injustice"

69. Biggar, *In Defence of War,* 7–8.

70. Johnson, "Just War I," 30. Other authors backing a similar line of argument are Helmut David Baer and Joseph E. Capizzi, "Just War Theories Reconsidered," *Journal of Religious Ethics* 33, no. 1 (2005): 119–37; Weigel, in Paul J. Griffiths and George Weigel, "Who Wants War? An Exchange," *First Things* (April 2005), accessed May 15, 2013, https://tinyurl.com/yckt22dt. See also J. Daryl Charles, "Presumption against War or Presumption against Injustice? The Just War Tradition Reconsidered," *Journal of Church and State* 47, no. 2 (2005): 265–69.

71. Daniel M. Bell Jr., *Just War as Christian Discipleship: Recentering the Church in the Tradition Rather Than the State* (Grand Rapids, MI: Brazos, 2009), 34.

72. See Kristopher Norris, "'Never Again War': Recent Shifts in the Roman Catholic Just War Tradition and the Question of 'Functional Pacifism'," *Journal of Religious Ethics* 42, no. 1 (2014): 108–36. Gregory M. Reichberg agrees in his *Thomas Aquinas on War and Peace* (New York: Cambridge University Press, 2017), 279–80.

73. *The Odyssey* 8.

74. Reinhold Niebuhr, "When will Christians Stop Fooling Themselves," in *Love and Justice:*

is certainly shared by those holding a presumption against war and, in fact, would seem a *sine qua non* of social ethics as such.[75]

Yet Johnson, Biggar, and others reject the presumption against war because they think it overestimates the degree to which conflict resolution without force will be possible and because they have a strong antipathy to the influence of pacifism in the mainline churches. Just war theorists who accept the presumption assume that better means can often, if not always, be found. Like all just war theorists, they grant that gospel ideals do not directly govern historical political action. Responsibility for neighbors and society may sometimes demand resort to force as the lesser evil. Yet Augustinians typically expect that this will happen more often than Thomists do. Aquinas's discussion of war is titled, "Is it *always* a sin to wage a war?"[76] providing a clue to the extreme caution that today characterizes official Roman Catholic teaching.

The debate about a shared presumption against war is rooted partly in different understandings of political society, politics, and political power, as well as in possible misunderstandings of the views of interlocutors. Those who repudiate this presumption repudiate not only a Christian ethical withdrawal from politics, but also a utopian view of society in which peace, harmony, and justice can be accomplished through political action short of force. They are also skeptical that the political action can order power in such a way that the use of force is minimized. Their view of politics reflects Augustine, who thought the historical prospects of justice are very limited.

Those who endorse the presumption also have a view of politics and political power. They would agree with Joseph Capizzi that governments are responsible for "those neighbors bound together by a common will and commitment to a common good" (not excluding diversity within those common commitments) and that any use of force should be ordered toward the political ends of "justice, order, and peace."[77] Contrary to what some critics suggest, they do not claim that force is never necessary, nor that perfect peace and justice can be achieved historically, with or without force. But their view of politics includes greater confidence that political action can make significant progress toward justice and peace without resorting to direct violence and killing. Nonviolent strategies to achieve governments' political ends are available, can be

---

Selections from the Shorter Writings of Reinhold Niebuhr, ed. D. B. Robertson (Louisville, KY: Westminster John Knox, 1957), 40–46.

75. This was pointed out to me by Richard Miller in a personal communication, 2017.

76. Aquinas, *Summa Theologiae*, II-II. 40. Italics added.

77. Capizzi, *Politics, Justice and War*, 26–27. Fewer would agree that the use of moral force is by divine providence part of "the morality of day to day politics" (34).

effective, and should be the recourse of first resort. The presumption is that more limited and moderate coercive measures should be used before direct violence and killing, after negotiations have failed. Theologically, the political ethic and view of power of those who hold a presumption against war are informed by a belief in humanity's God-given (albeit sin-marred) ability to act justly and in the transformative effect of salvation in the world.[78]

In any genuinely Christian view of politics, politically legitimate force and coercion do not necessarily and should not usually amount to killing, necessary though war and killing may sometimes be. Ultimately, the presumption against war not only should be shared, but implicitly is shared, by any ethicist, Christian or not, who maintains that war should and can be a "last resort." The "presumption against war" debate is more fundamentally a debate about whether it is easy or hard to override the prima facie duty to avoid war and killing, about whether war should be an instrument of politics frequently or rarely, not about whether it should be used at all.

The presumption against war can find little better defense than Karl Barth's reaction to contemporaries who argued such things as that war is neither Christian nor unchristian, neither moral nor immoral, and that Christians can have in principle no objection to it. Barth's post–World War II verdict: "Surely we cannot really continue to believe all this."[79] The basic error of such viewpoints is "their utter oblivion to the relative power of the pacifist thesis," and their failure to see that "peace is the real emergency," for a defective peace sows the seeds of war.[80]

In sum, the fact that the political vision behind Christian just war theory views coercion and even war as justified historical dimensions of politics does not mean that there is no presumption or bias against war. War should be avoided *unless* it is truly necessary for the common good (just cause, last resort, and proportionality), is placed in service to the Christian ideals of peace and love that will be fully embodied only escha-

---

78. H. David Baer argues that most just war theorists fail to locate their criteria within a larger vision of politics, and that a Christian political ethic excludes a presumption against war. For Baer, this ethic is a Lutheran "two kingdoms" theory, in which political authority is grounded in divine command, and must be implemented by violent force, even though informed by love. See Baer, *Recovering Christian Realism: Just War Theory as a Political Ethic* (Lanham, MD: Rowman & Littlefield, 2015), 13–16, 98–99. But this is not the only Christian political ethic. Christian ethicists who defend the presumption have a political ethic that centers on human dignity and just peace, grounded in doctrines of creation and redemption, and that recognizes yet relativizes the power of sin, thus marginalizing violence and killing as Christian political instruments.

79. Karl Barth, *Church Dogmatics*, vol. 3, part four, *The Doctrine of Creation* (Edinburgh: T&T Clark, 1961), 457.

80. Barth, *Church Dogmatics,* vol. 3, part four, 458–59.

tologically (right intention), and is judged to promote a relatively just temporal order by political authorities whose responsibility is to safeguard the common good (legitimate authority). And when these criteria have been met, the warriors' cause may not be judged immoral, but the fact of killing still leaves what James Childress calls moral "traces or residual effects" on agents that should be reflected in the restraint of their action and in subsequent restorative measures.[81] A bias against war and killing stands, then, as a link among just war theory, pacifism, and peacebuilding.

A Christian literature that does provide a striking contrast to these three is the crusade or "holy war" mentality (chapter 7). Historical examples are the medieval papal crusades and the seventeenth-century English Puritan revolution. These examples subvert the Christian presumption against war by seeing violence as directly commanded by Christ and as taken up in Christ's name with no regret. Today's Christians might view the Crusades as a past aberration, but the very existence of holy war as a Christian project should remind all of the humility, caution, and even remorse called for whenever Christians justify armed force. Familiarity with Christian history also teaches the broader lesson that holy war ideologies in any faith, or the cooptation of religion to validate unjust violence more broadly, is not a sufficient reason to label an entire religion or people as violent.

In my view, a presumption against violence, including war, is necessary to Christian social ethics. Positively, Christian social ethics prioritizes structures of justice informed by compassion, solidarity, mutual respect, and special regard for society's most vulnerable. If the presumption against violence is withdrawn, it becomes difficult or impossible not only to approximate this goal but even to limit violence according to basic standards of justice, much less Christian norms.

LOOKING AHEAD

In the chapters going forward, various thinkers in Christian tradition and recent debates will be considered in light of some common threads, already addressed in this introduction. The next chapter will be devoted to Jesus's ministry of the reign of God in the synoptic gospels, and the interpretation of texts such as the Sermon on the Mount, in which the "hard sayings" (Matt 5:38–48) are often taken as the charter of Christian pacifism and the stumbling block of just war theory. The chapter will argue that Jesus's ministry of the reign of God not only establishes ideals

---

81. Childress, "Just-War Theories," 433, borrowing from W. D. Ross and Robert Nozick.

that Christians should strive to attain, but that it empowers Christians to begin to turn eschatological ideals into social realities.

Historically speaking, authors who are most insistent on the inbreaking presence of the kingdom tend to be pacifists in their dedication to kingdom faithfulness, and their political expectations are diverse. Some early Christian writers; Reformation thinkers such as Menno Simons; the peace churches, including Mennonites, Anabaptists, and Quakers; and modern pacifist authors such as Stanley Hauerwas, John Howard Yoder, Dorothy Day, Daniel Berrigan, and John Dear believe discipleship permits no compromise with the violence that a sinful world employs to achieve historical ends. Jesus illustrates the meaning and cost of loving enemies with his life and death.

Many modern pacifists are citizens of world powers like the United States. These pacifists often create a counterculture whose purpose is to call members of the churches to resist government policies favoring war. Although these authors are not necessarily sectarian, they do hold that social change is contingent upon and secondary to fidelity in the life to which Jesus calls. Some, like Yoder and Hauerwas, believe a radically different Christian way of life is possible for individuals and the church, but not for a world held captive to the powers of evil. Others, like Day, Dear, and John Paul Lederach, hope that Christian pacifism may lead societies to appreciate the inhumanity and ultimate futility of using violence as a political means.

Another group of theologians, including those promoting some version of political "realism," see the kingdom as more distant even for Christians, and the Christian obligation to intervene in present injustice as more pressing. Thus gospel nonviolence and love of enemies can be set aside provisionally or in some circumstances, given a spiritual or figurative meaning, limited to intention rather than action, or focused on actions as protecting the innocent or the common good. Authors in this stream include Augustine, Aquinas, Luther, Calvin, Reinhold Niebuhr, Paul Ramsey, and some modern Roman Catholic authors such as John Courtney Murray, Bryan Hehir, and some documents of Catholic social teaching. These thinkers do not necessarily abandon attempts to live in the kingdom as inaugurated in history, but they do see the demands of love and justice as entailing measures that would not be required were the kingdom present in its fullness. These measures can include political coercion, violence, and even killing.

Authors who defend the just war do not deny the New Testament mandate to disciples to live a transformed life. But they give the nonviolent reading of that mandate less practical force through a process of translation that gives great weight to the social context and more free-dom to the biblical and ethical interpreter. That interpreter then devel-ops more complex lines of relationship between the New Testament's depiction of kingdom life and the community's embodiment of it in his-tory.

Many just war authors incorporate into their positions some particular qualification intended to safeguard the importance of the nonviolent ideal. Augustine and Luther, for example, give up the Christian indi-vidual's right to self-defense even while maintaining it for a Christian nation. Erasmus holds the nation itself to Christian values, such as a com-mitment to peacemaking or mercy toward the vanquished. Paul Ram-sey insists that noncombatant immunity is a derivative of the gospel. In their pastoral letter *The Challenge of Peace: God's Promise and Our Response*,[82] the US Catholic bishops acknowledge that the pacifist stance is an integral component of the Christian perspective on war and peace, even while reserving the practical application of it to a minority within the religious tradition. Only a very few in the tradition—the Crusaders, Thomas Müntzer, Heinrich Bullinger, and William Gouge, and possibly contemporary thinkers who deny any presumption against war—have seen violence as in some situations an unambiguous good that is wholly consistent with and straightforwardly demanded by their religious faith.

Yet, in my view, both just war thinkers and pacifists tend to underes-timate the genuine moral dilemma posed by the choice to use or not use force. Just war thinkers underestimate the reality that, in practice, war is never fully just and, in fact, invariably entails profound evils.[83] They also fail to take seriously enough the warning of the US Catholic bish-ops that "the possibility of taking even one human life is a prospect we should consider in fear and trembling."[84] To kill even an unjust aggressor involves an assault on the dignity of human life, even if killing accom-plishes the greater good of protecting innocent lives, and may be con-sidered just in view of the total constellation of circumstances in which it occurs.

The basic and universal wrongness of killing, no matter what the cir-cumstances, can be based on religious teaching, such as the New Tes-tament love command or the idea that all persons are created in God's image. The Catholic bishops believe that the duty to respect all human

82. United States Conference of Catholic Bishops, *The Challenge of Peace: God's Challenge and Our Response* (Washington, DC: United States Catholic Conference, 1983), accessed July 19, 2017, https://tinyurl.com/y9yaw85a.

83. This is recognized by, for example, John Langan, "The Just-War Theory after the Gulf War," *Theological Studies* 53, no. 1 (1992): 95–112.

84. USCCB, *The Challenge of Peace*, 80.

lives derives from basic human dignity, not only Christian teaching. And so do I. Addressing the immunity of noncombatants and the moral equality of soldiers, the philosopher Seth Lazar argues that all people have "moral status." Moreover, the inherent and inalienable moral status of all human beings is generally recognized, even though "explaining this is no easy task."[85] In a book on human equality, Jeremy Waldron takes up the challenge, arguing that human equality is based on a range of complex capabilities such as love, reason, and moral agency, not realized to the same degree or in the same way in every individual. Basic equality is not lost on account of wrongdoing.[86] Yet, says Seth Lazar, people can lose their right not to be killed when they pose an unjustified threat. I do not disagree with that, but I maintain that killing a human being with equal basic status still remains morally problematic, even if and when it may be justifiably regarded as the lesser evil. Therefore, even in the rare instance in which killing may be seen as just and necessary, it is properly accompanied not only by regret but remorse and compensatory efforts.

A theme of this book is that a decision either to undertake just war, or to renounce any use of lethal force, constitutes an *irreducible moral dilemma*. Either course of action will involve responsibility for evils caused that cannot be fully resolved by defining the targets as unjust aggressors, by the principle of double effect, by saying that agents have an intention of love, or by renouncing violence whenever it will cost innocent lives. This helps create a stronger case for nonviolent conflict transformation (peacebuilding) as a practical political strategy that can be effective and should be taken seriously, even though it cannot resolve every situation.

The concept of even "just" war as a moral dilemma, properly evo-king not only regret but also remorse and remediation, will be addressed further in the chapters on Augustine and Aquinas. Augustine seems to imply without stating it directly that moral dilemmas exist in which agents are caught in inevitable wrongdoing. Thus chapter 4 on Augustine will include a substantial introduction to the nature and consequences of irreducible moral dilemmas, referencing the work of contemporary philosophers. This discussion will be operative in later chapters, particularly chapter 5 on Aquinas and chapter 9 on twentieth and twenty-first century thought. The Aquinas chapter will consider further the bearing of double effect on the problem. Chapter 6 will take up the contributions of Luther and Calvin to a Christian ethics of war,

85. Seth Lazar, "Evaluating the Revisionist Critique of Just War Theory," *Daedalus* 146, no. 1 (Winter 2017): 119.

86. Jeremy Waldron, *One Another's Equals: The Basis of Human Equality* (Cambridge, MA: Harvard University Press, 2017).

arguing that their theologies of union with Christ in the Spirit might have enabled a more violence-transforming social ethics on their part, and thus they offer a resource for later generations of readers. Chapter 7, on the Crusades and holy war, with Joan of Arc as a contrast case, will portray the disastrous effects for Christianity when violence is related to Christ unambiguously and all restraint abandoned.

Pacifists, in contrast yet analogously to just war proponents, may not take seriously enough the moral responsibility involved in the case of an immediate assault on innocent life or on several lives that a force-bearing agent would have the power to deter. Contemporary pacifists seem more to target the militarized politics of nation-states, and the ruthless violence of ongoing civil conflicts, than they do the possibility of intervention in genocides or other human rights crises. Pacifists also face moral dilemmas when the renunciation of violence arguably involves responsibility for the violence done by others that proceeds unimpeded. Chapter 3 on the early church, chapter 8 on the historic peace churches, and chapter 9 on twentieth-century figures such as Dietrich Bonhoeffer and Dorothy Day will illustrate that pacifist Christianity is not a monolithic tradition and that many of its representatives recognize the dilemmas that a commitment to nonviolence can entail.

Despite these complications, Jesus's ministry of inclusion and reconciliation, his command to love neighbors and enemies, and his nonviolent death on a cross establish beyond a doubt that compassionate, forgiving, and reconciling love is a hallmark of gospel identity (chapter 2). For those who have carried the Christian moral tradition, the question is not *whether,* all things considered, Jesus represents and calls us to peacemaking (positively) and nonviolence (negatively). That much is established, even in just war thinking from Augustine and his teacher Ambrose onward.

The question is, rather, *how* the mandate to live in love, peace, and forgiveness is to function in the practical moral life and in community-building. Does love determine in a clear and specific way every decision a Christian may face in which violent action is a possible outcome (pacifism)? Is love (especially love of enemies) an ideal that encourages us onward, but whose fragmentation in this life requires preparation to use violence (just war theory)? Or does the gospel center Christian attention on active work for reconciliation and justice, embodying the reality that God rules even now among us (peacebuilding)? Can disciples become messengers of mercy, forgiveness, long-suffering—yet ultimately of hopeful action to transform the societies in which they live? This question captures the overriding challenge to Christian pacifism, to Christian just war thought, and now to worldwide peacebuilding movements.

Peacebuilding authors and movements undertake the biblical "ministry of reconciliation" with the conviction that the advent of Christ really does renew the whole creation (2 Cor 5:19). It is then incumbent upon all Christians who are members or allies of violence-torn communities, or communities whose policies and interventions are encouraging or tolerating violence internationally, to actively and creatively seeks ways to build justice, peace, and reconciliation, both personally and politically (chapter 10). The final chapter, on peacebuilding and hope, will turn the lens from international conflict zones to violence that is closer to home for North American readers. It will look at racially motivated violence in the United States, showing how domestic peacebuilders reflect the experiences and principles of peacebuilders globally, and how they are contributing to the Christian cause of peace, justice, reconciliation, and the dignity and voice of oppressed groups.

What peacebuilding distinctively highlights is the practical, located, "ground up," and in many ways pragmatic and provisional nature of Christian responses to the realities of injustice, violence, and human suffering. It embodies active hope that these realities can be changed nonviolently. Peacebuilders see engagement with overlapping and interactive civil society and governmental structures and organizations as part of the call of the gospel. Relationships of mutual recognition, reconciliation, and collaboration, embodied in concrete practices, are foregrounded by peacebuilders as importantly defining what Christian discipleship is called to be and do. They see peacebuilding practices as interconnected with and vital to networks and structures of political responsibility that give respect and cooperation normative force. Their work not only expresses gospel compassion, but it expands the scope of justice within local, national, regional, and global institutions.

2.

Jesus
The Reality of God's Reign and the Possibility of Peace

Historical-critical study of the roles played by the early churches and evangelists in authoring the gospels has cast doubt on many traditional Christian assumptions about the identity and career of Jesus. Yet scholars can still agree that at least on one point the gospels give unanimous and authentic testimony. Even "the most skeptical historian would agree that if Jesus spoke about anything, he spoke about the kingdom of heaven," the Israelite way of referring to "the kingdom of God."[1] Indeed, the kingdom of God "pervades the entire proclamation of Jesus," and "appears largely to have determined the course of his ministry."[2] The biblical symbol of the kingdom (or reign) of God is thus an obvious starting point for ethical reflection on what it means to be a follower of Jesus.

As indicated in the last chapter, it is crucially important for Christian discernment of the ethics of war and peace to know what kind of practices Jesus exemplified in his own ministry. Taking this ethics to the practical level, it is also important to know, on a biblical basis, why Christian disciples should believe that they not only should but can follow his example and, in so doing, transform historical conditions of violence and war. This chapter argues that Jesus not only embodies the inbreaking reign of God, he enables his followers to do likewise with transformative political effect.

"Kingdom of God" is a political and territorial phrase with dynamic connotations. It means that the God of Israel will soon reign in the land

---

1. Bruce J. Malina, *The Social Gospel of Jesus: The Kingdom of God in Mediterranean Perspective* (Minneapolis: Augsburg Fortress, 2001), 1.

2. G. R. Beasley-Murray, *Jesus and the Kingdom of God* (Grand Rapids, MI: William B. Eerdmans, 1986), x.

and that wherever God's kingdom is being inaugurated, God is already exercising God's own sovereignty.[3] In the Hebrew Bible, God is king of the universe, whose justice and peace will ultimately prevail.[4] "His kingdom is an everlasting kingdom" (Dan 4:3). In the earliest gospel, Mark, Jesus proclaims the good news that God's reign is "at hand"; it is the single reality in which human beings are now to live (Mark 1:14–15).[5] The sayings, parables, and deeds of Jesus show that kingdom life reverses ordinary expectations: the lowly are lifted up, displacing the powerful (Matt 25:31–46; Luke 1:46–55; 16:19–31); enemies are forgiven (Matt 5:43-45); and sinners and outcasts are brought into one community with the righteous (Mark 2:13-17). According to the love command found in all four gospels, the rule of the kingdom is love of God and neighbor, inclusively understood (Mark 12:28–34; Matt 22:34–40; Luke 10:25–28; John 15:12). As Paul conveys this message less than a generation after Jesus's death, "there is no longer Jew or Greek, there is no longer slave or free, there is no longer male or female; for all of you are one in Christ Jesus" (Gal 3:28).

Despite the fact that in the Hebrew Bible (the Christian Old Testament), God is sometimes portrayed as a warrior, or as leading his people in holy war, the indisputable biblical anchor of Christian tradition on war and peace is the teaching and example of Jesus. The gospels sometimes portray Jesus as bringing division with his challenging teachings (Matt 10:34–36; Luke 12:51), or as commanding obedience to Roman imperial authorities (Mark 12:13–17; Matt 22:15–22; Luke 20:20–26). All four gospels portray Jesus as intervening aggressively to expel merchants and money changers from the Jerusalem temple (Mark 11:15–19; Matt 21:12–17; Luke 19:45–48; John 2:13–16).

Conversely, Jesus commands his followers to love their enemies and "turn the other cheek," among other "hard sayings" (Matt 5:38–48). He is also depicted as explicitly rejecting the idea that anyone should defend him by the sword, even when faced with unjust arrest (Matt 26:51–52). However, he does not explicitly apply these teachings to

3. Malina, *Social Gospel of Jesus*, 1; James D. G. Dunn, *Jesus' Call to Discipleship* (Cambridge: Cambridge University Press, 1992), 10.

4. Eric M. Meyers and John Rogerson, "The World of the Hebrew Bible," in *The Cambridge Companion to the Bible*, ed. Bruce Chilton et al., 2nd ed. (Cambridge: Cambridge University Press, 2008), 308–9. For a discussion of instances of the concept of kingdom of God in Hebrew sources, see David P. Gushee and Glen H. Stassen, *Kingdom Ethics: Jesus in Contemporary Context* (Downers Grove, IL: InterVarsity, 2003), 23–28; and Bruce Chilton, *Pure Kingdom: Jesus' Vision of God* (Grand Rapids, MI: William B. Eerdmans, 1996), 32–41.

5. See Virgil Howard and David B. Peabody, "Mark," in *The International Bible Commentary: A Catholic and Ecumenical Commentary for the Twenty-First Century*, ed. William R. Farmer et al. (Collegeville, MN: Liturgical Press, 1998), 1339.

those acting in public roles, such as soldiers, judges, governors, emperors, or kings. When the gospels portray him interacting with such people (Matt 8:5–13; John 4:46–54), he does not condemn their professions. David Carroll Cochran is right that the question of "the Christian's relationship to the coercive power of the state—its claim to the legitimate use of violence by its agents—is one of the oldest and most fundamental in the Christian tradition."[6]

Yet Jesus's most characteristic teaching is undoubtedly the arrival of God's reign, establishing an inclusive community of reconciliation and nonviolence. Jesus conveyed this reality through his words and actions, performatively making of his whole life a parable of the kingdom.[7] As I will argue, Jesus's ministry of the reign of God has clear social implications and consequences. Therefore, after a brief discussion of war in the Hebrew Bible, this chapter will focus on Jesus's preaching of the reign of God, especially on the so-called "Sermon on the Mount," with its evangelical commands to turn the other cheek, go the second mile, and love one's enemies (Matt 5:38–48). Chapter 6 will return to the relatively few Christian movements that have taken Old Testament warfare as a model for sanctioning violence in their own day. The majority tradition—whether in its just war, pacifist, or peacebuilding manifestations—accepts the normative value of the nonviolent ideal and interprets the rejection or qualified justification of violence in relation to it.

A GOD OF WAR?

The Bible's books of Genesis and Exodus tell the ancient stories of the calling of Abraham and God's promises to make of his descendants a "great nation" (Gen 12:1–3; 18:18–19), the enslavement of the Israelites in Egypt, their rescue by God through the leadership of Moses, and God's establishment of a covenant with the people at Sinai (Exod 19:4–6; 34:10). The Deuteronomic "history" of these events instructs the people to remember God's faithfulness when celebrating the harvest in the land that shall be given to them:

"A wandering Aramean [Jacob] was my ancestor; he went down into Egypt and lived there as an alien, few in number, and there he became a great nation, mighty and populous. When the Egyptians treated us harshly and afflicted us, by imposing hard labor on us, we cried to the Lord, the God of our ancestors; the Lord heard our voice and saw our affliction, our toil,

6. David Carroll Cochran, *Catholic Realism and the Abolition of War* (Maryknoll, NY: Orbis, 2014), 8.
7. Meyers and Rogerson, "The World of the Hebrew Bible," 309.

and our oppression. The Lord brought us out of Egypt with a mighty hand and an outstretched arm, with a terrifying display of power, and with signs and wonders; and he brought us into this place and gave us this land, a land flowing with milk and honey" (Deut 26:5–9).

This account did not reach its final form until after the exile in the sixth century BCE, and the historicity of many of its aspects is uncertain. Nevertheless, it represents a formative memory for Israel, inspiring trust that the God of Israel rules over the earth, and that special favor has been and will be shown to God's covenant people.

Of note in the discussion of just war, pacifism, and peacebuilding is the exercise of divine power in "terrifying" ways, including the drowning of the troops of Egypt's Pharaoh (Exod 14:28), the visiting of plagues upon his nation (Exod 7–11), and the eventual military conquest of the land of Canaan by the Israelite warrior Joshua (Josh 12). Indeed, the Lord himself "is a warrior" (Exod 15:3). As the reader is told repeatedly, Joshua "utterly destroys" every king, town, and living person, "as the Lord God of Israel had commanded" (Josh 10:40). Indiscriminate killing in God's holy cause is mandated in the instructions passed on by Moses from the Lord: "as for the towns of these peoples that the Lord your God is giving you as an inheritance, you must not let anything that breathes remain alive. You shall annihilate them" (Deut 20:16–17).

The ideology of "holy war" was not confined to ancient Israel. Other nations too construed war as a struggle between ultimate powers, the gods of warring nations, and also adopted policies of totally exterminating enemy peoples as a sacrifice to the winning god or gods. Biblical texts about a warring God and his warring people are part of a larger cultural milieu and bear its imprint. To what degree these policies were implemented is not clear from the historical evidence, but they exist at least to the extent of inscriptions that archeological explorations have uncovered in the ancient Near East. Yet Israel did not, in point of actual fact, destroy every inhabitant of Canaan, as is obvious if only from later events in the biblical story itself (e.g., Judges 1, where the Israelites do battle with the Canaanites).

When faith communities explore the Bible for resources with which to reflect on a given ethical issue—whether it be violence, wealth, government, slavery, or gender equality—they are likely to find perspectives and precedents that both confirm and affront contemporary ethical convictions. Therefore it is important to compare a given text or teaching to the biblical witness overall, with Christians giving precedence to the New Testament. Richard B. Hays is representative of the way many Christians deal with the problem of holy war in the Old Testament when he says that "the New Testament witness is finally normative" and that witness counsels love of enemies.[8]

To avoid supersessionism and to give Jesus his due as a Jewish teacher, it is nevertheless important to examine whether the Hebrew Bible itself qualifies the seemingly straightforward endorsement of what today would be considered genocide or otherwise undeserved or disproportionate violence. The controlling theme of the Hebrew Bible is God's election of Israel, including Israel's role as a "light to the nations" (Isa 42:6; 49:6; 60:3), both of which are understood in terms of righteousness, harmony, and peace (Isa 2:3–4; 11:1–9). And love commands are not absent in the scriptures by which Jesus himself was formed (Deut 6:4–5; Lev 19:18). In Israelite perspective, the idea of an all-consuming holy war is a subordinate theme, and it is meant to serve other elements in the overarching story of covenant.

In larger perspective, and despite the objections that are rightly raised against it, holy war serves as a testament to three religious convictions key to the covenant with God. First, any victory won by military efforts is attributable to divine grace and power, not purely human strength, weapons, or wit (Josh 26:12). Second, the Israelites are always to resist and remain separated from foreign peoples, and their tempting rituals and gods (Deut 20:18). Third, neither war nor any other divinely commanded activity is waged for human profit, pride, or booty, but for God's purposes alone.

In addition, the Hebrew scriptures themselves cast some doubt on the ideology of holy war as a pure expression of the covenantal relation to God. Susan Niditch argues that some strands or authors show discomfort with unrestrained war and brutality and that they offer implicit critiques of it. Before waging all-out war for the "promised land," the Israelites are instructed to offer cities terms of peace (including the enslavement of inhabitants; Deut 20:10–11); if war is waged, women and children may be taken captive rather than killed, and orchards should be spared (Deut 13–14; 19). Numbers 31 justifies and ritualizes war as holy, but the ensuing killing nevertheless defiles, thus requiring cleansing and sacrifices of atonement.[9] The author of 1 and 2 Chronicles leaves out details of cruel behavior by King David—for example, the arbitrary killing of prisoners—that appear in an earlier account of the same events in 2 Samuel, which the Chronicler otherwise adopts entirely.[10] And a rabbinic

---

8. Richard B. Hays, *The Moral Vision of the New Testament: Community, Cross, New Creation: A Contemporary Introduction to New Testament Ethics* (New York: HarperCollins, 1996), 336.

9. Susan Niditch, *War in the Hebrew Bible: A Study in the Ethics of Violence* (New York: Oxford University Press, 1993), 89.

10. Niditch, *War in the Hebrew Bible*, 133.

tradition portrays God as enjoining heaven's angels from rejoicing jubilantly when Pharaoh's soldiers are lost in the Red Sea.[11]

After the monarchy and exile, when Israel was under the successive control of the Persians, the Greeks, and the Romans, the ideology of holy war no longer had practical relevance, given Israel's lack of political sovereignty. It was even a dangerous idea, since revolts against the powers ruling Israel generally ended in failure, with the qualified exception of the Maccabean victory (of relatively brief duration) in the second century BCE.[12] In time the holy war ideology of Israel faded away, to be replaced by an imagery of divine victory over evil that lived on in biblical writings such as the prophets, Daniel, and the New Testament book of Revelation.[13]

THE REIGN OF GOD AND ITS SOCIAL IMPACT

The mission of Jesus was to renew the people of Israel under God's covenant, and he was not primarily a political reformer, much less a revolutionary or a warrior. Nevertheless, as Daniel Harrington remarks, "his teachings had political and economic implications that got him into trouble with the Jewish political and religious leaders as well as the Roman imperial officials. His teachings about the kingdom of God and justice were surely factors in his arrest, condemnation and execution."[14]

In the circumstances of Jesus and his first hearers, a religious message such as his would necessarily have meanings and consequences far beyond the "spiritual." The social implications of Jesus's ministry of the reign of God derive not only from his convictions about the divine character and will for humanity but also from the ways in which politics, religion, and economics were interdependent in the first-century Mediterranean world, as well as for Jews living under Roman rule.

After the death of David's son Solomon, and the dissolution of the Davidic dynasty around 925 BCE, Israel divided into the northern king-

---

11. Niditch, *War in the Hebrew Bible*, 150.

12. Reuven Firestone, *Holy War in Judaism: The Fall and Rise of a Controversial Idea* (New York: Oxford University Press, 2012).

13. Meyers and Rogerson, "The World of the Hebrew Bible," 125; Bernhard W. Anderson, *Understanding the Old Testament*, assisted by Katheryn Pfisterer Darr, abridged fourth edition (Upper Saddle River, NJ: Prentice Hall, 1998), 128. For a contemporary exploration of a biblically based "just war" theory in Judaism, see Sarah Bohman, "Laying Down One's Swords—Judaism's Just War," *University of St. Thomas Journal of Law and Public Policy* 3, no. 1 (2009): 99–106, accessed July 15, 2013, https://tinyurl.com/yadm5ym2.

14. Daniel J. Harrington, SJ, *Jesus: A Historical Portrait* (Cincinnati: St. Anthony Messenger, 2007), 61–62.

dom of Israel and the southern kingdom of Judah, but these both fell to external powers by the early sixth century BCE.[15] The ministry of Jesus took place in Galilee, in the north of Judea, which by that time was under Roman occupation. Rome maintained control through local intermediaries, who were expected to make swift retaliation against threats and perceived threats to the imperial order. Bruce Malina sees the underlying violence that sustained this entire order as symbolized and publicized by the ubiquitous presence of Roman troops and the bloody public games in which animate beings, animal and human, were sacrificed cruelly for entertainment in the public amphitheater.[16]

Yet Jesus lived during the Pax Romana, not in a time of violent social upheaval or war. While some scholars like John Dominic Crossan and Richard Horsley have said there was considerable ongoing violence in Palestine in Jesus's environment,[17] more recent work on the "Jewish Jesus" has gone back into the historical evidence about Jews in Galilee and argued that, although imperial government could certainly be brutal in wiping out perceived threats to its power and order (why Jesus was crucified), daily life in Galilee was culturally Jewish and Roman force was more at a distance.[18] It required and enforced the cooperation of Jewish "client kings" like Herod the Great and Herod Antipas and local governors like Pilate.

The main social problem Jesus addresses is oppression of the poor by the elites, especially via the taxation system needed to run the Pax Romana. Judea came under the authority of a Roman governor, Pontius Pilate; Galilee was ruled by a Jewish king, Herod Antipas, who was "a political tool" of the Romans.[19] In Jesus's time, the Jewish king served at the Romans' discretion. Only the Romans had the authority to impose the death penalty, and they did not hesitate to use it. Herod and the officials of the Jerusalem temple colluded with Roman interests in exploiting the natural and agricultural resources of subject peoples, keeping the peace, and collecting onerous taxes. This included a tax to support the

15. J. Maxwell Miller and John H. Hayes, *A History of Ancient Israel and Judah* (Philadelphia: Westminster, 1986), 220.

16. Malina, *Social Gospel of Jesus*, 27.

17. See John Dominic Crossan, *God and Empire: Jesus against Rome Then and Now* (San Francisco: HarperSanFrancisco, 2007); Richard A. Horsley, *Jesus and the Spiral of Violence: Popular Jewish Resistance in Roman Palestine* (San Francisco: Harper & Row, 1987).

18. Sean Freyne, *Jesus, a Jewish Galilean: A New Reading of the Jesus Story* (London: T&T Clark, 2004).

19. Harrington, *Jesus*, 63.

operation of the Jerusalem Temple, including the High Priest, various levels of other priests, the Levites, and their retainers.[20]

While all societies can be seen as organized around the four institutions of kinship, politics, economics, and religion, kinship and politics were by far the dominant focal points in ancient Mediterranean societies, whereas the economy and religious roles and structures were embedded in them.[21] In other words, one's economic status and religious identity followed from one's membership in the family and the *polis*. Economics and religion were not regarded as freestanding realities or concerns. One's political roles and status were tied to the standing of one's family and to one's standing within the family by age, marital status, and especially gender.[22] One's religion was the religion of one's people, ethnic group, and family. Religious identity or ethnicity was also tied in to political standing, since the Roman Empire recognized only one state religion, the worship of the traditional Roman gods. Political status determined access to material and social goods.

The political religion of the Roman state, as of the temple aristocracy, expressed religious loyalties and values in ways that furthered the extant political hierarchy. The roles of religious officials were embedded in this hierarchy and benefitted from it. The "focus was on the deity(ies) as the source of power and might, expected to provide order, well-being, and prosperity for the body politic and its power wielders (elites) to the benefit of subjects."[23] Therefore to speak of or act in favor of religious reforms was necessarily to adopt an agenda about family or ethnic group, power politics and government, and differences in economic status or routes of access to goods.

The Galilean society in which Jesus lived had an agricultural economy, in which land was the basis of wealth and was transmitted by patrilineal inheritance. Many small landholders were driven off their land by debt. Since enhanced wealth and power for elite families required the acquisition of more territory, internal political struggles among rulers of territories resulted in ruthless, corrupt, and rapidly changing regimes, as

20. Anthony J. Saldarini, "Jewish Responses to Greek and Roman Cultures, 322 BCE to 200 CE," revised by Amy-Jill Levine, in *Cambridge Companion to the Bible*, 412–15, 422–26, 432–33.

21. For a more detailed discussion of the ancient embedded economy, see Ekkehard W. Stegemann and Wolfgang Stegemann, *The Jesus Movement: A Social History of Its First Century*, trans. O. C. Dean Jr. (Minneapolis: Augsburg Fortress, 1999), 15–52.

22. Stegemann and Stegemann, *Jesus Movement*, 65: "Indeed, membership in the female sex in the ancient societies of the Mediterranean region placed one on the wrong side of a fundamental social asymmetry, which diminished not only the social status of women but also their possibilities for participation in social power and the acquisition of privileges."

23. Malina, *Social Gospel of Jesus*, 24.

displayed in the frequent displacement of Roman rulers (who were the empire's largest land owners).[24]

Galilee was organized around the interests of powerful rural landowners, on whom the peasant majority was dependent. These large landowners had their primary residences on country estates, and they maintained houses clustered with others of high rank in the city. City residences afforded people the opportunity to socialize (e.g., to establish social status by hosting and attending banquets); to maintain political positions through participation in institutions such as the senate and intermarriage; and to access the system of taxation by which money was extorted from the vast majority eking out a living as small land owners, tenant farmers, and day laborers.[25] The relatively small elite in the cities, where power and wealth were concentrated, was dominant in the political, economic, religious, and cultural domains, to the disadvantage of the rural population. "Confiscations, appropriations, taxes or demands for tribute, compulsory labor and the payment of rent all enrich the rulers," driving up protests and rebellions and evoking even greater brutality from the ruling classes.[26]

In traditional peasant societies, social goods (both material and nonmaterial) are perceived to be limited, so that any improvement in the situation of one person or family is considered to be at the expense of another. Obvious consequences for the subsistence-level economy of the peasant village are high levels of anxiety, subservience, resentment, envy, and competition, as well as in-group loyalty centered on the family. Peasants and poor urban dwellers also competed for the favor of the powerful and prosperous. In Roman society, relations between elites and nonelites could be formed for mutual advantage in terms of "patron-client" roles. Patronage is a system by which well-placed persons use their reputation, influence or wealth to obtain benefits for a lower-status person or family, the "client." In return, patrons receive honor, information, and political support.[27] Patron-client relationships characterized by hierarchy, asymmetry, inequality, power, and status largely determine the way in which resources are channeled.[28] Jesus challenges this entire

24. Stegemann and Stegemann, *Jesus Movement*, 11.

25. Malina, *Social Gospel of Jesus*, 24–27; see also Stegemann and Stegemann, *Jesus Movement*, 99–100.

26. Stegemann and Stegemann, *Jesus Movement*, 14.

27. K. C. Hanson and Douglas E. Oakman, *Palestine in the Time of Jesus: Social Structures and Social Conflicts* (Minneapolis: Augsburg Fortress, 1998), 70–71; Bruce J. Malina and Richard R. Rohrbaugh, *Social-Science Commentary on the Synoptic Gospels* (Minneapolis: Augsburg Fortress, 1992), 74–76.

28. Halvor Moxnes, *Economy of the Kingdom: Social Conflict and Economic Relations in Luke's Gospel* (Minneapolis: Fortress, 1988), 36–47.

system in his practice of sharing meals ("table fellowship" or "open commensality") with the socially disreputable, regardless of social status.[29]

When the message of Jesus is placed in its concrete historical, political, economic, and religious circumstances, it is easy to see why "kingdom of God" could symbolize social renewal. Ultimately God rules, not the emperor, the governor, or their Jewish client-kings. Jesus is the patron of all, hosting the social riff-raff at his banquets without any expectation of personal return. Local communities could become new iconoclastic "families" that were nonpatriarchal and noncompetitive, providing concrete cooperation and care for one another. Such communities were not limited to reconciliation with external political enemies, but brought renewed reciprocal generosity among households.[30] A modern-day analogy might be found in Latin American "base communities" that bolster local agency and mutual support, while posing a tacit challenge to the interests and control of superior classes.[31]

From the Roman perspective, Jesus was a popular preacher who looked to be undermining the status quo or perhaps, with his talk of a new "kingdom," even calling for a revolution.[32] In fact, Jesus is reported to have called for the destruction of the temple in Jerusalem (Mark 13:1–2; Matt 24:1–2; Luke 21:5–6), and his disruptive challenge to its operations was quickly followed by his capture and execution (Mark 11:15–19, 27–33; Matt 21:12–17, 23–27; Luke 19:45–48; 20:1–8; John 2:13–16).[33]

Although Jesus was not in reality calling for a violent social movement, his "good news" was still a threat to the religious and political authorities. Appealing to Isaiah, he proclaims good news and liberation to the poor, the captives, and the oppressed (Luke 4:16–19). This message carried "a fundamental transvaluation of values, an exalting of the

29. For a discussion of recent controversies regarding the historicity of this practice and a defense, see Craig Blomberg, "Jesus, Sinners, and Table Fellowship," *Bulletin for Biblical Research* 19, no. 1 (2009): 35–62.

30. Richard Horsley, *The Liberation of Christmas: The Infancy Narratives in Social Context* (New York: Crossroad, 1989), 92, 122–25. On families and households in early Christianity, and the challenge to the patriarchal family posed by Christian family symbolism, see Elisabeth Schüssler Fiorenza, *In Memory of Her: A Feminist Theological Reconstruction of Christian Origins* (New York: Crossroad, 1989), 150; Carolyn Osiek, *Families in the New Testament World: Households and House Churches* (Louisville, KY: Westminster John Knox, 1997); and Osiek, "The Family in Early Christianity: 'Family Values' Revisited," *Catholic Biblical Quarterly* 58, no. 1 (1996): 1–25.

31. Moxnes, *Economy of the Kingdom*, 27–43.

32. Harrington, *Jesus*, 63.

33. For a discussion of the complex political factors that may have led to Jesus's arrest, see Howard Clark Kee, "The Formation of Christian Communities," in *Cambridge Companion to the Bible*, 592–96.

humble and a critique of the mighty."[34] As Jesus's parables illustrate, to live in the kingdom is to replace trust in power and wealth with an attitude of repentance, generosity, and dependence on God (see the parables of the good Samaritan, prodigal son, and unjust steward in Luke 10:30–37; 15:11–32; 16:1–8). The kingdom reverses expectations and breaks religious and social boundaries by including the poor, the outcast, the sinner, and even the enemy within the community's fellowship (Matt 21:31).

Next we will turn to the concrete impact that the eschatological reality of the kingdom is meant to have in the lives of disciples, in the church, and in their social worlds. On this basis we will examine more closely the significance of the biblical passage most widely cited in relation to the problem of war—the Sermon on the Mount.

ESCHATOLOGY AND SOCIAL ETHICS: INTERPRETIVE MODELS

To recognize the importance of the kingdom concept as characteristic of Jesus's preaching does not settle the issue of what difference it can or should make in the life of discipleship in the first century or today. Although the terminology of "kingdom present," "future," and "already/ not yet" that has been the vehicle for much discussion about practical discipleship and the use of force is a twentieth-century innovation, the problem it captures is as old as the gospel.[35] The issue is essentially that of eschatology. Certainly for Jesus as for other Jews, the fullness of God's reign is a future reality, completed by God's hand alone. If so, what impact does the nearness of God's reign as proclaimed by Jesus (Mark 1:15) have on our lives now? In what way does it affect individual relationships, the community of the church, and the roles that Christians and Christian communities play in their larger social worlds?

This problem has received varied resolutions, even within the New Testament. As we shall see in subsequent chapters, differences in eschatological vision underlie much of the diversity in the Christian tradition over whether war can be justified or whether biblical nonviolence makes an immediate practical claim on Christian action. All mainstream authors take love of God and neighbor seriously and envision the fullness of God's kingdom as righteousness, love, and peace. Yet they disagree over

---

34. Hays, *Moral Vision of the New Testament*, 163.

35. The terminology is associated with two mid-twentieth-century figures, Gerhard Vos (1862–1949; Princeton Theological Seminary) and George Eldon Ladd (1911–1982; Fuller Theological Seminary).

whether under present historical conditions, love of enemies, forgiveness, and reconciliation are always realistic, prudent, and just.

The relation between the social dimensions of the kingdom of God and its eschatological character has been a fraught topic in biblical research and in Christian social ethics for well over a century. The liberal Protestant social gospel movement of the late nineteenth century (as exemplified by Albert Ritschl and Walter Rauschenbusch) placed Jesus's teaching to love the neighbor in the context of an ethical mandate to transform unjust social relationships. The kingdom of God is present, in this view, in the lives of individuals and groups who achieve social reform by following and extending Jesus's example of brotherly love. The optimism of Christian social liberalism was shattered by the First World War. Even before that, however, the development of historical-critical research on the Bible encouraged Johannes Weiss and Albert Schweitzer to criticize the equation of the biblical kingdom of God with programs of social change.[36] These two authors marked a major modern shift in twentieth century interpretation of the kingdom, "by their discovery of the eschatological Jesus, preacher of the apocalyptic kingdom of God."[37]

Although their views are not identical, Weiss and Schweitzer agreed that Jesus expected that the kingdom was to be established by an apocalyptic act of God, probably after Jesus's own death. Though imminent, they said, it was not a reality in his own ministry; Jesus called his hearers to repent and to love one another in preparation for the coming judgment. His message to his contemporaries was therefore not intended "for us," nor are we in a comparable situation of "interim" expectation. Richard Hiers demonstrates the immensity of the problem that this historical reinterpretation created for biblical theology and for Christian ethics:

> The central problem was that Jesus had apparently expected the kingdom of God to come in the near future. If he had been mistaken about that, how could he and his first-century message be relied on in the twentieth? Moreover, what could the kingdom of God mean to people today who do not share the eschatological world-view?[38]

36. Johannes Weiss, *Jesus' Proclamation of the Kingdom of God* (Philadelphia: Fortress, 1971; originally published in 1892); Albert Schweitzer, *The Mystery of the Kingdom of God* (New York: Schocken, 1914); *The Quest for the Historical Jesus* (New York: Macmillan, 1968; originally published in 1910).

37. Wendell Willis, "The Discovery of the Eschatological Kingdom: Johannes Weiss and Albert Schweitzer," in *The Kingdom of God in Twentieth-Century Interpretation,* ed. Wendell Willis (Peabody, MA: Hendrickson, 1987), 1.

38. Richard H. Hiers Jr., "Pivotal Reactions to the Eschatological Interpretations: Rudolf

Rudolph Bultmann and C. H. Dodd replied to this dilemma by emphasizing the presence of the kingdom of God in Jesus's own ministry and, by extension, in the lives of those who are converted.[39] Jesus's message is not limited to his first-century audience but is for all times. However, overcorrecting for Weiss and Schweitzer, Bultmann and Dodd downplayed the future aspect of the kingdom so much as to virtually eliminate it. With it also went most of the transcendent and divine basis of the kingdom's reality and power. Bultmann did not deny that there was a future element to Jesus's own preaching, but he translated it into a timelessly relevant call to decision and conversion, an essence that should be extracted from Jesus's mythological (including eschatological) concepts.[40] Dodd adopted the solution of "realized eschatology"—that is, the kingdom of God and its blessings were already present in Jesus's own ministry and continue to remain present in the life of faith.[41] According to Dodd's student Norman Perrin, the futurity of the kingdom in the New Testament is largely the product of "early Christian apocalyptic" and did not even originate with the teaching of Jesus himself.[42]

The contentious issue among biblical scholars at the turn of the century and shortly thereafter seems to have been, then, not so much the practicability of nonviolence, but the credibility to the modern religious sensibility of any supernatural meaning that might be attached to the notion of the kingdom. For its part, the social gospel movement did not hinge so much on reasserting the supernatural realm over against historical-critical skeptics. Rather, it insisted that Jesus's message about God could (and should) be enacted in more just relationships and social structures, combatting the abuses of the industrial revolution. The tacit premise or implication of the claim that Jesus's ministry and gospel can transform social injustice, however, is both supernatural and eschatological: Jesus embodies divine power, and that power, the power of the inbreaking reign of God, is also available to Christians working for justice in every later era.

The issue of the presence/distance of the kingdom has continued not

Bultmann and C.H. Dodd," in *The Kingdom of God in Twentieth-Century Interpretation,* ed. Wendell Willis (Peabody, MA: Hendrickson, 1987), 31.

39. Rudolf Bultmann, *Theology of the New Testament,* 2 vols. (New York: Scribners, 1954–55); *New Testament and Mythology* (Philadelphia: Fortress, 1984); *Jesus and the Word* (New York: Scribners, 1958); *Existence and Faith* (New York: Meridian, 1960); C. H. Dodd, *The Gospel in the New Testament* (London: National Sunday School Union, 1926); *The Parables of the Kingdom* (New York: Scribners, 1961); *The Founder of Christianity* (New York: Macmillan, 1970).

40. Hiers, "Pivotal Reactions," 25.

41. Hiers, "Pivotal Reactions," 18–19.

42. Norman Perrin, *Jesus and the Language of the Kingdom: Symbol and Metaphor in New Testament Interpretation* (Philadelphia: Fortress, 1976), 30.

only to interest biblical scholars but also to be of vital importance to political theologians, liberation theologians, and Christian social ethicists. One concern may still be to restore the credibility of an otherworldly religion by giving it some political traction. But a more important factor is the practical investment of global Christianity in transforming the distortions and dysfunctions so pervasive in social life. Jesus came not only to promise eternal life but to live and die on the side of the poor, and to enact and enable their historical liberation. The transformative social function of Jesus's kingdom of God is not a substitute for faith in a transcendent God. Instead it is a manifestation of real salvation from God in Jesus Christ. The cross signifies the power of sin, the sacrificial nature of Christian love, and the reality that the gospel will meet fierce opposition from the "powers that be" of any era. The risen Christ, present in the Spirit, empowers the social and political missions of the church. Global poverty and violence challenge all biblical scholars and theologians to draw every possible connection between the gospel of the reign of God, the cross as divine solidarity with human suffering, the risen Christ, and the real political world.

Whether or to what degree that world can be affected positively by eschatological harmony and righteousness is crucial to any consideration of violence as an option for a Christian. The Christian just war tradition has been built on the premise that the present world so entangles the disciple in conflict and "brokenness" that gospel fidelity requires compromise action. Christian pacifism is premised instead on the accessibility of kingdom life now and the reality of a community in which the kingdom already begins, whether or not that community may be limited to the church. Peacebuilding takes kingdom life beyond the church, and while not denying the inevitable evil in political institutions and actions, emphasizes the historical accessibility of reconciliation and justice. Taking the interpretation of Cyril of Alexandria as still the most plausible—"it is in the scope of your choices, and it lies in your power to receive it"—G. R. Beasley-Murray suggests that the gist of Luke 17:20–21 is that the kingdom is within the reach of all those who have heard the good news. They need not concern themselves with trying to determine when, where, and with what signs the kingdom will arrive, but rather with earnestly, gratefully, and hopefully living its reality.[43]

43. Beasley-Murray, *Jesus and the Kingdom of God*, 102, citing Cyril of Alexandria, *Commentary on Luke*, section 368.

JEWISH APOCALYPTIC BACKGROUND

Biblical scholars writing around the turn of the twenty-first century offer a new avenue to reclaim Jesus's eschatology. Affirming or rediscovering Jesus's Jewish heritage, and his indebtedness to it, they recognize his teaching to be a form of Jewish apocalyptic. Yet this does not mean that Jesus's kingdom preaching is irrelevant to social change. Though Jesus is in continuity with Jewish apocalyptic, he distinctively develops or reinterprets its recurrent themes.[44] The points of contrast between Jesus and his background illuminate his own characteristic message. Jesus shared the Jewish idea that God would vindicate Israel with a future, decisive act. Yet he also believed that God's action is even now enabling a new life for his people. This idea is not absent among Jesus's Jewish contemporaries, but it is much more central and pronounced in Jesus's own ministry.

The background of Jesus's use of the symbol kingdom of God is divine faithfulness to God's covenant with Israel. The people of Israel returned to their land from exile in the sixth century, but they were thenceforth subject to foreign rule. The restoration of the Davidic kingship seemed an increasingly unlikely possibility given programs of forced Hellenization with which some of the Jewish leadership cooperated and the undiminished political impotence of the Israelites, even in their own land.[45] Trust in God's providence turned from anticipation that God would anoint a new king like David, and it largely assumed the form of an eschatological hope. Either God would fulfill God's promises to the righteous in Israel by a spectacular action in the last period of history, or God would do so by ending the world as we know it and inaugurating a wholly new age. Jewish apocalyptic favors the latter scenario, and it was the dominant (though not the only) vision in Jesus's time. In any event, evildoers will be destroyed by God's mighty act, righteousness and justice will reign, and God's kingdom will be made fully visible.[46]

John Collins points out that even when apocalyptic literature condemns the powers of the day and expects an ultimate utopia, it can still adopt a quietist politics, subservient to worldly authorities for the time being. This strand existed in Second Temple Judaism and conveys a mood reflected in Daniel 2. Although corrupt foreign rule is eventually

44. Sean Freyne, "Jesus the Jew," in *Jesus as Christ: What Is at Stake in Christology?*, ed. Andrés Torres Queiruga et al. (London: SCM, 2008), 24–32; E. P. Sanders, *Judaism: Practice and Belief, 63 BC – 66 AD* (London: SCM, 1992).

45. Stegemann and Stegemann, *Jesus Movement*, 145–46.

46. Harrington, *Jesus*, 22–23. For a general definition of apocalyptic with Jewish and Christian examples, see Meyers and Rogerson, "The World of the Hebrew Bible," 306.

to be destroyed by the hand of God and replaced by an eschatological kingdom, the seer respects and even flatters the Babylonian king (Dan 2:38). "In fact, apocalyptic hopes for a judgment and a utopian kingdom have often been deferred. . . . The revolutionary implications of the kingdom of God have often been muted in both Jewish and Christian tradition."[47]

A different, revolutionary stance informs the more urgent apocalyptic vision of Daniel 7. Although apocalyptic by definition expects that the new world order will be constructed by divine action, the condemnation of the present political order may motivate resistance rather than cooperation. If so, future hope can issue in historical agitation for radical change, even though the focus of apocalyptic as such remains the future order, not the reform of the present.[48]

Many of the themes and images that Jewish apocalyptic drew from earlier traditions to depict the signs and events surrounding the end time were re-appropriated by New Testament writers to convey the significance of Jesus: the contest of two ages or powers of light and darkness, a cosmic battle, judgment upon the world, the coming of "the son of man," the figure of a messiah (anointed one, like David), "the holy ones of the Most High," a final period of tribulation, a new heaven and earth, and (in the later Second Temple era) the resurrection of the dead. Jesus's own affinity with a dimension of future expectation is heard in his call to repent in view of the nearness of the kingdom (Mark 1:17); and in the prayer he taught his disciples, beseeching, "Your kingdom come. Your will be done, on earth as it is in heaven" (Matt 6:10; Luke 11:2).[49]

On the one side, Jesus rejects the idea that his followers can or should try to overcome Roman imperial rule. Yet on the other, he also rejects the idea that the kingdom will not come until cosmic signs and wonders have been manifest. As he tells the Pharisees, "the kingdom of God is among you" (Luke 17:21). God's reign is already felt in the community of his followers when they live in the grace of God's love, justice, and mercy, and in so doing they reflect the divine character in their own acts of compassion, forgiveness, reconciliation, and generosity.

As seen in Jewish apocalyptic of the more revolutionary variety, the idea that God's eschatological reign might result in changes now is not entirely unique to Jesus. Consider as well Isaiah's vision of Jerusalem as Zion, now healed of divisions, a place where "the servants of Yahweh" already enjoy his blessings, while those who have worshiped idols or

47. John J. Collins, *Encounters with Biblical Theology* (Minneapolis: Fortress, 2005), 136.
48. Collins, *Encounters with Biblical Theology*, 138–39.
49. Harrington, *Jesus*, 23–24.

oppressed the poor are punished (Isa 65:1–15; 66:14).[50] In the first century, the Essene community at Qumran envisioned a future warrior messiah who liberates Israel from the Gentiles. Their writings—as seen in the Dead Sea Scrolls found at Qumran—describe a community meal of bread and wine that anticipates the messianic banquet of the eschatological age. Yet the Essene writings also describe present communion with heavenly beings, as if community members "were already living the risen life with the angels."[51] Jesus may have had a connection with the Essene movement through John the Baptist. Like the Essenes, John withdrew to the desert for an ascetic existence, and he focused on present repentance for a coming judgment. But where John stressed the futurity and imminence of God's reign, Jesus also gave expression in word and deed to its present manifestations.[52]

JESUS'S MINISTRY EMBODIES THE REIGN OF GOD

That the kingdom is already dawning in Jesus's own ministry, by the power of God, is demonstrated strikingly in his miracles of healing and exorcism. "More than any other teacher of morality, the Matthean Jesus teaches with *exousia*, i.e., divine power and authority, and by this empowerment makes possible a new existence."[53] Several confirmatory miracles are collected together by Matthew (8–9). They include the healing of a man with leprosy, two blind men, the paralyzed servant of a Roman centurion, another paralyzed man, the mother-in-law of Peter, a woman with a flow of blood, and a man unable to speak. Jesus even raises his friend Lazarus from the dead (John 11:38–44) and brings back to life the daughter of Jairus, a leader in the synagogue (Mark 5:21–43).

The synoptics include stories in which people are healed of demons, for example, Mary Magdalene (Mark 16:91; Luke 8:2), the Gerasene demoniac (Mark 5:1–20; Matt 8:28–34; Luke 8:26–39), the daughter of a Syrophoenician woman (Mark 7:25–30; Matt 15:21–28), and a man in Jesus's hometown of Capernaum (Mark 1:21–28). "If it is by the finger of God that I cast out demons, then the kingdom of God has come to you" (Luke 11:20). Jesus also has power over nature, calming storms, walking on water, multiplying fish, and making water become wine. These

---

50. Freyne, *Jesus*, 103–8.

51. Collins, *Apocalyptic Imagination*, 174.

52. Harrington, *Jesus*, 18.

53. Raymond E. Brown, *An Introduction to the New Testament* (New York: Doubleday, 1997), 178.

miracles are signs of the presence of the Messiah who acts with the power of God (Matt 7:22; 11:15).[54]

These miracles prepare the way to see Jesus as, even more astonishingly, acting with the authority of God to forgive sins. If Jesus can heal the body and mind, he can heal the spirit and restore the person's relation to his Father in heaven (Matt 9:2–8). According to Mark and Matthew, Jesus heals a man who could not walk "so that you may know that the Son of Man has authority on earth to forgive sins" (Mark 2:10; Matt 9:6). This claim brings the accusation of blasphemy against Jesus, and it helps propel the machinery of rejection and persecution that will end in his death. Jesus evoked such a reaction not because of his insignificance but because of his power. He was not a political figure in the typical sense, but his words and deeds inaugurated a new and divinely willed order that is deeply threatening to oppressive structures, whether religious or political.

God's effective reign makes it possible for the disciples to experience a divine transformative presence in the midst of ordinary experience (Luke 17:21). God's promises of liberation and freedom are "now fulfilled in your hearing" (Luke 4:21). As remembered by the evangelists, Jesus is not a sectarian; he travels about Galilee, engaging the common people in their quotidian existences. He expects them to enact the availability of God's rule in familiar relationships among parents and children, friends and neighbors, travelers and robbery victims, masters and servants, vineyard owners and workers, observant Jews and tax collectors. Jesus does not see the world in extreme dualisms, nor does he preach hatred or rejection to opponents, sinners, and outsiders. He shares with Paul a stance toward God's eschatological action that Daniel Harrington calls "modified apocalyptic dualism."[55] Yes, the kingdom is in contrast to this world, standing over against it; yet by God's power, evil relationships and patterns of control are already being replaced. It is because of its anticipatory yet real presence, not its absence, that the kingdom has faced violent opposition (Matt 11:12; Luke 16:16). Jesus's belief that change should begin now, first and foremost in the holy city of Jerusalem, accounts for his final pilgrimage and confrontation, first with Temple practices, then with religious and imperial authorities.

This is not to deny the continuing truth and political value of the "kingdom distant" accent in much biblical apocalyptic, present also as an aspect of Jesus's message, considered overall. Certainly Jesus, like the

---

54. Brown, *Introduction to the New Testament*, 39–43.

55. Daniel J. Harrington, SJ, and James F. Keenan, SJ, *Paul and Virtue Ethics: Building Bridges between New Testament Studies and Moral Theology* (New York: Rowman & Littlefield, 2010), 114. Each chapter is single-authored.

more quietist varieties of apocalyptic, recognized that the powers of the world are often provisionally dominant over the righteous, and that efforts to embody God's reign in history will bring suffering and death. Apocalyptic assures the faithful that even though they may seem to suffer defeat, God rules over the whole universe, and God's justice will prevail. Apocalyptic is an answer to the problem of the historical intransigence of evil, the destruction of the innocent, and the endlessness of human suffering.[56]

THE SERMON ON THE MOUNT

Nowhere in New Testament interpretation are eschatology, theology, and ethics bound more closely together than in approaches to Matthew's Sermon on the Mount (Matt 5–7). When ethical concerns are foremost, the so-called "hard sayings" (5:38–48) command attention. By demanding nonresistance and love of enemies, Jesus seems both to hold the faithful to impossible standards of concrete action and to break up the foundations of justice on which social cooperation is built. Also problematic are the equally direct and at points more impractical imperatives to avoid anger, lust, divorce, and swearing (5:21–37). The Beatitudes (5:3–11) generally have been of secondary ethical interest, while the Lord's Prayer (5:9b–16) has remained peripheral in most accounts of Christian morality. Before the development in the nineteenth century of a historical-critical method of studying and correlating biblical texts, the ethical attention given to the remainder of Matthew 5–7 was occasional at best, and the gospel setting of the Sermon was virtually ignored. Undoubtedly the greatest impact of the historical-critical method on ethical interpretations of the Sermon on the Mount has been made by the discovery that the early church expected the imminent return of Jesus, risen Lord and judge, to complete the reign of God begun in his lifetime.

The interpretive typology proposed by Joachim Jeremias in 1963 is simple, yet still captures the basic contours of classic readings of the Sermon, although more complex models have been proposed.[57] According

---

56. See J. Matthew Ashley, "The Turn to Apocalyptic and the Option for the Poor in Christian Theology," in *The Option for the Poor in Christian Theology*, ed. Daniel G. Groody (Notre Dame, IN: University of Notre Dame Press, 2007), 132–54.

57. Joachim Jeremias, *The Sermon on the Mount,* trans. Norman Perrin (Philadelphia: Fortress, 1963); see also broader schematizations by Harvey K. McArthur, *Understanding the Sermon on the Mount* (New York: Harper, 1960), which has twelve categories; Krister Stendahl, "Messianic License," in *Biblical Realism Confronts the Nation*, ed. Paul Peachey (Nyack, NJ: Fellowship of Reconciliation, 1963), 139–52, which adds a thirteenth; and the historical survey in Robert A. Guelich, *The Sermon on the Mount: A Foundation for Understanding* (Waco, TX: Word, 1982).

to Jeremias, the Sermon usually is seen in one of three ways: (1) as a set of literal demands to which disciples should strive to be faithful; (2) as an impossible ideal meant to drive the believer first to desperation and to trust in God's mercy (following Martin Luther); or (3) as an "interim ethic" meant for what was expected to be a brief period of waiting in the end time, which is now obsolete. Most major interpreters can be understood in relation to the options posed by Jeremias.

It would be virtually impossible to find any representative of the position that every single injunction of the Sermon on the Mount, including the destruction of morally offensive bodily members (Matt 5:29–30), should be taken literally and strictly. Jeremias himself calls the literalist reading a "perfectionist code," still in line with the supposed legalism of rabbinic Judaism. Yet not all are so quick to dismiss the literally binding character of the hard sayings (nor to stereotype rabbinic teaching). There is a strong tradition of gospel-based nonviolence that takes the command to love the enemy to the point of nonresistance. Early proponents include Tertullian and Origen; the best Reformation examples are the radicals (such as Menno Simons) who faced extreme persecution for wanting to return to primitive Christianity and the cross of Christ. In more recent times, the Quakers, Mennonites, and other pacifists follow in this current.

Some theorists of just war, who obviously do not take the Sermon literally, also understand it as in a sense a new law that should directly guide behavior. Yet the scope of applicability of this law is called into question. Augustine, Aquinas, Luther, and Calvin all take Matthew 5:48, for example, as a direct moral precept commanding obedience. To find ways around the prima facie social and political implications of loving the enemy, they limit the law's range. Augustine applies it to attitude rather than to external action, and is followed by Calvin; Augustine also says defense of others or of social peace is legitimate while self-defense is not, and is followed by Luther; and Aquinas distinguishes precepts meant for all persons from counsels of perfection for the few, placing the hard sayings in the latter category.

The notion that the Sermon is impossible of fulfillment, but has a pedagogical function, is usually associated with Martin Luther or, as Jeremias puts it, with "Lutheran orthodoxy."[58] The main concern in this approach is not so much with ethics and society, as with maintaining a bulwark against "works righteousness." The evangelical demands of the Sermon bring home the point that there is no divine command that humans can fulfill on their own, for they are entirely dependent on God's

58. Jeremias, The Sermon on the Mount, 6.

grace. Yet when we move the focus from the nature of faith to actual social problems such as killing and war, it is important to think concretely about what norms do or should guide behavior, and in what way they are or can be based on Jesus's reported teaching. Jeremias himself concludes by stressing the concrete relevance of the Sermon, as will be addressed below.

Finally, the position that the Sermon on the Mount is an interim ethic reflects early twentieth-century historical-critical work on primitive Christian eschatology, but it also surfaces a concern still present in contemporary thought. Many recent interpreters of the Sermon on the Mount share the dilemma of Albert Schweitzer: How to build a bridge from the eschatological worldview of the primitive church to our own?[59] As we have seen, ethicists as well as exegetes have rephrased the question: What is the continuing relevance of the presence/absence eschatology that is so definitive a part of the early Christian religious experience?

By far the majority in the Sermon's history of interpretation have decided that the radical demands of the Sermon are not binding mandates for concrete ethical action today. As Richard Hays comments, their "ingenious interpretations" often ignore the plain meaning of Jesus's words and do not take his challenge seriously. For Hays, it is important that the Sermon on the Mount is an instruction for the *disciples* (5:1–2), and although the *crowds* are astounded by it (7:28–29), the disciples are to put it into action.[60]

A similar sentiment may be behind Jeremias's addition of his own fourth thesis: the Sermon is an indicative depiction of incipient life in the kingdom of God, which presupposes as its condition of possibility the experience of conversion. In other words, the Sermon assumes that faithful disciples have experienced God's reign now. The sayings of the Sermon depict the ways, occasions, or outcomes of that experience. Hence the Sermon does indicate a way of life that should take concrete shape in human relationships. Jeremias reappropriates one of Luther's key insights. Faith is active in works of love, and it is precisely faith that loving service presupposes and of which it is a sign.[61]

---

59. Albert Schweitzer, *The Mystery of the Kingdom of God* (New York: Schocken, 1914).

60. Hays, *Moral Vision of the New Testament*, 321; on the variety of interpretations, citing Horsley, *Jesus and the Spiral of Violence*, 272–73.

61. Martin Luther, *Christian Liberty*, ed. Harold J. Grim (Philadelphia: Fortress, 1957), 28.

SALVATION EMPOWERS RENEWAL OF LIFE

A key theme of the Sermon's depiction of the kingdom is imitation of God—that is, to act as God does, with inclusive forgiveness and mercy, is to embody God's reign (5:48).[62] The Sermon's portrayals of discipleship, while not literal prescriptions, create ideals and set burdens of proof for all concrete embodiments of Christian discipleship, insofar as the Christian life is claimed to be grounded in a real experience of salvation from God in Jesus Christ. Matthew presents Jesus "as the Messiah and divine agent of renewal of God's people."[63] "More than any other teacher of morality, the Matthean Jesus teaches with *exousia*, i.e., divine power and authority, and by this empowerment makes possible a new existence."[64]

Righteousness in God's eyes is not narrowly interpreted purity and law-abidingness, but mercifulness effective in compassionate action. The "pure of heart" shall see God (5:3). The Golden Rule (7:12) urges the disciple to identify with the other, to perceive the other's concrete need as though it were the disciple's, to act toward the other as though the other were oneself. The morally right act is simply but radically the act that demonstrates the forgiving attentiveness to the needs of others disclosed by Jesus as the will of God. Love is defined in Matthew's Sermon as a way of acting, not as an emotion. However, inferable from the deeds done is an attitude toward others that might be characterized as empathy, kindness, generosity, or compassion. With this, the dilemmas said to be posed by an ethic of love, such as the conflict between love and justice or the impasse of a choice between two neighbors, are set aside if not answered. The mandate is not to settle such conflicts in the most prudent or effective way, but to enter into them by identifying the needs of those concerned as one's own.

Love of enemies characterizes all who are "children of your Father in heaven" (5:45). Not just obedience but solidarity and compassion are important as responses to the mercy and forgiveness that are characteristic of God. The disciple loves not simply as a matter of duty, but because the other is perceived "as a member of one's own family in the family of being," as "one whose life and joy or sorrow touch our own."[65] This is the keynote of Jesus's command to love neighbor and enemy. Attentive

62. Elsewhere in Matthew, kingdom "righteousness" also is constituted by forgiveness and mercy—e.g., the parable of the king and the wicked servant (18:23–35) or the giving of a cup of cold water to one of the "little ones" (10:42).

63. Kee, "The Formation of Christian Communities," 595.

64. Brown, *Introduction to the New Testament*, 178.

65. Wolfgang Schrage, *The Ethics of the New Testament,* trans. David E. Green (Philadelphia: Fortress, 1988), 157.

concern for the other in need is not first of all self-sacrifice, a still self-centered focus on one's obligation, loss, suffering, or righteousness. It is an identification, an empathy captured in the "as yourself" of the double love command (Matt 22:39). Wolfgang Schrage calls this compassionate openness "the comprehensive solidarity of love," a "fundamental, all-encompassing attitude" and also "the quintessence of all the individual commandments."[66]

Love as attentive forgiveness fleshes out the concrete meaning of the "hard sayings," including the baffling instruction not to resist the evildoer (5:39). It can be concluded minimally that the disciple does not approach the enemy or evildoer in hard, resistant, alienating, and self-righteous judgment, but in a compassionate desire to meet the needs of wrongdoers and victims as well as possible in difficult circumstances. This of course does not abolish the importance of attending first to the most vulnerable or most endangered and empowering those whose agency has been suppressed or violated. Jesus's sayings and parables consistently identify the one who is least well-off or most in need as the most urgent object of concern. The parable of judgment in Matthew 25 exhorts hearers to serve Jesus by attending to the needs of the hungry, thirsty, homeless and imprisoned.[67] Appeal is made to the powerful, hard-hearted, and apathetic so that they may be converted to compassion, justice, and mercy.

For Matthew the end time has been inaugurated in the life, death, and resurrection of Jesus. "So too, after the historical ministry of Jesus, when the Son of Man is hidden in the least of the brethren, the true order of justice is maintained when those acts of mercy and loving-kindness characterize the life of discipleship."[68]

66. Schrage, *Ethics of the New Testament*, 78–79.

67. Scholars have debated whether the "brethren" references the needy universally (the modern reading), or fellow members of the Christian community (the traditional reading). John Donahue proposes that the brethren are not the needy in general but the disciples, as exercising their missionary role and facing rejection. Nevertheless, he argues, the parable reveals the universal standards by which all people shall be judged, including Christians themselves when confronted with generalized poverty and need. See John R. Donahue, SJ, "The 'Parable' of the Sheep and the Goats: A Challenge to Christian Ethics," *Theological Studies* 47, no. 1 (1986): 25–31.

68. Donahue, "The 'Parable' of the Sheep and the Goats," 24–25. See also John Meier, *The Vision of Matthew: Christ, Church and Morality in the First Gospel* (New York: Paulist, 1978), 26–39.

THE COVENANT IN MATTHEW'S GOSPEL AND
READING THE SERMON TODAY

Matthew's Gospel was written toward the end of the first century (80–85 CE), after the Romans had destroyed the temple in Jerusalem in 70 CE. With the loss of its common cultic center and its leadership, Judaism was to experience dramatic changes. Nationalist movements gradually died out; priestly collaboration with Rome that had enabled political control in Palestine was disabled; the Essene settlement was destroyed by the Roman army. The surviving group with most influence was the Pharisees, who even before the Temple's destruction had begun to redefine Jewish purity around gatherings in homes and local settings, rather than in terms of temple ritual alone.[69]

The Gospel of Matthew reflects struggles over the reformation of Judaism during this time. Matthew is determined to show how God has reconstituted his covenant people around Jesus; how Jesus brings the authentic interpretation of the law and the prophets, building on what has gone before; and how God's rule over the whole earth is being accomplished through Jesus's agency.

An obvious new element for Matthew—as for the other evangelists, Paul, and the Jesus movement in general—is the inclusion of non-Jews in the covenant community. Matthew not only defends the mission to the Gentiles but he sees Jesus as commissioning the apostles with a mission to the whole world, fulfilling Isaiah's vision of Israel as a "light to the nations" (28:19–20). The Gentile mission was a notorious flashpoint within the early church, with some Jewish followers of Christ insisting that Gentile converts be circumcised, a view that did not ultimately win the day (Acts 15). Unfortunately for the historical record of Christianity as an inclusive and reconciling force, Matthew stands out among the evangelists for characterizing opponents (whether other Jewish groups or more traditionalist Jewish Christ-followers) as "the Jews," then painting them in highly negative terms in his story of Jesus (Matt 23:1–36; 27:24–25). This rhetoric is, to say the least, at cross-purposes with Matthew's intention to draw Jews and Gentiles together in one community, and it ultimately provides fuel for later Christian anti-Semitism.

At the same time, Matthew makes a strong connection between Jesus and Judaism, albeit in contrast to the (post–70 CE) Pharisaic tradition. As Anthony Saldarini writes, "The members of Matthew's group combine a sharp critique of some community attitudes and practices with a deeply

69. Kee, "The Formation of Christian Communities," 580–81.

renewed sense of fundamental Jewish values, that is, divine rule (king-dom of God) and care (justice/righteousness), which has been commu-nicated by God's emissary and son, Jesus."[70] Jesus, unlike the Pharisees, is the teacher of true righteousness who grasps the essential meaning of the law (Matt 23).

The Sermon on the Mount elaborates the way of life represented by Jesus, focused around the love commandments, forgiveness, mercy, and justice. It does so in a way that speaks to debates going on in Matthew's own day about Christian identity in relation to Judaism. Similarly to the ascent of Moses on Sinai, Jesus goes up a mountain to deliver his dis-course on the true and greater righteousness that fulfills the law and the prophets (Matt 5:17). Righteousness must come from the heart as well as external behavior (Matt 5:17–20), and this teaching is contrasted with the teaching of the Pharisees on many points, including divorce, swear-ing oaths, hoarding wealth, forgiveness and reconciliation, ostentatious piety, nonretaliation, and love of enemies.

The disciples are instructed to love their enemies and pray even for those who persecute them—an especially radical command in Matthew's historical context, given violent Roman repression of the Temple cult and continuing vitriol between his community and other Jewish groups.[71] Yet, in Matthew's time (or in any age, for that matter) such realities must not disrupt the creation of a new family in God's name.

Importantly for social ethics and for continuing contextual interpreta-tions of the Sermon on the Mount, Matthew models the expansive reap-propriation of the gospel to meet the demands of new generations. In fact, he carries the gospel and its promise of communal renewal beyond the original disciples to include Jews and Gentile converts. For his Christian-Jewish community, Matthew's Gospel "emphasizes both the continuities between Jesus and the biblical tradition, and the radi-cally new dimensions of covenantal identity and obligation that God has introduced through Jesus."[72] This opens the possibility of further expan-sion to multiple religious traditions, and, especially at the level of social

---

70. Anthony J. Saldarini, *Matthew's Christian-Jewish Community* (Chicago: University of Chicago Press, 1994), 89.

71. The precise original referent of "enemies" or "the evil one" (5:39, 44) is disputed. This may not have referred to national or political enemies but rather to personal ones. See Richard A. Horsley, "Ethics and Exegesis: 'Love Your Enemies' and the Doctrine of Non-Violence," *Journal of the American Academy of Religion* 54, no. 1 (1986) 3–31; Guelich, *Sermon on the Mount,* on the "evil one," 219, and on religious enemies, 227; Stephen Charles Mott, *Biblical Ethics and Social Change,* 2nd ed. (New York: Oxford University Press, 2011), 143–64; and Luise Schot-troff, "Non-Violence and the Love of One's Enemies," in *Essays on the Love Commandment,* ed. Reginald H. Fuller (Philadelphia: Fortress, 1978), 12–13.

72. Kee, "The Formation of Christian Communities," 583.

relationships, to all those seeking a more just and compassionate political society. This move is crucial to contemporary peacebuilding—and the Sermon on the Mount, if seen in its gospel context, provides a warrant for it.

THE BEATITUDES AND LORD'S PRAYER

The Beatitudes proclaim the fulfillment of the Sinai covenant in Jesus, announcing blessings on the faithful who keep the covenant, and confirm the renewal of life proclaimed in the Sermon as a whole.[73] The Beatitudes (Matt 5:2–12) emphasize that the future blessings of the kingdom will reverse present suffering and reward mercy, peacemaking, and righteousness; yet the kingdom already belongs to those who enact these virtues (5:3). Those blessed with the kingdom are "poor in spirit" (5:3), "meek" (5:5), "merciful" (5:7), and "pure in heart" (5:8).

The phrases of the Beatitudes may well have reference to minority social position as well as to discipleship attitudes, and thus they fit well with the many sayings of Jesus (e.g., 6:19–21) about the dangers that wealth and power present to the greater righteousness expected of the disciple.[74] The more position and prestige one has to protect, the less likely one is to enter with compassionate action a situation in which one's assets are required for the well-being of others. Indeed his inclusive attitude toward the poor, including the socially rejected person and the sinner against the law, is a key to Jesus's teaching. It may even be said that Jesus's primary purpose was to "preach the good news to the poor" and that, according to the Beatitudes, "the first characteristic of God's people in the new age is that they are the poor."[75] This sentiment is certainly reflected in the work of many liberation theologians, with Jon Sobrino and later Pope Francis insisting explicitly that it is only in the "church of the poor" that the crucified and risen Christ is historically present today.[76] The concern of the Beatitudes with the poor, and with the reversal of suffering, is also key for peacebuilding. Christians have long recognized that they must be willing to carry Christ's cross and bear worldly defeat. But Christian social ethics today goes further. Christians

---

73. Adrian Leske, "Matthew," in *International Bible Commentary*, 1270.

74. Guelich, *Sermon on the Mount*, 97–109.

75. Dunn, *Jesus' Call to Discipleship*, 33, 36.

76. Jon Sobrino, *Jesus the Liberator: A Historical-Theological Reading of Jesus of Nazareth* (Maryknoll, NY: Orbis, 1993), 30; Joshua L. McElwee, "Pope Francis: 'I would love a church that is poor'," *National Catholic Reporter*, March 16, 2013, accessed July 19, 2017, https://tinyurl.com/y9p374vs.

take on risks for the gospel, but the cause in which they assume those risks has a social justice dimension.

The Beatitudes may originally have concerned relations within the community, where—as today—divisions, mischaracterizations, and hostility are continuing dangers. In light of the ideal of the kingdom, "all peoples and nations will eventually be part of God's universal family acknowledging God as Father." Because all people are the recipients of God's love, they are also to be loved by disciples, love "shown in an earnest desire for the good of the other."[77]

The expansiveness of the Sermon and the Beatitudes is particularly seen in the blessing on peacemakers. Peacemakers are "children of God" (5:9). While "love of enemies" seems to call for a radical conversion of the personal and collective attitudes that produce attempts at domination, retaliation, and violent self-vindication, "peacemaking" names the communal and political processes that follow from this conversion. The commitments and practices of peacemaking gradually knit enemies and competitors together, as well as those who have been harmed and excluded by violence. Involving reconciliation, reparations, and the restoration of trust, peacemaking is necessary to create viable patterns of social coexistence and cooperation that can sustain just and inclusive communities going forward after conflict and division.

Surrounding the Lord's Prayer are admonitions (6:1–8,16–24) not to pray or do good works for worldly motives, especially in order to increase one's own importance, but rather out of a desire to imitate God's generosity. The often cited and seemingly naive "lilies of the field" passage can be understood in context as an exhortation not to be caught up anxiously in one's own daily needs but to seek first God's kingdom and God's righteousness. Action that is righteous the way God's attentive care, mercy, and forgiveness are righteous is the most basic condition of the goodness experienced in the life of the disciple.

The Lord's Prayer, an appeal for the fullness of the kingdom, closely associates it with doing on earth the will of the Father (6:10) and especially with forgiving as God does. It is one's forgiveness of neighbor on which one's own forgiveness by God explicitly depends (6:15); the disciple prays to be forgiven as one who also forgives (6:12, 14–15). The command not to judge others' failings (7:1–5) bears out the forgiveness theme of the prayer for the kingdom; it is our attitude toward others that will determine God's attitude of judgment or forgiveness toward us. It is not too much to say, with James Dunn, that Christian love "can be measured by" forgiveness, and that "Jesus clearly saw such readiness to

---

77. Leske, "Matthew," 1276.

forgive as the mark of discipleship and of the community of disciples."[78] No one has to wait for political liberation or religious intermediaries to experience the kingdom; it is open to all who seek it (Matt 7:7–12), if they are faithful to the covenant as conveyed by Jesus.

MERCY AND JUDGMENT IN THE GOSPEL AND TODAY

An obvious next question is: What sustains a compelling connection between relation to God and acts toward others? To insist, as did Luther and some recent interpreters, that action flows necessarily and spontaneously from conversion and the virtues it brings, seems right but inadequate once the incompleteness of the kingdom is acknowledged. Also needing attention are the eschatological themes of warning and judgment that accompany those of salvation, freedom, and blessing.[79] When the radical, conversion-based injunctions are placed in the context of the three chapters of the Sermon, and more broadly, in that of the gospel, they derive much of their forcefulness from accompanying warnings of the consequences for those who fall short of the law's fulfillment and of the greater righteousness enjoined by Jesus (5:17, 20). Those who fail "will never enter the kingdom of heaven (5:20), "will be liable to judgment" (5:22a); "will be liable to the hell of fire" (5:22), or "thrown into hell" (5:29; cf. 30b).

The insistent pairing of the twin themes of righteous action and judgment is central to Matthew 7; these themes are amplified by those of efficacious prayer and mission. As we have seen, action is an important component of spreading the gospel. It is the life of good works that gives "glory to your Father in heaven," and by which the disciples will be "salt" and "light" to the world (5:13–16).[80] Doing the good works commended is not a distant ideal but necessary now. "Not every one who says to me, 'Lord, Lord,' will enter the kingdom of heaven, but only the one who does the will of my Father in heaven" (7:21). Although doing what is heard is hard, Jesus assures that "good things" shall be given to those who

78. Dunn, *Jesus' Call to Discipleship*, 85.

79. See Allen Verhey, *The Great Reversal: Ethics and the New Testament* (Grand Rapids, MI: William B. Eerdmans, 1984), 88–89, 92; Guelich, *Sermon on the Mount*, 405–13; Herman Hendrickx, *The Sermon on the Mount*, Studies in the Synoptic Gospels (London: Geoffrey Chapman, 1984), 160–74.

80. Possibly also 7:6 is a mission saying; see Guelich, *Sermon on the Mount*, 353–54, and Hendrickx, *Sermon on the Mount*, 155. If so, it may be illumined by 6:1–8, 16–21. In other words, Christian discipleship and respectable religious practice are not the same; do not be religious for earthly reward and do not prostitute the gospel to those who will use it for worldly respect or power.

earnestly ask (5:1). The Sermon's exhortation to pray counteracts exaggerated "gift" interpretations of the kingdom, since the petitioner has a role in securing the blessings from which action springs. The warnings not to be taken in by false prophets in sheep's clothing (7:15), or by trees that do not bear good fruit (7:16–20), or by those who perform showy works in Jesus's name (7:22–23); or the admonition not to build one's house on "sand" by not living up to Jesus's words (7:24–27) suggest choice, responsibility, difficulty, and the possibility of delusion in the life of would-be discipleship. The allusions to the "narrow gate" (7:13–14) and the Lord's repudiation of "evildoers" on the last day (7:22–23) are explicit references to judgment.

Useful though these eschatological warnings may be in sustaining the disciple's attention to the nature and seriousness of his or her moral obligations, they raise for Christian ethics an unsettling question similar to one already considered in relation to the Hebrew Bible. Upon precisely which depiction of the divine character are the faithful to model their behavior? On the one hand, Jesus teaches his disciples to imitate God's love, forgiveness and mercy by showing compassion to neighbor and enemy alike. On the other hand, he or she who fails to do so will be "accursed" on the last day, and sent away "into the eternal fire prepared for the devil and his angels" (Matt 25:41). This seems not to be a message of imitation of God, but a divine version of "Do as I say and not as I do."

Taking this dilemma as her point of departure, Barbara Reid questions whether on the basis of Matthew's Gospel, violence might considered a situationally justified response to evil.[81] She contrasts the gratuitously loving God of Matthew 5:38–48 with the violent God who punishes evildoers in eight of the parables: the weeds and wheat (13:40–43), the dragnet (13:49–50), forgiveness aborted (18:23–35), the final judgment (25:31–46), treacherous tenants (21:33–46), the wedding feast (22:1–14), faithful servants (24:45–51), and the talents (25:14–30). After considering a few other possible explanations for the discrepancy (different strands in the tradition, an ethics that tries to meet its audience where it is, and misinterpreting violent male characters as representing God), she turns to an interpretation that she considers to be more adequate.

All eight parables with violent endings are either explicitly eschatological or contain eschatological symbols and themes. Hence the reader should draw a distinction between what humans should do when they

81. Barbara E. Reid, OP, "Violent Endings in Matthew's Parables and an End to Violence," *Catholic Biblical Quarterly* 66, no. 2 (2004): 237–55. For a further argument that New Testament texts promoting violence should be given more attention and weight, see Michel R. Desjardins, *Peace, Violence and the New Testament*, Biblical Seminar 46 (Sheffield, UK: Sheffield Academic, 1997).

confront this-worldly violence, and what God will do "when the time for conversion is past and the time for final reckoning has arrived."[82] God does not give approval for humanly caused violence toward people that those in authority deem to be evildoers. Goodness and evil are mixed in every person and community, including one's own. Reid also considers that violent imagery may be a metaphorical way of making vivid the seriousness of the call to imitate God's love and forgiveness, and it may well be a language that owes more to the creative hand of the evangelist that to the original rhetoric of Jesus. If so, it would be well to replace the imagery with nonviolent versions.

Reid acknowledges further problems. Is God's graciousness ever exhausted? "Does God at the end-time set aside compassion and engage in vindictive violence?"[83] Cautioning that these questions cannot be answered on the basis of biblical exegesis alone, she turns to constructive and systematic theology, suggesting that a possible perspective is that humans who participate in cycles of violence cause violence to redound to themselves. She also recognizes that the biblical counsels of nonviolence or nonretaliation assume some freedom and power on the part of the person injured to decide among different options available. But this may not always be the case. What is to be done then, or if the "enemy" is "an international foe"?

Reid concludes by asking whether just war theory and pacifism can both be correct interpretations of Matthew, given different situations.[84] While this may be true, I would argue that peacebuilding is an even more appropriate interpretation, for it engages parties to a conflict in a way that includes both judgment and forgiveness in an ongoing process of community-building. Reconciliation and restorative justice are necessary to peacebuilding, but so is ending impunity for perpetrators of human rights violations, restoring the rule of law, and establishing just and stable institutions. This will require some coercive measures, though not "vindictive violence." From a gospel perspective, the burden of proof is certainly on the advocates of violence. Political and economic resistance and constraint may be justified, as is righteous anger. Yet both must be controlled by the Sermon's normative ideals of justice, compassion, mercy, and forgiveness, applied to the righteous and unrighteous alike and directed not only at individual relationships but at the inclusion of all in just and peaceful societies.

82. Reid, "Violent Endings," 253.
83. Reid, "Violent Endings," 253.
84. Reid, "Violent Endings," 255.

THE CHURCH AND SOCIAL TRANSFORMATION

The idea that Jesus's admonitions and blessings can be formative for the disciples' roles in other communities and larger spheres of relationship is assumed and implied by peacebuilding efforts across cultural, ethnic, and religious differences. Yet some depictions of biblical ethics by biblical exegetes follow John Howard Yoder and Stanley Hauerwas (see chapter 1) in seeing the evangelical counsels of the Sermon as directed almost exclusively to the church. Richard Hays's *The Moral Vision of the New Testament* lies in this vein.[85] Hays emphasizes that the cross is the center of the Christian life.[86] He understands Matthew to represent Jesus as the one who chooses "the way of suffering obedience" rather than violence, and who is thus persecuted, dying "powerless and mocked."[87] The church must "embody the costly way of peace," exemplifying "the reality of the kingdom of God in a pluralistic and sinful world."[88] Since the way and the fate of Jesus are normative for his disciples, they too can expect persecution and worldly failure. "New creation" for Hays does not mean social change now, but rather that the countercultural lifestyle of disciples in the church will be "vindicated by the resurrection of the dead."[89]

However, Hays's observation that Jesus's message threatened the establishment of his day seems to lend itself to the opposite interpretation: although Jesus's kingdom preaching brought suffering, it was not entirely powerless. Nor were its effects confined to a countercultural discipleship community. Although the Sermon does not plainly dictate social objectives, it implies them. As Wolfgang Schrage puts it, "Personal renewal must occasion a corresponding structural renewal,"[90] because the imminence of the kingdom, now accessible in the risen Christ and the Spirit, motivates and empowers people to act in ways appropriate to it. As communicated by the political nature of the symbol kingdom or reign, as well as by the imagery of family, Christian action has an integral corporate dimension. The inclusive religion of Jesus challenged the status distinctions on which secular cultures depend, thus destabilizing traditional Roman society and provoking persecution.[91] "Jesus' teachings are of crucial importance, according to Matthew, because they have an

85. Hays, *The Moral Vision of the New Testament*.

86. Hays, *The Moral Vision of the New Testament*, 340.

87. Hays, *The Moral Vision of the New Testament*, 322.

88. Hays, *The Moral Vision of the New Testament*, 344, 321.

89. Hays, *The Moral Vision of the New Testament*, 338.

90. Schrage, *Ethics of the New Testament*, 3.

91. Stephen C. Mott, "The Use of the Bible in Social Ethics II: The Use of the New Testament: Part II: Objections to the Enterprise," *Transformation* 1, no. 3 (1984): 24.

effect on life, come from God and the Bible, and are essential to the welfare of the Jewish community and the world."[92]

As early as the letters of Paul, the kingdom is understood to span races, cultures, and nations. The Synoptic Gospels, John, later epistles, and Revelation envision the mission of the church across generations. The situation is no different for subsequent eras. God's rule requires expansive social-political identification with the oppressed, mutual solidarity, noncondemnation, liberation from fear, and praxis that enhances human welfare.[93] Inasmuch as the disciple today has increased capacity to affect whole groups of socially and economically disadvantaged persons globally, the broader social duties of discipleship hardly can be ignored. Luise Schottroff sees aggressive love of enemy as resistant to social evil and as "a combative and evangelistic means for the salvation of all,"[94] consistent with gospel inclusiveness and Jesus's manifest intent to cut across religious and social boundaries. Biblically oriented authors writing after the turn of the twenty-first century are even more insistent on the Christian responsibility and ability to work for more just societies.

The work of Glen Stassen and David Gushee on Jesus's kingdom and politics is illustrative. Taking the kingdom of God and the Sermon on the Mount as his points of departure, Stassen proposes a theology of "incarnational discipleship" that is politically engaged for the sake of justice. Incarnational discipleship begins with a historically informed understanding of the life and ministry of Jesus Christ that can guide the moral life concretely and realistically. It sees the incarnation as pertaining to "*all of life and all of creation*." And it designates active practices that can function as strategies of repentance and conversion from "ideologies *such as nationalism, racism, and greed*."[95]

These practices or strategies can also be seen as "transforming initiatives" that are modeled in and validated by the Sermon on the Mount. Jesus neither ratifies traditional teaching nor simply rejects it. Instead he recommends original and unexpected actions that break cycles of violence: go the second mile, turn the other cheek, offer your tunic as well as your cloak, and so on. The disciples are encouraged to find a constructive response "that points the way of deliverance from being mired in powerlessness in the face of oppressive power."[96] In *Kingdom Ethics*,

---

92. Saldarini, *Matthew's Christian-Jewish Community*, 161.

93. Hendrickx, *Sermon on the Mount*, 3, 87.

94. Schottroff, "Non-Violence and the Love of One's Enemies," 28.

95. Glen Harold Stassen, *A Thicker Jesus: Incarnational Discipleship in a Secular Age* (Louisville, KY: Westminster John Knox, 2012), 16–17, italics in the original.

96. Stassen, *A Thicker Jesus*, 186. Gushee and Stassen again present the transforming initiatives in *Kingdom Ethics*, 132–43.

Gushee and Stassen call for *"a Christ-following countercultural community that obeys God by publicly engaging in working for justice."*[97] To be
light and salt for the world (Matt 5:13–16) means to provide "leadership to the whole human family."[98] Direct-aid "mercy ministries" grow
out of pastoral concern and are important ways in which churches help
the downtrodden and heartbroken. They also provide direct experience
of the importance of just structures, institutions, and policies. Concrete
forms of "brokenness, need and injustice" clarify that broader social and
political action is essential to following Christ, thus placing activism and
advocacy within the ambit of the church's social mission.[99]

To summarize, community and praxis are key in connecting the Bible
to ethics and in giving substance to the Bible's eschatological message
with its clear social overtones. As revealed by historical and sociological
studies, the New Testament itself emerges from, makes sense of, and
forms a community of discipleship and moral practice. The contribution of the Bible to ethics is at the level of community formation, not
primarily at that of rules or principles, and this applies in the case of
nonviolence[100]. Christian solidarity and equality challenge exploitative
socioeconomic relationships whereby some are deprived of basic necessities of life. Yet they also challenge resort to violence as a means of
changing such relationships. Both biblically and historically, nonviolent
peacebuilding is grounded in and experienced as consistent with a committed communal practice of forgiveness, forbearance, and fellowship.

The very multivocity of the Christian vision, and the variety of contexts in which it is put into practice, however, may mean that although
a nonviolent and actively reconciling way of life is most consistent with
Christian identity as scripturally and experientially tested, debates about
how specifically to bring that identity together with a more public identity of person or group will be ongoing.[101] The variety of literary gen-
res, religious symbols, and budding theologies in the New Testament
points to an ongoing and moderately pluralistic project of community

97. Gushee and Stassen, *Kingdom Ethics*, 467, italics in the original.

98. Gushee and Stassen, *Kingdom Ethics*, 474.

99. Gushee and Stassen, *Kingdom Ethics*, 478–79.

100. On whether any general moral principles or specific moral rules may be grounded in the
New Testament, compare Verhey, *The Great Reversal*, 174–78, 187–95; and Richard N. Longe-
necker, *New Testament Social Ethics for Today* (Grand Rapids, MI: William B. Eerdmans, 1984),
14–15, 26–28.

101. Ulrich Mauser, *Gospel of Peace: A Scriptural Message for Today's World* (Louisville, KY:
Westminster John Knox, 1992), 167: "It is not possible, therefore, to extract from the New Testament a set of direct instructions about peacemaking. On this point, as on any other, the New
Testament, as much as the Old Testament, cannot be treated like a code of law whose content
requires only contemporary interpretation and application."

formation, always subject, as today, to incompleteness and failure. At the same time, the New Testament makes it abundantly clear that to love and forgive one's enemies is not only intrinsic to the kingdom but that a life of such love and forgiveness is a concrete alternative now. Ulrich Mauser includes with the biblical message on peacemaking "the discipline of being radical," by which he means a constant struggle against the idolatries and violence in the public order. "Precisely as a community of peace, the Christian community must constantly be expected to infuse an element of disquietude into public life."[102] Above all, Christians must challenge the tendency of just war theory to function as an "opiate," lulling citizens into submission to the decisions of leaders whom they assume to have not only moral responsibility for the public good but also superior knowledge about morally defensible means by which to exercise responsibility.[103]

In relation to debates about war and peace, these claims imply that followers of Jesus and the church as a whole ought to live first and foremost by the virtues of compassion, mercy, forgiveness, and justice; that the normative character of nonviolence ought not easily be set aside on grounds of the impossibility of experiencing the reign of God historically; that the acts and practices that kingdom life sponsors should extend across social and religious boundaries; and that God's judgment will fall on individuals and communities who hear Jesus but turn aside from the actions his teaching implies.

102. Mauser, *Gospel of Peace*, 179.
103. Mauser, *Gospel of Peace*, 186.

3.

Early Christian Pacifism
Tertullian and Origen

Although the New Testament offers no concentrated or direct analysis of the ethics of war, it clears the ground for Christian pacifism by establishing compassion and forgiveness—as well as care for "the poor"—as defining the lives of Jesus Christ's followers. Jesus's ministry of the reign of God empowers the church and its members to love neighbors and even enemies, sacrificing their own needs for the welfare of others when necessary. Christians are to be peacemakers, and peacemaking begins a process with broad social reverberations. Yet a key problematic of Christian social ethics has been to define and discern at the practical level the meaning of Christian love, reconciliation, and peacemaking in a sinful world, a world in which responsibilities can be uncertain or can conflict.

Christians in the first centuries after Christ responded to a question that has been essential to Christian social ethics ever since. How can Christian persons and the church integrate their religious identity with their membership in a particular culture, civil society, form of political order, and type of government? The agenda of transforming society, later so important in Christian ethics, is not a prominent theme in early Christian writings, which are colored more by the expectation of Christ's impending return and the incompatibility of Christian and cultural values.[1] The first Christians' question was rather: How should Christians and the church relate to the imperial government, including the use of military force to sustain the *Pax Romana*?

An obvious nexus of the Christian struggle with these questions is the problem of participation in institutions, such as the military, that have as their function the protection and perpetuation of the empire, and that

---

1. James Turner Johnson, *The Quest for Peace: Three Moral Traditions in Western Culture and History* (Princeton, NJ: Princeton University Press, 1987), 12–17.

will likely entail a lifestyle or practices that undermine the new relation to God and neighbor embodied by Jesus. The Christian response to the problem of coercion and violence has never been univocal and clear. Moreover, Christian identity itself is contextual, taking shape interactively with cultural presuppositions, values, opportunities, and pressures. A good example is the influence of the establishment of Christianity by Constantine in the fourth century upon the attitudes of Christian thinkers toward the legitimacy of violence on behalf of the emperor.[2] The trend after Constantine was to legitimize military service, though Christian presence in the military apparently was more than minimal even before his reign. Earlier Christian teaching on military service and support of the government was complex, if not ambiguous. Yet killing was unanimously and clearly forbidden for Christians.[3]

In a critical overview of the complicated evidence for the views of early Christian writers, as well as of the practices of ordinary Christians, Ronald Sider reminds readers that in the Greco-Roman culture of the first three centuries, killing was widespread and accepted in the forms of abortion, infanticide, suicide, capital punishment, gladiatorial sports, and that at the hands of the Roman army. Christian teaching and the Christian way of life provided a protest and an alternative, and killing by Christians in any circumstances is widely and without exception denounced by extant Christian writers.[4]

Nevertheless, there is a "disconnect" between the unanimity of such teaching and "the clear evidence that more and more Christians were in the army," especially toward the third century, at the borders of the empire where threats by armed forces were more frequent.[5] Christian solders in the Roman army have been identified by gravestone inscriptions identifying their religion. Notably, they were permitted to be

2. See, for instance, Roland Bainton, *Christian Attitudes toward War and Peace: A Historical Survey and Critical Re-evaluation* (Nashville: Abingdon, 1960), 85–93; John Howard Yoder, *The Original Revolution: Essays on Christian Pacifism* (Scottdale, PA: Herald, 1971), 64–70.

3. See Knut Willem Ruyter, "Pacifism and Military Service in the Early Church," *CrossCurrents* 32, no. 1 (1982): 54–70; John Helgeland, "Christians and the Roman Army from Marcus Aurelius to Constantine," *Aufstieg und Niedergang der römischen Welt* (ANRW), part 2, vol. 23/1, *Vorkonstantinisches Christentum: Verhältnis zu römischem Staat und heidnischer Religion,* ed. Wolfgang Haase (Berlin: Walter de Gruyter, 1979), 724–834; John Helgeland, Robert H. Daly, and J. Patout Burns, *Christians and the Military: The Early Experience* (Philadelphia: Fortress, 1985); Francis Young, "The Early Church, Military Service, War and Peace," *Theology* 92 (1989): 491–503; David G. Hunter, "A Decade of Research on Early Christians and Military Service," *Religious Studies Review* 18, no. 2 (1992): 87–94; and Ronald J. Sider, *The Early Church on Killing: A Comprehensive Sourcebook on War, Abortion, and Capital Punishment* (Grand Rapids, MI: Baker Academic, 2012).

4. Sider, *Early Church on Killing*, 190–91.

5. Sider, *Early Church on Killing*, 193; cf. 185–90.

buried as Christians.[6] Churches have been discovered inside Roman army fortresses, as at Megiddo in Israel.[7] Celsus and others recount an incident in the army of Marcus Aurelius in which a foe withdrew due to a sudden and seemingly miraculous thunderstorm of rain and hail, which was attributed to the prayers of the Christian soldiers (the story of the "Thundering Legion").[8] Sider concludes that although it was certainly possible for Roman soldiers living far from any battlefront to escape violence, there was a significant number who did participate. "Those in the 'Thundering Legion' in 173 very probably did. Julius the veteran (d. 304) clearly did. So did the large number of Armenian soldiers who helped defeat the pagan emperor Maximin Daia in 312."[9]

In fact, the evidence regarding whether Christian thinkers condemned imperial wars in general, or the participation of Christians in the military if they refused to kill, is also mixed. For example, while Christians were forbidden to join the army, soldiers who wished to be baptized were not required to leave. According to Irenaeus, the government rightly uses the sword, and Origen (to be discussed further below) distinguishes between just and unjust wars, though clearly forbidding Christians from either.[10]

Moreover, Christian martyrdom was exhorted and celebrated in militaristic terms. In a mid-third century letter by Cyprian encouraging Christians to bravely withstand persecution, a glorification of martyrdom, along with demonization of the adversary, even took shape as a story about an army of Christian soldiers who rushed into battle without weapons and were massacred for the glory of God and their own eternal bliss.[11] One commentator likens this "cosmic war" ethos to the mentality of contemporary suicide bombers who not only seek glory in a violent death, but wage war against an entire culture that they see as opposed to God's will.[12] Though this earlier version may not have resulted in actual violence, it does provide an obvious connection in Christian narrative,

---

6. C. John Cadoux, *The Early Christian Attitude toward War* (New York: Seabury, 1982), 105–6, 13; Bainton, *Christian Attitudes*, 69.

7. See Peter J. Leithart, *Defending Constantine: The Twilight of an Empire and the Dawn of Christendom* (Downers Grove, IL: IVP Academic, 2011), 261–62.

8. For the details, see Young, "Early Church," 498.

9. Sider, *Early Church on Killing*, 193.

10. Sider, *Early Church on Killing*, 181–84, 192.

11. On these themes, see also Young, "Early Church," 494–96 and Sider, *Early Church on Killing*, 180–81.

12. Jonathan Koscheski, "The Earliest Christian War: Second- and Third-Century Martyrdom and the Creation of Cosmic Warriors," *Journal of Religious Ethics* 39, no. 1 (2011): 100–124.

symbolism, and emotional timbre to the "holy war" ethos of the Crusades and Puritan revolutionaries (see chapter 8).

Yet, compared to later writers, especially after Constantine, Christian teachers of the first three centuries were generally adamant that Christians should emulate the nonviolent and countercultural example of Jesus's own life and of his sayings about the nature of the kingdom as the present inbreaking of God's reign. They were ready to assume that the one who follows Jesus will be at odds in significant and dangerous ways with the prevailing societal ethos. This is not to say that the church fathers did not borrow from the ideals of contemporary philosophical schools, which were often also countercultural. But the Christian authors associated displacement from the larger social order precisely with the reality of salvation in Jesus Christ and with the nature of the church as body of Christ. However, both the degree of tension between Christianity and society and the function of Scripture as an authority for theology and practice were understood variously. Still, there is a well-substantiated theological and pastoral consensus in the centuries before Constantine that compassion, forgiveness, peace, and peacemaking are regulative Christian ideals, and that killing by Christians is never acceptable.

Two figures representative of the pacifist themes in early Christian teaching are Tertullian of Carthage, a late second-century Latin (Western) father, and Origen of Alexandria, a Greek (Eastern) theologian whose life began about a quarter century later. An important point of comparison will be their attitudes toward the grounding and implications of what they agreed was the nonviolent vision of the New Testament. Among the early church fathers, they address the questions of participation in the military and in war most directly. Even at this relatively early stage of the tradition, biblical interpretation is not always direct and literal. Both Tertullian and Origen are philosophically influenced in their appropriation of the gospel. Their pacifism neither consists in nor even focuses on an absolute rule against violence derived directly from biblical texts; it is a feature of a multidimensional portrait of the Christian way, inspired by the Scriptures as mediating Christ's presence and teaching, but also received within an ongoing community that brings to that depiction its own coloration.

TERTULLIAN

The details of Tertullian's life are not known with precision. He apparently was born about 160 CE in the city of Carthage, situated in the then-prosperous Roman province of Africa. He was the well-educated son of a Roman centurion. Military and legal images pervade his writings, suggesting that he may have been a lawyer. One of Christianity's foremost apologists, he was converted as an adult but was eventually won to the rigorist, schismatic Montanists.[13] Preaching a strict asceticism as a preparation for the imminent return of Christ, they encouraged fasting, celibacy, and martyrdom, and forbade second marriages. Tertullian's Montanist writings reflect an austerity latent even in his earlier works.[14]

Throughout his career as a Christian author, Tertullian draws direct and demanding connections between Christian teaching and the practical moral life. The one treatise he devotes exclusively to the military, *The Crown,* is dated in his Montanist phase. However, the skepticism about military service he expresses there echoes earlier works such as *Apology.* At least three aspects of Tertullian's pacifism have been subject to debate: (1) whether he supported the function and endeavors of the state generally, as divinely mandated; (2) whether he forbade military service for Christians entirely, or only participation in anti-Christian practices, such as idolatry and the wearing of the ceremonial laurel crown in honor of imperial supremacy and even deity; and (3) whether he was actually a pacifist at all, or instead objected only to military practices other than killing. Further, it has been argued that Tertullian's antimilitary polemics may reflect a counterstrain in Christianity that accepted what he rejected, and that just warfare was warranted by some even before Constantine.[15]

To the contrary, Tertullian is typical of most early Christian writers in that he makes no explicit defense of Christian participation in battle

13. For an overview of Tertullian's life and his thought about Christian morality, see George Wolfgang Forell, *History of Christian Ethics,* vol. 1, *From the New Testament to Augustine* (Minneapolis: Augsburg, 1979), 44–60. Forell presents his documentation carefully, adding in a footnote, "Little is actually known about Tertullian's life. The biographical information here summarized represents the 'conventional wisdom'" (186n14). For an overview of Tertullian's views on killing and war, with supporting documentary selections, see Sider, *Early Church on Killing,* 42–63. See the "Introductory Note," in *The Ante Nicene Fathers,* vol. 3, *Latin Christianity: Its Founder, Tertullian,* ed. Cleveland A. Coxe (Grand Rapids, MI: William B. Eerdmans, 1951), 8–12, on the problems involved in dating Tertullian's works and in assigning them to his·orthodox and Montanist periods.

14. For example, Tertullian eventually came to agree with the heretical position that mortal sins such as adultery could not be forgiven after baptism (*Modesty*), as cited in Arthur Cushman McGiffert, *A History of Christian Thought,* vol. 2, *The West from Tertullian to Erasmus* (New York: Scribner's, 1933), 20. However, even in his pre-Montanist period, Tertullian had allowed the possibility of only one more repentance after baptism (*On Repentance* 7, p. 662). For a chronicle of Tertullian's works, see C. John Cadoux, *Early Christian Attitude,* xiii–xiv and Coxe, *Latin Christianity,* 11. Unless otherwise indicated, citations from Tertullian's works are taken from Coxe; page numbers will refer to that volume.

15. Hunter, "A Decade of Research," 93.

and sees military service as at least a temptation to sin, not only through violence but also through lewdness and idolatry.[16] He recognizes that any Christian soldier will likely be forced to an eventual choice between the requirements of his profession and those of his faith, and that if the latter win out, the likely penalty is death. Tertullian's foundational discussion of war occurs in *On the Crown* (the title refers to the soldier's crown of laurel), dating from the period when his sectarian inclinations are heightened. The idolatry involved in Roman military pageants primarily motivates his exhortation to Christian soldiers to repudiate the crown, which they were required to wear on ceremonial occasions.[17] Military life is not singled out in this regard, since the duty of obedience to God and the sin of idolatry are key themes throughout Tertullian's writings. Idolatry is named the "principal crime of the human race" and "the crowning sin."[18] Tertullian conveys well that indirect cooperation in pagan cults was a pervasive danger in second-century Roman society. He is disgusted by the circuses, games, and shows in honor of false gods and idols.[19] Festivals honoring the emperor are also idolatrous.[20] He is intolerant of the excuses of servant or tradesman or craftsman, noting, for instance, that the plasterer ought to be as able to mend a roof or lay on a stucco as to draw on walls the gods' likenesses.[21]

Tertullian is highly skeptical that a true Christian can hold public office, since the Christian would have to refrain from any participation in or support for temples, sacrifices, and tributes, as well as from judgments on life, condemnations, imprisonments, and torture.[22] Military service is so much more dangerous that Tertullian seems, in *On Idolatry*, to exclude it definitely, stating that there "is no agreement" between service to divine and human masters. He addresses specifically both the

---

16. Cadoux, *Early Christian Attitude,* cites ancient authors such as Lactantius and Eusebius to support his claim that there was a "strong disapprobation" of war in early Christianity, "both on account of the dissension it represented and of the infliction of bloodshed and suffering which it involved," and that warfare and murder were connected in Christian thought (57). The passages he quotes substantiate an abhorrence of bloodshed and other atrocities, but not necessarily the stronger case that all killing under any circumstances is forbidden on grounds of specifically Christian commitment. Sider, *Early Church on Killing,* confirms this general assessment, asserting "What we can say with confidence is that every extant Christian statement on killing and war up until the time of Constantine says Christians must not kill, even in war" (194).

17. Cf. Helgeland, Daly, and Burns, *Christians and the Military,* 48–55, for a general discussion of idolatry in Roman army religion; Sider, *Early Church and Killing,* 50; and Young, "Early Church," 497–98.

18. Tertullian, *Idolatry* 1, p. 61; *The Shows* 2, p. 80.

19. Tertullian, *The Shows* 5, pp. 81–82.

20. Tertullian, *Idolatry* 15, p. 70.

21. Tertullian, *Idolatry* 8, p. 65.

22. Tertullian, *Idolatry* 17, pp. 71–72.

question of the believer who volunteers and that of the soldier who converts to Christianity; he includes even the lower ranks who are not required to take part in sacrifices and capital punishment. Even if not direct participants, they wear the garb of a soldier, which represents the "unlawful action" of killing.[23] Tertullian is strict in his exclusion of all near occasions of sin, not so much because external association may contaminate the believer, as because he demands absolute and uncompromising purity of heart in devotion to the Christian life.

Tertullian grounds his prohibitions of killing and of military service on a literal interpretation of Scripture. Scripture leads not only to condemnation of any association with idolatrous practices, but also to the more basic question "whether warfare is proper at all for Christians."[24] In the Ten Commandments, God "puts his interdict on every sort of man-killing by that one summary precept, 'Thou shalt not kill.'"[25] Chronological sequence in the gospels is important to Tertullian in determining Jesus's attitude toward violence; even though soldiers had been received by John the Baptist (Luke 3:12–13); and a centurion had believed in Jesus (Matt 8:5; Luke 7:2), "*still* the Lord afterward in disarming Peter, unbelted every soldier."[26] In his rejection of the "occupation of the sword," Tertullian refers to the Lord's commands not even to avenge wrongs or to sue at law (Matt 5:38–39; on lawsuits, see 5:25, 40), and to the saying that those who take up the sword shall perish by it (Matt 26:52). Rather than betray the Lord, the faithful Christian is willing to suffer punishment and death in Christ's name, in imitation of the Lord and his disciples.[27]

Tertullian's use of biblical texts may be viewed in the context of a difference between two schools of thought in the early church regarding biblical interpretation. In the Eastern center of Alexandria, allegorical exegesis flourished, exemplified in the thought of Origen. In the West, at Antioch, there was a stronger influence of Jewish teaching, which tended to take more seriously the literal meaning of Scripture.[28] Alexandrian interpreters found freedom to uphold the intellectual coherence of the faith by finding the true meaning of some biblical events at a higher level than historical reality.

23. Tertullian, *Idolatry* 19, p. 73; cf. Cadoux, *Early Christian Attitude,* 107–9.
24. Tertullian, *The Crown* 11, pp. 99–100.
25. Tertullian, *The Shows* 2, p. 80.
26. Tertullian, *Idolatry* 19, p. 73.
27. Tertullian, *The Crown* 11, pp. 99–100; *Apology* 21, pp. 34–35; *Against Marcion* 28, p. 396.
28. See Robert M. Grant and David Tracy, *A Short History of the Interpretation of the Bible,* 2nd ed. (Philadelphia: Fortress, 1984), 52–82, on the contrasts between the Alexandrian and Antiochene schools.

Antiochene exegetes wanted to maintain both the historicity of these events and their relatively direct use as a standard for Christian theology and practice. Partly to combat some of the more whimsical excesses of unhistorical allegorization, the thinkers of Antioch, especially Irenaeus, insisted that no interpreter should simply take a biblical text and independently extrapolate theological meanings from it. The authoritative interpreter of Scripture—and the guarantor of fidelity to its true meaning—is the church, defined in terms of apostolic succession. This authority preserves the true faith in continuity with the biblical tradition. As R. M. Grant indicates, the authority of the church as interpreter becomes both internal and external to the texts interpreted.[29]

Tertullian develops the view of Irenaeus that the Scriptures are the property of the church as descended from the apostles. Against the Valentinians and Marcion, Tertullian claims that orthodoxy is the norm of interpretation. His interpretations are thus based on two principles: (1) the importance of the literal sense of Scripture as the foundation of all interpretations; and (2) consistency with the authoritative tradition of the church as the standard for the theological expansion of literal meanings.

An important foundation of Tertullian's teaching against killing is his stringent interpretation of the Sermon on the Mount, which he takes literally both on swearing and on nonviolence.[30] In *The Crown,* Tertullian goes so far as to say that avoiding those things forbidden by Scripture is not enough. What is not "freely allowed" by Scripture should be presumed "forbidden."[31] In his controversies with Marcion's followers, who denied the authority of the Old Testament, Tertullian avoids allegorizing interpretations of even the most inconsistent biblical texts. For example, he harmonizes the literal meanings of "love your enemies" and "an eye for an eye" by taking the latter as meant "for the purpose of restraining the injury in the first instance, which it had forbidden on pain of retaliation or reciprocity."[32] This purpose is furthered by the saying of Jesus rather than contradicted by it, so that the Old Testament is superseded by the New, though not nullified. The command to love the neighbor is gradually extended to strangers and even enemies, making the New Testament the final and authoritative norm. Although Tertullian forbids the Christian to take overt vengeance, he encourages the patient sufferer to anticipate the Lord's vengeance on her or his behalf, and to take immediate gratification in the fact that the attacker will be

29. R. M. Grant, *The Spirit and the Letter* (London: SPCK, 1957), 81–84.
30. Tertullian, *Idolatry* 11, p. 67; *Apology* 37, p. 45.
31. Tertullian, *The Crown* 2, p. 94.
32. Tertullian, *Against Marcion* 16, p. 371.

pained and disappointed by staunch passivity.[33] Although this consolation leaves something to be desired when measured against the Beatitudes, it was to enjoy some popularity among later authors, notably Augustine and Calvin.

The primacy of the teaching of Jesus regarding killing is developed in the context of Tertullian's polemics against Judaism, and by means of a distinction between the "old" and "new" divine laws. Although, on the one hand, Tertullian wants to preserve the Old Testament against Marcion, he also wants, against the Jews, to subjugate it to Christianity. Thus he includes it within divine revelation as the old law, diminishing its authority by claiming that the old law is "obliterated"[34] and "that the old Law has ceased."[35] In regard to the numerous Old Testament examples of divinely sanctioned warfare, Tertullian allows that the Israelites did well by fighting, even on the sabbath, but asserts that the "giver of the new law" who announces "the new kingdom which is not corruptible" is "already come," so that "service may have to be rendered him."[36] In this kingdom already present, swords are beaten into plowshares (Isa 2:4) and "fierce and cruel" dispositions become peaceable.[37]

This extension of meaning from implements to attitudes shows us that Tertullian is not tied absolutely to literal meanings but uses them as the basis for theological and ethical proposals that are consistent with them. In fact, "some things spoken with a special reference contain in them a general truth . . . so that it is legitimate to move from *species* to *genus*," and also vice versa.[38] When, for instance, God reproves the Israelites, God speaks to "all men." Tertullian is willing to take some biblical references figuratively if to adhere rigidly to the literal meaning of one would make nonsense out of the literal meaning of another. Indeed, Scripture sometimes transfers names of persons or groups figuratively on the basis of similar characteristics.[39] Thus the various modes of discourse included in the Bible become models for contemporary theological and ethical discourse. In showing that Jesus's identification as the Messiah fulfills prophetic sayings, Tertullian is careful to dissociate him from the literal sword, battles, and weaponry. Even though Tertullian thinks that the psalms prophesy a "warrior," girt with a "sword," they also acclaim his "lenity" and "justice." Since these virtues are inconsistent with war

33. Tertullian, *Patience* 7, pp. 712–13.
34. Tertullian, *Against the Jews* 3, p. 154; 6, p. 157.
35. Tertullian, *Against the Jews* 4, pp. 55–56.
36. Tertullian, *Against the Jews* 6, p. 157.
37. Tertullian, *Against Marcion* 1, p. 346.
38. Tertullian, *Against the Jews* 9, p. 162.
39. Tertullian, *Against the Jews* 9, p. 162.

and killing, he concludes that the weapon must be meant of Jesus figuratively. Thus notions of justice and mercy that are not derived strictly from the Bible, or at least not from it exclusively, become the standards of the meaning of biblical references.

> See we, then, whether that which has another action be not another sword—that is, the Divine word of God, doubly sharpened with the two Testaments of the ancient law and the new law; sharpened by the equity of its own wisdom; rendering to each one according to his own action. Lawful, then, it was for the Christ of God to be precinct, in the Psalms, without warlike achievements, with the figurative sword of the Word of God.[40]

Tertullian demonstrates that specifically religious sources of ethical reflection rarely can be employed in total disjunction from more philosophical or cultural presuppositions and normative ideals. For the rules of Christian living, Tertullian turns first to Scripture, but also relies on "Tradition, and custom, and faith" and believes that reason will support rather than collide with these. The "true interpretation of reason" is, however, given by "authority," or "the apostle's sanction."[41] In *The Soul*, Tertullian intends primarily to vindicate Christian doctrine against the philosophers and heretics. But since Scripture and even church tradition do not speak extensively on the nature of the soul, he has to substantiate his literalist arguments from Scripture (for example, on the corporeal suffering of persons in hell) with references to such philosophers as the Stoics and Aristotle.[42] As Jaroslav Pelikan remarks, Tertullian's avowed aversion to rationalist thought did not prevent his "quoting the very philosophy against whose pretensions he had spoken so violently."[43] It was perhaps Tertullian's insistence on the literal sense of all Scripture, authoritatively defined, combined with his resort to more extrinsic supports when biblical texts or the tradition failed to coincide unambiguously with his agenda, that led the nineteenth-century scholar Frederick Farrar, in his Bampton Lectures, to exclaim impatiently: "The eloquent, fiery, uncompromising African practically makes Scripture say exactly what he himself chooses."[44]

Although Tertullian generally is regarded as a pacifist and definitely

---

40. Tertullian, *Against the Jews* 9, pp. 162–63.

41. Tertullian, *The Crown* 4, p. 95.

42. See Tertullian, *The Soul* 5, pp. 184–85. See also Jaroslav Pelikan, *The Christian Tradition: A History of the Development of Doctrine*, vol. 1, *Emergence of the Catholic Tradition (100–600)* (Chicago: University of Chicago Press, 1971), 49–50.

43. Pelikan, *Emergence*, 50.

44. Frederick W. Farrar, *History of Interpretation: Eight Lectures Preached before the University of Oxford in the Year MDCCCLXXXV* (New York: E. P. Dutton, 1886) 178–79.

holds up nonviolence as a Christian ideal, it is less clear that he is a sectarian pacifist who supports Christian withdrawal from the enterprise of government. On the one hand, Tertullian defines Jesus as a peacemaker whose power consists in the pursuit of peace (citing Isa 2:3–4).[45] He views most public roles as dangerous to Christian belief and practice. On the other hand, he appeals for tolerance of Christianity on the grounds that Christians pray for the emperor and for the stability of the Roman Empire. "We respect in the emperors the ordinance of God, who has set them over the nations. We know that there is that in them which God has willed."[46] Even though Christians refuse to worship him, the emperor is "called by our Lord to his office."[47] Tertullian does not expect that the kingdom of God, superseding all temporal authority, will be realized soon.[48]

Tertullian protests against the view that Christian citizens are "useless," contending that "we sail with you, and fight with you, and till the ground with you."[49] He twice tells with pride the legend of the "Thundering Legion" of Marcus Aurelius's army, which its Christian members supposedly saved from attack with their prayers.[50] On these two occasions, the story is mentioned in a group of other incidents demonstrating that Christian claims have merit and that wise and prudent rulers ought not persecute Christians. It is dubious that these references represent an acceptance of Christian military participation as such on Tertullian's part. They seem to demonstrate merely that he regarded it as a fact, and that the efficacy of Christian prayer at least was to be commended to the powers that be. In his somewhat later but pre-Montanist treatise *On Idolatry,* he states that a Christian may not enlist, not even in peacetime, and not even if he will not be involved directly in killing, for every soldier must wear the military uniform and weapon which are forbidden by Christ—and no one can serve two masters.[51]

In sum, Tertullian supports the legitimate and necessary function of the state and its rulers; he does not prohibit Christian participation in public roles to the extent that idolatry, killing, and other immorality can be avoided. He claims that Christians support by their spiritual endeavors

45. Sider, *Early Church on Killing,* 174, citing Tertullian, *Against Marcion* 3.21.

46. Tertullian, *Apology* 32, pp. 42–43.

47. Tertullian, *Apology* 33, pp. 43.

48. Tertullian, *The Resurrection of the Flesh* 24, p. 18.

49. Tertullian, *Apology* 4, p. 49 (pre-Montanist); cf. *Apology* 37; p. 37; and *To the Heathen* 1, p. 109.

50. Tertullian, *Apology* 5, p. 22; *To Scapula* 4, p. 107. See Helgeland, Daly, and Burns, *Christians in the Military*; and Sider, *Early Church on Killing,* 185–90, for discussion of other ancient attestation to this story of Christian presence in the military.

51. Sider, *Early Church and Killing,* 175; citing *Idolatry* 19.

even those officials whose actions they cannot always approve morally and religiously. A pacifist but not a separatist, Tertullian is concerned most of all with total obedience to God in every facet of life. For living obediently, the Christian must expect persecution that will be rewarded by God. But Tertullian does not repudiate the world in return for its rejection of Christians, and he continues to implore important political figures to consider justly the merits of the Christian faith and life.

The nature of that faith and life are defined in relation to Scripture, with the New Testament taking precedence over the Old. The guarantor of faithful Christian teaching is the tradition of the church. Tertullian understands "authoritative tradition" in light of his view of orthodoxy. He uses it to determine which texts, themes, or incidents in the Bible will be interpreted with strict literalness and which in a "deeper" or a figurative manner. Tertullian rarely (if ever) uses figurative interpretation to compromise biblical teachings that seem simply too difficult to fulfill in the present age. Rather, he fearlessly takes at their most literal level the "hard sayings" that presuppose the inbreaking reign of God.

ORIGEN

Origen is both similar to and quite different from Tertullian. Origen too interprets Scripture in the light of tradition (the "rule of faith") but defines the meaning of Scripture much more freely in relation to the individual text as well as to the canon, using the method of allegory. Like Tertullian, Origen counsels the Christian to refrain from violence and even from military service in general. At another level he supports as social necessities the government, its representatives, and its strategies.

Unlike Tertullian, Origen envisions the ideal Christian life as a goal that is attained only progressively. While the theme of sanctification is not worked out explicitly in relation to pacifism, it contributes to the context in which Origen's sayings about pacifism should be understood. His general support of the emperor is also part of this context, as it was for Tertullian. In neither author is a systematic Christian view of nonviolence or peace given sustained attention in relation to the exigencies of social life, in view of the partial historical presence of the kingdom. These themes are only beginning to appear in these church fathers, who do not develop the sorts of internally coherent positions that subsequent Christian pacifism (or just war theory) is likely to demand.

Born to an Alexandrian Christian family in the late second century (ca. 185 CE), Origen was inspired by the martyrdom of his father, Leonides, when Origen was about seventeen. The details of Origen's life are known largely from Eusebius of Caesarea's *Ecclesiastical History.* Eusebius's reliability may be compromised by his interest in portraying Origen as a Christian hero, but it is clear at least that Origen received a quality education in both philosophy and the study of Christianity and gained an unusual reputation as a priest, preacher, theologian, apologist, and participant in ecclesiastical controversy. As the result of a dispute (the details of which are unclear) with his bishop, Demetrius, Origen was expelled from the Alexandrian church. He died in Caesarea (ca. 254 CE), after having also suffered persecution as a Christian by the Emperor Decius.[52]

Although Origen's work was suppressed after his death because it suggested unorthodox ideas such as the preexistence of souls, the subordination of the Son to the Father, and universal salvation, it continued to exert a hold on great Christian thinkers, such as Gregory of Nazianzus, Basil, and Jerome. The attractive core of Origen's theology is his vision of the Christian life as a movement toward God, occurring within a cosmological drama of reunion with the divine, enabled by the *logos* or Word and guided by the Spirit. For Origen, the Word is incarnate not only in the historical Jesus, but also in Scripture, the full meaning of which is increasingly grasped as one is transformed by the Spirit.[53]

While the Alexandrian school did not deny the historical meaning of most biblical texts, it subordinated them to a higher meaning. It was this freedom over against the literal sense to which the Antiochene exegetes reacted so negatively. The ability to transcend the literal sense without rejecting it, however, allows interpreters such as Origen to retain the Old Testament while refuting both the Jewish tradition, which retained the Mosaic law, and gnostic Christians who rejected the Old Testament because of its ostensible incompatibility with the New.[54] Origen interprets the Old Testament spiritually, so that at a deeper level it is in keeping with the New Testament, and he also sees the New Testament as a higher stage of revelation that surpasses but is indicated by the earlier Scriptures.

Origen's method of interpretation is derived from classical sources,

52. A biography of Origen is provided in Joseph Wilson Trigg, *Origen: The Bible and Philosophy in the Third-Century Church* (Atlanta: John Knox, 1983), 3–30. See also Pierre Nautin, *Origene: Sa vie et son oevre* (Paris: Beauchesne, 1977).

53. For a discussion of the importance of Jesus Christ as Word, especially in relation to Origen's interpretation of Scripture, see Robert Daly's foreword in Hans Urs von Balthasar, ed., *Origen's Spirit and Fire: A Thematic Anthology of His Writings,* trans. Robert Daly (Washington, DC: Catholic University of America Press, 1984) xi–xviii, as well as Balthasar's introduction to the same volume.

54. Cf. Jean Daniélou, *Origen*, trans. Walter Mitchell (New York: Sheed & Ward, 1955), 140–44.

mediated into religious exegesis by Philo of Alexandria and Clement. Hellenistic allegorical techniques were quite intricate and included philology, etymology, and numerology. Allegory, for example, was used to enhance the acceptability of the escapades of the heroes and gods in the Homeric poems.[55] Clement of Alexandria, the first Christian thinker to attempt an explanation of the allegorical method, bases his exegesis on the Jewish thinker Philo. According to Philo, allegory is justified by Scripture itself, which, among other instances, uses the trees in Eden to stand for knowledge and for good and evil.[56] Clement's own interpretation is Christocentric, but he agrees with Philo that every word in Scripture is divinely inspired but not every part of Scripture need be taken at its most obvious meaning. Beyond the literal sense, Scripture can have meanings that are theological, moral, or even philosophical. The guide of the interpreter is faith in Christ; impossible meanings are rejected and hidden ones discovered on the basis of this standard.[57]

Origen's approach to Scripture is expounded primarily in the fourth book of *On First Principles*, composed between 220 and 240 CE.[58] After arguing that the success of the early Christian movement and the fulfillment in Jesus of Old Testament prophecies attest to Scripture's divine inspiration, Origen proceeds to the matter of interpretation. Adopting Philo's method, he assigns to the Scriptures a triple meaning corresponding to the body, soul, and spirit of humanity: the literal, the moral, and the mystical or theological.[59] Although Origen does not dispute the historicity of most biblical events, he maintains that their real significance transcends it. The simple believer grasps only the historical meaning or an obvious religious one, but those who have progressed to greater union with the Holy Spirit will discern deeper or higher levels of signif-

55. Trigg, *Origen*, 31–33; Karlfried Froelich, *Biblical Interpretation in the Early Church* (Philapelphia: Fortress, 1984), 18–19.

56. Grant and Tracy, *Short History*, 52–56.

57. Grant, *Spirit and the Letter*, 85–89; cf. Grant and Tracy, *Short History*, 55–56; Daniélou, *Origen*, 185; Froelich, *Biblical Interpretation*, 15–16; and Trigg, *Origen*, 54–65, which also includes a discussion of the influence of Platonism on Clement.

58. The edition used is *Origen: On First Principles*, ed. G. W. Butterworth (New York: Harper & Row, 1966). *First Principles* has been partly preserved in Greek by Basil of Caesarea, but much must be reconstructed from Rufinus's less reliable Latin translation. Butterworth arranges translations from the Greek and Latin in parallel columns. The translation from which quotations are taken here will be indicated in the notes as G or L. Selections from several relevant works by Origen are included, with an overview, in Sider, *Early Church on Killing*, 67–83.

59. This is to state the schema in basic terms. Actually, Origen did not have a particularly systematic or definitive set of principles for assigning interpretations. Daly points out that the three levels sometimes have different meanings: historical, moral, mystical; or historical, mystical, spiritual (Daly, foreword to *Spirit and Fire*, xvii). Note also Grant's contention that the distinction of levels "breaks down immediately" (*Spirit and Letter*, 94).

icance.[60] Indeed, many "hindrances and impossibilities" have been deliberately inserted into the biblical narratives as "stumbling blocks," with the purpose of leading the reader to reflect more carefully on the highest meanings that Scripture contains.[61] When the sequence of the actual events recorded does not correspond evenly to the spiritual truths to be communicated, the Holy Spirit occasionally has inserted less probable, impossible, or possible but fictitious events.[62]

Origen tells us that the "'key of knowledge' is necessary" to understand Scripture.[63] In fact, he uses multiple and not always consistent criteria to determine which of the narrative's literal meanings the Holy Spirit must have inserted gratuitously. If Origen discerns the immediately apparent sense of a text to be "absurd and impossible," things which "cannot be accepted as history," then these elements must have been intended to force inquiry to a higher level.[64] However, Origen's standard of the impossible varies. It can be science (there could have been no "morning and evening" on the first three days of creation if the sun and moon had not yet been created);[65] "irrationality" as uselessness (the Mosaic prohibition to eat vultures, since clearly no one would want to);[66] "irrationality" as immorality (the instruction to pluck out an eye if it is guilty of lust),[67] religious (the anthropomorphism "God walks" does not comport with the Christian view of deity);[68] or physical unlikelihood or impossibility (the devil could not have shown Jesus the whole world, for it would be impossible to see it all at once;[69] we cannot be expected to offer the "other" cheek, since an aggressor striking with the right hand will hit the left cheek a second time).[70] On the other hand, Origen does not qualify his assertion that there is no need to question the literal sense of "swear not at all" and the condemnation of hidden lust as adultery.[71] The credibility of the virgin birth, miracles of Jesus, and the appearance of the

60. Origen, *First Principles*, L: 1. preface. 8, p. 1.

61. Origen, *First Principles*, G: 4.2.9, p. 285. (L: "stumbling blocks," "impossibilities and incongruities.")

62. Origen, *First Principles*, G: 4.2.9, p. 286.

63. Origen, *First Principles*, G: 4.2.3, p. 274.

64. Origen, *First Principles*, G: 4.3.4, p. 294; L: 4.3.1., p. 290.

65. Origen, *First Principles*, L: 4.3.1., 288; cf. Gen 1:5–13.

66. Origen, *First Principles*, G: 4.3.2., p. 290; cf. Lev 11:14.

67. Origen, *First Principles*, G & L: 4.3.3, p. 293; Matt 5:28–29.

68. Origen, *First Principles*, G & L: 4.3.1, p. 288; Gen 3:8.

69. Origen, *First Principles*, G & L: 4.3.1, p. 289; Matt 4:8.

70. Origen, *First Principles*, G & L: 4.3.4, p. 289; Matt 5:39.

71. Origen, *First Principles*, G & L: 4.3.4, p. 295; Matt 5:34, 28. Butterworth indicates that the inclusion of the text on lust may be the work of Rufinus.

Holy Spirit as a dove are staunchly defended while the creation of Eve from Adam's rib is given an allegorical interpretation.[72]

Origen's calls for "considerable investigation" and an "open mind" are sometimes more appropriate than the interpretations themselves.[73] No wonder Origen compares scriptural interpretation to a hunt for lost treasure in a field, admitting that, even while using the allegorical method, the "final goal" of complete understanding is unattainable.[74] Obviously, selective interpretation of Scripture is nothing new. Nor should it be surprising or distressing. After all, the biblical narratives were written in historical contexts and for specific audiences. This leads to contradictions in the Bible itself, as well as cases in which an apparent biblical message is repugnant to later communal discernment of the demands of the Christian life. Warmaking, patriarchy and slavery, and even accommodation to the government are cases in point. The most important question is whether a given interpretation comports with the heart of the gospel, which is salvation from God in Jesus Christ; the virtues of faith, hope and charity; the inbreaking of God's reign in Jesus's prophetic ministry of inclusive fellowship, forgiveness of sins, and healing; and the sending of the Spirit to the church by the risen Jesus.

Origin's theological convictions about God, Jesus Christ, and the Spirit form the most important horizon for his biblical interpretations.[75] They interact with cultural, moral, and "scientific" premises that are context-dependent, if not simply reducible to context. Similarly to the contemporary thinker, Origen's theology is influenced strongly by the humanistic disciplines and intellectual currents of the day. In his case, it is Platonic philosophy and other elements of an educated Hellenism. For the Christian interpreter, the most important criterion of interpretation is the figure of Jesus Christ, both as mediated through biblical texts, and in light of ongoing communal appropriation and theological reflection. Tradition is as important to Origen as it is to Tertullian; the difference lies primarily in the degree of constraint placed on the methods used to bring the canonical literature into line with the rule of faith.

What Origin seeks is "the methods of interpretation that appear right to us who keep to the rule of the heavenly Church of Jesus Christ

---

72. Origen, *Against Celsus* 1.37, p. 36; 1:46, p. 42; 4.38, p. 213 in *Origen: Contra Celsum*, trans. Henry Chadwick (Cambridge: Cambridge University Press, 1980).

73. Origen, *Against Celsus* 1.42, p. 39.

74. Origen, *First Principles* G & L: 4.3.11, p. 306; Matt 13:44; L: 4.3.14, p. 311.

75. See Trigg, *Origen*, 13–14, for a summary of what the agreed "canon of faith" included in Origen's day. For example, doctrines of God, Christ, Spirit, spiritual beings, last things, and sacraments, but not yet precise doctrines of the Trinity, of the Son's relation to the Father, or of the relation of the two natures in Christ.

through the succession from the Apostles."[76] Origen states in *On First Principles* that the parameters of apostolic teaching can be understood "in plain terms" to include certain key documents such as the unity of the creator and the Father of Jesus Christ, author both of the Old Testament and the New; the true divinity and true humanity of Jesus; and the resurrection of the dead. Origen refers the questions whether the Holy Spirit is begotten or unbegotten, and how exactly it is that devils exist, to future investigation of the Scriptures, "with wisdom and diligence." Repeated references to the authority of apostolic and church teaching make it clear that understanding of Scripture occurs in an ecclesial and communal context, under the guidance of the Spirit.[77]

The most extended attention to the ethics of war or of the military profession occurs in *Against Celsus* (248 CE), written to refute the charges of a Greek philosopher that Christians undermine the common good by refusing to participate in the necessary activities of government. Like Tertullian, Origen does not deny the legitimacy of government. He does, however, object to Christian involvement with the professional violence of the military. While it can be taken for granted that military service at that time included idolatry, and that Origen found it objectionable, idolatry does not play a major role in Origen's writings as a reason against such service. Rather, he argues that Christ absolutely forbids any sort of homicide (or even vengeance), even against "the greatest wrongdoer." Jesus's followers are peaceful and love their enemies.[78]

For Origen, the dominance of the Roman emperor was a result of divine providence. The absence of international conflict facilitated the missionary teaching of the apostles, "which preaches peace and does not even allow men to take vengeance on their enemies."[79] As Tertullian had pointed out, Christians support the emperor even more effectively than do troops, through prayer, intercession, and asceticism, "composing a special army of piety."[80] Thus, like pagan priests, they should be exempt from killing and allowed to avoid public office, to serve both church and

76. Origen, *First Principles*, G: 4.2.2, p. 272 (L: "who keep to that rule and discipline delivered by Jesus Christ to the apostles and handed down by them in succession to their posterity, the teachers of the heavenly Church.").

77. Origen, *First Principles*, L: 1.preface, 4–7, pp. 1–5.

78. Origen, *Against Celsus* 3.8, p. 133. Cf. Louis J. Swift, *The Early Fathers on War and Military Service* (Wilmington, DE: Michael Glazier, 1983), 57, and Sider, *Early Church on Killing*, 67–83. Sider overviews Origen's views of war, including substantial selections from *Against Celsus*.

79. Origen, *Against Celsus* 2.30, p. 92.

80. Origen, *Against Celsus* 8.73, p. 509.

nation.[81] Christians are "gentle," are "killed 'as sheep'" and refrain even from defense against persecutors.[82]

The Old Testament presents hermeneutical difficulties for Origen, for "It was impossible for Christians to follow the Mosaic law in killing their enemies" and inflicting the death penalty.[83] In pursuit of a resolution, Origen cites Old Testament passages coinciding in spirit with New Testament nonviolence (Ps 7:4–6; Lam 3:27–29).[84] In addition, he insists that "concerning the promise to the Jews to the effect that they would massacre their enemies we would say that, if one reads and studies the words carefully, one finds that the literal interpretation is impossible."[85] The allegorical hermeneutic is centrally operative in Origen's pacifism, demonstrating again that pacifism does not depend on literalist or biblicist interpretations of the Sermon on the Mount. He examines what "secret mysteries" might be concealed under the historical "account of wars," and concludes that "the wars and conquests of Israel" and "the soldiers who appear . . . in scripture" are figures of heavenly things—for example, of souls fighting for God.[86] Origen sees the law and the Israelite revelation as a preparation for the New Testament, as typologically prefiguring the New Testament, and as eventually superseded by the New Testament. That is to say, the Jews represent a prior level of faith, and the events in their history, while literally true, stand for the religious or theological significance of the messiah who is to come.[87]

Although universal agreement among nations and peoples is historically impossible ("to those still in bodies"), things will change when the Word has destroyed all the evil in the world.[88] Origen hopes for a temporal victory of Christianity. "One day" Christianity will be the only religion "to prevail, since the Word is continually gaining possession of more souls."[89] In the present, however, Christians must avoid not only violence but also public service, leading progressively better lives. Through piety they become leaders in the salvation of all.[90] Those still outside the faith might in the meantime be involved in "necessary" wars, which should be kept as "just and ordered" as possible.[91]

81. Origen, *Against Celsus* 8.73–75, pp. 509–10.
82. Origen, *Against Celsus* 3.7, p. 132.
83. Origen, *Against Celsus* 7.26, p. 415.
84. Origen, *Against Celsus* 7.24–25, pp. 414–15.
85. Origen, *Against Celsus* 7.19, p. 410.
86. Origen, *First Principles*, L: 4.2.8, p. 284; L: 4.3.12, pp. 307–9.
87. See Daniélou, *Origen*, "The Typological Interpretation of the Bible," 139–73.
88. Origen, *Against Celsus* 8.72, p. 508.
89. Origen, *Against Celsus* 7.68, p. 505.
90. Origen, *Against Celsus* 8.74, p. 510.
91. Origen, *Against Celsus* 4.82, p. 249.

It is important in understanding Origen's position, that while morality is extremely important to him, he sees sanctification as a gradual process. This applies both to the individual, being united to the *logos* by the Spirit; and to the human race, gradually being converted. Origen knows that there is no one in whom Christ reigns so that the power of sin is completely broken. "And the Lord himself at the beginning of his preaching does not say: 'The kingdom of heaven has come,' but: 'The kingdom of heaven has drawn near' (Matt 3:12)."[92] The kingdom "draws near" to a person only as she or he increases in understanding of the Word.[93] The mission of Christians is to make the eschatological reality of the kingdom increasingly present in their lives and in the world.

Despite his absolute and insistent rejection of violence, Origen maintains a tension in his view of gospel existence in this life. The Holy Spirit is the agent of sanctification that is progressing. Origen differs in his moral demands or expectations not only from Tertullian but also from Menno Simons and the Quakers, who are committed to kingdom life without compromise, expecting repudiation by the world. Origen agrees with the norm of total nonviolence but is more accepting that failure is a reality. Nevertheless, for the Christian, participation in violence is a mark of sin, representing a lack of full conversion and unity with the Word.[94]

Although the theologians of early Christianity held up pacifism as an ideal and exhorted their hearers to embody the new life possible in Jesus Christ, not all Christians realized this ideal. Moreover, while killing another human being is always wrong for Christians (and is generally put in a bad light no matter who does it), civil government and the order it enforces are social goods. Use of force by the emperor or other authorities may be necessary, and while it is not condemned, neither is it praised. Christians are not subject to a blanket prohibition to avoid any and all public offices and roles. People such as soldiers—whose roles place them in an ambiguous or dangerous situation regarding this duty—are not necessarily excluded from the church. It is more accurate to say that early Christian teachers unanimously insist on the wrongness of killing for Christians, than that the early church as a whole was "pacifist." Early Christian writers do not systematically analyze the nature of the moral dilemma involved in being both a Christian and a citizen, a stakeholder

---

92. From Origen's *Commentary on Romans* 5:3, as cited in Balthasar, *Spirit and Fire*, 362.

93. From Origen's *Commentary on Matthew* 10.14, as cited in Balthasar, *Spirit and Fire*, 362.

94. Some authors have noted in Origen the seed of the later "two swords" theory of the relation of church and government. See Gerard E. Caspary, *Origen and the Two Swords* (Berkeley: University of California Press, 1979); Helgeland, Daly, and Burns, *Christians and the Military*, 40–41.

in the common good who benefits from the stability government provides. Yet ambivalence and unclarity about whether Christians must
remove themselves entirely from any public institutions connected to
government-sponsored killing reveal awareness that the dilemma exists.
That being said, given the tension between the duty toward government
and the common good, on the one side, and the duty not to kill, on the
other, the balance is struck in favor of the Christian duty not to kill.

The next chapter will consider Augustine's effort to retain the ideals
of self-offering love and redeemed Christian community, even while
accepting Christian use of violence in view of the reality of sin in the
world, and the practical need to maintain order in the "earthly city."

4.

Augustine and the Beginnings of Christian Just War Theory

Early Christian thinkers were likely to assume that Christian discipleship meant a distinctive way of life that, even if not deliberately separatist in relation to politics and government, would mark the Christian community and its members off against dominant cultural values. The early church was not unequivocally pacifist in practice, but major theologians did see military life as a threat to Christian ideals. Although an author like Origen can refer to Christians contributing an "army of piety" to society, the outlier nature of Christian social status is reflected in the very need for a bridging metaphor. Louis Swift contrasts the first two centuries with the age of Augustine by remarking, "It is a truism that the reign of Constantine (AD 306–37) represents a watershed in the development of Christian attitudes concerning war and military service," inasmuch as "the question is no longer whether participation in war is justified but what conditions should govern the right to declare war *(ius belli)* and what rules should be observed in waging it *(ius in bello)*."[1]

The focus of the present chapter will be Augustine's answer to the Christian problem of justifying war. It will also incorporate a discussion of the problem of irreducible moral dilemmas that arise in killing, war, and political responsibility. The reality of moral dilemmas that cannot be satisfactorily resolved is attested by both Augustine's ambiguous views of killing in war and torture and the flawed analysis by which he squares them with Christian virtue.

For Augustine, to be a "peacemaker" can involve using mortal force as a means to peace. Augustine enumerates three criteria for going to war: the goal of peace, lawful authority, and right intention (love). Augustine's views are the point of departure for many later authors, most

---

1. Louis J. Swift, *The Early Fathers on War and Military Service* (Wilmington, DE: Michael Glazier, 1983), 80.

notably Aquinas, and continue to anchor much of the contemporary debate about just war theory. Special points of concern will be Augustine's ambivalent view of society and politics in general; his validation of war as divinely authorized "punishment"; his requirement that war be conducted with an inward intention of love; and the effect that justification of war as loving punishment has on the ethics of going to war, of means in war, of limits of war, and on the moral identity of the warrior.

Augustine's legacy is constructive in that he sees love as a constitutive and indispensable Christian virtue, recognizes the sinful and conflicted nature of political life, regards Christian political participation as an obligation nonetheless, grants the ambiguous moral position in which this places the agent, and in his letters and sermons exemplifies concrete strategies of social change. Negatively, however, Augustine fails to confront directly, much less resolve, the inevitable contradiction between Christian love and killing, to recognize the inherent interdependence of intention and action, to set firm and adequate limits on the ends and means of war, and to take seriously enough in the context of violent conflict the transformative possibilities of the inbreaking reign of God. Nevertheless, certain tensions in his thought suggest that the reality of moral dilemmas was not entirely outside Augustine's frame of reference. Ultimately this chapter will argue that some of his other writings on social problems (not just war) open the door to practical strategies that resemble peacebuilding.

FROM EARLY CHRISTIAN PACIFISM TO JUST WAR

Christian pacifists emphasize the present possibility of enacting God's reign now, and the absoluteness of Jesus's teaching on love and nonviolence (Matt 5:38–48). If force is necessary and even useful in the real political world, then Christian participation in that world must in the pacifist view be limited and the use of force repudiated. As we have seen in early Christian writings, pacifists seek to realize a biblical and communal vision of sacrifice and nonviolence. They tend to overlook or downplay the occurrence of violence in the Old Testament, especially Yahweh's leadership in battle. They not infrequently come to terms with biblical violence by construing a nonviolent message behind the war imagery. Their priority is reinforcement of Christian identity as constituting a contrast society against broader social acceptance of power politics and coercive force.

While pacifists stress the literal following of Jesus's nonviolent message, those who justify government by coercive means stress Christian responsibility in a broken or fallen world, as well as the possibility of ordering that world more justly. The Christian's conformity to the kingdom's radical nature is qualified by his or her coexistence as a citizen of the present world and the necessity of fulfilling the obligations of justice, seen as another way of expressing neighbor love. Just war theory is oriented toward establishing and protecting the stable social structures and authorities that serve just peace. Most just war theorists take the nonviolent thrust of the Sermon on the Mount quite seriously and do not attempt to set aside nonviolence as such. Yet they usually transmute its practical impact to another level or sphere than that of practical politics. Christian discipleship has a social as well as a spiritual meaning, but Christian social ethics must be guided not only by sacrificial love but also by the common good of society and the possibility of limiting injustice and building greater justice.

The mainstream or dominant tradition on war and peace has justified limited uses of violence, yet it has also acknowledged their tension with the evangelical ideal of peace and attempted to recognize the latter in some practical way. Contrasts among the pacifism of earlier figures and later just war (and even "holy war") positions can be gauged by distinctions, described by James Childress, employed to recognize the obligatory character of nonviolence, while limiting its practical scope: higher/lower, for oneself/for others, inner/outer, private/public.[2] In other words, Christian authors restrict the force of New Testament sayings against violence ("turn the other cheek," "go the second mile," "love your enemies") by making one or more of the following assertions: that the sayings define a "higher" Christian life (of the clergy, for example) but need not be taken literally on the "lower" plane (by the laity); that they must be interpreted strictly regarding actions on one's own behalf but not if one is removing or preventing harm to others; that they apply to the inner realm of loving intention but not to the outer realm of just action; that they apply to the decisions of private citizens but not to those of public authorities acting in an official capacity (who have the right to command their subordinates, such as soldiers). Augustine avoids the first of these strategies, while adopting the last three—and arguing somewhat inconsistently that Christian love is *directly* expressed in wartime killing as loving punishment of a sinner.[3]

All these maneuvers are attempts to construe a distinctive Christian

2. James F. Childress, "Moral Discourse about War in the Early Church," *Journal of Religious Ethics* 12, no. 1 (1984): 12.

3. Augustine, *On Christian Doctrine*, trans. D. W. Robertson (Indianapolis: Bobbs-Merrill, 1958), 3.18.25. Augustine, unlike Ambrose and Aquinas, does not seem to distinguish explicitly between clergy and laity on participation in violence.

identity as compatible with other social obligations of the Christian. The life of kingdom discipleship is negotiated historically to accommodate the responsibilities, possibilities, and tensions entailed by membership in multiple, intersecting communities of identity. The critical theological, biblical, and ecclesial question, of course, is whether any given process of negotiation is also a process of dilution or distortion.

AUGUSTINE

Christian just war tradition begins with Augustine, who appropriated from Roman politics the idea of a "just war" for defense or punishment. Augustine did not invent a coherent theory comparable to modern versions, but he did germinate some of the key ideas or issues around which subsequent theories are constructed.

Augustine was born in North Africa (modern-day Algeria), a Roman province, at a time (354) when Christianity was finally enjoying imperial favor, but Roman rule was itself in decline. In 313 Constantine had granted Christianity full legal status and protection, and in 391 his successor Theodosius went so far as to outlaw traditional Roman worship and rites. Yet Rome came under threat from "barbarian" invaders, and in 410 Rome fell to the Visigoths. As a result, many Roman refugees—both Christian and "pagan," some of them wealthy—fled across the Mediterranean to North Africa.[4] While Christians blamed the empire's ill fortune on persistence of idolatrous rites, the adherents of Roman religion blamed Christian abandonment of the ancestors' gods.

Augustine was a Christian leader whose reputation beyond the North African church was sustained by correspondence, often polemical, with prominent figures like Jerome and Julian of Eclanum. These letters, his homilies, and his theological treatises provided opportunities to counter pagan accusations, to consolidate his own views of the relation between the church and political society, and to attract new patrons from among the noble Christian refugees. He argued eloquently, in one of his greatest and longest works, *The City of God*, that any true republic must serve the welfare of the people, that to do so requires justice, and that true justice is only possible where the God of Jesus Christ is shown true piety (*pietas*) and worship (*latreia*).[5] Following his mentor Ambrose (ca. 339–97), rather than the historian Eusebius (ca. 260–339), Augustine argued that while Christian emperors and the state could support the

4. See Peter Brown, *Augustine of Hippo: A Biography* (Oakland: University of California Press, 1970), 299–312.

5. Augustine, *City of God*, trans. Marcus Dods (New York: Random House, 1950), 19.21.

church, the historical paths of the two will never converge, and the emperor lacks authority in ecclesial affairs.[6]

Augustine embraced Christianity in adulthood. He had long questioned Christianity's implausible claims and resisted its virtues, dedicating himself to a rhetorician's career in the imperial court of Valentinus in Milan. As a young man, Augustine was attracted to Manichaeism, an aberrant Christian sect that was to have a lasting effect on his attitudes. Contemplating the evil in the world and the struggle in the human soul, the Manichaes resorted to a simple if dualistic explanation. They held two different gods responsible for the creation of darkness and light, as well as the human soul or mind and the body or baser nature, and they associated these divine principles respectively with the deities of the Old and New Testaments. Known for its ascetic ideals and strict antiprocreative morality (at least for elite members), the Manichean way of life appealed to Augustine's introspective sense of personal moral (especially sexual) conflict.[7]

Augustine gave up Manichaeism after nine years of initiation, and he went to Rome to teach rhetoric and to study Platonist philosophy. Later he accepted a position as a teacher of rhetoric in Milan. There he was baptized by Ambrose, the bishop of Milan and a compelling preacher and teacher. After his conversion, Augustine turned toward teaching to a life of study, prayer, and writing in a small community of friends, at first in Italy and later upon his return to Africa. But only about four years after his baptism, Augustine was pressed into service as pastor in the port city of Hippo, from which he came to exercise great influence as a prolific theologian and active bishop.

Augustine saw Christianity as the one true philosophy. The ancient philosophers such as Plato, Aristotle, and Cicero had asked what constitutes true happiness, a happiness that can never be taken away, and responded that happiness lies first of all in virtue. Replying that the only good that can never be lost is God, the highest good (*summum bonum*), Augustine translates all the virtues as forms of love of God; that is, in God we find true and lasting happiness.[8] But no mere human reasons or virtues can lead one to God. Augustine knew from his own struggle, as recounted in the *Confessions*, that only God's touch and calling can move

---

6. Augustine, *City of God*, 5.24–26; see Kenneth R. Himes, *Christianity and the Political Order: Conflict, Cooptation, and Cooperation* (Maryknoll, NY: Orbis, 2013), 63–71.

7. See J. Kevin Coyle, "Mani, Manichaeism," in *Augustine through the Ages: An Encyclopedia*, ed. Allan D. Fitzgerald, OSA (Grand Rapids, MI: William B. Eerdmans, 1999), 520–25.

8. Augustine, *City of God*, 14.4; *On the Morals of the Catholic Church*, in *Basic Writings of St. Augustine*, vol. 1, ed. Whitney J. Oates (New York: Random House, 1948), 15.

the sinner to a new way of life. Only God's healing grace can convert the self-enclosed will, centering all one's loves on God.[9]

John Mahoney characterizes Augustine's mentality as "dyadic," an approach to reality that tends to highlight dualities, polarizations, and extremes.[10] In his determination to rebut Pelagius's view that human beings are morally responsible and thus, despite sin, retain a natural free will adequate to choose good,[11] Augustine stated in the strongest terms possible that all human virtue is entirely dependent on God.[12] Perhaps most evident in Augustine's interpretations of sexual desire as "lust," a certain dualism also colors his grand social paradigm of the "two cities"— earthly and heavenly.[13] The heavenly city is formed by love of God, but the earthly city by love of self; one seeks human glory, while the other finds glory only in offering worship to the one true God.[14]

The theme of ordered goods and loves is central to Augustine's social ethics, as framed particularly in *The City of God*. The heavenly city of the title is contrasted with the earthly city whose loves are distorted by pride, the quest for worldly honor, and the drive to dominate others (*libido dominandi*).[15] The heavenly city is "a captive and a stranger in the earthly city," though it obeys the earthly city's laws in order to secure the common life of both cities in this world.[16]

When a society orders its loves in relation to the highest good, God, its internal relations and practices are harmonious, having been blessed by the "well-ordered concord" and "tranquility of order" that define true peace.[17] However, the sinful impulse of most to dominate others makes the peace of the unjust a poor imitation of the real thing.[18] Though nec-

---

9. See Augustine, *Confessions*, trans. Henry Chadwick (New York: Oxford University Press, 1991), 1.1; 9.1.

10. John P. Mahoney, SJ, *The Making of Moral Theology: A Study of the Roman Catholic Tradition* (Oxford: Clarendon, 1987), 69.

11. Eugene TeSelle, "Pelagius, Pelagianism," in *Augustine through the Ages*, 633–40.

12. See Augustine, *The Spirit and the Letter*, in *Augustine: Later Works*, ed. John Burnaby (Philadelphia: Westminster, 1955), 7.5.

13. Augustine, *City of God*, 14.7; but see a late letter, Epistle 6, to bishop Atticus of Constantinople (ca. 421), in which Augustine defends "the concupiscence of conjugal purity," because it serves procreation and "the social bond" of the sexes. See Elizabeth Clark, ed., *St. Augustine on Marriage and Sexuality*, Selections from the Fathers of the Church 1 (Washington, DC: Catholic University of America Press, 1996), 99–105.

14. Augustine, *City of God*, 14.28. See also his comparison of Roman virtue and Christian virtue in *City of God*, 2.21; 5.15–16.

15. Augustine, *City of God*, 4.4; 14.28; 19.17.

16. Augustine, *City of God*, 19.17.

17. Augustine, *City of God*, 19.13.

18. Augustine, *City of God*, 19.10, 12.

essary to the ordering of temporal life, the peace of the earthly city is fragile, containing within itself the seeds of injustice.[19]

INFLUENCE OF AMBROSE

In the background of Augustine's politics and just war thought stands Ambrose, who was elected bishop while serving as governor of a province in northern Italy, and so had an experience-based appraisal of political service and its costs.[20] While struggling from Manichaeism toward Christianity, Augustine listened to Ambrose's sermons, which suggested ways to reconcile evangelical nonviolence with limited political violence within a coherent biblical narrative.[21] The Manichaes rejected the anthropomorphically depicted god of the Old Testament, particularly the deity's apparent endorsement of immorality and violence, seemingly so inconsistent with the spirit of the God of the New Testament, Father of Jesus. Augustine learned from Ambrose that Old Testament events could be allegorized and thus made to yield a higher religious meaning, consistent with the Pauline maxim, "The letter kills but the spirit gives life."[22]

Ambrose depicts the Christian life as answering a higher calling than that ordinarily considered virtuous, just, and honorable. Although he avoids sharp opposition between the Christian and Roman lifestyles, he makes it clear that Christian standards will be sometimes at odds with worldly wisdom. At the same time, many common moral ideals are shared, especially loyalty and service to one's country. Fundamental virtues are justice and courage. "The splendor of justice is great. Justice exists for the good of all and helps to create unity and society among us."[23] "Those who love justice must first direct it to God; second, to their country; third, to parents; and last, to all people. This is the way in which nature reflects it. Courage reflects justice when it protects one's country in time of war or defends the weak and the oppressed."[24]

And yet Christian morality does not stop at conventional understand-

---

19. Augustine, *City of God*, 19.17.

20. Swift, *The Early Fathers,* 97.

21. Eugene TeSelle, *Augustine the Theologian* (New York: Herder & Herder, 1970), 30–31.

22. TeSelle mentions Augustine's claim to have heard Ambrose cite frequently this text (*Confessions*, 6.4.6), cited TeSelle, *Augustine the Theologian*, 31. TeSelle also notes (265) that after about 405, Augustine probably had access to all the works of Ambrose, which had been brought to Carthage by a former secretary of Ambrose who participated in the controversy against the Pelagians.

23. Ambrose, *The Duties of the Clergy*, in *Morality and Ethics in Early Christianity,* trans. and ed. Jan L. Womer (Philadelphia: Fortress, 1987), 1.28.

24. Ambrose, *Duties of the Clergy,* 1.27.

ings of justice. "The very duty that the philosophers see to be primary to justice, we reject. They say we should hurt no one except when responding to wrong received. The gospel has taught the opposite"—that is, "to give grace and not harm."[25] Ambrose commends compassion as the trait that most helps the Christian to imitate the Father's perfection, reminding his audience: "It is also written that the Lord has commanded us to love our enemies, to pray for those who plot against us, who persecute us, or who spread false scandal about us."[26]

In regard to the compatibility of defending one's country and enemy love, Ambrose makes a distinction between self-defense and national defense or defense of allies, considering the latter, as actions on behalf of the common good, to be instances of "courage" and "wholly just."[27] The Old Testament provides examples in figures such as Joshua, Jonathan, and Judas Maccabeus.[28] "There is nothing that goes against nature as much as doing violence to another person for the sake of one's own advantage," but "any man wins a glorious reputation for himself if he strives for universal peace at personal risk to himself."[29] Ambrose follows the standard Roman view of the right to declare war and the morality of conduct within war, allowing defensive or punitive wars and insisting that the conventions of war be kept.[30] Ambrose also adheres both to civil law and to the example of the Old Testament (Moses's slaying of an Egyptian to defend a Jew) in holding up a duty of courage to come to the aid of innocent third parties.[31]

Ambrose often draws parallels between Christian morality and the morality of "nature" regarding these basic obligations, including the duty to forego personal self-defense—harming another to save oneself appears ignoble as well as unchristian. But although the virtues of peace and mercy are admired generally, the gospel command to love even the enemy colors the moral life of the Christian differently: "The law calls for reciprocal vengeance; the Gospel commands us to return love for hostility, good will for hatred, prayers for curses. It enjoins us to give help to those who persecute us, to exercise patience toward those who are hun-

---

25. Ambrose, *Duties of the Clergy*, 1.28.
26. Ambrose, *Duties of the Clergy*, 1.11, p. 90.
27. Ambrose, *Duties of the Clergy*, 1.27.129, quoted in Swift, *The Early Fathers,* 98.
28. Ambrose, *Duties of the Clergy*, 1.40.195 (Swift, 98).
29. Ambrose, *Duties of the Clergy*, 3.3.23 (Swift, 98).
30. Ambrose, *Duties of the Clergy*, 1.176; 3.19.110, 116; 1.35.176–77; 1.27.129; 2.7.33; 3.8.54 (Swift, 99–100). See also *Duties of the Clergy,* 1.29, in *Morality and Ethics,* 99, on fidelity to agreements in war.
31. Ambrose, *Duties of the Clergy,*1.36.178 (Swift, 102).

gry and to give thanks for a favor rendered."[32] The repudiation of self-defense is stated especially strongly on the basis of the gospel: "Indeed, even if a man comes up against an armed thief, he cannot return blow for blow lest in the act of protecting himself he weaken the virtue of love. The Gospel supports this position in a clear and obvious way: 'Put up your sword; everyone who kills with the sword will be killed by it' (Matt 26:52)." Ambrose proposes the example of David, said to have hated evildoers rather than their deeds, and to have to lived a violent life without loss of loving attitude.[33]

While Christian morality demands a consistently loving intention, Ambrose also presupposes the compatibility of civic responsibility and Christian commitment. The Sermon on the Mount does demand radical spiritual reversal, but this very conversion makes it possible for the Christian to bring peace in the world. "In the area of peace begin with yourself so that when you have established peace there, you can take it to others."[34]

Ambrose recognizes that the total conversion of the Christian's life, attitudes, and actions remains an incomplete project until history's end, while in the meantime both the inner and the outer struggle continue.[35] The difficulty of persevering in the Christian life while resorting to violence is reflected in Ambrose's exclusion of participation in war for the clergy. According to Ambrose, "the thought of warlike matters seems to be foreign to the duty of our office [as clergy], for we have our thoughts fixed more on the duty of the soul than on that of the body, nor is it our business to look to arms but rather to the forces of peace."[36] Augustine too explicitly contrasts Christian righteousness with the virtue of the courageous and noble pagan, insofar as the motive and intention are concerned (self-glorification vs. glory of God).[37] He reflects Ambrose insofar as he allows for the justification of war but disallows self-defense, and attempts to reconcile an evangelical intention with a violent outward action.

32. Ambrose, *Discourse on Luke's Gospel*, 5.73 (Swift, 100). See also *Discourse on Psalm 118*, 12.51 (Swift, 100).

33. Ambrose, *Discourse on Psalm 118*, 15.22 (Swift, 103).

34. Ambrose, *Discourse on Luke*, 5.58 (Swift, 109).

35. Ambrose, *Discourse on Psalm 36*, 22 (Swift, 110).

36. Childress, "Moral Discourse about War," 12, quoting *Duties of the Clergy* (place unspecified).

37. Augustine, *City of God*, 5.13–16,

AUGUSTINE'S POLITICS OF THE TWO CITIES

Ambrose's distinction between the present realm and its eschatological fulfillment is made more explicit and central through Augustine's imagery of the "two cities." For both Ambrose and Augustine, the peace of the reign of God lies far beyond history, yet civic peace and political order are important goods and historical imperatives.

The City of God, written in Augustine's later years, is an occasional work of polemical intent, a deliberate confrontation with Roman culture, its religions, and the great classical traditions of the Roman Empire. The author's pessimism about the justice and ultimate value of politics and the careers of earthly kingdoms reflects his firsthand experience of the disintegration of a mighty power. Augustine defends the merits of the Christian religion over competitors by illustrating the positive relation of the Christian church to the common good. Christianity is infinitely superior to other interpretations of society, virtue, and happiness.

Augustine contrasts two cities that "have been formed by two loves," the earthly city by "the love of self" manifested in love of ruling, strength, and profit; the heavenly city by "the love of God."[38] According to Augustine, the Christian citizens of God's "heavenly city" are only transient sojourners in the "earthly city." At the same time, the happiness of the heavenly community is not wholly inaccessible, even in this life. Civil government is a God-given means of protecting peace and social order.[39] Augustine asserts that there is no true justice without God's grace, but suggests nevertheless that the Romans have natural virtue on which Christian virtue may build.[40] True peace belongs to the heavenly city alone, but "peace of one kind or other" still can be attained by citizens who live in civil concord.[41] A more negative counterpoint in Augustine's characterization of temporal peace is his remark that "the peace which we enjoy in this life, whether common to all or peculiar to ourselves, is rather the solace of our misery than the positive enjoyment of felicity."[42]

The opposition and interdependence of the two cities form the con-

---

38. Augustine, *City of God,* 10.28.

39. For a discussion of whether Augustine sees civil government as natural or as instituted by God only after the fact of sin, and whether such grace is inherently coercive, see Peter J. Burnell, "The Status of Politics in Augustine's City of God," *History of Political Thought* 13, no. 1 (1992): 13–29.

40. Compare Augustine, *City of God,* 2.21; 19.21 with *On Free Choice of the Will,* trans. Anna S. Benjamin and L. H. Hackstaff, The Library of Liberal Arts 150 (Indianapolis: Bobbs-Merrill, 1964), 1.6. See Burnell, "Status of Politics," 15.

41. Augustine, *City of God,* 19.13.

42. Augustine, *City of God,* 19.27.

text for Augustine's approach to politics and social ethics. Behind this friction of spheres lies a single standard of human virtue: the love of God and of all other things in relation to God and for God's sake. Augustine establishes this clearly at the outset of book 19 of *The City of God,* which contains his central discussion of the historical relation of the two cities: "the end of our good is that for the sake of which other things are to be desired, while it is to be desired for its own sake."[43] The one thing to be desired for its own sake is God, as Augustine states repeatedly.[44]

The heavenly city is Augustine's metaphor for the kingdom of God; "peace" is his term for its inner and definitive nature. Theologically, peace is the corollary of love; it is the inner perfection or harmony of all things in their relationships to God, when those relationships are characterized as they should be by an orientation to God above all else. Perfect peace and happiness come to fruition in the heavenly city where love and worship are given to God alone. "The peace of the celestial city is the perfectly ordered and harmonious enjoyment of God, and of one another in God. The peace of all things is the tranquility of order."[45] Christian piety will be fulfilled by an "eternal peace which no adversary shall disturb."[46] Ordered love of God, "true virtue," can exist only in those who have "true piety,"[47] and true piety (recognition of God as the supreme good) is possible only for those who have been divinely enabled to respond in faith, to pray, and to live rightly.[48] Peace is realized only provisionally and defectively in the harmony of earthly relationships. The aims and loves of the earthly city fall far short of, and

43. Augustine, *City of God,* 19.1.

44. A concise representative example is his definition in *On Christian Doctrine* of the grace-inspired love of God called *caritas* or charity: "I call 'charity' the motion of the soul toward the enjoyment of God for His own sake, and the enjoyment of one's self and of one's neighbor for the sake of God; but 'cupidity' is a motion of the soul toward the enjoyment of one's self, one's neighbor, or any corporal thing for the sake of something other than God." See Augustine, *On Christian Doctrine,* 3.10.16. See also *On the Morals of the Catholic Church* 3–6, in *Basic Writings of St. Augustine,* vol. 1, ed. Whitney J. Oates (New York: Random House, 1948), 320–24; and *The Spirit and the Letter,* in *Augustine: Later Works,* ed. John Burnaby, Library of Christian Classics 3 (Philadelphia: Westminster, 1955), 39.24; 49.28.

45. Augustine, *City of God,* 19.13.

46. Augustine, *City of God,* 19.10. Or again, "we shall one day be made to participate, according to our slender capacity, in His peace, both in ourselves, and with our neighbour, and with God our chief good" (19.29).

47. Augustine, *City of God,* 19.4; see also 14.15, where Augustine comments that eternal life will not be given to those who practice "virtue" without "true piety . . . which the Greeks call *latreia.*" However, pagan virtue may yet deserve "a punishment less severe" in eternity (*The Spirit and the Letter,* 48.28).

48. Augustine, *City of God,* 19.4. See also *Spirit and the Letter,* 60.34: "Assuredly then it is God who brings about in a man the very will to believe, and in all things does his mercy anticipate us."

indeed pervert, the love of God that alone confers real order in human affairs. The noblest forms of self-mastery are "inflated with pride . . . so long as there is no reference to God in the matter," they are "rather vices than virtues."[49] Pagan civic virtue will receive sufficient reward in earthly glory and success.[50]

Nevertheless, temporal harmonies are to be valued and sought, whether among members of the body, between body and soul, among members of a family, among citizens and rulers, or between humanity and God.[51] After all, the "greatest ornament" of life on this earth is "temporal peace, such as we can enjoy in this life from health and safety and human fellowship."[52] Although neither the "supreme good" nor true happiness can be attained "in the present life," still, with God's help, the lusts of the flesh—cupidity or concupiscence—can be restrained.[53] Earthly societies approximate the perfect harmony of the heavenly city to the extent that self-gratification is overcome and lesser beings and enjoyments are ordered in relation to those that are greater. Yet all of these approximations of peace are judged in light of the highest peace.

The peace of this world, even when requiring force or violence, is of instrumental value to members of the heavenly city in their earthly journey. In addition, finite goods are objective goods, though they should be loved in their proper relation to God and one another. They are rightly defended.[54] But Augustine concedes the usefulness of the relative peace of the earthly realm only with strong caveats. "The heavenly city, or rather the part of it which sojourns on earth and lives by faith, makes use of this peace only because it must, until this mortal condition which necessitates it shall pass away."[55]

John Langan notes that the adequacy of concrete instantiations of earthly peace "depends on the gradations of similarity to the ultimate peace one is prepared to recognize."[56] Critics have argued that Augustine was prepared to accept far too great a range. For example, Augustine's depiction of a "wise judge" has caused many to conclude that Augustine cloaks with the name "peace" egregious policies and practices that fall dismally short of justice. The judge, in the course of ensuring the civil peace, cannot avoid perpetrating "numerous and important evils," such

49. Augustine, *City of God*, 19.25.

50. Augustine, *City of God*, 5.15.

51. Augustine, *City of God*, 19.13; 19.16.

52. Augustine, *City of God*, 19.13.

53. Augustine, *City of God*, 19.4.

54. Augustine, *City of God*, 19.13, 17.

55. Augustine, *City of God*, 19.17.

56. John Langan, SJ, "The Elements of St. Augustine's Just War Theory," *Journal of Religious Ethics* 12, no. 1 (1984): 29.

as the torture of the innocent in the effort to ascertain whether they are in fact guilty. These evils are not sins on his part, according to Augustine, not only because he does not intend them maliciously, but also because human society demands the judicial role. Dilemmas like that of the torturing judge are inevitable, in Augustine's view, and lead him to "condemn human life as miserable." The judge himself will "recognise the misery of these necessities, and shrink from his own implication in that misery," crying piously to God, "'From my necessities deliver Thou me.'"[57]

In my view, it is difficult to read this account as implying that the judge is morally "off the hook," in view of a greater good served, even though Augustine refuses to call him a sinner outright.[58] Augustine's very point is to stress the entanglement of duty and misery in a situation in which the agent cries to God for mercy. The so-called peace and justice of the earthly order are maintained only with tools and at costs that are abhorrent to the citizen of God's city, and they are employed and paid with revulsion—yet employed.

Augustine's treatment of this example suggests that the judge's moral integrity is compromised, even though he is morally compelled to act as he does. Many modern readers will judge that torture crosses a clear line between moral and immoral means of pursuing important political ends—and that if torture were to be justified it would take a much larger social threat to justify it than the possibility that one criminal might escape without due punishment. This raises a question that Augustine does not here address: Are there any moral norms that should never be transgressed because ensuing benefit could never outweigh the evil done? However, if we grant for the sake of argument that, from Augustine's perspective, torture in this case was both proportionate and a last resort, then we might infer that Augustine paints the judge as caught in an internal moral turmoil. It is not that it is impossible to determine the better course, for Augustine depicts the torture as "necessary" and "guiltless." Yet the judge seems to experience a moral trauma that goes beyond simple regret that his job requires him to harm gravely another human. Significantly, Augustine questions whether the judge can be happy; for Augustine, true virtue based on love of God is both a necessary and a sufficient condition of happiness. If the judge is unhappy, he must be a man of compromised virtue.

57. Augustine, *City of God*, 19.6.
58. Here I disagree with Edmund Santurri, in Edmund N. Santurri and William Werpehowski, "Augustinian Realism and the Morality of War: An Exchange," in *Augustine and Social Justice*, ed. Teresa Delgado, John Doody, and Kim Paffenroth, *Augustine in Conversation: Tradition and Innovation* (Lanham, MD: Lexington, 2016), 170–71.

Contrast Augustine's position on lying. Augustine disallows the morality of any lie whatsoever, even a lie told in order to avoid grave and unjust harm that will otherwise befall another. He rejects any excusing distinction between what may be falsity in one's speech and what may be purity in the intention of one's heart. In time of temptation, one may be fortified by recalling the contemplation of the "luminous good," real unity, that permits not even the shadow of a lie.[59] Yet Augustine's judicial torturer evidently represents a different perception: some actions and policies necessary to temporal peace and order are both morally obligatory and offensive to Christian virtue, especially the virtue of love. Yet public officials are obliged to uphold them nonetheless. This possibility, and its relevance to killing in war, will bring us later in the chapter to consider whether irreducible moral dilemmas exist, and how they might be relevant to Christian ethics. In any event, Augustine's schema of the "Two Cities" assumes a large gap between the ideal realization of divinely ordained peace and the historical circumstances of Christianity in which the struggle against sin is waged. Order in both the political and the ecclesial spheres is urgently important but fundamentally unstable, so that Augustine is willing to justify extreme measures to maintain it.

Natural and even necessary to human society as orderly government is, however, Augustine never forgets that it is at bottom vicious. When Augustine compares kingdoms to robberies that take place with impunity, he raises the possibility that politics and government exist only after the fact of sin, thus restraining injustice only to the extent useful to those in power. We are left with the question not only whether and how Christians should be politically active but even whether such action will have any significant positive result.[60]

Augustine's interpretation of the historical possibility of a transformationist politics to which Christians may contribute has been extensively debated and never decisively settled.[61] Is Augustine more disposed to critically appreciate or critically distance himself from the goal of an ordered political peace?[62] Augustine himself "constantly changed his mind on the matter" and may ultimately have opted for realistic ambi-

59. Augustine, "Lying," trans. Mary Sarah Muldowney, RSM, in *Treatises on Various Subjects*, ed. R. J. Deferrari, The Fathers of the Church: A New Translation 16 (Washington, DC: Catholic University of America Press, 1952), 1; 2; 18.

60. Augustine, *City of God*, 4.4.

61. See Burnell, "Status of Politics."

62. Eric Gregory poses these two options, citing Edmund Santurri, and pursues the former in his own version of "Augustinian civic liberalism." See Gregory, "Rawlsian Liberalism, Moral Truth, and Augustinian Politics," *Journal of Peace and Justice Studies* 8, no. 1 (1997): 1–36; *Politics and the Order of Love* (Chicago: University of Chicago Press, 2008), 107.

guity over theological consistency.[63] Augustine recognized many para-
doxes in the human condition, and he did not always draw straight lines
from Christian principles to the expected social behavior.[64] Augustine's
political theory "can point in different directions," and though fecund
and profound, "turns out to be indecisive."[65]

One of the foremost authorities on Augustine's politics, Robert
Markus, made the proposal in 1988 that, for Augustine, justice as attained
by human social arrangements is an illusion.[66] The realm of the "secular"
(the *saeculum*) is an interim reality in which the earthly and heavenly
cities overlap. The two kingdoms and their standards of justice are
interwoven and mixed.[67] Hence the situation of the Christian and of
Christian politics is ambiguous. Christianity's ultimate frame of value
is radically different from that of "pagan" politics. But since the goods
whose limited value is distorted in the earthly frame of reference are still
real if relative goods in light of the *summum bonum*, the Christian shares
a political commitment to protect them. Thus the Christian is a committed "member of a temporally limited society," in which shared "needs
and concerns" are "sufficient to mobilize . . . loyalties" and create a "sense
of belonging."[68]

As if to underwrite the difficulty of pinning Augustine down on the
question of social transformation, Robert Markus published a revision
thirty-six years after his landmark *Saeculum*. In the vision of the newer
work, the secular realm is not so much mixed and ambiguous as it is
neutral and autonomous.[69] Markus expresses "no doubt that an imperfect but useful virtue can be found among citizens of the earthly City.
The same goes for justice: an imperfect or relative version of justice may

63. Burnell, "Status of Politics," 13.

64. William R. Stevenson Jr., *Christian Love and Just War: Moral Paradox and Political Life
in St. Augustine and His Modern Interpreters* (Macon, GA: Mercer University Press, 1987), 8.
Stevenson adds, "The proper human response to the complexities and perplexities of international politics, for Augustine, would not be prudential deduction from principle, whether a
principle of end *or* means, but rather a prudential induction from circumstance. This response
would humbly withhold self-confidence in enduring human achievement and place its hope in
a merciful providence" (pp. 8–9). Whether such an approach leaves moral judgment so loose
and open that excluding the immoral becomes a rather tenuous possibility remains a question
to be answered. For example, see Stevenson's own suggested defense of nuclear deterrence (p.
46).

65. Eugene TeSelle, "Toward an Augustinian Politics," *Journal of Religious Ethics* 16, no. 1
(1988): 98.

66. Robert A. Markus, *Saeculum: History and Society in the Theology of St. Augustine* (Cambridge: Cambridge University Press, 1970), xi.

67. Markus, *Saeculum*, 63, 101.

68. Markus, *Saeculum*, 102.

69. Robert A. Markus, *Christianity and the Secular* (Notre Dame, IN: University of Notre
Dame Press, 2006), 6, 37.

be found in all sorts of places. . . . Being imperfectly just is not the same as being unjust."[70] One critic, Anthony Meredith, notes that Markus's revised reading of Augustine furnishes an openness to the secular and a positive appreciation of the justice available within its scope. Yet, he concludes laconically, "Whether Augustine would have gone quite as far is not absolutely certain."[71] Augustine, it seems, is perennially hard to figure out.

THE KINGDOM OF GOD AND THE LOVE COMMAND

To the extent that Augustine does justify Christian political and military roles—and that extent is considerable—he must also address how policies, practices, and actions that seem flatly inconsistent with the Christian virtue of love can be squared with the gospel. Unlike the modern Christian "just war" thinker, he rarely grounds his views of the social use of violence in commonly held values but sets as his explicit foundation the definitive Christian text, the Holy Scriptures, especially the New Testament. Augustine does not avoid the challenge of Jesus's nonviolent example by turning instead to the heroes of the Old Testament, and certainly not by averring (anachronistically) that a revealed text is not an appropriate resource for normative reflection on public behavior. Instead he uses the gospel as a lens through which to envision the meanings both of Israelite examples and of social responsibility in his own age and culture. The moral meaning of the gospel is captured for Augustine, as for Christianity in general, in the love command, including the challenging sayings about nonresistance in Matthew 5.[72] Augustine's theology as a whole is constructed around the idea of love of God and of creation in relation to God. For Augustine, love is the indispensable center of Christian morality, whatever the concrete dilemma.

He appreciates the challenge that Jesus's teaching of love of enemies poses to Christian justification of killing. Therefore, he strives to explain why biblical texts need not be taken literally, and how both love and killing can be accommodated within a unified Christian vision and mission. In his treatise *On Christian Doctrine,* Augustine claims that the canon is unified in God's intention and in the doctrine and life of the church, which provide the "rule of faith."[73] Under the influence of

70. Markus, *Christianity and the Secular,* 43–44.

71. Anthony Meredith, SJ, review of *Christianity and the Secular,* by Robert A. Markus, *Journal of Theological Studies* 59, no. 1 (2008): 379.

72. Augustine, *On Christian Doctrine,* 1.35–36; 2.7.

73. Augustine, *On Christian Doctrine,* 1.35–36; 2.7; 3.1–3. See also Hamilton, "Augustine's Methods," 113.

Ambrose and Neoplatonist philosophy, Augustine adopted an allegorical method of exegesis, according to which biblical texts may have multiple meanings and some elements of the Bible are construed as signs of divine things.[74] Augustine also advocated typological or figurative interpretation—understanding the meaning of one thing by means of another—cautiously using the rules of a Donatist author, Tyconius.[75] Yet Augustine did not allegorize unrestrainedly, and his reliance on the literal readings of texts increased in his later works.[76]

Augustine's concrete context directed his attention to the importance of squaring Christian political and military participation with the gospel. He moves toward this goal using two different strategies. First, he refers to Jesus's teachings about nonviolence and love of enemies to the sphere of internal intentions and actions. In his *Commentary on the Sermon on the Mount*, he interprets Jesus's call to be "peacemakers" to mean internal control of one's desires and dispositions, regeneration of the person in the image of God, and "contemplation of the truth."[77] The command and virtue of love are thus largely disconnected from politics, at least as far as direct action is concerned. Second, Augustine claims that Christian love *is* directly expressed by killing, if killing is intended as solicitous punishment of the offender. Both strategies will be addressed further in the next section on war.

In effect, Augustine departs from the emphasis on the inbreaking character of the kingdom or reign of God as embodied in the ministry in Jesus (as presented in chapter 2). Augustine does not see the power of the incarnation, the risen Christ in history, or the Holy Spirit active in church and creation as entailing an immediate, historical possibility of altering institutionalized violence to any significant or lasting degree. He is more impressed by the compromises necessary to fulfill what he regards as social and political responsibilities. So often Augustine stresses not the incomplete but real presence of the kingdom in history but the absence from the historical struggle of the harmony that will characterize the *eschaton*. A theological rationale for the kingdom's distance is a

---

74. G. W. H. Lampe, "The Exposition and Exegesis of Scripture: To Gregory the Great," in *The Cambridge History of the Bible*, vol. 2, *The West from the Fathers to the Reformation*, ed. G. W. H. Lampe (Cambridge: Cambridge University Press, 1969), 172–83.

75. Gordon J. Hamilton, "Augustine's Methods of Biblical Interpretation," in *Grace, Politics, and Desire: Essays on Augustine*, ed. Hugo Maynell (Calgary, AB: University of Calgary Press, 1990), 111.

76. Hamilton, "Augustine's Methods," 110.

77. Augustine, *On the Sermon on the Mount*, trans. William Findlay, *Nicene and Post-Nicene Fathers*, First Series, vol. 6, ed. Philip Schaff (Buffalo, NY: Christian Literature, 1888), 1.1.20, revised by Kevin Knight, *New Advent*, accessed February 21, 2017, https://tinyurl.com/ybb5yppt.

view of history as a time of trial and testing.[78] The fullness of kingdom life is delayed, not because of failures of discipleship, but because God's providence designates history as a field on which Christian courage and steadfastness are tried, as the furnace in which impurities are purged, and humility forged.

In the *Retractions*, Augustine corrects any impression he might previously have given in *On the Sermon on the Mount* that the kingdom the Sermon announces can now be present fully, even in the lives of the dedicated few.[79] Even the apostles can realize the eschatological blessings only with "the kind of perfection of which this life is capable, not as those things are to be realized, with that absolute peace for which we hope."[80]

It is difficult to resolve the question whether Augustine begins experientially with the perceived historical necessity of waging war to preserve the civil order, and so tries to square it with the New Testament; or sets out from the Christian ideal of love of neighbor and enemy but meets up with the difficulty of how best to put this ideal into practice in a fallen world. It is undeniable, however, that his interpretation of Scripture was heavily influenced by his respect for the social goods protected by the Roman empire and his aim to enlist Christians in its defense.

Precedent can be found for Augustine's strong and pessimistic contrast between divine and earthly kingdoms in the letters of Paul, who expected that the Lord might return in his own lifetime and did not envision that in the meantime the church would or could make a large difference in society. The work of the Spirit was to be found within the community, and in the lives of individual believers, called to give their "undivided devotion to the Lord" (1 Cor 7:35). Although Christians have already died with Christ, they will share in his resurrection only eschatologically (Phil 3:10–11). The present in no way compares to what God will do in the future.[81] Like Augustine, Paul does not expect disciples to withdraw from the world. Instead they should fulfill their duties as citizens in a way consistent with the gospel of Christ (Phil 1:27), even while

78. Augustine, "Letter 189, to Boniface," in *Saint Augustine: Letters,* vol. 4 (165–203), trans. Wilfrid Parsons, SND, The Fathers of the Church 30, ed. Roy J. Deferrari (New York: Fathers of the Church, 1955), 269.

79. The *Retractions*, often published as *Retractations*, consists of "reconsiderations" in which Augustine both defends and revises earlier positions.

80. Augustine, *Retractations,* trans. Mary Inez Bogan, The Fathers of the Church 60, ed. Roy J. Deferrari (Washington, DC: Catholic University of America Press, 1968), 18.2. Augustine, in *On the Sermon on the Mount,* 1.4.12, had explained Jesus's saying "Blessed are the peacemakers for they shall be called children of God" by adding, "And these things can be realized even in this life as we believe they were realized in the apostles."

81. J. Paul Sampley, *Walking between the Times: Paul's Moral Reasoning* (Minneapolis: Augsburg Fortress, 1991), 17–24.

realizing that Christian identity and citizenship are dissonant.[82] How one should live in two fundamentally opposed worlds is not spelled out by Paul, who offers varied counsel such as paying taxes (Rom 13:7), and remaining in slavery (1 Cor 7:17). According to Paul Sampley, "Paul's focus on the end time had a profound effect on what receives his attention," and "there is no indication Paul ever saw the larger social implications inherent in his gospel."[83]

A major contrast with Augustine is that it would have been obvious to the latter that the return of Christ was significantly delayed and that Christians were in a then-unprecedented position to make their mark on the course of history. Yet Augustine organizes his social vision around maintenance of the imperial order, and he does not envision that Christian emperors, generals, soldiers, and citizens could begin to reorder some of the political and institutional vices of the earthly city in any systemic way.

CHRISTIAN JUSTIFICATION OF KILLING AND WAR

Christians in the fourth century not only depended on the Roman Empire for protection from barbarian invasion but they also received from this same government public recognition and protection wholly unanticipated by earlier pacifist theologians. This new situation provided an incentive for Christian participation in the institutions of imperial administration, including war. This is true to some extent of all members of a society or state (even pacifists) who live within and benefit from the conditions of human security and rule of law the government provides. Augustine believed that Christians who benefit from the peace of the earthly city have a duty to help secure and maintain it.

Augustine did not have a full-fledged, systematic theory of just war. His views on war are communicated within discussions of other issues, which were never compiled into a unified treatment. Yet he provides "the origins of a specifically Christian just war ethic," that would be consolidated in the twelfth and thirteenth centuries, especially under the influence of Gratian and Aquinas.[84] According to Richard B. Miller, the key to Augustine's logic of war is his "overarching theory of the meaning of peace," which is "not the absence of violence, but tranquility,

82. Sampley, *Walking between the Times*, 28
83. Sampley, *Walking between the Times*, 112–13.
84. James Turner Johnson, "Just War, as It Was and Is," *First Things* (January 2005), accessed March 1, 2017, https://tinyurl.com/y8om7hxt. See also Gregory M. Reichberg, "Historiography of Just War Theory," in *The Oxford Handbook of Ethics of War*, ed. Seth Lazar and Helen Frowe (Oxford: Oxford University Press, 2018): 64–65.

concord, a set of properly ordered relations within or between human beings" that is essential to social fellowship.[85] For Augustine, political tranquility, concord, and fellowship will never conform to the order of all things in relation to God that is necessary for genuine peace. "Peace between man and man is well-ordered concord," reflecting if imperfectly the "tranquility of order" with which God orders the universe.[86] Augustine sees war as necessary to avenge injuries, punish wrongs, restore property or violated rights—in other words, to restore or preserve peace.[87] "Your will ought to hold fast to peace, with war as the result of necessity, that God may free you from the necessity and preserve you in peace. Peace is not sought for the purpose of stirring up war, but war is waged for the purpose of securing peace."[88] The motives of emperors and warriors are not always pure, and imperial institutions are infected by the *libido dominandi*; thus Augustine's attitude to war is regretful and ambivalent. Wars of domination are "robbery."[89] Even wars that are legitimate responses to aggression or injustice are still waged to gain victory, "conquest of those who resist us," and "peace with glory" for the victors.[90] Yet war, for all its "misery," is justified by Augustine when and if necessary to rectify wrongdoing and restore provisional peace to a relatively just historical order.[91]

The conditions Augustine sets for war are threefold: it must be commanded by a legitimate civil authority (understood to have authority from God); be necessary to punish crime in light of securing peace;

---

85. Richard B. Miller, *Interpretations of Conflict: Ethics, Pacifism, and the Just-War Tradition* (Chicago: University of Chicago Press, 1991), 21.

86. Augustine, *City of God*, 19.13.

87. Frederick H. Russell offers as Augustine's "formula for the just war" a definition adapted from Cicero: "'just wars are usually defined as those that avenge injuries (*ulcisi injurias*)' (qu. *Hept.* 6.10). War was justifiable 'when a people or a city neglected either to punish wrongs done by its members or to restore what it had wrongly seized.'" See Russell "War," in *Augustine through the Ages*, 875. John Langan specifies the component parts of Augustine's view of war: "St. Augustine's just war theory involves eight principal elements: a) a punitive conception of war, b) assessment of the evil of war in terms of the moral evil of attitudes and desires, c) a search for authorization for the use of violence, d) a dualistic epistemology which gives priority to spiritual goods, e) interpretation of evangelical norms in terms of inner attitudes, f) passive attitude to authority and social change, g) use of Biblical texts to legitimate participation in war, and h) an analogical conception of peace. It does not include non-combatant immunity or conscientious objection. A contemporary assessment of the elements is offered." See Langan, "The Elements of St. Augustine's Just War Theory," *Journal of Religious Ethics* 12, no. 1 (1984): 19–38.

88. Augustine, "Letter 189, to Boniface," in *Saint Augustine: Letters*, vol. 4 (165-203), trans. Wilfrid Parsons, SND, The Fathers of the Church 30, ed. Roy J. Deferrari (New York: Fathers of the Church, 1955), 269.

89. Augustine, *City of God*, 4.6.

90. Augustine, *City of God*, 19.12.

91. Augustine, *City of God*, 19.7.

and be intended to establish justice rather than hatefully to inflict suffering on enemies.[92] Like Ambrose, Augustine applies Jesus's "hard sayings" (Matt 5:38–48) strictly in personal relationships, thereby excluding killing in self-defense.[93] Private citizens may not kill, not even in self-defense or to shorten the suffering of a dying person.[94] Yet if John the Baptist told soldiers to be content with their pay (Luke 3:14), this must mean military service is acceptable.[95] In the case of authorized killing by a public official, "he does not do it for his own sake, but for others or for the state to which he belongs, having received the power lawfully."[96] Rulers wage wars, and soldiers fulfill their military duties, to serve "the peace and safety of the community."[97] Wars waged by and for the good root out vices and curb disordered passions.[98] Augustine minimizes the requirement of restraint in wars undertaken for a just cause. The real evils in war, he maintains, are not death and destruction but "interior" vices, such as "love of violence, revengeful cruelty, fierce and implacable enmity, wild resistance, lust of power and such like."[99] To kill to save one's own life represents an inordinate attachment to a personal temporal good; but to kill selflessly for the common good may be justified both by those who have responsibility for maintaining the temporal order, and by those obedient to their authority. In such cases, killing is a form of love of God and neighbor—even, Augustine maintains, a form of love for the one killed.

In order to arrive at this oxymoronic conclusion, Augustine depicts killing as divinely mandated punishment of evil or sin, necessary both for the safety of society and for the reform of the evildoer.[100] John Langan surmises that Augustine focuses on punishment rather than on self-

92. Augustine, *Reply to Faustus the Manichean*, in *Writings in Connection with the Manichean Heresy*, trans. R. Stothert (Edinburgh: T&T Clark, 1953), 22.74.

93. Augustine, *City of God*, 1.20. See also *On Free Choice of the Will*, 1.5.

94. Augustine, "Letter 204, to Dulcitius," in *Saint Augustine: Letters*, vol. 5 (204–70), trans. Wilfrid Parsons, SND, The Fathers of the Church 32, ed. Roy J. Deferrari (New York: Fathers of the Church, 1956), 6.

95. Augustine, *Reply to Faustus*, 22.74.

96. "Letter 47, to Publicola," *Saint Augustine: Letters*, vol. 1 (1–82), trans. Wilfrid Parsons, SND, The Fathers of the Church 12, ed. Roy J. Deferrari (New York: Fathers of the Church, 1951), 230.

97. Augustine, *Reply to Faustus*, 22.75.

98. Augustine, "Letter 138, to Marcellinus," in *Saint Augustine: Letters*, vol. 3 (131–64), trans. Wilfrid Parsons (Washington, DC: Catholic University of America Press, 1953), 47.

99. Augustine, *Reply to Faustus*, 22.74.

100. For discussions of war as punishment in Augustine, see Frederick H. Russell, *The Just War in the Middle Ages* (Cambridge: Cambridge University. Press, 1975), 12–18; Stevenson, *Christian Love and Just War*, 104–13; and N. Phillip Wynn, *St. Augustine on War and Military Service* (Minneapolis: Fortress, 2013), 328–31.

defense in his discussion of war, because defense to the death of finite goods, which are eventually to be lost anyway, is intrinsically suspect as the motive of a Christian.[101] A related reason is that the Christian is always to be motivated by love, as ordering all goods in relation to God. A favorite simile for killing in war is the loving father punishing his son. Both the warrior and the father "act with a sort of kindly harshness," considerate of the welfare of the object of restraint. "For, in punishing a son, the father's love is certainly not cast aside"—he sees, rather, that the son "can be cured only by unwilling suffering."[102] When the purpose of punishment is "correction," "it is not to be feared that parents would seem to hate a little son when, on committing an offense, he is beaten by them that he may not go on offending." Those with earthly authority can and should punish with the same fatherly "goodwill."[103] Few Christians would regard killing as an acceptable form of parental discipline. Yet, in the case of war, Augustine asserts that violent coercion is punishment that protects the common welfare by discouraging future infractions and removing the present causes of discord. As "kindly harshness" punishment can encourage reform, and even if death results, punishment cannot harm its object in any essential (spiritual) way.

Contemporary Augustinians have grappled with the centrality of punishment to Augustine's view of just war, with uneven results. Nigel Biggar ardently defends the punitive function of war as sufficient cause, but strongly tends to envision it as part of a larger program of justice involving the defense of "genuine and important human goods," including the reestablishment of peace.[104] Oliver O'Donovan and Joseph Capizzi both make the basic point that to be just a war must be intended to serve the objective long-term common good as including all concerned, which implies that punishment should be limited appropriately and have some kind of a restorative function. In other words, it is not an end in itself.[105] Capizzi explicitly alludes to the implausibility of seeing violent force against an aggressor as rooted in Christian love for that person.[106] Yet while he wants to retain Augustine's domestic analogy, he also rightly notes both that the destruction of war rarely targets the real perpetrators proportionately, and that we today are wary of any idea of collective guilt. In fact, even combatants usually assume that they are fighting in a

101. Langan, "Elements of St. Augustine's Just War Theory," 27.

102. Augustine, "Letter 138, to Marcellinus," 46.

103. Augustine, *Sermon on the Mount* 1.1.20.63.

104. Nigel Biggar, *In Defence of War* (New York: Oxford University Press, 2013), 160, 170, 212.

105. Oliver O'Donovan, *The Just War Revisited* (Cambridge: Cambridge University Press, 2003); Joseph E. Capizzi, *Politics, Justice and War* (New York: Oxford University Press, 2015).

106. Capizzi, *Politics, Justice and War*, 129, 133.

just cause, lack the ability to evaluate its justice, or believe it their duty to follow authoritative orders. Finally, then, punishment should not be seen apart from the other traditional aims of war, defense and restoration of right order.

When aligned with the larger common good, violent coercion construed as punishment might protect the common welfare by removing present threats and discouraging future ones. Yet it is difficult to see how it is of any direct benefit to individuals killed, and how it can possibly be an act of Christian love toward those individuals. Certainly, death interrupts any ostensibly reformatory purpose of punishment. The only role punishment can have in a just war, from a Christian perspective, is a restorative one: "an actual restoration of human flourishing among victim, communities, and perpetrators."[107] In fact, arguing on another topic, mercy rather than the death penalty, Augustine admits, "there is no other place but this life for correcting morals. . . . Consequently, we are forced by our love of humankind to intercede for the guilty, lest they end this life by punishment."[108]

Some of those with whom Augustine corresponded, the general Boniface and the tribune Marcellinus, worried about how public roles that require the infliction of death and destruction could coexist with Christian virtue. Marcellinus questioned whether genuine Christianity is compatible with the prevention of evil to the state.[109] Augustine reports that Boniface was similarly anxious that someone in military service would be unable to please God.[110] Augustine grants that the ideal solution to social conflict and crime is to overcome evil with good, to convert wrongdoers with an example of patience and mercy.[111] But he reassures Boniface that he can be a peacemaker (following Matt 5:9) "even while you make war," and expresses more concern about Boniface's chastity and wine consumption than about the effects on his character of killing people and of ordering others to do so.[112] He assures Marcellinus that there is no essential conflict between the Sermon on the Mount and "the customs of the state."[113]

107. See Daniel Philpott, *Just and Unjust Peace: An Ethic of Political Reconciliation* (New York: Oxford University Press, 2012), 208. Arguing more from Aquinas than Augustine, John Finnis concludes that no state or ruler can claim the right to punish, and that the only legitimate rationale for war is defense. See Finnis, *Human Rights and the Good* (New York: Oxford University Press, 2011), 206.

108. Augustine, "Letter 153, to Macedonius," in *Letters*, vol. 3, 282.

109. Marcellinus, "Letter 136, Marcellinus to Augustine," in *Letters*, vol. 3, 16–17.

110. Augustine, "Letter 189, to Boniface," 4.

111. Augustine, "Letter 138, to Marcellinus," in *Letters*, vol. 3, 44.

112. Augustine, "Letter 189, to Boniface," 269.

113. Augustine, "Letter 138, to Marcellinus," 41–42.

As if tacitly aware that this argument about kindly or loving punishment is unpersuasive, Augustine argues along a different line that the Sermon on the Mount requires "not a bodily action, but an inward disposition."[114] In the case of just warriors, Christ's command not to return evil for evil refers not to nonviolence much less nonresistance, but to interior virtue and "abhorrence of the passion of revenge."[115] On this basis, Augustine instructs Marcellinus that he should give up, not killing, but vengefulness.[116] From this point of view, the command to love one's enemy does not require that killing itself be interpreted as an act of kindness or love. Instead, the love command can be read as a "precept with regard to the preparation of the heart, and not with regard to the visible performance of the deed." The Christian "should have his heart prepared for everything."[117] Along these same lines, patience and kindness should be "preserved in the heart, to keep it in readiness."[118] They do not need to be expressed directly in action.

With this move, Augustine creates a wide space between preparedness to act on the Lord's commands and the actual embodiment of their literal meaning. In this space it is important to determine exactly when and how the disciple moves from preparation to action. Exactly which actions—if not the ones literally mentioned as exemplifying the kingdom ideal—are the means to move from preparation to action, and when is that move to be made? How far away from the literal meaning can Christian action move and still be claimed to lie within the symbolic range of Jesus's illustrations?

Another more basic problem is that separation of the inner experience of the soldier from his (or today, her) destructive action circumvents the problem of the unity of action and intention in moral character.[119] As Eugene TeSelle remarks of Augustine, violent paternalism has corrosive effects on perpetrators as well as victims. "We have learned to be suspicious of intentions that are too markedly at odds with the external circumstances."[120] In various writings on the interaction of Jesus with the

114. Augustine, *Reply to Faustus*, 76.
115. Augustine, "Letter 138, to Marcellinus," 42.
116. Augustine, "Letter 138, to Marcellinus," 41–42.
117. Augustine, *Sermon on the Mount* 1.19.58–59.
118. Augustine, "Letter 138: To Marcellinus," 46.
119. The integrity of the warrior's interior kindliness is further called into question by Augustine's comfort to the individual Christian who shows patience toward his or her oppressor. God, says Augustine (echoing Tertullian, and Calvin will echo both), will repay our enemy even if we do not: "A final just vengeance is looked for, that is, the last supreme judgment only when no chance of correction remains." See Augustine, "Letter 138: To Marcellinus." Here the correspondence of violent act to loving intentionality is reversed; when the Christian refrains from personal self-defense, he or she takes comfort in the foe's perdition.
120. TeSelle, "Towards an Augustinian Politics," 91.

woman caught in adultery (John 8:3), Augustine himself makes the point that those whose actions do not conform to their true, interior identity and knowledge are unrighteous hypocrites, and applies this specifically to those who administer the law in the name of justice.[121] In recent decades, those counseling combat veterans have come to recognize the reality of "post-traumatic stress syndrome" and even "moral injury" as devastating consequences of war for the identities, moral integrity, and psychological function of many returning participants.[122] Yet Augustine seems oblivious to the potential personal effects of repeated engagement in ongoing violent practices or in particularly brutal actions that override a soldier's formative moral convictions and the standards of human respect.

These conundrums result from the fact that, for Augustine, love (caritas) controls the entire moral life, even when violent coercion is required to protect the innocent, punish the enemy, and serve the common good. The paradox or tension in his approach to war (and to social ethics more generally) arises because he both advocates Christian political participation in a fallen world and retains Christian love as the ground and measure of all specific moral actions. As Frederick Russell sums it up, "the pacific precepts were transformed so that love of neighbors could legitimate their deaths, and not to resist evil became an inward attitude compatible with outward belligerence."[123]

This unsatisfactory outcome is addressed by a modern Augustinian, Paul Ramsey, who explains wartime killing as the work of love in a different way. Ramsey agrees that love is the determinative guide of the Christian life, but abandons the rationale that killers show love to the one killed by killing. No, the love expressed by military violence is love for the innocent victims of aggression.

> The change-over to just-war doctrine and practice was not a 'fall' from the original purity of Christian ethics; but . . . a change of tactics only. The basic strategy remained the same: responsible love and service of one's neighbors in the texture of the common life. . . . Christians simply came to see that the service of the real needs of all the men for whom Christ died

121. See Robert J. Dodaro, OSA, and John Paul Szura, OSA, "Augustine on John 8:3–11 and the Recourse to Violence," *Augustinian Heritage* 34 (1988): 35–62.

122. See Brett T. Litz, Nathan Stein, Eileen Delaney, Leslie Lebowitz, William P. Nash, Caroline Silva, and Shira Maguen, "Moral Injury and Moral Repair in War Veterans: A Preliminary Model and Intervention Strategy," *Clinical Psychology Review* 29 (2009): 695–706; Rita Nakashima Brock and Gabriella Lettini, *Soul Repair: Recovering from Moral Injury after War* (Boston: Beacon, 2012); and Tobias Winright and E. Ann Jeschke, "Combat and Confession: Just War and Moral Injury," in *Can War Be Just?*, 169–87.

123. Russell, "War," 875.

required more than personal, witnessing action. It also required them to be involved in maintaining the organized social and political life in which all men live. Non-resisting love had sometimes to resist evil.[124]

Ramsey also emphasizes the role of love in transforming the norms of justice, and, he claims, shaping the secular political doctrine of just or limited warfare. In particular, it is the pressure of love in just-war ethics which in the Western political tradition placed limits on the conduct of war, especially the prohibition on killing noncombatants.[125] Oliver O'Donovan, like Paul Ramsey, sees just war principles as extensions of the gospel, amounting to a "counter practice" within the reality of war, one with the potential to radically correct it and lead to reconciliation.[126] Yet Ramsey believes Augustine gives warrant in the just war tradition to see right and wrong as always mixed or at least ambiguous in the decision to go to war.[127] This makes it especially important to restrain the means, a concern neglected by Augustine.

Augustine's struggle to rectify love and violence surfaces an ongoing important question for ethics. Are there any moral situations—personal or social—that involve agents in irreducible conflicts that cannot be satisfactorily aligned with virtue and right action? In fact, attempts fully to align conflicted actions with true virtue might not only falsify the moral reality but also distort the meaning of virtue itself. If selves and their agency are partly constituted by the conditions and opportunities of action, then agency and the agent might be unavoidably compromised by dilemmas in which every alternative carries a moral cost. Although Augustine may be right that the use of coercive means is a lesser evil than permitting injustice, it would seem that the use of violence still calls for some measure of regret and even repentance, as suggested in the example of the torturing judge. Violence and killing have a negative impact on the coherence of Christian identity, even when motivated by good intentions—and even when the agent or agents have no better alternative, so that the act considered as a whole cannot be judged blameworthy.

In an assessment of what he sees as Augustine's developing views on the evils suffered by those who make prudential decisions to go to war, Kevin Carnahan claims that Augustine's early writings (*On Order*; *On*

---

124. Paul Ramsey, *War and the Christian Conscience: How Shall Modern War Be Conducted Justly?* (Durham, NC: Duke University Press, 1961), xvii–xviii; see also *The Just War: Force and Political Responsibility* (Lanham, MD: University Press of America, 1983; originally published 1968), 142–45.

125. Ramsey, *War and the Christian Conscience*, xvii.

126. O'Donovan, *Just War Revisited*, 5.

127. Ramsey, *War and the Christian Conscience*, 30–32.

Free Choice of the Will) present a Christian version of Stoic detachment from the suffering caused by evil. By the time he wrote *The City of God*, however, he realized at an existential level that suffering in earthly life is both unavoidable and deeply affecting.[128] Carnahan points out that in the very same treatise in which Augustine dismisses deaths in war as not a "real evil," he describes David as mourning the death of his son Absalom, especially because those who die in a state of guilt miss their opportunity for "'repentance and submission,'" and hence meet "'eternal doom.'"[129] This is obviously at odds with any depiction of war as kindly punishment of those killed. "For the mature Augustine," continues Carnahan, "the evils in war are real evils." This is why, in *The City of God* 19.7, Augustine laments the scale of wars, "'the slaughter of human beings,'" and the quantities of blood shed.[130] Citing Augustine's example of the miserable torturing judge, as well as Augustine's letters to Christian military leaders, Carnahan draws this conclusion: "Evil suffered penetrates the person who is forced to make decisions under the conditions of sin. This evil erodes the extent to which we can speak of any person who must make such decisions as living a good life."[131]

Later in this chapter I want to take this insight further. The greatest evil that comes through this discussion is evil suffered because it is also perpetrated, through the making of decisions and the undertaking of actions that "must" be made and done. Deliberate agential implication in the "necessary" evil suffered by others is the most excruciating cause of the suffering endured by the judge and the warrior. Before turning to further discussion of the nature of moral dilemmas, we will take up another use of force regarding which Augustine's position is both ambiguous and notorious: violent coercion of religious belief.

128. Kevin Carnahan, "Perturbations of the Soul and Pains of the Body: Augustine on Evil Suffered and Done in War," *Journal of Religious Ethics* 36, no. 2 (2008): 269–94.

129. Carnahan, "Perturbations," 281, citing *Reply to Faustus*, 22.66.

130. Carnahan, "Perturbations," 288. It is often said that Augustine regards war as something that should be undertaken "mournfully," but with no specific citation from Augustine. See Alan J. Watt, "Which Approach? Late Twentieth-Century Interpretations of Augustine's Views on War," *Journal of Church and State* 46, no. 1 (2014): 101. Watt attributes this characterization to Roland Bainton, *Christian Attitudes toward War and Peace: A Historical Survey and Critical Re-Evaluation* (Nashville: Abingdon, 1979), 98. Bainton uses the word "mournfully" of Augustine, but does not tie it back to any text in Augustine that uses the same term. Therefore, it seems to have originated with Bainton, who invokes it in extrapolating from Augustine's view of the judge to his presumed view of the general.

131. Carnahan, "Perturbations," 290.

VIOLENT DEFENSE OF RELIGION

Augustine did not limit his justification of armed force to the defense of a country from outside threats, he also supported violent containment of social unrest, such as that inspired by disruptive religious convictions. The Roman Empire is certainly not to be identified with the City of God for Augustine, and its "peace" is always shadowed by defect. However, Christianity had achieved protection and eventual hegemony in Roman society. Augustine paints "Christian emperors" as "gaining splendid victories over the ungodly enemies, whose hope was in the rites of idolatry and devil worship."[132] The later Markus even hypothesizes a "euphoria" among Christians who saw "the new order of Christianity superseding the ancient Roman traditions."[133]

Augustine's struggle with the Donatist heresy provides a fascinating nexus of his views of Christian identity, ecclesial realities, and practical political power. The Donatist controversy had to do with the nature of the church as a holy community, membership in which is marked by a distinctively different lifestyle, a higher moral and religious standard. It may also have had to do with Augustine's concern that, as schismatics with terrorist tendencies, the Donatists threatened the political as well as the ecclesial order.[134] The Donatists claimed that the validity of the sacraments is affected by the holiness of the minister, and that the church will be unworthy if it permits unworthy leaders, especially those who cooperated with the civil authorities during Diocletian's persecution (303 CE).[135] Augustine, on the other hand, was committed to the expansion of Catholicism's size and influence, not just to preservation of its purity and traditions. He saw it as part of the Christian calling and responsibility to turn back the social effects of sin as far as possible by participating in political affairs.

In combating the Donatists, Augustine resorted to political and physical coercion as well as to theological argument. In the process of aligning church and political community, he imports into the religious community the tools for establishing order in civil society. Although he prefers conversion over coercion, he does see a place for fear as motivating dissenters to return to the orthodox communion.[136] A defense of Augus-

---

132. Augustine, *Reply to Faustus*, 22.76.

133. Markus, *Christianity and the Secular*, 32.

134. O'Donnell, *Augustine*, 220–22.

135. J. N. D. Kelly, *Early Christian Doctrines* (New York: Harper & Row, 1958), 410.

136. Augustine, "Letter 93, to Vincentius," 3; 16, accessed November 22, 2017, https://tinyurl.com/yddsnmau. On Augustine and the use of coercion against the Donatists, see Johannes Brachtendorf, "Augustine: Peace Ethics and Peace Policy," in *From Modern Just War to*

tine on coercive force could rest only on the possibility that his actions against the Donatists were primarily a reply to their own violence and attacks on other Christians, in which case coercion of them could be seen to further peace in the practical social order.[137]

Augustine's views on the Donatist threat are summarized in a letter to Boniface, Christian governor of Africa, with whom Augustine corresponded frequently regarding the reconciliation of political duty with Christian faith. Not unaware that his own view of the church does not emerge easily from the New Testament, Augustine calls attention to the necessity of adapting the teachings of the apostles to different historical circumstances. Those who resist the enactment of civil laws punishing heresy by appealing to the apostolic era "fail to notice that times were different then, and that all things have to be done at their own times." Expanding with an observation on the New Testament context that also would apply to early Christian pacifism, Augustine notes, "At that time there was no emperor who believed in Christ, or who would have served Him by enacting laws in favor of religion and against irreligion."[138] A sovereign serves God by legally commanding goodness and true worship of God.[139] Through such laws "all will be called to salvation," either by fear or conversion.[140]

The purpose of coercive laws is to achieve the peace and unity of Christianity, as the church on earth embodying "Jerusalem."[141] This argument is flawed by two points of incongruity, given the manner in which Augustine elsewhere expects the peace of the heavenly city to be completed only eschatologically, as well as his belief that the reality of that kingdom is present in history only where there is genuine love of God. First, in Augustine's attack on the Donatists the metaphor "Jerusalem" is used to cover the church on earth, understood not as a holy sect or a transhistorical ideal but as an institutional, ecclesial, and even sociopolitical body encompassing believers at disparate levels of commitment. The practical effect is to dislocate Augustine's ecclesiology so that the limitations of the historical church (and its need to live with imperfection) are no longer so well illuminated against an eschatological horizon of judgment and transformation. Second, the methods for

Modern Peace Ethics, ed. Heinz-Gerhard Justenhoven and William A. Barbieri Jr., Arbeiten zur Kirchengeschichte 120 (Berlin: De Gruyter, 2012), 65–70.

137. For evidence in favor of this motive, see O'Donnell, *Augustine*, 228, and Stevenson, *Christian Love and Just War*, 101–4.

138. Augustine, "Letter 185, to Boniface," in *Letters*, vol. 4, 19.

139. Augustine, "Letter 185, to Boniface," 19.

140. Augustine, "Letter 185, to Boniface," 8.

141. Augustine, "Letter 185, to Boniface," 46. See also "Letter 195, to Boniface," 9, and the letter fragment "185A, to Count Boniface," in *Letters*, vol. 4, 190.

enforcing order in political bodies become means of control over the church—for enforcing the unity of "Jerusalem" in earthly incarnation. Augustine thus places himself in the position—whose anomalous character he half admits[142]—of espousing violent coercion when persuasion fails to induce religious conversion, an event in which *caritas* supposedly is to order all things through God's grace-filled healing of the will.

First, he relies heavily on Old Testament examples of divinely sanctioned force and bloodshed to characterize the Donatist debate, thus justifying violence against the offenders. Second, he returns to the theme of loving punishment, so prominent in his discussion of secular warfare, to reconcile violence on behalf of religion with the evangelical commands. The persecution of Hagar by Sarah is said, for instance, to have "prefigured" the affliction of the heretics by "Jerusalem," the "true Church of God";[143] the Donatists are compared to the persecutors of Daniel and to Saul acting wickedly toward David.[144] David himself wept over the death of his son Absalom, but that death was the price of the latter's participation in a war against his own father.[145] Augustine protests, "if the good and holy never persecute anyone but only suffer persecution, whose voice do they think that is in the psalm where we read: 'I will pursue after my enemies and overtake them, and I will not turn again until they are consumed'?"[146] It is God's voice, but Augustine identifies it not only with the Catholic church, but also with civil authorities acting cooperatively with ecclesial officials.

Returning to the themes that guided his discussions of war, Augustine again tries to retrieve the love command by connecting it with an intention of reform. He cites other Old Testament texts that urge punishment as a means of education of the child.[147] The church punishes the Donatists as a father beats a rebellious son; the motivation is "Christian charity" and "fraternal love," which hopes that the wayward will be converted and saved.[148]

Mark Doorley comments regarding the Donatist incident that Augus-

142. "Does anyone doubt that it is better for man to be led to the worship of God by teaching rather than forced to it by fear of suffering? Because the former group is preferable it does not follow that those of the latter, who are not like them, should be neglected" See Augustine, "Letter 185, to Boniface," 21).

143. Augustine, "Letter 185, to Boniface," 11. Not a few modern critics have instead read the persecution of Hagar as evidence of the sinfulness of the so-called models of faith, Abraham and Sarah. See Delores Williams, *The Challenge of Womanist God-Talk* (Maryknoll NY: Orbis, 1995).

144. Augustine, "Letter 185, to Boniface," 7; 9.

145. Augustine, "Letter 185, to Boniface," 32.

146. Augustine, "Letter 185, to Boniface," 11, citing Ps 17:38 (18:38).

147. Augustine, "Letter 185, to Boniface," 21, citing Prov 23:14; 13:24.

148. Augustine, "Letter 185, to Boniface," 7; 11; 14.

tine's primary concern was not to save souls but to maintain peace (with the added hope of converting the offenders). Yet "the violent response does not seem a faithful testimony to 'enemy love.'" The contradiction here reminds all that the realm of the political is always a realm calling for continual repentance.[149] From Augustine's perspective, the Donatist controversy could be interpreted as a moral dilemma. He thought violent coercive action was necessary to the social good and the good of the church; yet he recognized that religious coercion wrongs its objects insofar as freedom of conscience and faith are concerned. The Christian begins in this world to live by the transcendently ordered love that is *caritas*. Yet the potential for embodying that love socially is severely limited by the radically disordered loves of the community in which the Christian has practical responsibilities. That said, the responsibility to make restorative efforts is evidenced in some of Augustine's letters, which will be treated after the consideration of moral dilemmas.

MORAL DILEMMAS AND AUGUSTINE

On the whole Christian theologians and ethicists have assumed that a good and providential God would not permit human agents to be placed in a position in which immorality and sin are unavoidable. The Creator beholds that everything divinely made is "very good" (Gen 1:31). Evil and suffering arise from human disobedience (Gen 3); human choices to violate the order of creation are the very definition of sin. In this sort of view, choices cannot be simultaneously moral and immoral, though they may have regrettable dimensions. When a lesser good must be sacrificed for a greater good, the agent might feel sorrow or regret, but should not experience guilt or remorse. As long as his or her decisions and actions respect the right ordering of the goods at stake in a given moral situation, the agent is blameless. A dilemma might arise from the difficulty in discerning the right choice, or from lack of knowledge and foresight about aspects of the situation and its consequences. But these are not true moral dilemmas, in the sense of situations in which it is impossible for the agent to make a choice that in no way wrongs another, a wrong for which the agent bears some moral responsibility. From such a perspective, moral quandaries always have definitively right or definitively wrong answers, however difficult it might be to determine what they are and to act upon them. To believe otherwise, it is claimed, would impugn God's justice,

149. Mark Doorley, "The Pursuit of Social Justice: Some Augustinian Sources of Caution," in *Augustine and Social Justice*, 24.

and undermine the concepts of free will and personal responsibility, so necessary to the very idea of morality in the first place.[150]

Post-Enlightenment philosophers have largely followed suit. One reason irreducible moral dilemmas are a problem to many is that people confronting tough decisions don't want to think we might be given more than we can handle or explain. We also want to attribute blame to those we regard as responsible for wrongs and injustices. Hence one of the main objectives of ethical theory is to clarify how to resolve moral conflicts fully. Modern philosophy has been influenced by the Kantian maxim "ought implies can."

Yet in the past few decades a philosophical literature has emerged that questions these assumptions and premises as untrue to moral experience.[151] For example, Martha Nussbaum speaks of "the fragility of goodness" to indicate that virtue depends to some extent on circumstances beyond one's control.[152] In 1930, W. D. Ross proposed that a choice between conflicting prima facie duties can leave a "moral residue." Even if the agent believes the choice to have been justified, he or she can still feel "not indeed shame or repentance, but certainly compunction, for behaving as we do; we recognize, further, that it is our duty to make up somehow."[153] Following Ross, Bernard Williams uses the term "moral residue" to refer to the remorse and guilt an agent may appropriately feel when he or she chooses between two bad options, either of which will involve his or her agency in bringing about evil.[154] For Williams, "moral

---

150. Related to this debate is the question of theodicy—that is, the possibility of arguing that God is good and just when conditions in the world God created are often not, either through no fault of human beings or no fault of the human beings they trap and even crush. An excellent work defending theologically and ethically the existence of irreducible moral dilemmas (against Aquinas), giving a more thorough treatment of the philosophical literature than will be offered here, is Katherine Jackson-Meyer, "Tragic Dilemmas and Virtue: A Christian Feminist View" (PhD diss., Boston College, 2018). For an insightful and provocative discussion of how limited agency and forced choices can be reconciled with free will and moral accountability, see Jesse Couenhoven, *Stricken by Sin, Cured by Christ: Agency, Necessity, and Culpability in Augustinian Theology* (New York: Oxford University Press, 2015). A trenchant critique of theodicy is Terrence W. Tilley, *The Evils of Theodicy* (Portland: Wipf & Stock, 2000).

151. For a general discussion, see Terrance McConnell, "Moral Dilemmas," *Stanford Encyclopedia of Philosophy* (Fall 2014), ed. Edward N. Zalta, accessed February 24, 2017, https://tinyurl.com/yatmpy9b.

152. Martha C. Nussbaum, *The Fragility of Goodness: Luck and Ethics in Greek Tragedy and Philosophy* (Cambridge: Cambridge University Press, 1986). Carnahan is partly informed by Nussbaum.

153. William David Ross, *The Right and the Good* (Oxford: Oxford University Press, 1930), 28. On possible interpretations of Ross's theory of prima facie duties in relation to moral residue, see James J. Brummer, "Ross and the Theory of Prima Facie Duty," *History of Philosophy Quarterly* 19, no. 4 (2002): 401–22.

154. Bernard Williams, "The Inaugural Address: Consistency and Realism," *Proceedings of the Aristotelian Society*, Supplement 40 (1966): 1–22.

conflicts" can involve genuine conflicts of moral obligation.[155] He rejects the Kantian idea that there is a moral realm and moral will that are ultimately immune to fortune.[156] Similarly to Nussbaum, he uses the concept "moral luck" to refer to aspects of moral-decision making that are beyond one's control, but that factor nevertheless into how a decision is evaluated and an agent held accountable. These can include the circumstances in which one must decide, a decision's unforeseen results, one's own inherent personality traits, and the personal history that determines one's outlook and inclinations. In some cases, especially in the political realm,

> We can have reason to approve of the outcome, and of the agent's choice to produce that outcome, and of his being an agent who is able to make that choice, while conscious that there has been a 'moral cost'. . . . The idea that there is moral cost itself implies that something bad has been done, and, very often, that someone has been wronged.[157]

Rosalind Hursthouse writes of "genuinely tragic irresolvable dilemmas," from which "not even the most virtuous agent can emerge with her life unmarred."[158] Such an agent "acts with immense regret and pain," although because Hursthouse holds such an agent "blameless," she avoids attributing to her "remorse or blame."[159] Lisa Tessman uses the term "burdened virtues" to refer to qualities that are necessary to struggle against oppression, but also detract from the flourishing of those who cultivate them. She advises that "when good actions are unavailable," there is even a type of virtuous trait that "enables its bearer to choose as well as possible, with the appropriate feelings, such as regret or anguish, toward what cannot be done."[160]

There are resonances of this newer strand of philosophical questions with Augustine's theology and ethics. As Augustine insisted against the Pelagians, no one can live a sinless life and this is in part because even "good" agency is tangled in "bad" situations and conflicts.[161] Yes, love should be the overriding Christian virtue, and it should inform all virtue, but Christian virtue will be burdened or compromised to the extent that

155. Bernard Williams, *Problems of the Self* (Cambridge: Cambridge University Press, 1973), 170–71.
156. Bernard Williams, *Moral Luck* (Cambridge: Cambridge University Press, 1981), 20–21, 38.
157. Williams, *Moral Luck*, 37.
158. Rosalind Hursthouse, *On Virtue Ethics* (New York: Oxford University Press, 2001), 63.
159. Hursthouse, *On Virtue Ethics*, 76–77.
160. Lisa Tessman, *Burdened Virtues: Virtue Ethics for Liberatory Struggles* (New York: Oxford University Press, 2005), 163.
161. Augustine, *Spirit and the Letter*, 2.37.

the agent willingly participates in violent activity, even if doing so is a "forced choice" between two morally repugnant options. Augustine hopes that a true and integral peace will come to characterize relationships originally ordered by violence. Yet it might be better simply to grant that even with an intention to strive for the right, the Christian may inevitably be caught up in—and need at some level not only to regret but to repent of—the contradictions that characterize agency in the political world with which he or she must engage. (A modern Augustinian theologian, Reinhold Niebuhr, who sees ambiguous moral decisions as unavoidable, will be taken up in chapter 9.)

Sometimes these contradictions place the agent in a situation where all options seem equally intolerable from a moral point of view, a situation we might term an *absolute moral dilemma*. It is impossible to give a reasonable defense of one choice over another. In other cases, one option, though abhorrent, can be defended as the lesser evil. A moral dilemma can exist here too, insofar as the moral considerations cannot all be reduced either to right or to wrong. We can call this an *irreducible moral dilemma*. No matter what the agent does, even if on the whole "right," he or she will still be implicated in wrongdoing. In fact, his or her intentions, motivations, planning, and will have been engaged in bringing it about.[162]

Irreducible moral dilemmas are different from situations of complicity, since complicity refers to one's degree of cooperation with or facilitation of the action of another.[163] But the sort of moral dilemmas here under discussion involve the agent in choosing a course of action in which he, she, or it is a or the primary perpetrator of a morally offensive outcome, albeit for the protection of an equal or greater good—and feels responsible or accepts responsibility for it.[164] Jesse Couenhoven uses a similar analysis of agency to grapple with a different theological-ethical issue, original sin and human responsibility. Couenhoven defends as "Augustinian compatibilism" the idea that we can be "at least minimally responsible and at least somewhat blameworthy" for things that are outside our control, but are part of us, that we "own."[165]

I affirm explicitly a point suggested by Williams, which is that an irreducible moral dilemma should be understood as one in which the agent not only causes an undesirable outcome but does so in the stronger sense of having committed a "wrong" or injustice toward another. This char-

---

162. On this point, see Jackson-Meyer, "Tragic Dilemmas," 156–62.

163. On complicity, see M. Cathleen Kaveny, "Complicity with Evil," *Criterion* (2003): 20–29, accessed March 2, 2017, https://tinyurl.com/ychy5ppm.

164. Couenhoven, *Stricken by Sin*, 10–12, 188–224.

165. Couenhoven, *Stricken by Sin*, 10–12.

acterization fits Augustine's judge. It also fits the causation of collateral damage and unintended consequences in waging war. More controversially, I maintain that the killing of even an unjust aggressor still involves an offense against the dignity of human life. Such killing is justified only when necessary to protect other innocent lives, yet it still carries a "moral cost."

Most of the philosophical literature on moral dilemmas has in view decisions and actions of individual agents. Augustine's ethics reminds us that individuals are social and political actors and that their social responsibilities can be a major cause of moral conflict, a direction of thought also voiced by Tessman. The moral conflict that may arise when individuals fulfill morally compromising social roles is embodied in the torturing judge, and captured philosophically by Michael Walzer, who poses the problem as one of "dirty hands."[166] A key and controversial aspect of this problem is whether such an agent is morally culpable (blameworthy and properly remorseful), even if he or she had no reasonable alternative, and was even acting for compelling "political" reasons. Hursthouse and Tessman do not go this far, and Williams prefers to use the term "agent-regret" over remorse, but he acknowledges that some "moral conflicts are neither systematically avoidable, nor all soluble without remainder."[167] Similarly to Augustine, Walzer applies the term guilt to the example of a public official whose role requires the use of torture for the sake of the greater good. Though he rightly prioritizes his political responsibilities, "he committed a moral crime and he accepted a moral burden. Now he is a guilty man."[168] Stephen de Wijze, agreeing that "unavoidable wrongdoing is part of our moral reality," proposes the term "tragic-remorse" to characterize the specific emotion proper to the situation of dirty hands.[169]

Considered overall, what defines morality in Augustine's ethics is the proper order of goods in relation to one another, and ultimately to God.

166. See Michael Walzer, "Political Action: The Problem of Dirty Hands," *Philosophy and Public Affairs* 2, no. 2 (1973): 160–80. Walzer refines this concept further in *Just and Unjust Wars: A Moral Argument with Historical Illustrations* (New York: Basic, 1977), 267–68, and *Arguing about War* (New Haven, CT: Yale University Press, 2004), 46.

167. Williams, *Problems of the Self*, 179.

168. Michael Walzer, "Political Action," 167. As C. A. J. Coady points out, a paradox in the dirty hands scenario is that both "ordinary" morality and role morality are grounded "in a deeper moral outlook that gives sense to the role itself." See Coady, "The Problem of Dirty Hands," *Stanford Encyclopedia of Philosophy* (Spring 2014), ed. Edward N. Zalta, accessed February 24, 2017, https://tinyurl.com/ydhlk32v. Although the moral demands of political office may be exceptional, they are not beyond the realm of the moral. If both the role and the violated duty exist in a common moral framework, that either invalidates the role-related obligation or the duty; or generates the problem of a moral dilemma.

169. Stephen de Wijze, "Tragic-Remorse—The Anguish of Dirty Hands," *Ethical Theory and Moral Practice* 7, no. 5 (2004): 454.

Such ordering is governed by the virtue of love. Therefore, if any moral action—political or otherwise—violates the order of love, it is immoral. The tension between protecting the good of political order by destroying a human life or by a perpetrating a great wrong like torture, both of which violate proper love for human beings and Jesus's direct command to love our neighbor, is exactly what creates the "dirty hands" problem for Augustine. The inability to fulfill both his political duty and his duty to the individual tortured leads the judge to pray for deliverance from "miserable necessities," even when he is fulfilling the obligations of his role. It is plausible to interpret Augustine's example as a tacit recognition of the possibility of irreducible moral conflict. Admittedly, moral conflicts in which we unavoidably wrong another, can exist on a spectrum of gravity. The considerations entertained by Augustine and the philosophers here under discussion obviously focus our moral attention on those at the more radical end of the spectrum, especially killing and torture, other enduring traumas of war, and the kind of wartime destruction that undermines conditions for recovery and reconciliation.

The literature on moral dilemmas and dirty hands is extensive and complex. It certainly has not been analyzed conclusively here. The primary aim of this discussion has been to raise the possibility that even when a moral decision, action, or practice is defensible, or even the best option available, it can still have *morally* evil dimensions, not just unfortunate and regrettable ones. In such a case, an agent's agency, intention, and will may be involved in such a way that the agent not only perceives or is perceived to be responsible but is, in fact, responsible for the evil caused. This may be true, even granting that the responsible agent is attaining a greater good and would have avoided the evil caused if possible. In such cases, his or her responsibility for violating a duty toward or the dignity of another human being or beings is diminished but does not disappear. To protect the dignity and rights of some, the agent has engaged in action that unavoidably treats another or others unjustly. While onlookers may, and probably should, hesitate to assign blame (for the choice was forced and the outcome justifiable), the honest and anguished agent may well surmise that the decision in some way violates his or her moral integrity, commitments, and true values. Indeed, it is arguable that only a conflict of this nature could be one from which, in Hursthouse's estimation, "not even the most virtuous agent can emerge with her life unmarred."[170]

170. Hursthouse, *On Virtue Ethics*, 63. A contrary view is that irreducible moral dilemmas do not exist—that it is logically impossible for them to do so—because if an act is justified, then the agent is not *culpable* for any regrettable aspects or consequences. Agents who in such situations claim to feel guilt and remorse should be helped to understand that they are not blameworthy.

In the case of unavoidable and irreducible moral dilemmas, remorse is an appropriate response. Remorse is an emotional and psychological state of distress and self-reproach, arising from a sense of guilt for wrong done. Remorse entails "some sense of voluntariness," although in some cases (moral dilemmas) "a person is not held by others or themselves to have acted fully voluntarily but still feels a very real kind of remorse for what was done."[171] Steven Tudor explains, similarly to Williams, that remorse comes from knowledge of having wronged the Other and from a keen sense of "the frightfulness of the wrong done." A major cause of the suffering of the remorseful agent is "the kind of internal rift experienced in remorseful self-reproach."[172] The agent feels that "there is now something which is a part of me but which I reject and oppose."[173] In a moral dilemma, one both undertakes and rejects one's own action, exacerbating the sense of an internal division and turmoil.

Remorse reflects an accurate assessment by the agent of his or her responsibility for causing evil, as well as—and importantly—a resolution to take compensatory future action of some type. Arising both from the frightfulness of the wrong done to another, and from the frightfulness of the agent's divided moral identity, remorse involves a desire to make amends and an intention to avoid future wrong. This process may also be termed repentance, which is a necessary outcome and test of true remorse.[174] The remorseful agent seeks redemption (of his or her "true" self and of his or her standing in the estimation of others) through a process involving elements such as remembrance, confession, apology, repentance, reparation, and receiving just reproach and punishment.[175]

The so-called "principle of double effect" (to be discussed further in the next chapter) seeks to further specify conditions under which wrong-causing agents are or are not guilty, in situations in which they are intending a greater or proportionate good. A key condition is that if the wrong involved is grave enough (for example, the death of an innocent person), it cannot be the agent's primary goal, nor can it be the means by which the good end is accomplished. In such cases, agents are forbidden to act, no matter how great the evil that results from refraining to act. If these conditions are met, however, the agent is absolved from all guilt and need feel no remorse. I question both whether these conditions adequately protect the agent from guilt and whether, if they cannot be met, the agent should be forbidden from acting. I maintain, to the contrary, that agents may still be obligated to act and may act rightly, but at the same time they bear some level of culpability and are properly remorseful for having violated the rights of or just obligations to another. This is what constitutes an *irreducible*, even if not *absolute*, moral dilemma.

171. Michael Proeve and Steven Tudor, *Remorse: Psychological and Jurisprudential Perspectives* (Burlington, VT: Ashgate, 2010), 39. Literature on remorse typically envisions a single agent, which the language here reflects.

172. Steven Tudor, *Compassion and Remorse* (Leuven: Peeters, 2001), 143. See also Proeve and Tudor, *Remorse*, 33.

173. Proeve and Tudor, *Remorse*, 43.

174. Proeve and Tudor, *Remorse*, 35.

175. Tudor, *Compassion and Remorse*, 189–206.

COLLECTIVE AGENCY, DIRTY HANDS, AND POLITICAL REMORSE

The philosopher C. J. A. Coady brings up the fact that public officials with "dirty hands" can be regarded as authorized by the citizenry, particularly in a democratic society. Coady quotes Martin Hollis to this effect: "'Political actors, duly appointed within a legitimate state, have an authority deriving finally from the People. Currently that means from you and me. . . . when their hands get dirty, so do ours.'"[176] Even if the responsibility of citizens for morally questionable actions of their leaders is less direct and more diffuse, it is still responsibility. This takes the problems of moral dilemmas and dirty hands to another level. As usually employed, the vocabulary of moral dilemmas addresses irreducible conflicts faced by individuals, and that of dirty hands envisions conflicts faced by officials responsible for the good of a political society. The problem of war demands an ethical analysis that can account for collective agency, as well as the social responsibilities and dilemmas of individuals. It must recognize the participation of all members of a society in its basic institutions and consider potential conflicts among society's organizing institutions and policies, for which participating members generally are responsible.

Such conflicts could arise either because the direct purposes of institutions or policies are morally opposed to one another, or because subsidiary effects of institutional behavior or policy implementation contradict the moral values ostensibly defining the institution as a whole or embodied in other entities. Looking at the United States, the executive branch might sign on to UN Climate agreements, while the legislative branch loosens environmental controls on business. The State Department might advocate for human rights abroad, while the Department of Homeland Security refuses refugees and deports immigrants who, because they are not citizens, are not regarded as having equal rights in the United States. The Department of Education might administer free public education for all, while the Congress establishes a tax system that strongly favors the wealthy and the school districts in which they reside. Most Americans have had the experience of voting for a candidate while not supporting all of the policies for which he or she stands—realizing that a vote for the platform they do support entails a vote for the positions they do not. A political party or its collective leadership may

---

176. Coady, "The Problem of Dirty Hands," citing Martin Hollis, *Reason in Action: Essays in the Philosophy of Social Science* (Cambridge: Cambridge University Press, 1996), 146–47.

endorse a candidate partly on the basis of his or her chances of election, despite objectionable aspects of his or her history or current views.

War is a collective action for which there is both collective and individual responsibility. Conflicts within and around the enterprise of war as not only a political but a social-ethical enterprise can arise from many directions—for example, between the pressing obligations of an individual agent; between or among an agent's moral commitments and his or her roles; between and among the coordinated forms of agency within the war enterprise itself; or between and among social institutions or enterprises that are acting simultaneously within a society. War, it would seem, provides ample verification and illustration of the fact of irreducible moral dilemmas.

A dynamic analogous to the individual moral dilemma can occur within collective agency, responsibility, and identity. If a group or organization has failed to live up to its mission, even granting that some other aspect of its mission has in the process rightly been fulfilled, the group leadership and membership bear a (differentiated) burden of guilt, and leaders and spokespersons properly offer public explanations and apologies. The identity and trustworthiness of the group do not "emerge unmarred." A possible example here is humanitarian aid agencies working in conflict zones, who are caught between maintaining political neutrality to gain access and serve all in need; and at the same time, providing resources to perpetrators of human rights violations, and even facilitating further violations by organized criminals or combatants who receive, steal, or extort donated goods or cash. Nations or other entities such as ethnic groups or political organizations whose leaders wield violence for political ends, even justified political ends, are in a similar situation. Even humanitarian intervention brings with it the injustices and moral costs of war.

In what way can or should political collectives take responsibility for wrong caused, wrong that has both been done to others and damaged the agents' own moral identities? Collective responsibility in such situations is in some ways similar to cases in which political representatives make public apologies for wrongs committed by a nation or other entity, even if not every individual member is a perpetrator, and even if (though less frequently) the wrongs have been done in the course of pursuing an otherwise defensible course of action. Aaron Lazare claims that "apologies have the capacity to positively transform relationships between individuals, groups, and nations," by providing processes for overcoming hostilities, "while also preserving or restoring the dignity of both parties."[177] He offers three paradigmatic examples of direct, sincere, and effective apologies: the decision of the Roman Catholic Church (under the pontificates of John XXIII and Paul VI) to eliminate and reject all vestiges of anti-Semitism, whether in its own teachings and policies or in other social forms (I note that the Church never directly apologized for anti-Semitism, though an apologetic stance could be inferred); the 1985 speech of the president of the Federal Republic of Germany, Richard von Weizsacker, confronting and renouncing Nazi crimes; and the 1988 action of the US government in apologizing and making reparations to Japanese Americans interned during World War II. Of importance in the last instance is the recognition by Congress that moral obligations that come into conflict with political considerations do not lose their moral force, and that violations of these obligations call for acknowledgment and apology.[178]

None of these cases constitutes an irreducible moral dilemma in the sense of a wrong that was unavoidable in the justified pursuit of an overriding good, but they do illustrate ways in which collective remorse can be recognized and embodied. Daniel Philpott affirms that the possibility and effectiveness of apologies drives from the fact that political injustices have collective dimensions for both victims and perpetrators. Apologies, however, may not represent all members of a political body, and they may produce debate and backlash. Hence the greater the degree of popular consensus, the more representative of the collective it will be, and the greater the likelihood of the success of the apology as an act of political reconciliation.[179]

In this light, it is helpful to consider how remorse is a "political emotion," and how that emotion might be nurtured and enlarged within a political body that bears collective responsibility for wrongs.[180] Although treatments of remorse usually focus on the emotions and related actions of individual agents, remorse is also applicable to the agency of groups, organizations, and societies, such as the United States, the Democratic Party, and the Roman Catholic Church. Augustine was himself a rhetorician who served the emperor, presumably by using the art of persuasive speaking to create a social and political ethos amenable to the

---

177. Aaron Lazare, "The Future of Apologies," *New England Journal of Public Policy* 21, no. 1 (2006): 87. See also Aaron Lazare, *On Apology* (New York: Oxford University Press, 2004), from which the article is taken.

178. Lazare, "Future of Apologies," 89.

179. Daniel Philpott, *Just and Unjust Peace* (New York: Oxford University Press, 2012), 204.

180. See Janet Staiger, Ann Cvetkovich, and Ann Morris Reynolds, eds., *Political Emotions* (New York: Routledge, 2010); Martha C. Nussbaum, *Political Emotions: Why Love Matters for Justice* (Cambridge, MA: Harvard University Press, 2013).

emperor's political values and goals. As some contemporary social theorists pose the question, "What contributions can the study of discourse, rhetoric or framing of emotion contribute to understanding the political sphere, civil society and the political?"[181] Noting an "affective turn" in cultural studies, they observe that the political sphere is not one of rationality and reasoned argument, so much as one of feeling and emotion.[182]

The political philosopher Martha Nussbaum believes that compassion and even love are accessible and constructive political emotions, and that they are in fact necessary to sustain justice. The emotion of fear, properly directed, can support compassion; but "fear is too often excessively narrow," focused on "oneself and one's immediate circle."[183] Fear exaggerated and misdirected is not only an obstacle to compassion, it is a frequent motivation for war. Augustine attunes us to the fact that emotions and the loves and loyalties they support can be rightly or wrongly ordered, virtuous or vicious, and that the ordering of loves has political as well as personal origins, contexts, and consequences.[184] Public rhetoric urging support for war or other forms of coercive violence against "outsiders" and "enemies" is a notorious tool of politicians with ulterior interests and other warmongers. Remorse as a political emotion opposed to distorted fear can be an ally of compassion and justice. Remorse acknowledges the ambivalent moral status of even the well-meaning agent, and it directs individual and collective agency to repentance and the repair of relationships, while forming agents in habits of humility, compassion, and justice.

Augustine's ambivalence toward war, along with recent literature developing the notions of moral dilemma and dirty hands, confirm that remorse and atonement are fitting in political circumstances as well as individual ones, and that they pertain to war as a "miserable necessity," implying the need for compensatory and restorative social practices. In the case of "just war," remorse and repentance could be viewed as appropriate social responses in light of lives taken and of the economic and social destruction war is sure to leave in its wake. A historical illustration is the medieval practice of requiring penitence on the part of soldiers returning from war, whether or not they had violated any of the rules of "just war."[185] Soldiers kill other human beings, albeit in service of a legitimate authority, one who had set war as a necessary condition of peace,

---

181. Staiger et al., *Political Emotions*, 1.

182. Staiger et al., *Political Emotions*, 4–5.

183. Nussbaum, *Political Emotions*, 322.

184. On this point, see Richard B. Miller, *Friends and Other Strangers: Studies in Religion, Ethics, and Culture* (New York: Columbia University Press, 2016), 122–34.

185. See Bernard J. Verkamp, *The Moral Treatment of Returning Warriors in Early Medieval and*

and even if they manage to sustain a personal intention of love. Soldiers were required to repent of, and not only to regret, the violence perpetrated against other human beings. Moreover, war inevitably brings lasting social evils, including injury to and traumatization of noncombatants, dismantling of government and law, devastation of civil society, and ruin of means of sustenance and livelihood. The penance borne by soldiers could be regarded as a role-specific vicarious expression of remorse on the part of the whole community, for which the soldiers represent the part of the collective agent that acted necessarily and yet is rejected and opposed.

In addition to ritual repentance, or representative public apologies, remorse should also be expressed in terms of reparations made to offended or harmed parties, even if the remorseful party considers its actions ethically and politically justified. An example might be the Marshall Plan following World War II, although it was promoted more in the name of future peace and security than in acknowledgment of unjust suffering caused by US military action. Reparation can take either material or symbolic form. It can constitute direct restitution to victims or some other type of compensation, especially when the harm done cannot simply be reversed. Another expression of remorse is proactive peacebuilding that seeks to avoid future violence, partly by reforming and reorienting individual and social characters disposed to resort to violence. In addition, a remorseful war-waging body politic (or the leadership within it) should develop and heighten a critical public discourse about war, other uses of military force, and the incidence of violence domestically. Rational discourse must be backed up by rhetorical appeals, public symbolic actions, expressions of support by respected public figures, and aesthetic reinforcement by art, music, and creative literature.

AUGUSTINE'S LETTERS AND ADVOCACY

Augustine was not totally oblivious to the fact that if one truly regrets or even is remorseful about the violence done in the name of political order, an obligation follows to remedy the fallout as far as possible. On politics as on other issues, Augustine can affirm seemingly contradictory positions, and some of his stronger theological claims are undermined at the pastoral level. The *Confessions*, for example, ostensibly illustrates the thorough dependence of Augustine's faith on God's initiative and God's absolute sovereignty and efficacy in bringing Augustine to love

Modern Times (Scranton, PA: University of Scranton Press, 1993); and Michael Griffin, *The Politics of Penance: Proposing an Ethic for Social Repair* (Eugene OR: Wipf & Stock, 2016), 148–62.

of God as the highest good (*summum bonum*). Yet, as James O'Donnell observes, the "staying power" of the book lies in its narration of an uncertain process and outcome "that speak against the doctrine the book serves." He writes: "The poignancy of the narrative, the fragility of the triumphs it achieves, and the anxiety that lingers in the wake of the storytelling are unmistakable."[186] Augustine's memoir communicates both a sense of divine power, and the urgency of human anguish, questing, responsibility to seek the truth, and evanescent consolation.

Similarly for Augustinian politics, support for a more constructive and hopeful Augustine is being accessed through renewed interest in the many letters he wrote throughout his career, abetted by the discovery in France in 1981 of a trove of thirty-one previously untranslated and unpublished letters by, to, or concerning Augustine. They come from the last part of his life.[187] Robert Dodaro has called attention to the politically active bishop of Hippo behind many of these messages. In them, Augustine is "reflecting on practical issues as they arise, as he answers a request, intercedes with authority, debates with an opponent or advises a friend. We also hear him encouraging, teaching, and chastising his congregation from the pulpit in reaction to current events."[188] Augustine's correspondence with public officials shows not only that he envisions the promotion of civic virtue and justice as the role of the statesman, but also that he urges Christian officials, motivated by Christian values, to exploit their public roles in order to mitigate the effects of unjust laws and policies and to militate for the enactment of more just ones.[189]

Under the explicit rubric of "Augustine and politics," Dodaro develops the specific ways in which Augustine networked with fellow bishops and made alliances with Christians in positions of influence and authority to exercise "political activism" on behalf of Christian social values.[190] For example, Augustine participated in a "bishops' tribunal" in which bishops adjudicated civil cases in their local churches. An episcopal council originally developed to coordinate a response to the Donatist threat evolved

---

186. O'Donnell, *Augustine*, 76.

187. Robert B. Eno, SS, "Epistulae," *Augustine through the Ages*, 306. For primary sources, see E. M. Atkins and R. J. Dodaro, eds., *Augustine: Political Writings* (Cambridge: Cambridge University Press, 2001). For a review of the contents of this collection, see Paul C. Burns, Review of *Augustine: Political Writings*, ed. E. M. Atkins and R. J. Dodaro, *Bryn Mawr Classical Review*, 2001.10.32, accessed September 18, 2017, https://tinyurl.com/y9shl5cf.

188. E. M. Atkins and R. J. Dodaro, "Introduction," in *Augustine: Political Writings*, xii.

189. Robert Dodaro, *Christ and the Just Society in the Thought of Augustine* (Cambridge: Cambridge University Press, 2004), 25, 217–18.

190. Robert Dodaro, "Between the Two Cities: Political Action in Augustine of Hippo," in *Augustine and Politics*, ed. John Doody, Kevin L. Hughes, and Kim Paffenroth, Augustine in Conversation: Tradition and Innovation (Lanham, MD: Lexington, 2005), 99.

into a forum from which to pressure the imperial administration. Augustine personally sent letters to imperial officials—especially Christians like Macedonius, Donatus, Marcellinus, and Boniface—and made common cause with other bishops to urge clemency on the death penalty, the avoidance of torture, enforcement of prohibitions on the kidnapping and sale of persons into slavery, and church sanctuary for people in danger of imprisonment and torture for nonpayment of burdensome taxes.

Contrasting with the positions on war and torture he espouses elsewhere, Augustine in his occasional writings tries to modify killing and torture used by legitimate state authorities as instruments of social order. In a series of letters (133, 134, and 139), Augustine urges fellow Christians Marcellinus and his brother Apringius, proconsul of Africa, not to torture or execute Donatist clergy who had attacked or killed Catholic priests. To the latter he explains, "we so love our enemies that we would appeal against your harsh sentence."[191] Augustine appeals to Marcellinus to intervene with the proconsul for leniency, since "it lies in the power of the just to soften a sentence or to punish more mildly than the laws suggest."[192] To Nectarius, an imperial official at Calama, Augustine promises that he will himself advocate for lesser penalties for pagans accused of burning a Catholic church and killing a member of the congregation.[193] And to Macedonius, imperial vicar for Africa, Augustine argues (contrary to his view of killing in war as kindly punishment) that valid penalties for illegal activities should aim at reform of the offenders, and that torture and capital punishment are therefore counterproductive.[194] Augustine's view of the virtue of the ideal Christian emperor, mentioned while praising Constantine and Theodosius, hints at larger transformative possibilities: rulers "rule justly . . . if they are slow to punish, ready to pardon; if they apply that punishment as necessary to the republic, and not in order to gratify their own enmity; if they grant pardon, not that iniquity may go unpunished, but that the transgressor may mend his ways."[195] That Augustine believes that Christian virtues can influence the conduct of war and its aftermath concretely (and not only in terms of an inward intention) is evident when he exhorts the general Boniface: "You must be a peacemaker, even when you go to war, and help those whom you defeat to know the importance of maintain-

191. Augustine, "Letter 134: To Apringius," in *Augustine: Political Writings*, 66.
192. Augustine, "Letter 139: To Marcellinus," in *Augustine: Political Writings*, 68.
193. Augustine, "Letter 91: To Nectarius," in *Augustine: Political Writings*, 2–7.
194. Augustine, "Letter 153: To Macedonius," in *Augustine: Political Writings*, 71–78.
195. Augustine, *City of God*, 5.24.

ing peace. . . . Mercy must be shown to those who have been defeated or captured, especially when they pose no threat to the future peace."[196]

Augustine's activism is not programmatic, and it does not overturn his generally pessimistic view of the course of human history as a whole. Yet he does appreciate that the power and expertise of ordained church ministers and laypeople can be orchestrated to accomplish improvements in specific areas, including government-sponsored killing. In his letters, there is visible "an African church capable, against almost all the odds, of undertaking an extremely limited level of coordinated political activity in support of social justice."[197] Along with modifying policies and practices, Augustine also thereby invites others to consider "the roots of social and political ills" and perhaps instigate more far-reaching changes.[198]

With a twenty-first century awareness of modern movements for democracy and civil rights, of global interdependence, and of transnational problems and responsibilities, some scholars of Augustine are taking another look at his social pessimism and suggesting that the transformationist element in his thought must be recovered and enhanced. For example, Eric Gregory's *Politics and the Order of Love* proposes a theological rationale for Christian participation in liberal democracies, as well as for the modification of a liberalism of noninterference by the cultivation of the civic virtues necessary to a good society.[199] With the caveat that not all his own conclusions can be identified with the politics of Augustine, Gregory draws on liberation theology, Martin Luther King Jr., and the feminist ethics of care to advocate for a Christian political participation that is transformative. But he also draws support from Augustine's depiction of the incarnation in book 10 of *The City of God*.[200] In the Word all creation is made, sustained, and redeemed; thus all things may be loved and enjoyed, if not exactly for their own sakes, then for the divine reality in which they participate. Neighbor-love can nourish the virtues necessary for political citizenship. I would add that what Augustine does not bring is a theological rationale for expecting that interfaith (or "pluralistic") cooperation can be based on shared religious or humanistic values and insights, or that it can bring significant and lasting social change. Yet Gregory holds out the hope that Christians can share in and be committed with others to a just society (which Gregory equates with a "liberal democratic polity"), supporting without

196. "Letter 189: To Boniface," 5.
197. Dodaro, "Between the Two Cities," 108.
198. Dodaro, "Between the Two Cities," 111.
199. Eric Gregory, *Politics and the Order of Love* (Chicago: University of Chicago Press, 2008), 8–11, 28–29, 60.
200. Gregory, *Politics and the Order of Love*, 286–87, 379–81.

reservation the genuine forms of justice it can achieve, yet conscious of the limits and pitfalls to which Augustine rightly calls our attention.

CONCLUSION

Eugene TeSelle refers to Augustine's "political realism," his "refusal to hold illusions about the nature of political life."[201] Augustine's eschatology of deferral, his reading of biblical narratives, and his construal of the historical meaning of Christian love are generated at the practical level by his investment as a Catholic bishop in the stability that had been provided by the Roman imperial order, a stability that during his lifetime had come under serious threat. The distance of the eschatological kingdom is particularly pronounced in Augustine's advocacy of force to preserve the unity of the City of Jerusalem on earth. There are undoubtedly dualist tendencies in Augustine's thought about Christian love, the kingdom of God, and political ethics. Augustine develops the contrast model of the two cities primarily to account for the "miserable necessities" of this life. At the same time, he recognizes and struggles with moral ambiguity, as well as ambiguous and even conflicted moral responsibility.

Augustine sets limits on violence, and he tries to bring permission to commit violence into constant contact with the evangelical norm of love by specifying that the Christian warrior must always act in a loving way even when acting violently. Thus, "love" means not nonviolence but a particular attitude motivating violent acts. In a contrasting line of thought, it can also mean violent punishment, which has in view the good of the offender. Neither of these strategies places much confidence in the power of the reign of God as already transforming historical conflicts, a possibility better represented in Augustine's letters, and the practical commitments and activism the letters facilitate.

For later generations of theologians and believers, Augustine can reinforce realistic awareness of the limits of politics and imbue all political endeavors with humility and caution. Augustine knows that "any exercise of power that involves imposition tends to feed violence," and so to destroy love of God and neighbor.[202] Augustine's is an ethic by and for people and societies who know the suffering and costs of war firsthand, who are cynical about the selective identification of "just" causes by governments with military power, who lament the frequency with which just war criteria are invoked and the rarity with which they are followed,

---

201. TeSelle, *Augustine the Theologian*, 272.

202. Jean Bethke Elshtain, *Augustine and the Limits of Politics* (Notre Dame, IN: University of Notre Dame Press, 1995), 101.

and who know that peace accords are likely to disintegrate in new outbreaks of violence.

In an era of widespread civil conflicts around the globe, it is more important than ever to look at the criteria of "just war" and their application in light of the real effects they have on societies and peoples, and especially of their likelihood of "spiraling into unceasing violence for entire populations."[203] An Augustinian caution is that even Christians who struggle honestly and at personal cost to use violent interventions only for humanitarian aims, those with a sincere motivation toward serving the vulnerable neighbor, will find themselves implicated in causing further destruction. It may be necessary to repent of and not only regret the "collateral damage" countenanced in service of a larger justice, even that of the "responsibility to protect." It is also necessary to interrogate decisions about entering war to save the peace from the perspective of those who most suffer war's brunt and live its consequences.[204]

Augustine's letters reveal that he was active in a network of bishops, influential laypersons, and imperial officials in North Africa, striving to be an agent of social change to a greater extent than his theological writings and historical reputation suggest. Augustine did not give up on the ability of Christians to enhance relations of justice in their immediate cultural and political environments. Provisionally successful efforts to bring about change are set against the critical horizon of a transcendent future. In the grand scheme of things, no claims can be made for a progressive view of history, but it is still morally obligatory and practically possible to take action toward love-informed justice within whatever local opportunities arise. Augustine presents proactive social advocacy not only as an ecclesial opportunity but as a Christian obligation. This is especially the case when other alternatives present inherent and ultimately irreducible moral dilemmas—and when there is cause for remorse in view of past choices and actions.

203. Maria Teresa Dávila, "Breaking from the Dominance of Power and Order in Augustine's Ethic of War," in *Augustine and Social Justice*, 158.
204. Maria Teresa Dávila, "Breaking from the Dominance," 156–59.

5.

War and the Common Good
Aquinas and the Just War Tradition

Thomas Aquinas (1225–74) was born in the empire of Frederick II, at the castle of Roccasecca near Aquino, a small town between Naples and Rome. From the eleventh to the fifteenth centuries, the rise of powerful Italian city-states led to internal conflicts, as well as conflicts with the Holy Roman Emperor, who was frequently at war with the pope. Thomas's father was a knight, and his brothers pursued military careers. But as the youngest son of a large and noble family, Thomas was as a small child sent off to the Benedictine abbey of Monte Cassino for schooling and in the expectation that he would follow the monastic vocation of his uncle. When armed confrontations between the pope and the emperor affected the abbey, Thomas's parents sent him at age fifteen to the University of Naples. About four years later, he joined the Dominicans, a mendicant order of preachers, who had a growing presence at the university. Originally hosted in Naples by a small Benedictine monastery, the Dominicans and their influence grew so quickly that the monastery church was eventually rededicated to Saint Dominic. Thomas persevered in his vocational choice, despite strenuous familial efforts to redirect him toward a more promising and politically advantageous ecclesiastical career with the Benedictines.

What parent today would be surprised that a teenager, for the first time leaving his childhood home and the close supervision of relatives and monks, would resist departing his exhilarating new neighborhood, a port city and one of the largest Christian hubs of medieval Europe? Especially since Thomas's older brothers were free to test their mettle in military exploits, as did Francis of Assisi and Ignatius Loyola before they realized that the Spirit's call led in a different direction.

Thomas's adult life as a city-based academic and preacher did not disappoint. At the University of Paris and later at the Dominican school of theology in Cologne, Thomas studied with Albert the Great, who was creatively—and controversially—introducing the thought of Aristotle alongside theological texts. Thomas himself eventually served as one of the University of Paris's greatest professors and scholars. In his later years, he traveled on assignments from his order and the pope, in addition to extensive writing. He died at the age of forty-nine, on his way to participate in the Council of Lyons, which was to begin in the spring of 1274.[1]

Aquinas was first and foremost a theologian, and his ethics is informed by insights from the Bible, tradition, and his historical Christian community of spiritual, moral, and liturgical practice. Yet Aquinas's ethics also responds to aspects of the human reality that endure over place and time. Adapting Aristotle's scientific method of analysis for theological use, Aquinas brings to Christian ethics an orderly infrastructure, based on the natures and ends of beings. Like Aristotle, Aquinas sees humans as inherently social and political. How human political nature (created good, now sinful) relates to humanity's graced or "supernatural" destiny will be a main question of this chapter.

If Augustine operates out of an intellectual milieu colored by a new alliance between Christianity and the political order, Aquinas operates out of a milieu equally indebted to the interpenetration of Christian theology and the academy. In the twelfth and thirteenth centuries, university faculties were established at Bologna, Cambridge, Naples, Oxford, Paris, Salerno, and Salamanca. Of the thirteenth-century university, Marie-Dominique Chenu writes, "Intellectual corporation of the city, the university was at the same time an official body of the Church, with its own proper 'office,' and with rights and liberties that it enjoyed pursuant to charters granted by authority of the collective Christianity it meant to serve."[2] Moreover, "it was the faculty of theology that formed the soul of the university." For the first time the role of expounding revealed truths was extended from the episcopacy to the competency "of professors, of a school of men who were professionals in their work, whose energies were devoted to developing a science, and whose juridi-

---

1. For biographical information, see Thomas F. O'Meara, OP, *Thomas Aquinas: Theologian* (Notre Dame, IN: University of Notre Dame Press, 1997), 1–40; Josef Pieper, *Guide to Thomas Aquinas* (New York: Pantheon, 1964), 11–22.

2. M.-D. Chenu, OP, *Toward Understanding St. Thomas*, trans. Albert M. Landry, OP, and Dominic Hughes, OP (Chicago: Henry Regnery, 1964), 19.

cal status depended on the corporation and was not, properly speaking, a function of the hierarchy."[3]

As today, this close cooperation between church and academy created problems as well as opportunities. Some of each arose from the fact that, in the Western church, Augustine was regarded as the authority for Christian doctrine, while Aristotelian philosophy opened new lines of intellectual inquiry. On the one hand, Aquinas achieved an unparalleled synthesis of Christian teaching and philosophical reflection. On the other, Aristotle's account of nature posed significant challenges to the Augustinian doctrines of providence and grace.

SYNTHESIS OF AUGUSTINE AND ARISTOTLE

Since the eleventh century, Aristotle had been known in the West as a logician, but in the thirteenth, his works in natural science and philosophy of nature gained currency: the scholar's "attention now focused on the world of matter and sense, on the study of life and its laws, on the phenomena of generation. In brief, what now appeared was a world that was *real,* a world *capable of being understood.*"[4] The Aristotelian approach to nature—as containing its own principles of intelligibility—prescinded from any reliance on God, religion, or revelation. Not surprisingly, it met with resistance within the church and from the hierarchy, expressed by occasional condemnations within which even Aquinas was included (posthumously). These rejections obviously did not last.

The genius of Aquinas is that he set an appreciation of the intrinsic intelligibility of the universe and its laws within a framework of divine creativity and goodness, identifying reason and freedom as the very marks of the divine intention for humanity. Union with God through knowledge and love is the destiny that fulfills natural human capacities even as it elevates them to a qualitatively different level. Human abilities and enterprises are thus given a limited autonomy that permits the development of truly philosophical inquiry, even as the encompassing character of divine activity and providence is affirmed. In the thirteenth century, some interpreters of Augustine read his elevation of the heavenly city over the earthly city in such a way as to subsume civil government under ecclesial authority, in a unitary Christian society. This indeed describes the political agenda of the twelfth-century papacy,

3. Chenu, *Toward Understanding St. Thomas,* 20.
4. Chenu, *Toward Understanding St. Thomas,* 33.

which emerged as a stronger institution than the Holy Roman Empire—but this was not the goal of Aquinas.[5]

Because political life is envisioned on an Aristotelian model to have its own coherency and positive *raison d'être*, Aquinas feels less need to struggle constantly with the significance of Jesus's preaching of the kingdom or with the difference for ethics made by infusion of divine grace. His analyses of government and the political common good achieve a reasonableness and balance that eluded Augustine. The natural moral law and the cardinal virtue of justice guide and measure political life. Divine revelation corrects human error and reproves human wickedness, while the infused theological virtues bestow a human capacity for eternal friendship with God. Yet the fundamental requirements of civic life and government can be established by practical reason, formed in virtue by prudence.[6] The infused moral virtues augment the natural or cardinal virtues, and refer them holistically to friendship with God. They transform, rather than replace, humanity's created ability to know, will, and do the good. This view of the effects of grace is consistent with Aquinas's "fundamental realism" about goods, virtues, and morality.[7]

Aristotle's teleological and eudaimonistic construal of natures and virtues structures the way Thomas Aquinas approaches "right order" within political community. Aquinas's political ethics has deeply influenced Catholic traditions about justice, civic virtue, the preservation of peace, and the permissibility of killing in defense of self, the community, or the nation. Thomas Gilby notes that the modern state was at

5. Kenneth R. Himes, *Christianity and the Political Order: Conflict, Cooptation, and Cooperation* (Maryknoll, NY: Orbis, 2013), 104–5.

6. See the so-called "Treatise on Law" for Aquinas's fundamental exposition of the basic and rationally intelligible principles ordering human life. Aquinas, *Summa Theologica*, trans. Fathers of the English Dominican Province (New York: Benziger Bros., 1948), I-II, qq. 90–94. (Hereafter cited as ST.) For clarification and interpretation, consult Clifford G. Kossel, "Natural Law and Human Law (Ia IIae, qq. 90–97)," in *The Ethics of Aquinas*, ed. Stephen J. Pope (Washington, DC: Georgetown University Press, 2002), 169–93; James F. Keenan, "The Virtue of Prudence (IIa IIae, qq. 47–56)," in Pope, *Ethics of Aquinas*, 259–71; and Ludger Honnefelder, "The Evaluation of Goods and the Estimation of Consequences: Aquinas on the Determination of the Morally Good," in Pope, *Ethics of Aquinas*, 426–37.

7. Jean Porter, *Justice as a Virtue: A Thomistic Perspective* (Grand Rapids, MI: William B. Eerdmans, 2016), 161. On the infused moral virtues, see ST I-II, q. 63, a. 3. While some contemporary authors maintain that the theological virtues entirely replace the natural virtues, this would imply that grace destroys nature rather than "elevating" it, an interpretation that I believe goes implausibly against the stream of Thomistic interpretation as well as Aquinas's own moral and political sensibilities. See Porter, *Justice as a Virtue*, 29–31. For discussions of the contrary perspective, see William C. Mattison, "Can Christians Possess the Acquired Cardinal Virtues?," *Theological Studies* 72, no. 3 (2011): 558–85; Thomas J. Bushlack, *Politics for a Pilgrim Church: A Thomistic Theory of Civic Virtue* (Grand Rapids, MI: William B. Eerdmans, 2015), 98–108.

this time being born. "Soon the reflection followed that politics or state-craft constituted a special discipline with rules of its own" and an aspiration to "civic reasonableness," rather than being an eclectic combination of patristic theology, Stoic philosophy, Roman law, and various local folk customs.[8] All natural law and the human laws accountable to it are derived from eternal law.

But knowledge of the natural law is not fundamentally dependent on divine revelation. Despite the effects of sin and the importance of revelation as a corrective, truth is attained by human beings through their powers of reason and free will, as well as through human beings' basic inclinations to seek the ends that fulfill their natures, such as life, reproduction and education of children, and life in political society.[9] For Aquinas, the common good transcends the good of individuals, and it is the common good with which the virtue of justice and law in general are above all concerned.[10] Yet the common good also includes just treatment of individuals. In the *Summa Contra Gentiles,* Aquinas comments that "an ordered concord is preserved among men when each man is given his due, for this is justice."[11] The virtue of justice perfects the will, disposing the agent to act in favor of the objective goods of individual and social existence, and of the relations that realize and sustain these goods. Justice also acts as a "normative ideal" that inspires and regulates individual and social agency, by providing a paradigm of virtuous behavior.[12]

The most significant difference between the ethics of Aquinas and that of Augustine is the former's greater confidence in a reasonable moral order, known in principle by all human beings, which can form the basis of a common morality and politics. For Augustine, the emphasis is on the disruption of order in history by sin and the need for a divine restoration by grace, provided only within the church. Certainly, for Aquinas, the

8. Thomas Gilby, *The Political Thought of Thomas Aquinas* (Chicago: University of Chicago Press, 1958), xvi.

9. ST I-II, q. 94, a. 2.

10. ST II-II, q. 58, a. 5. See Jean Porter, "The Virtue of Justice (IIa IIae, qq. 58-122)," in *Ethics of Aquinas,* 273.

11. Aquinas, *Summa Contra Gentiles,* vol. 3, *Providence,* part 2, trans. Vernon J. Bourke (Notre Dame, IN: University of Notre Dame Press, 1975), q. 128, a. 6. This work (hereafter SCG), apparently directed to the conversion of non-Christians, in fact contains many arguments from "divine law" and even from the Christian Scriptures. Chenu speculates that Aquinas may have in mind, to an extent, the Islamic religion, which Christian missionaries had recently encountered in Spain and to which the scholarly world had been introduced through the influence of Arabic civilization. More likely, though, this work is presented more generally as "a defense of the entire body of Christian thought, confronted with the scientific Greco-Arabic conception of the universe, henceforth revealed to the West." See Chenu, *Toward Understanding St. Thomas,* 292.

12. Porter, *Justice as a Virtue,* 19, 31, 36.

transcendent grounding and healing of human political life are important. He is well aware of the reality of sin and the need not only for the
theological virtues of faith, hope, and charity but also for infused moral
virtues to supplement the imperfect natural ones.[13] Nevertheless, for the
most part, ordered relations among persons and things are understood in
terms of those entities' finite, particular, and divinely created natures.

In his synthesis of theology and philosophy, Aquinas places considerable trust in human reason and evinces a comparable degree of optimism
about the potential of natural humanity, hindered though it may be by
sin and ignorance, to establish justice in personal and social relationships
and thereby achieve a peaceful political order governed by law. This is
not to say that Aquinas disagrees with Augustine that the peace of this
world is partial, imperfect, and easily corrupted. The preservation of just
relations between citizens and nations occasionally will require resort to
force. Nonetheless, the kingdom of God builds on and transforms communities and relationships that are not naturally uncongenial to it.[14] In
Aquinas's ethical writings, direct obedience to Christ's evangelical commands is subordinated in the political sphere to the requirements of just
human communities and the common good. The Christian is at home
within political society, and the gradual sanctification by the Spirit in
Christ takes place within it, not over against it.

Gilby cautions that Aquinas's political thought was always subordinate
to his philosophical and theological interests, and hence it cannot be
expected to constitute "a complete and self-contained system."[15]
Nonetheless, four principles lie at the heart of Aquinas's approach to the
political order. First, political authority and the law do not exist merely
because of original sin, but they correspond to needs and purposes inherent in human nature itself. Second, political authority, although flawed
by sin, is distinct from and not in principle subordinate to the authority of the church in the realm of temporal affairs. This, of course, does
not resolve the practical problem of coordinating two distinct sources of
power without subsuming one under the other. Third, temporal power
is directed to temporal affairs, including the cultivation of social virtue.
"The foremost task of government was to establish and maintain those
objective conditions, principally matters of justice, which allowed citizens to lead the good life."[16] Finally, political judgment is more like an

13. ST I-II, q. 63, a. 3.
14. Porter even argues that, because Aquinas sees all persons as made in the image of God, it
can be inferred that he envisions equality and love of neighbor as self-evident to reason (*Justice
as a Virtue*, 5, 116ff., 214, 153, 221).
15. Gilby, *Political Thought*, xxii.
16. Gilby, *Political Thought*, xxiii.

art than a deductive science. Because they answer to practical and contingent matters, government and legislation can never be deduced from abstract premises, nor totally legitimated by philosophy or theology.

The decision to go to war is a good example. Kevin Carnahan argues that prudence, a virtue of practical moral reason, is a higher-order guide to decision-making about war than just war criteria.[17] General precepts against unjustified killing can never change, but the determination of whether specific acts should count as murder can change.[18] War is a type of killing that, according to just war theory, does not always count as unjust homicide or murder. While there may be in principle good moral reasons for going to war, the venture itself is justified only if, at the practical level, it will serve peace and the common good, is initiated by a legitimate political authority, and is carried out with a good intention. Since the Jesus of the gospels does not sanction any taking of human life by other humans, Aquinas's natural law justification of war in exceptional cases runs up against a clear biblical contradiction. Whether Aquinas resolves this problem satisfactorily, and what its implications are for just war thinking in general, are questions addressed below.

JUSTIFICATION OF WAR

Aquinas's basic terms in analyzing social and political obligations are temporal peace, the common good, and justice. War is placed in this moral framework. Aquinas understands violence to be permissible in exceptional situations, on the basis of natural obligations and prerogatives, established divinely in the creation of what is natural to humanity. In the *Summa Contra Gentiles,* Aquinas asserts, "it is apparent that things prescribed by divine law are right, not only because they are put forth by law, but also because they are in accord with nature."[19] Although the perfection of the Christian life transcends the natural (acquired) virtues, Aquinas presents the moral choices that respect human nature as such as coherent with those to which the Christian person is ordinarily obliged. There are some exceptional examples, in which a higher expression of charity might seem to go against natural human ends or virtues, such as martyrdom, fasting, and celibacy.[20] But these are supererogatory actions, and therefore they are required only in specified circumstances, if at all.

Given his framing of ethics in terms of reason, the natural law, and

17. Kevin Carnahan, *From Presumption to Prudence in Just-War Rationality* (London: Routledge, 2017).
18. ST I-II, q. 100, a. 8, ad 3.
19. SCG 3/2, q. 129, a. 1.
20. See ST I-II, q. 64, a. 1, ad 3; q. 65, a. 5; II-II, q. 124, a. 2; q. 152, a. 4.

an ordered hierarchy of goods, Aquinas in principle would not envision that there could be any such thing as a truly irreducible moral dilemma. There are good reasons to think, however, that he came up against the "paradox" of joining the gospel and war that his Thomistic natural law heir, John Courtney Murray, was to recognize seven centuries later.[21] Aquinas's awareness of the ambiguous morality of war, at least from a Christian perspective, is evident from the way he places it in relation to charity and from the fact that he tenaciously sticks to natural law grounds for justifying it, sidelining possible biblical considerations as not relevant in this case. After addressing Aquinas's ethics of war specifically, I will turn at the end of the chapter to his larger vision of the effects of charity on the moral life, arguing that, to be consistent, he should have taken up the question whether and how charity and related dispositions affect the conduct of war. Were he to have done so, such a move would have provided resources for an ethic of peacebuilding.

Following Augustine, Aquinas retains in his comprehensive theological work, the *Summa Theologiae,* a negative, provisory context for the discussion of war. He raises the subject under the virtue of charity, against which it seems a self-evident offense, perhaps the greatest imaginable. The title of the article which has war as its topic puts the enterprise of war on dubious footing from the outset: "Whether it is *always* sinful to wage war?"[22] Though the title was supplied by a later editor, it captures the tone of the article it heads.[23] The phrasing seems to assume that war is *usually* sinful; even though the negative answer to be pursued in the article makes it clear that justified war is possible. Aquinas has a parallel strategy to distance capital punishment and killing in self-defense from ready moral approbation, by bringing them up under "murder" as a sin against the virtue of justice.[24]

Another alternative would have been to place war within the discussion of either justice (as an illustration) or peace (as a means). However, the peace gained by war is often neither truly just nor authentically peaceful. Elaborating on Augustine's premise that "peace is tranquility of

---

21. John Courtney Murray, "Remarks on the Moral Problem of War," *Theological Studies* 20, no. 40 (1959): 40–61. "The effort of the moral reason to fit the use of violence into the objective order of justice is paradoxical enough; but the paradox is heightened when this effort takes place at the interior of the Christian religion of love" (57). And even though Murray elsewhere strenuously defends the viability and reasonableness of the doctrine of natural law, he admits that war "remains always fundamentally irrational" (52). Cf. Murray, *We Hold These Truths: Catholic Reflections on the American Proposition* (Kansas City: Sheed & Ward, 1960), 251, 257.

22. ST II-II, q. 40, a. 1. Italics added.

23. Gregory M. Reichberg, *Thomas Aquinas on War and Peace* (Cambridge: Cambridge University Press, 2017), 42–43.

24. ST II-II, q. 64, a. 2, 7.

order," Aquinas explains that true peace includes the harmony and ful-fillment of all one's desires, properly ordered. When peace is inspired and informed by grace, "man loves God with his whole heart, by referring all things to Him, so that his desires tend to one object," and so that "we love our neighbor as ourselves, the result being that we wish to fulfill our neighbor's will as though it were ours."[25] Ultimately, "the complete fulfillment of the law depends on love."[26] This does not describe earthly, political peace.

Yet, unlike Augustine, Aquinas does not believe all earthly peace is corrupt. Temporal peace can be at least imperfectly just, and greater peace and the common good are what are sought by just war. Hence, "those who wage war justly aim at peace, and so they are not opposed to peace;"[27] and "all wars are waged that men may find a more perfect peace than that which they had heretofore."[28] But Aquinas does not pre-sent war primarily either as an instrument of justice, or a means of peace. Instead, war appears under charity (as a probable violation), with the effect of making war morally and religiously questionable, creating a burden of proof for those who want to justify it, and suggesting that, in fact, war is quite hard to justify.

Yet contemporary scholars have debated the significance of Aquinas's decision to treat war under charity. Some want precisely to counteract the idea that war is in any essential way a moral problem. Gregory Reichberg argues that Aquinas places war under charity, *not* as a vio-lation, but because war seeks peace, and peace is an effect of charity. Aquinas, he claims, places just war in a positive relation to the virtue of charity, as a means of defeating offenses against peace, and establishing the conditions of temporal peace.[29] Reichberg's goal is to defend the jus-tice of war, as over against those who, like James Childress and Richard

---

25. ST II-II, q. 29, a. 3.

26. SCG 3/2, q. 128, a. 8. See also Matthew A. Tapie, "'For He Is Our Peace': Thomas Aquinas on Christ as Cause of Peace in the City of Saints," *Journal of Moral Theology* 5, no. 1 (2016): 111–28.

27. ST II-II, q. 40, a. 1, ad. 3.

28. ST II-II, q. 29, a. 2, ad. 2; cf. II-II, q. 29, a. 4.

29. Gregory M. Reichberg, "Aquinas' Moral Typology of Peace and War," *The Review of Metaphysics* 64, no. 3 (2011): 468, 473, 486. See also Gregory M. Reichberg, *Thomas Aquinas on War and Peace* (Cambridge: Cambridge University Press, 2017), 17–41, 266. Reichberg refers his claims to II-II, q. 26, a. 3, ad 3, but the quotes he gives actually appear in II-II, q. 29, a. 3, ad 3. Darrell Cole also interprets the placement of war within the treatment of charity to mean that war embodies charity. See Cole, "Thomas Aquinas on Virtuous Warfare," *Journal of Religious Ethics* 27, no. 1 (1999): 57–80.

Miller (see below), want to line Aquinas up on the side of skepticism about war's justice in practice.[30]

Reichberg's reading of war's relation to charity, however, can be questioned from two directions. First, as noted above, Aquinas is careful to distinguish the peace that flows from charity from temporal peace. Second, in the text Reichberg cites in support of the alliance of just war with charity, Aquinas only maintains that those formed by the virtue of charity will produce peace; not that all efforts toward civil peace—much less killing—embody the theological virtues.[31] In other words, even if charity can inform various types of social communion, this does not imply that, or explain how, killing to protect the common good is validated by charity. In fact, as will be developed below, Thomas Aquinas primarily uses arguments from justice and the common good to justify war, while setting aside gospel nonviolence as not applicable in the situation of just war.[32] In my view, interpretations such as those of Reichberg, Biggar, and Johnson (see Chapter 1) underplay the tension between Christian love and violence, even when violence is, all things considered, justified.

The tension between love and killing is better reflected in Richard Miller's assessment. Following James Childress, he places Aquinas among those who see war as prima facie wrong, precisely because it does involve violence.[33] All other things being equal, killing people is not morally neutral but evil, because it violates the basic good of life and undermines the common bonds of society. This does not mean that killing cannot be justified in certain exceptional circumstances, the stipulation of which is the point of just war theory, according to Aquinas.

Aquinas invokes Augustine to argue that war can be justified if and only if certain conditions are met. "In order for a war to be just three things are necessary," the authority of the sovereign (as public and role-related, not merely individual, authority),[34] a just cause, and a right

30. Gregory M. Reichberg, "Is There a Presumption against War' in Aquinas's Ethics?," *The Thomist* 66, no. 3 (2002): 337–67.

31. Reichberg, *Aquinas on War and Peace*, 266, citing ST II-II, q. 23, a. 3, ad 3.

32. See the first two objections and replies in ST II-II, q. 40, a. 1.

33. Richard B. Miller, "Aquinas and the Presumption against Killing and War," *Journal of Religion* 82, no. 2 (2002): 173–204. James F. Childress, *Moral Responsibility in Conflicts: Essays on Nonviolence, War, and Conscience* (Baton Rouge: Louisiana State University Press, 1982), 67. The Childress essay cited by Miller originally appeared as "Just-War Theories: The Bases, Interrelations, Priorities and Functions of Their Criteria," *Theological Studies* 39, no. 3 (1978): 427–45. As presented in the previous chapter, Childress relies on W. D. Ross's theory of prima facie duties and the "moral residue" that can result when duties conflict.

34. ST II-II, q. 64, a. 1, ad 1. See also Aquinas, *The Commandments of God: Conferences on the Two Precepts of Charity and the Ten Commandments,* trans. Laurence Shapcote, OP (London: Burns, Oates & Washbourne, 1937), 58. Citing Augustine, Aquinas argues that the sense of the fifth commandment is "Thou shalt not kill on thine own authority." Thus, "it is lawful for the

intention aiming to advance the good.[35] This implies that in all other cases war is unjust and wrong. It is striking and important, that, unlike Augustine, Aquinas explains the reasons justifying war primarily in terms of the common good or "common weal." He repeats the term "common weal" four times in validating the declaration of war by the authority who has the responsibility to take care of it, to watch over it, and to lawfully defend it from internal and external enemies.[36] The provision that war can be declared only by a legitimate public authority serves to limit war. Lower lords, knights, and bands of men avenging the honor of family or city are not authorized to use violence.

Justifying war in relation to justice and the common good undermines Augustine's idea that war is primarily or largely punitive. Augustine seems to see punishment as a sufficient condition for war; Aquinas cites Augustine on punishment as an intention in war but does not repeat this point in his own elaboration of the three criteria of a just war. He deemphasizes punishment and situates it in the larger context of war as serving the common good. While war punishes wrongdoers, and those against whom war is waged are culpable ("deserve it on account of some fault"), the governing reason for undertaking war, according to Aquinas, is the common good, not retribution as such. The necessary "rightful intention" for going to war is to "intend the advancement of good, or the avoidance of evil."[37] Here Reichberg concurs, arguing that it is extremely doubtful that for Aquinas culpability alone is a sufficient reason for

judge who kills at God's command, since then it is God that kills: because every law is a command of God" In ST II-II, q. 64, a. 2, Aquinas also justifies the killing of a criminal to safeguard the common good. (The same point is made in the SCG 3/2, q. 148, a. 4.) In ST II-II, q. 64, a. 3, he stipulates that this is the prerogative of a public authority only, not of a private individual. The execution of the wicked can be both for "the chastisement of the offender" and for "the good of the state"; see Aquinas, *The Commandments of God*, 23.

35. ST II-II, q. 40, a. 1. Roland Kany points out that Aquinas probably took his citations of Augustine from a collection of excerpts, such as Gratian's *Decretals*, and did not necessarily interpret them in the context of the entire work in which they appear. Yet unless it can be shown that the context reverses the meaning of the specific statements about war, this fact does not amount to an argument that Aquinas's just war theory is not based on Augustine's ideas (granting that Augustine does not have a full, systematic theory of just war). See Roland Kany, "Augustine's Theology of Peace and the Beginning of Christian Just War Theory," in *From Just War to Modern Peace Ethics*, ed. Heinz-Gerhard Justenhoven and William A. Barbieri Jr., Arbeiten zur Kirchengeschichte 120 (Berlin: De Gruyter, 2012), 34. Like classic just war theory in general, Aquinas accepts "offensive war" in the sense of righting a wrong that has already been done, but whose effects continue. This is distinguished from "aggressive war," an unprovoked war waged for reasons such as conquest of territory. See Reichberg, *Aquinas on War*, 276–77.

36. ST II-II, q. 40, a. 1.

37. ST II-II, q. 40, a. 1.

waging war.[38] Punishment or retribution is not a stand-alone rationale for killing people, even from a natural law perspective.[39]

Another way in which Aquinas goes beyond Augustine's three criteria for going to war, is that, in addition to limiting the reasons for waging war (*jus ad bellum*), he demands at least some restraint of means in war (*jus in bello*). Just war will not entail direct falsehood or the breaking of a covenant with the enemy; but ambushes in war are acceptable because the deceptions they require are anticipated by both sides.[40]

Aquinas, then, maintains that war is not always a sin against charity, but he does not make his case primarily in terms of that virtue. Instead, he turns to the virtue of justice. Aquinas's treatment of war in terms of three criteria of justice becomes more complex, nuanced, and perhaps ambiguous if the first article of the question, "Of War" (ST II-II, q. 40)—Whether It Is Always a Sin to Wage a War?—is read in light of two other questions on related subjects. The first is his treatment of self-defense (ST II-II, q. 64, a. 7: "Whether It Is Lawful to Kill a Man in Self-Defense?"). The second is his treatment of religious orders dedicated to military life (ST II-II, q. 188, a. 3: "Whether a Religious Order Can Be Directed to Soldiering?"). The first of these raises the possibility that just wars are imperfectly just; the second the possibility that just wars could embody charity as well as justice. Self-defense will be addressed here in relation to the justice of war. The religious vocation of soldiers will be addressed in the next section, on war and the gospel.

The way Aquinas handles the morality of individual self-defense is different from the way he handles self-defense of a people, nation, or state. Unlike the legitimate sovereign authority, the private individual does not have divinely delegated authority to kill in order to protect the common weal. Yet if the natural law envisions protection of human life as one of

38. Reichberg, *Thomas Aquinas on War and Peace*, 154. Reichberg covers an extensive historical debate on the question whether culpability in itself is an adequate cause for going to war.
39. Arguing to the contrary, along with Biggar, is James Bernard Murphy, "Suarez, Aquinas and the Just War: Self Defense or Punishment?" in *From Just War to Modern Peace Ethics*, 178, citing Aquinas's view that those who are punished must deserve it on account of wrongdoing as evidence that Aquinas sees punishment as a sufficient purpose of war, and that the "core meaning" of punishment is retribution. However, Murphy also acknowledges that punishment is a complex notion that "includes elements of deterrence, remediation, protection, and rehabilitation." If so, then just war as punishment seems ineluctably connected to the criterion of furthering the common good, especially since it is the "common weal," not "punishment," that is the concept that shapes Aquinas's appropriation of Augustine's three criteria for going to war.
40. ST II-II, q. 40, a. 3. Augustine, in contrast, says that once a war is engaged justly, it is permissible to deceive the enemy by "ruses." See Augustine, *Questions on the Heptateuch*, 6.10, Corpus Scriptorum Ecclesiasticorum Latinorum (CSEL) 28: 428; as cited in Swift, *Early Fathers*, 138.

the most fundamental moral and social goods,[41] then why are public officials entirely justified in killing to protect the common good—directly,
intentionally, and with no hint that intention should somehow be distanced from such a horrendous act? Recall that Michael Walzer believes
public officials can have "dirty hands, though it may be the case that they
had acted well and done what their office required." "They have killed
unjustly, let us say, for the sake of justice itself," and they "bear a burden of responsibility and guilt."[42] The purpose of just wars is to preserve
peace, the common good, and the conditions of ordered political society—but war also endangers these very goods and conditions.

Aquinas's analysis of killing in self-defense includes a distinction and a
provision that might be revisited usefully in relation to war, a suggestion
made by Richard Miller.[43] The distinction is between private citizens and
public authorities as agents of justified killing, a distinction also operative in Aquinas's treatment of war. The provision is that, while lawful authorities may directly and intentionally kill to protect the common
good, a private citizen may kill in self-defense only if his or her intention
is focused on saving his or her own life, if killing the aggressor is truly
necessary to self-defense, and remains "beside the intention."[44]

Self-defense, viewed by Aquinas as requiring that infliction of death
as such remain "beside the intention," could be seen as an internally
ambivalent yet unitary action for *the whole of which* the agent bears
responsibility, albeit in different ways and degrees for different aspects.
Killing must be beside the intention precisely because *in itself* it always
has a morally objectionable dimension. Yet even when killing is not the
dominant motive or goal of the self-defending agent, killing is directly if
repugnantly *intended as a means*, subordinate to the goal of saving one's
own life. So redescribed, killing in self-defense represents the unavoidably mixed moral character of forced actions where one or another
obligation must be violated. Why doesn't the provision that the death of
a human being must be distanced from the primary intention ("beside
the intention") of the agent apply on both sides of the distinction—that
is, between the agency of the individual and that of the public official?

Supporting the thesis that public officials and soldiers indeed carry
responsibility for in some way violating the dignity of the aggressor

41. ST I-II, q. 94, a. 2.

42. Walzer, *Just and Unjust Wars*, 323.

43. Richard Miller argues that it is appropriate to generalize from individual self-defense to
killing in war "on analogy" ("Aquinas and the Presumption," 198–200). I agree that the analogy should be made and that Aquinas himself did not make it. If it *is* made, then killing in war
becomes a moral dilemma.

44. See ST II-II, q. 64, a. 3; a. 7.

who is killed, Nigel Biggar argues that "even the life of a wrongful aggressor is a good that deserves care and not hostility."[45] Thus, like Aquinas's self-defending individual, warriors should not "want" the deaths of adversaries. While neither the deaths of individual soldiers nor those of civilians are as such the purpose of killing in war, killing is part of the enterprise of war a whole, the means to the primary political outcome, and indeed the immediate intended effect of actions by soldiers: "wounding or killing is surely integral and not accidental, to what they [soldiers] are choosing to do."[46] Killing in war is war's definitive means, and warriors must and do choose it. Thus, killing is something governments, military officers, and soldiers all "choose with reluctance," yet they are still responsible for it.[47]

My argument begins from a similar premise, although, unlike Biggar, I am not trying to increase moral approbation of war, by confronting and "owning" the wrongness of the killing involved as necessary to and justified by the war enterprise as a whole. Instead, I am arguing that the necessity to choose killing as a means to a greater good constitutes a moral dilemma, *because* "even the life of a wrongful aggressor is a good that deserves care and not hostility."[48] Knowingly killing other human beings always involves the agent in directly wronging another person, and killing is an inherent means of war. Moreover, war always involves civilian deaths, atrocities, and destruction of social infrastructure. This diminishes the moral justifiability of war.

Ultimately, there is no good reason to see killing as less problematic in war than in individual self-defense. In fact, given the erosion of moral constraints in war, the magnitude of its collateral effects, and the cycles of violence to which it leads, killing in war is more problematic, especially so for Christians. This is why, compared to Augustine, Aquinas is highly wary of portraying killing as an outcome of charity. I would put great emphasis on a presumption that war should be avoided in the first place, as I understand Aquinas to have done.

Given Aquinas's treatment of self-defense, one can infer that, since causing a death is not a good in itself, the intention, even of a rightful public authority, should be focused on the good of protecting the common weal—i.e., avoiding the evils that endanger it. Causing deaths in war is no more a proper primary intention for the declaring authority and for the obedient soldier, than it is for the individual facing a threat

---

45. Biggar, *In Defence of War*, 108.
46. Biggar, *In Defence of War*, 103.
47. Biggar, *In Defence of War*, 106. See also Nigel Biggar, "In Response," *Soundings* 97, no. 2 (2014): 254–55.
48. Biggar, *In Defence of War*, 108.

to his or her own life. Aquinas's hesitation and provisionality regarding private killing should be extended to officials who kill or command subordinates to kill in the name of the common good, even if their role demands this and even if the community as a whole has legitimated their authority to do so (as in a modern democracy).

Aquinas's distinction between directly intended killing and killing that, though not accidental, is still something one does not fully "want," might be interpreted—by later readers, not Aquinas himself—as not totally exonerating the agent from culpability for the evil effect that is supposedly "beside the intention." Interestingly, Aquinas's definition of the proper intention of a sovereign declaring a just war opens the door to precisely such a provision in the case of the public authority (not only of the individual): for the legitimate authority to have a "rightful intention" in waging war requires intending "the advancement of good or the avoidance of evil."[49] Neither the private nor the public agent should "want" death in itself, not even the death of the unjust aggressor. Though it may be justified as a necessary means to the greater good, killing (considered in itself) is always a wrong against the basic good of life, and against the irrevocable dignity of a human person.

Gregory Reichberg adds to the plausibility of seeing killing in war as an activity of mixed moral character, when he notes that "on at least one occasion, the term *praeter intentionem* is used by Aquinas to signify an agent's choice of an unwanted means," such as tossing overboard a ship's cargo to avoid capsizing. This is a regrettable choice for which Aquinas creates the category "mixed voluntary." This concept applies to acts that are "repulsive" and "against the will," but that "can nonetheless be rationally desired (chosen) under circumstances of imminent danger." Reichberg sees this as similar to killing in self-defense, for Aquinas.[50] He continues, Aquinas's "purpose is not necessarily to exclude all intentionality whatsoever from the resulting [evil] effects," but rather to deny that they are "desired as the very goal of the agent's action."[51]

Even from the standpoint of justice, there is always something deeply problematic about killing human beings. Aquinas stipulates that killing not be the primary intention in self-defense, presumably because killing violates the basic good of life. The same is implicitly true of authorities declaring war (who he says should intend only the good or avoiding

---

49. ST II-II, q. 40, a. l.

50. Reichberg, *Aquinas on War and Peace*, 181, citing SCG 3/1, q. 6. Here Reichberg references his disagreement with Joseph Boyle, who envisions that the evil effects are outside the intentionality and responsibility of the agent.

51. Reichberg, *Aquinas on War and Peace*, 182.

evil), and of ordinary soldiers, who are taking human life at their superiors' command.[52]

Next, we will turn to the problem of war, considered from the perspective of the gospel and Christian morality. Aquinas seems either to set the virtue of Christian love aside when considering morally necessary wars, or to assign the concrete realization of love's demands to a Christian elite that should not be involved in wars at all. This may be preferable to Augustine's attempted assimilation of killing to love; but it does not capture the sense of real tragedy and wrongfulness that Christians should and do have when killing their fellow human beings, even in a just cause.

WAR AND THE GOSPEL

Although Aquinas defends the reasonableness and justice of war within limited circumstances, he appreciates the difficulty of reconciling just war with the New Testament, which supersedes the "Old Law."[53] In addition to the inherent moral ambiguity of destroying the basic good of life (reflected in Aquinas's treatment of self-defense), the gospel presents even greater challenges to the legitimacy of killing. In the case of war, it seems especially difficult to reconcile the demands of the common good (measured by justice) with those of the gospel (inspired by charity).

Aquinas does not cite Jesus's command to love one's enemies (Matt 5:44; Luke 6:27) as one of the four objections he gives to his justification of war. However, he has treated the obligatory nature of love of enemies earlier in his discussion of charity, in effect categorizing it as a "supererogatory" act, not one to which we are obliged by justice and natural law. Love of enemies constitutes the "perfection of charity," which is "not necessary for salvation." There is no absolute requirement to feel a special attitude of love toward enemies, nor to show them "the signs and effects of love."[54] Nevertheless, "we should be ready to love our enemies individually, if the necessity were to occur," and thus "the mind" should be "prepared to do so."[55] Yet readiness to assist need become action only "in a case of urgency," such as extreme hunger or thirst.[56]

This strategy of relegating obedience to evangelical commands to a

---

52. In Aquinas's view, soldiers are not responsible to evaluate whether the war as a whole is just. Michael Walzer persuasively defends the equality of combatants on the grounds of their relative inability to evaluate the justice of the cause and dissent from it. See Walzer, *Just and Unjust Wars: A Moral Argument with Historical Illustrations* (New York: Basic, 1977), 335–46.

53. ST I-II, q. 107, a. 2.

54. ST II-II, q. 25, a. 8–9.

55. ST II-II, q. 25, a. 8.

56. ST II-II, q. 25, a. 9.

state of mental "readiness" and preparation comes in again in Aquinas's treatment of further biblical objections to war in the question on war. As specific objections to the idea that war is not always a sin, Aquinas brings up two additional precepts attributed to Jesus. Jesus seems to threaten warriors with punishment, because war violates a divine command: "'All those who take the sword shall perish by the sword'" (Matt 26:52). Jesus seems to rule out self-defense entirely in his instruction, "'I say to you not to resist evil'" (Matt 5:39).[57]

To the first objection Aquinas replies that the prohibition of the sword only applies to individuals using it on their own authority, not to authorized public officials or soldiers acting at their command. As argued above, it might have been more consistent with Aquinas's general perspective on the evils attendant on war, if he had applied to killing in war the same caveat he applied to an individual killing in self-defense: protecting the good, rather than causing death in itself, should be the agent's intention. More importantly, Aquinas does not consider whether, apart from the natural law basis for justifying war, a further moral obligation might impinge on the responsibilities of Christian officials and Christians acting at their command.

In replying to the second objection, Aquinas returns to the idea that some gospel commands require only mental preparation to act under special circumstances, not when justice demands a course of action other than what charity ideally prescribes. Following Augustine, Aquinas maintains that nonresistance and similar precepts "should always be borne in readiness of mind, so that we be ready to obey them, and, if necessary, to refrain from resistance or self-defense."[58] Yet justice can still make it necessary "for a man to act otherwise for the common good, or the good of those with whom he is fighting [on the same side]." On self-defense as against the gospel, he makes a similar argument regarding Romans 12:19, "not defending yourselves." He explains that Paul refers only to defense in "vengeful spite."[59] Both these interpretations resemble Augustine's hermeneutic of "inward intention" to define the place of love when killing in war.

Richard Miller suggests that even when carried out by the agents of justice, "war involves justice with regret," or should do so, especially because of its negative relation to charity.[60] Miller is right that an aura of

---

57. ST II-I, q. 40, a. 1, obj. 1–2.
58. Here Aquinas cites Augustine's *Sermon on the Mount*, 1.19.
59. ST II-II, q. 64, a. 7, ad 5.
60. Miller, "Aquinas and the Presumption," 190, 203. Miller concludes that war involves "justice with regret" (203), whereas I am arguing further that it involves or should involve both remorse and active compensatory measures.

moral ambivalence can and should shroud war as presented in Thomistic terms. Yet apparently Aquinas's public authorities do not share the moral quandary of Augustine's judge. After framing war as a potential sin against charity, Aquinas does not elaborate further on ways war could be regrettable because it endangers Christian virtue.

Aquinas partially reinstates the obligatory nature of Jesus's commands about killing, nonresistance and love of enemies by making them binding on certain classes of people. Aquinas combines this with the idea—extending back to Ambrose's discussion of military service—that the calling of the priest is privileged. Clerics and bishops must not fight because "warlike pursuits . . . hinder the mind very much from the contemplation of Divine things." The clergy have a special vocation to imitate the nonviolence of Christ, one not binding without exception for the laity.[61] The ordained cleric—the eucharistic celebrant—must refrain from violent action. In effect, the New Testament ideal of love of neighbor and enemy is simultaneously protected and reduced in the strategy of designating it a special responsibility of those Christians most highly called to live the gospel—but not of ordinary Christians or those involved in war.

Yet in discussing the vocation of religiously dedicated soldiers, Aquinas seems to contradict this distinction. There he does affirm that all Christians are called to serve God in charity, though in the ways suited to their states of life. Not only in the "contemplative life," but also in the "active life" the Christian is dedicated to "helping our neighbor," and that includes Christian soldiers for whom military life can be a religious vocation.[62] He cites Augustine's counsel to Boniface, recalling that, like David, "those can please God who handle warlike weapons." And he explicitly brings the profession of the soldier under the love command, by including protection of the common good under service to one's neighbor: "Now the occupation of soldiering may be directed to the assistance of our neighbor, not only as regards private individuals, but also as regards the defense of the whole commonwealth."[63] Implicitly, then, love of neighbor (protection of the innocent) can be a motivation and purpose of war, though this is not a line of argument that appears in Aquinas's primary analysis of war, in the first article of the question "Of War." Like Augustine, Aquinas entertains the idea that use of armed force could be an act of love, though he specifies it (contrary to Augustine) as love for the ones protected, not love for the target.

---

61. ST II-II, q. 40, a. 2; q. 64, a. 4.
62. ST II-II, q. 188, a. 3: "Whether a Religious Order Can Be Directed to Soldiering?" The types of active service for which (nonclerical) religious orders were established included "the purpose of soldiering."
63. ST II-II, q. 188, a. 3; citing Augustine, "Letter 189, to Boniface."

Moreover, in the question on military service as a religious vocation, Aquinas confronts the challenge of Jesus's saying about nonresistance differently than in the question on war.[64] Instead of distancing Christian love from the practical morality of the situation by making it a mental attitude, he argues that, while the gospel duty of nonresistance might apply to individual self-defense, defending the vulnerable can be a duty that it would be wrong to neglect. It might actually be vicious to refrain from acting when the welfare of others is at stake. Using armed force is better than "tolerating patiently the wrongs done to others."[65]

This idea that armed force could express the love command connects to an intriguing comment that Aquinas does make in II-II, q. 40 ("Of War"), not in the first and main article ("Whether It Is Always a Sin to Wage a War?") but in the second article on clerics and bishops. There he takes up the objection that if clerics can counsel others to fight, they should be allowed to fight as well. Aquinas does not accept that clerics can fight (for the reasons cited above). However, he does agree that clerics can advise others to do so, for (just) war as undertaken by Christians is not only not a sin but it should be considered to serve "the Divine spiritual good to which clerics are deputed."[66] This idea does not occur in his first and primary response to the justice of war in relation to charity, and he does not explain exactly how war relates to any spiritual good. Does the question of religious soldiering shed any light on this question? Could the Christian sovereign's cause and intention in declaring war be analogized to the Christian soldier's service of the vulnerable neighbor?

Aquinas does not use this strategy to explain how it is that war is not always a sin against charity in the question "Of War." Yet in a different question, on soldiers, Aquinas says not only that their act of gospel service "may be directed to the assistance of our neighbor" but also that the neighbor served in war is not limited to "private individuals, but also . . . regards *the defense of the whole commonwealth*."[67] Defense of the commonwealth is specifically the responsibility of public authorities and is the cause that makes war just. Taken together, these remarks seem to

64. ST II-II, q. 188, a. 3.obj.1. Here Aquinas considers the argument that "our Lord said with reference to the perfection of Christian life (Matt 5:39): *I say to you not to resist evil; but if one strike thee on the right cheek, turn to him also the other,* which is inconsistent with the duties of a soldier."

65. ST II-II, q. 188, a. 3, ad 1; citing Ambrose's *On Duties* 1.27.

66. ST II-II, q. 40, a. 2, ad 3. Darrell Cole regards this text as significant to his argument that war is an expression of charity. (See Cole, "Thomas Aquinas on Virtuous Warfare," 67.) I agree that it is significant but believe that Aquinas's reliance (in the main body of this article) on reasons having to with justice and the common good, while bracketing gospel sayings against violence, is more significant for deciding his general or dominant view of the relation of war to charity.

67. ST II-II, q. 188, a. 3. Italics added.

imply that the just cause and intention of legitimate authorities making war could be forms of love of neighbor.

In summary, in the one question devoted to the ethics of war, Aquinas does not explicitly envision killing in war as an expression of Christian love. Whereas Augustine's primary justification of war is love, Thomas Aquinas's is justice. He argues that war avoids being a violation of charity (and thus a sin) when it meets three criteria of justice: lawful authority, right intention, and just cause—all of which center on protecting and furthering the "common weal." Gestures toward the incomplete justice of war and the function of love in motivating war show that Aquinas saw connections of war to Christian responsibility, was ambivalent about the morality of war, was in an ongoing process of reflection on war, and/or that he saw the inherent contradictions in Christian justifications of war. But the fact remains that, after placing war under charity, Aquinas does not then proceed by showing how war fulfills the virtue of charity. He uses various tactics to distance war from love, justifying it instead in terms of justice and the common good.

On the one hand, removing love from the justification of war guards against distortions of the meaning of Christian charity. On the other hand, it also prevents Christian love from having any recognized effect on decisions about war and its conduct (as one might infer it should have, from Aquinas's question on Christian military orders). But there is a possibility that, in Aquinas's larger and less systematic vision, war could be *both* a just and even charitable means of last resort; *and* killing, considered in itself, could always be a wrong against the good of human life. If so, then killing in war might be an irreducible moral dilemma—even though Aquinas argues in II-II, q. 40, a. 1 for its unambiguous justice. We will return to killing in war as a moral dilemma after considering Aquinas's view of the armed coercion of religious belief.

RELIGION AND COERCION

Modifying his three criteria of a just war, Aquinas, like Augustine, accepts the use of force in safeguarding true worship of God, because it is necessary to peace and the common good as having both a natural and a spiritual dimension. "For it is a much graver matter to corrupt the faith which quickens the soul, than to forge money, which supports temporal life. Wherefore if forgers of money and other evil-doers are forthwith condemned to death by the secular authority, much more reason is there for heretics." Beside the defense of "public safety" and of "the poor and oppressed," the profession of soldiering "can also be directed to the upkeep of divine worship."[68] Like Augustine, Aquinas bolsters this claim with reference to Old Testament figures (Judas Maccabeus and Simon).[69] But Aquinas is more reluctant than Augustine to justify the actual use of force to protect religion. Although he considers pagan and even Jewish rites to be sinful, he advises moderation in measures to eliminate them. The comprehensive common good must be the aim of human government, as of divine government, and the common good may recommend toleration. The rites of unbelievers "may be tolerated, either on account of some good that ensues therefrom, or because of some evil avoided," for instance, "scandal or disturbance."[70] Moreover, it is unjust to baptize the children of unbelievers without parental consent: "it would be contrary to natural justice, if a child, before coming to the use of reason, were to be taken away from its parents' custody, or anything done to it against its parents' wish."[71]

Unbelieving persons or groups are to be constrained by force only when necessary to put an end to blasphemy and persecution of Christians: "these are by no means to be compelled to the faith, in order that they may believe, because to believe depends on the will." Heretics are a separate case, because they once embraced the faith, then willfully turned away.[72] They are to be twice admonished before they are excommunicated, in the hope that they will return to the church and be saved. Aquinas connects exhortation rather than violence with the hope of conversion. Yet if heretics refuse to retract, death (at the hands of the temporal authority) is not an excessive measure to spare the common good their influence.

In sum, Aquinas is unlike Augustine in his approach to war, because Aquinas does not assume that the Christian community is fundamentally at odds with the requirements of the common good, reasonably established. Christians can articulate and endorse reasons for and limits on war that make sense in the light of justice. This is why a twenty-first century Thomistic social ethics can work on the premise that Aquinas has "no obvious sectarian bias," and does not say "the fundamental principles of justice or morality depend on any kind of Christian revelation."[73] For Aquinas, peace in political community, while always in progress and never perfect, is furthered by justice and the rule of law much more

68. ST II-II, q. 188, a. 3.
69. ST II-II, q. 188, a. 3. For a discussion of other texts in which Aquinas defends the protection of religion by civil authority, see Russell, *War in the Middle Ages*, 261.
70. ST II-II, q. 10, a. 11.
71. ST II-II, q. 10, a. 12.
72. ST II-II, q. 10, a. 8.
73. Porter, *Justice as a Virtue*, 56–57.

emphatically than for Augustine, for whom the possibility of a genuine earthly peace is constantly overshadowed by the distant peace of the Heavenly City, of which it is a "miserable" approximation.

Aquinas certainly agrees with Augustine that charity, as friendship for God, surpasses the capacity of natural virtue and depends on the grace of the Holy Spirit.[74] And charity means the Christian "makes an earnest endeavor to give his time to God and Divine things, while scorning other things except insofar as the needs of the present life demand."[75] Yet the present life demands a lot. For Aquinas, the "needs of the present life" include fairness, justice, and a reasonable attempt to discern and live by the obligations of the natural law, the fulfillment of which brings not only virtue and happiness, but a just and cooperative mode of social living.

Augustine more overtly retains the eschatological ideal of love, by banishing self-defense and struggling to press violence into love's direct service. Aquinas strives for a prudent balance of justice and love by regarding conflict in the light of natural law and the common good, by subjecting violence to the test of justice, and by assigning perfect fidelity to the love command to a designated Christian subset. Unlike Augustine, Aquinas does not try to explain how exactly charity could be forming justice as killing in war. Aquinas's approach has the merit of keeping a distance between even justified force and the commands and example of Jesus. At the same time, however, he places those commands at the margins of Christian social ethics, seeming to envision that in some spheres or situations of life they need only be remotely formative of Christian character and action. Neither Aquinas nor Augustine ventures clear criteria to determine when and how the Christian disciple will practically realize his or her ostensible "readiness of mind" to live up to Jesus's nonviolent word and example, which seem to require the sacrifice of at least some goods that could be defended "justly."

MORE ON WAR AS A MORAL DILEMMA

I argued in the last chapter that, despite his depiction of the torturing judge as morally compromised, Augustine avoids the problem of a true moral dilemma in war by reconciling the requirements of Christian love and of temporal justice by means of two inconsistent and ultimately unconvincing strategies. He claims that justly punitive killing is an expression of love for the one killed, while also maintaining that the Ser-

74. ST II-II, q. 23, a. 1; q. 24, a. 3.
75. ST II-II, q. 24, a. 8.

mon on the Mount speaks to the Christian's internal attitude rather than his or her outward actions. In my view, even if killing is sometimes justified insofar as it protects the innocent, it is never wholly and unequivocally justified, especially from a Christian perspective, as it involves the destruction of human life. Remorse is an appropriate response even when killing seems justified as the lesser of two evils. Augustine does realize that the Christian priority is to avoid war and other types of violence, not to justify them, and that all practical measures possible should be taken to avoid war, reduce its destruction, end conflicts, and forgive and rehabilitate combatants and other offenders. Thus, as a bishop, he made strenuous efforts to influence imperial policy and the behavior of Christian officials to reduce the violent nature of civil government.

Although Aquinas's theological-ethical outlook is not beset by internal conflict as much as Augustine's, it does hint at a lower-intensity ambivalence on the approval of war and killing as tools of civil government. For Aquinas, justice requires the protection of earthly peace, entailing measures sufficient to protect society's basic institutions and the lives and welfare of society's members. Yet how can killing be aligned with the Christian virtue of charity, the Christian vocation to love all neighbors, or even the natural obligations to protect life and to recognize that individual human lives can never be subordinated entirely to the "body politic"?[76]

As we have seen, in the context of his most explicit discussion of the morality of war, Aquinas's way out of this quandary is to set the practical expression of Christian love outside the enterprise of justified war. Like Augustine, he sees the Christian warrior as "ready" to express love rather than called to do so in practice. Furthermore, Aquinas assigns the virtues of love and justice to different roles (clerical and military) in the Christian community. This solution is not much more satisfying than Augustine's division of intention and act. If charity furnishes the basic form of the Christian life, it is hard to see how its practical embodiment can be bracketed for some Christians—or for all Christians some of the time.

At the very least, I believe, it must be recognized that if killing in war can be justified at all, it still presents an irreducible moral dilemma, especially (though not only) from the standpoint of Christian ethics. As argued in chapters 1 and 4, an irreducible moral dilemma is a situation in which any option involves the agent in wronging others, *even if* so doing is part of a course of action chosen over others on the grounds of "lesser evil" and proportion. In war, the dilemma consists in the reality that respect for human life, as well as love of neighbor and enemy, exclude

76. ST I-II, q. 2, a. 2, ad 3; q. 21, a. 4, ad 3.

violence; but love of and justice for the innocent neighbor (or self, or community) require protection from deadly assault, by violent force as last resort.

If the use of violent force that results in human deaths can be accepted at all, it must be accepted as the product of a moral conflict, in which it may be possible but never easy to make a choice, and one in which even a justifiable choice involves some degree of moral culpability. Coming to the aid of the vulnerable neighbor is a moral imperative; respecting the lives of all human beings (including enemies) is a moral imperative too. Conversely, turning aside from a neighbor in need is a dereliction of duty and a betrayal of virtue; killing another human being violates a commandment and contradicts the example of Jesus. These are biblical warning signs, even granting that Scripture does not provide an absolute guide to specific moral behavior.

When aid takes the form of lethal force, love is operative in the choice to lend aid, but the will and intention are ambivalent in that they are simultaneously directed to killing as a means. Aquinas provides that even when one is justifiably killing an aggressor in self-defense, the death must remain beside the intention, a caveat that should be extended to killing in war. Yet when killing is chosen as a means, injury and destruction of life are not literally "beside" the intention, they are regrettable *and* remorse-worthy subsidiary aspects of it.

If the situation of choice is an irreducible moral dilemma, the agent can both have acted rightly and have intended and caused unjust harm to another. The greater good has been chosen and attained, but the intention and will of the agent have still been engaged in causing a harm that is wrongful if one regards the one harmed in his or her own right (even unjust aggressors retain dignity and their lives value). Even if and when killing can be justified, the agent will have failed in treating the one killed with full justice, and that agent will have failed to express Christian love in direct relation to that person. In such a case, the agent should not be condemned, but may justifiably experience remorse, and deserve human empathy, compassion, solidarity, forgiveness and mercy. The agent is also obliged to take compensatory and restorative measures, as are the social bodies or authorities on whose behalf the agent acts.

Contrary to this reading, most later interpreters of what came to be known as "the principle of double effect" have used it to set conditions under which an act with both a good and an evil effect may be justified without any culpability or remorse whatsoever, provided the good effect only is directly intended and done.[77] Many later interpreters add the

---

77. See John Finnis, "War and Peace in the Natural Law Tradition," in John Finnis, *Human*

stipulation that the evil effect cannot be a means to the good effect, a condition that would not be met in Aquinas's instance of killing in self-defense.[78] For Aquinas, killing is precisely the means in self-defense, even though the agent regrets that such an extreme measure is called for; the death of the assailant is not wanted as an outcome in its own right (which would be "unlawful," according to Aquinas), and it would be avoided if possible.

The function of double effect (both in Aquinas's prototype and in later developments) is to acknowledge that a virtuous agent properly oriented to objective goods can still be involved in the causation of evil, while keeping that evil away from the core of moral identity. But even though the agent may emerge with basic integrity intact, the fact that sometimes agents are, as Rosalind Hursthouse says, permanently "marred" by what they have done, reveals that forced choices can be profoundly morally conflicted, and that the rubric of double effect may not adequately capture the relation of the agent to the evil done. James Keenan argues that it is "disturbing" and "dangerous" to presume that double effect can by itself and neatly "rescue us from otherwise regrettable courses of action," inventing, if necessary, "solutions that are convoluted simply to conform to the principle's conditions."[79] Dilemmas involving both good and evil cannot always be resolved by partitioning intentionality, and in some cases they can undermine the self's sense of moral integrity, of being one who is at peace with one's moral history.

John Bowlin likewise supports the idea that irresolvable conflicts of goods play a bigger part in Aquinas's ethics than is usually granted. Bowlin argues that the roles of contingency and fortune are so great in Aquinas's ethics that virtues should be understood precisely as enabling humans to negotiate difficult and distressing circumstances. "Hence it is essential to virtue to be about the difficult and the good."[80] Thomas does not expect, according to Bowlin, that any particular rules (such as those

Rights and the Natural Law Tradition, vol. 3 (Cambridge: Cambridge University Press, 2011), 206.

78. For discussions see Joseph T. Mangan, SJ, "An Historical Analysis of the Principle of Double Effect," *Theological Studies* 10, no. 1 (1949): 41–61; John C. Ford, SJ, "The Morality of Obliteration Bombing," *Theological Studies* 5, no. 3 (1944): 261–309; and Alison MacIntyre, "The Doctrine of Double Effect," *Stanford Encyclopedia of Philosophy*, accessed April 9, 2017, https://tinyurl.com/ybugfq27.

79. James F. Keenan, "The Function of the Principle of Double Effect," *Theological Studies* 54, no. 2 (1993): 294, 311. Keenan argues that the principle of double effect is not a formula for guaranteeing moral certainty, but a set of generalizations from cases that have been prudently resolved in the past. It is important to assess each case in light of other cases that are similar to it, not just in terms of the provisions of the principle.

80. John Bowlin, *Contingency and Fortune in Aquinas's Ethics*, Cambridge Studies in Religion and Critical Thought (Cambridge: Cambridge University Press, 1999), 30–31; see also 5.

of just war or double effect) can guide us through the perplexing and distressing contingencies we face. Knowing and willing the good are prohibitively difficult, so much so that happiness in this life is impossible. While I believe this overstates the futility of rules and the pervasiveness of happiness-destroying moral uncertainty in Aquinas's own outlook, Bowlin does provide a needed reminder that for Aquinas, moral reason is practical reason. Practical reason is situated and contingent; real, compelling, and competing goods can in concrete situations tear the agent in different directions.

Yet it is just because competing goods *can* be clearly known and desired, and even felt to be equally commanding, that circumstances in which they are irreconcilable amount to moral dilemmas. Furthermore, even when it is possible reasonably to choose one competing good over another in a given situation, the violated good still exerts a moral claim and morally burdens the agent. Aquinas does presuppose a knowable order of goods for human beings, an order in light of which they can and should order their choices. He evidently believes that moral reason can in principle unknot any practical dilemma.[81] Yet his discussions of war, self-defense, and intentionality internally undermine those premises as not "true to life." Killing, even when to save an equal or greater good than life or to avoid a greater evil, presents a genuine moral quandary, intensely so for Christians. This quandary is tacitly acknowledged when Aquinas suggests that the gospel does not apply in the realm of just war and argues that self-defensive killing should not be seen as key to one's intention.

While a long and strong tradition in Christianity entirely rules out the use of violence as a contradiction of the gospel, a less long but historically stronger tradition has, as a last resort, accepted and even advocated violence aimed at ordering society and protecting the innocent. The former tradition is morally unsatisfactory in that it accepts (and exempts the Christian agent from responsibility for) grievous harm to the innocent, as well as to social structures essential to human well-being. The latter tradition is likewise unsatisfactory in that it deliberately undertakes the destruction of human life (albeit for a "just cause") and inevitably entails the deaths of innocent human beings and harm to essential social struc-

81. I see Aquinas as assuming that in general humans can successfully discern, choose, and do the good even in complicated cases; that the virtuous life is on the whole the happy life; and that politics and government can be sufficiently guided by the cardinal (and implicitly the theological) virtues to represent or accomplish respect for individual humans and for the common good. For more on Aquinas and irreducible moral dilemmas, including why he denies them and why there are contrary hints in his ethics, see Katherine Jackson-Meyer, "Tragic Dilemmas," 72–136.

tures. This tradition, the just war tradition, is especially problematic for Christians, who are called to imitate Christ and embody the virtue of charity in the whole of life. Pacifism cannot be established unambiguously as the definitive Christian vocation; yet just war theory and practice present Christians and Christian ethics even more acutely with an irreducible moral dilemma—that is, one that cannot be fully resolved, analytically or practically. Yet agents must act. Regret, remorse, and remediation are appropriate responses in such instances, most certainly so when actions responsive to social disorder involve Christians in killing.

Rosemary Kellison has argued, drawing on feminist critiques of intention theories, that the use of double effect and indirect intention in the historical development of just war theory have made the just war tradition too permissive of war.[82] A particular concern is the justification of civilian deaths in war as indirectly intended "collateral damage" accompanying directly intended attacks on military targets. Kellison's discussion is germane to Aquinas's analysis of the morality of war, particularly considering that if his view of intentionality in self-defense were applied to his discussion of just war, the result would be a more ambiguous ethics of war.

Kellison proposes that neither the circumstances nor the effects of our actions are fully under our control—there is no such thing as "pure agency," and we are all at the mercy of "moral luck" to some extent. This resonates with Aquinas's view of the situatedness and contingency of practical reason.[83] Nevertheless, according to Kellison, agents are held responsible—and hold themselves responsible—for responding to unforeseen events and for the causation of unintended effects.[84] The moral quality of an action should not be judged by an untenable and opaque inward agential division of the intended and unintended components of one action, but by the actual character of the action taken, complete with its conditions and effects, whether foreseen or not. Responsibility is relational, historical, and dynamic. "We can evaluate intention by looking at what an agent in war does, what level of care the agent takes, and how well the agent learns from past mistakes and implements changes that demonstrate commitment to the right intention as the war progresses."[85] Even though there might not be direct moral or legal culpability for destructive actions taken in war, communities participating in war "take

---

82. Rosemary B. Kellison, "Impure Agency and the Just War: A Feminist Reading of Right Intention," *Journal of Religious Ethics* 43, no. 2 (2015): 317–41.

83. ST I-II, q. 90–94, especially q. 94, a. 4–5.

84. Kellison, "Impure Agency," 327. Here Kellison uses the work of Thomas Nagle, Bernard Williams, Claudia Card, and Margaret Urban Walker.

85. Kellison, "Impure Agency," 337.

on a responsibility to engage in moral repair, responding to the suffering and harm they cause," and "restoring the moral relationships."[86]

Julie Rubio confirms this conclusion in a social-ethical critique of the moral-theological categories of complicity and cooperation in Catholic moral theology. She maintains that it is not enough to debate the conditions under which an individual agent might be excused for facilitation of social evil. Rubio builds on the work of African American womanist theologians to make the case that prophetic resistance to evil is also necessary.[87] Traditionally, agents could be absolved of complicity (willing and hence culpable facilitation of wrongdoing) under certain conditions having to do with limitation of freedom of choice, one's moral attitude to the wrong done, and the causal relationship of one's own action to the evil outcome.[88] But today we have a new sensitivity to our responsibility for patterns of social injustice, however indirect or unwilling our involvement in them is. "If assessing responsibility is complicated, denying all responsibility for social sin seems inadequate."[89] Womanist theologians such as Shawn Copeland, Delores Williams, and Jamie Phelps put more emphasis on resistance to structural evil than avoidance of personal sin. Even if any one action or initiative may be limited, and even if goods do truly conflict, radical theologians and Christian activists urge us to take personal and collective responsibility for "noncooperation with evil, engagement with local communities and alternative ways of living."[90]

When applied to military violence, all this means that remorse and repentance are not sufficient "solutions" to the moral dilemma of war. The damage of war must be limited and repaired as far as possible; even more importantly, all efforts must be made to avoid war and killing of any kind. Christians and the Christian churches must resist cooperation with divisive, exploitative and hate-mongering social forces; must engage with or within local communities that are divided, oppressed, or enduring the scourge of violence; and must seek alternative, nonviolent, peace-seeking modes of resolving conflicts and building community.

---

86. Kellison, "Impure Agency," 337.

87. Julie Hanlon Rubio, "Cooperation with Evil Reconsidered: The Moral Duty of Resistance," *Theological Studies* 78, no. 1 (2017): 96–120.

88. See Thomas R. Kopfensteiner and James F. Keenan, "The Principle of Cooperation," *Health Progress* (April 1995): 23–27; M. Cathleen Kaveny, "Complicity with Evil," *Criterion* (Autumn 2003): 20–29.

89. Rubio, "Cooperation with Evil Reconsidered," 100.

90. Rubio, "Cooperation with Evil Reconsidered," 109.

AQUINAS AND PEACEBUILDING?

In the case of Augustine, we have seen that pastorally and practically, he did strive to mediate conflicts and avoid the infliction of death as a tool of government. Aquinas has a more positive view of the potential of government to attain justice than Augustine. Yet he doesn't seem to place equal confidence in the ability of Christian leaders to work with government and civil society to reduce violence and avoid killing, a consequence that would seemingly follow from his presumption against war and his commitment to the common good. This difference between Aquinas and Augustine might be more apparent than real, in that Augustine's letters provide records to his political activities that we lack from Aquinas.

Judging by the writings we do have, however, Aquinas was not engaged in and did not exhort others to proactive mediation of conflict and remediation of the consequences of violence. Why not? An obvious answer is that Aquinas lived in an era in which the pope wielded worldly power and the emperor claimed the mantle of Christianity in using force. Aquinas himself came from a family of knights. Perhaps he was not disposed to question the basic legitimacy of military force as consistent with a Christian vocation. Still, it is regrettable that Aquinas did not rise above his culture on this issue, as he did in appropriating elements of Aristotle's philosophy. Instead of confronting military force on the basis of Christian identity, he allowed the legitimacy of the former to sideline the practical expression of the latter. As a contemporary commentator laments in concluding a discussion of Aquinas's position, "Nothing is more characteristic of the classic just war tradition than the doctrine that state officials are emancipated from the most basic norms of Christian morality."[91]

But if we look more broadly at Aquinas's theology, can we find resources to support the idea not only that war is a moral dilemma but that charity can and does remain active in Christian politics and in decisions about just war? Aquinas does not argue this himself—or, at most, he argues it only in a marginal way. But are there in his theological ethics grounds to argue that Christians can and should be conflict-mediators and peacebuilders who make it their priority to influence governments and civil society to utilize nonviolent means, rather than killing, to fend off threats to the common good? Can it be argued, with Augustine, that charity is operative in all Christians' decisions and actions, including those surrounding the prospect of war?

91. Murphy, "Suarez, Aquinas and the Just War," 186.

A promising lead in this direction is the way in which Aquinas indicates, in his writings on grace and virtue, the constant effects of charity, enabling and elevating the natural virtues throughout the Christian moral life. Arguably, Aquinas's deflection of the effects of charity in the just warrior (in his primary treatment of war) is not consistent with his portrayal of Christian moral agency overall.[92] First, the graced versions of the moral virtues that are supposedly "infused" with charity should enhance the potential of even natural justice to achieve peace and reconciliation in human society, insofar as natural justice is served by Christians. In addition to the infused moral virtues (prudence, justice, fortitude, and temperance), Christians also receive the gifts of the Spirit (wisdom, understanding, counsel, courage, knowledge, piety, and fear of the Lord), and the fruits of the Spirit (charity, joy, peace, patience, long-suffering, goodness, benignity, meekness, faith or fidelity, modesty, continence, and chastity).

The infused virtues transform the natural virtues by placing them within one's friendship with God, making the agent more ready and able to do "each different kind of good work."[93] The gifts are "inner promptings that additionally dispose Christians to follow the guidance of the Spirit, even where reason and justice are concerned.[94] The fruits are actions inspired by the Spirit, realizing the effects of grace (the agent's friendship with God) in the entire moral life of the Christian, including its social, political, and institutional dimensions.[95] The infused virtues, fruits, and gifts represent the active, transforming presence of God in the entirety of Christian existence. Certainly this presence entails an unwavering commitment to reconciliation and peace, even when Christians are convinced that refusal to take up arms against evil would render them "guilty bystanders" (Thomas Merton's phrase).

Obviously both charity and justice require that armed violence be a last resort, since there is a presumption against it. The overriding goal must always be the protection of innocents, and resort to violence minimized. Violence is more likely to lead to spirals of violence than a peaceful and just future for all—showing why the criteria of last resort and proportion are essential. The infused moral virtues, gifts, and fruits of the Spirit attune the Christian agent situationally to exercise mercy, spare suffering, seek reconciliation, and build community within war-torn regions and among enemies, before and during conflicts, as well as after open violence has subsided.

---

92. ST II-II, q. 40, a. 1.
93. ST I-II, q. 65, a. 3.
94. ST I-II, q. 68, a. 3; II-II, qq. 45; 52; 57.
95. ST I-II, q. 70, a. 1.

SUBSEQUENT DEVELOPMENTS

Although both Augustine and Aquinas emphasize the right to go to war over temperance within it, attention to right means was also on the agenda by the end of the Middle Ages, finally yielding the key principle of noncombatant immunity. James Turner Johnson notes that the *jus ad bellum* was affirmed within the church by canon law and by scholastic theology, while two secular sources contributed to the *jus in bello*: (1) the chivalric code of conduct prescribing that warfare and warlike contests of valor were to be conducted with tightly regulated gamesmanship and (2) the gradual and increasingly detailed specification of the Roman concept of *ius gentium,* which became a sort of common law for Christendom.[96]

The extension of the criteria of the just war beyond this cultural boundary, as well as the recognition that both parties to a conflict may have some right on their side, are the contributions of the sixteenth-century Spanish Dominican Francisco de Vitoria (ca. 1492–1546). Johnson refers to Vitoria's formulation of just war doctrine as "the first clear and complete statement of what has come to be conceived as the classic requirements of the doctrine of just war."[97] These requirements, although variously formulated, are generally understood to include, under *jus ad bellum,* legitimate authority (expressed in a declaration of war), just cause, right intention, and the purpose of peace or the common good (with regard to the attainment of which there must be a "reasonable hope of success") and, under *jus in bello,* discrimination or noncombatant immunity, and proportionality of damage caused to good achieved as a limitation on the weapons or tactics of war.

Born in Burgos, Vitoria was educated by the Dominicans there, and later at a Dominican college in Paris and at the University of Paris. Ultimately, he achieved a distinguished professorship in theology at the University of Salamanca. In Vitoria's era, not only did Europeans discover "the New World" and subject its native inhabitants to the rule of the Spanish emperor Charles V (also the Holy Roman Emperor), they experienced destabilizing changes on their own continent. Francis I of France weakened Charles's control over Europe at a time when the unity of the Latin Church was disrupted by the Protestant Reformation. In the early sixteenth century, European intellectuals debated whether "the Indians"

96. James Turner Johnson, "Morality and Force in Statecraft: Paul Ramsey and the Just War Tradition," in *Love and Society: Essays in the Ethics of Paul Ramsey,* ed. James Johnson and David Smith (Missoula, MT: Scholars, 1974), 96–101.

97. Johnson, "Morality and Force in Statecraft," 95.

were wild human beings without civilization and so could be treated as slaves, a position that conveniently supported their exploitation by the Europeans.[98]

Around 1540, Vitoria authored two works dealing with war, specifically with the conquest of the native populations by the Spanish in the New World. These are *De Indis (On the Indians)* and *Dejure Belli (On the Law of War)*. Appalled at reports of plundering and massacres, particularly in Peru, Vitoria drew on scholastic theology to establish a common law of nature, entailing reciprocal obligations between the Europeans and the "Indians."[99] He was also influenced by the demonstrated capacity of many of the Indians to receive the gospel. Following Aquinas's view that grace fulfills nature, Vitoria draws the conclusion that the Indians must have been created with a rational nature suited to the gift of salvation.[100] The peoples of the New World are included in the fundamental unity of humankind.

Although Vitoria does not abandon the idea that religious authority can command war legitimately, the morality of war is adjudicated largely on universalistic grounds, backed by doctrines of creation and redemption.[101] According to Vitoria, the *ius gentium* (the law of nations) originates in reason, is common to all peoples, and includes the rights to hospitality, free travel, and trade. The *principes* of the early modern states had the obligation not only to preserve the common good within their own states, but to seek and protect it in the international order.[102] Regarding the rights of (European) princes to declare war, Vitoria cautions that even the authorities "should first of all not go seeking occasions and causes of war, but should, if possible, live in peace with all men." Moreover, even potential adversaries are "neighbors, whom we are bound to love as ourselves." "For it is the extreme of savagery to seek for and rejoice in grounds for killing and destroying men whom God has created and for whom Christ has died. But only under compulsion and reluctantly should he come to the necessity of war."[103] While medieval

---

98. Heinz-Gerhard Justenhoven, "Francisco de Vitoria: Just War as Defense of International Law," in *From Just War to Modern Peace Ethics*, 122–23.

99. See also LeRoy Walters, "Historical Applications of the Just War Theory: Four Case Studies in Normative Ethics," in *Love and Society*, 120–24.

100. Justenhoven, "Vitoria," 124.

101. For an argument that religious war remains central for Vitoria, see Melvin Endy, "Francisco de Vitoria and Francisco Suarez on Religious Authority and Cause for Justified War: The Centrality of Religious War in the Christian Just War Tradition," *Journal of Religious Ethics* 46, no. 2 (2018): 289–331.

102. Justenhoven, "Vitoria," 130–33.

103. This passage occurs near the conclusion of *De Jure Belli*. Franciscus de Vitoria, *De Indis et de Iure Belli Relectiones*, ed. Ernest Nys (Washington, DC: Carnegie Institution, 1917), 187.

just war discussion had for all practical purposes occurred within Christian cultures, Vitoria uses both humanitarian and religious grounds to extend it to non-Christians, while excluding religion as a valid cause of war.

Finally, Vitoria realizes that both sides in a war maybe legitimately believe themselves to be fighting in a just cause, which raises the prospect that the criteria of just war may not provide a clear resolution of its morality in a given case. Therefore, every head of state must be exceedingly circumspect in justifying war, and the victor in a war has a continuing obligation to adjudicate matters impartially for the common good after hostilities have ceased. Any war and any action in war must be undertaken with a view to the peace and security not only of the individual state but of the international community.[104] Vitoria uses criteria of the international common good, of the humanity of all combatants, and of the caution required given the dubious justice of war to establish a presumption against war that is more explicit, more grounded in the gospel, and also more universalistic than that proposed by Aquinas.

CONCLUSION

To view just war in terms of a conflict of duties means that even when the duty to avoid violence is overridden, it continues to function in the course of actions via restraint and eventual efforts at restoration. Hence just war criteria may challenge the status quo and, at least ideally, undermine cultural assumptions that violence is always warranted in pursuit of political goals. I have argued that the duty not to kill can never be overridden unambiguously, constituting killing in war as at best a genuine and irreducible moral dilemma. If this is so, then the duties to find alternatives to war, to restrain war, and to remedy the consequences of war, are even more urgent.

Although neither fully resolves the paradox of Christian justification of war, both Augustine and Aquinas continue in subsequent centuries to influence the unfolding just war tradition. From the Augustinian side, the extension of love to cover killing the "loved" victim is taken up by the Protestant Reformers. Twentieth-century authors like Reinhold Niebuhr and Paul Ramsey also build violence out of love, though more narrowly and plausibly as service to the victimized but innocent neighbor.

In the Thomistic tradition, the killing of aggressors is legitimated as a requirement of natural justice and right order. This rationale is taken

104. Justenhoven, "Vitoria," 134–35.

up in Roman Catholicism, for example, by John Courtney Murray and Bryan Hehir. From one point of view, it could be more dangerous to remove access to armed conflict from the realm governed by love than to subject it to that most stringent criterion. But from another, it is safer to make the steps of war accountable to clearly defined and "reasonable" standards and to refrain from claiming that destruction of life is a straightforward application of Jesus's command to love others as oneself. I believe that in either case—whether one holds war to the standard of love or to that of justice—the standard cannot be unambiguously met. War is an irreducible moral dilemma. This is not a rationale for excusing war, but rather a cause of remorse and remediation. War—understood as always involving agents in some level of moral culpability—should motivate even more intense and urgent transformational and compensatory action than war viewed as clearly justified (though regrettable).

The next chapter will deal with the Reformation development of Augustinian thought. The subsequent one will take up the crusading ideology that was prevalent during the Middle Ages and lasted into the religious wars of the Reformation period. For crusade and holy war apologists, the sense of paradox about violence is heightened by and finally submerged in a righteous sense that a divinely mandated cause demands the most extreme measures. As will be shown, the crusade ethic leaves few traces of the tradition's sense of contradiction inherent in the Christian use of violence, affirmation of the humanity of the foe, or ideal of Christian love as transforming antagonistic relations.

6.

Reformation Interpretations of Just War
Luther and Calvin

Historians agree that European society in the fifteenth and sixteenth centuries was defined by change: economic, political, social, religious and theological. Differing and even antagonistic schools of thought in the late-medieval European universities represented intellectual diversification and hence a challenge to the authority of the papacy. Northern European humanist thinkers subverted contemporary religious authorities by championing a "return to the sources" of antiquity. The conciliarist movement was an attempt at reform from within the Church, and its failure as well as the destabilizing effect of the Great Schism (1378–1417) was a stimulus toward the acceptance of Reformation ideas.[1]

Parallel developments precipitated political and economic unrest. Secular rulers sought greater national power and gained increasing control of church affairs. Even the power of the independent "states" of Europe was not always solidly constructed over against some of the more wealthy or influential nobles or subjects, although rulers did have more authority over territories than in the medieval feudal system. In many areas of northern Europe, peasants and agricultural workers swelled urban areas, as they sought relief from food crises brought on by the Black Plague. Meanwhile, the cities gained new independence from larger structures of imperial government and from the control of local princes. City councils began to function as the independent governments of urban areas. The Reformation caught on primarily within

1. Alister McGrath, *Reformation Thought: An Introduction*, 4th ed. (New York: Oxford University Press, 2012), 40–44; David Little, "Religion, Peace, and the Origins of Nationalism," in *The Oxford Handbook of Religion, Conflict, and Peacebuilding*, ed. R. Scott Appleby, Atalia Omer, and David Little (New York: Oxford University Press, 2015), 65–66.

cities, whose local leadership often had the power to accept reform or expel its proponents.[2]

The development of capitalist economic practices permitted the emergence of a new middle class and created much greater opportunity of mobility for some, even as "discontent grew" among "the new urban proletariat."[3] It was the peasants' new consciousness of their disadvantaged status and of their potential to change it, as well as the Reformers' empowering of ordinary believers, that led the peasants to demand on earth the justice of the kingdom of God and resulted in the violent upheavals of the Peasants' Revolt (1524–25).[4] The rising bourgeoisie were likely to lend their financial support (on which monarchs depended) to those who represented the attainment of social stability through programs of law and order.[5]

RELIGIOUS AND SOCIAL BACKGROUND

The drastic social shifts occurring in Europe did not sit well with the medieval presupposition of a harmonious created order, or with a cosmic pattern of changeless, divinely established hierarchy. The yearning for political stability by those who had something to fear from change lends intelligibility to the Reformers' valuing of peace guaranteed by the sword, and to their insistence on the unassailable authority of the sovereign in determining just cause for war. "In theory as in practice, the need of the age was for authority rather than liberty, for order first and freedom afterward."[6]

The political situation in Germany in Luther's day illustrates that the strong government to which many aspired was far from the actuality. The largest part of the Holy Roman Empire, Germany was divided into practically independent, sometimes aligned and sometimes warring, political units, including duchies, bishoprics, walled cities, and territories of knights. Although the Hapsburgs had managed through prudent marriages to keep the empire in the family, the emperor did not actually inherit his position. During the period of Luther's first revolutionary stirrings, the prospect of a new election was in the offing. When Emperor Maximilian died in 1519, he was succeeded by his grandson, Charles

---

2. McGrath, *Reformation Thought*, 16–17.

3. McGrath, *Reformation Thought*, 16.

4. David M. Whitford, "Luther's Political Encounters," in *The Cambridge Companion to Martin Luther*, ed. Donald K. McKim (Cambridge: Cambridge University Press, 2003), 185–86.

5. E. Harris Harbison, *The Age of Reformation* (Ithaca, NY: Cornell University Press, 1955), 15.

6. Harbison, *Age of Reformation*, 16.

V. Charles was to command a considerable dynasty, but because it comprised relatively autonomous political entities in Europe and the New World, he also was to have difficulty exercising control and in responding to problems in his far-flung holdings.[7] Charles was a devout Catholic, loyal to Rome, and opposed Luther; he also may have wished to avoid the turmoil that the popular spread of the Reformation would bring.[8]

Meanwhile, the church of the sixteenth century had its own political and economic difficulties. Papal jurisdiction (for example, over trials of ecclesiastical cases) and power of taxation had been increasingly curtailed by the monarchs of the national states and by the Holy Roman Emperor. For example, Francis I of France won the right to appoint senior clergy by prevailing over Swiss and papal forces at a battle near Milan in 1515; and Charles V pressured the Medici pope Clement VII not to annul the marriage of Henry VIII and Catherine of Aragon, who was Charles's aunt. Financial burdens were created by the defense of the papal states, continuing though waning crusades against the Turks and the support of the papal court. Costs were passed from the Vatican to the higher clergy, to the parish clergy, and finally to the laity, who were charged heavily for clerical services. The indulgences controversy that inflamed Luther arises in this context. Even before Luther, there were calls for reform of the power of the pope, of the corruption of ecclesiastical institutions, and of the high level of living of some monastic orders. For instance, the conciliarists had proposed reform through decentralization of church administration and teaching.[9]

Theologically speaking, the fourteenth and fifteenth centuries yielded a legacy of doctrinal pluralism, particularly regarding the Eucharist and the role of Mary.[10] Doctrinal diversity prepared the way for questions about church authority and uniformity in relation to the insights of the

---

7. Harbison, *Age of Reformation*, 32. See also Volker Press, "Constitutional Development and Political Thought in the Holy Roman Empire," in *The New Cambridge Modern History*, vol. 2, *The Reformation, 1520–1559*, 2nd ed., ed. G. R. Elton (Cambridge: Cambridge University Press, 1990), 505–25.

8. David Dwyer Corey, "Luther and the Just-War Tradition," *Political Theology* 12, no. 2 (2011): 307.

9. For background, see Bernhard Lohse, *Martin Luther's Theology: Its Historical and Systematic Development* (Minneapolis: Augsburg Fortress, 1999), 11–27; Press, "Political Thought in the Holy Roman Empire"; McGrath, *Reformation Thought*, 1–7, 16–32, 40–41; Kenneth R. Himes, *Christianity and the Political Order: Conflict, Cooptation and Cooperation* (Maryknoll, NY: Orbis, 2013), 116–121; Scott H. Hendrix, *Luther and the Papacy: Stages in a Reformation* (Minneapolis: Fortress, 1981); and a critical Catholic review of the latter, including comparison to other scholarship: Jared Wicks, review of *Luther and the Papacy*, by Scott H. Hendrix, *Archivum Historiae Pontificiae* 20 (1982): 427–30.

10. Jaroslav Pelikan, *The Christian Tradition*, vol. 4, *Reformation of Church and Dogma*

individual theologian or believer. Other intellectual and religious move-ments may also have helped to undermine the relative medieval unity of Christian life—for example, mysticism, nominalism, and humanism.[11] The Christian mystical tradition confirmed the capacity of the individual person to experience God directly. Nominalism emphasized the unique-ness of all individual beings in contrast to their unity in a natural, hier-archical order characterized by universality. By emphasizing revelation over reason, the nominalists may in one respect have enhanced church authority, but they diminished the sense of the unity of reality, truth, and knowledge. Another line of challenge to the monocentric, hierarchical church of the medieval period came from humanism, with its confidence in human rationality and moral potential. Humanism also may have con-tributed to the erosion of the perceived need for ecclesiastical mediation of Christian truths.

Renaissance humanists studied classical scholarship in the original lan-guages, seeking to appropriate from antiquity its rhetorical techniques of written and spoken eloquence. According to Alister McGrath, "the liter-ary and cultural program of humanism can be summed up in the slogan *ad fontes*—'back to the fountainhead.'" For Christian authors, this meant a return to the New Testament and patristic sources, engaged directly and without the "filter" of medieval commentary and ecclesial interpretation. These texts could offer direct access to the "golden age" of Christianity, from the resurrection of Jesus Christ to the death of the last apostle. The experience of the apostolic era could be restored to the church, providing a new key to unlock the riches of the Christian faith and life, centered on the presence of the risen Jesus.[12]

Exploring the question, "What is the essence of Roman Catholicism?" from what is still fundamentally a pre–Vatican II worldview, the Jesuit historian Robert E. McNally focuses on its social nature. For him, Catholicism

is a religious reality of the social order, of the order of men and their con-cerns, which envisions and demands that, while human beings ultimately depend on God through faith and charity, they also depend on one another.

(1300-1700) (Chicago: University of Chicago Press, 1984), 10; McGrath, *Reformation Thought*, 27–30.

11. John Dillenberger and Claude Welch, *Protestant Christianity: Interpreted through Its De-velopment* (New York: Scribner's, 1954), 4–9; Denis R. Janz, "Late Medieval Theology," in *The Cambridge Companion to Reformation Theology*, ed. David Biagchi and David C. Steinmetz (Cambridge: Cambridge University Press, 2004), 5–14; McGrath, *Reformation Thought*, 27–30; and Scott H. Hendrix, "Luther," in *Cambridge Companion to Reformation Theology*, 40.

12. McGrath, *Reformation Thought*, 40–41.

In the historical and social order the distribution of the fruits of redemption is the cooperative work of man.[13]

In this worldview, the church as a community of believers is of crucial importance, both as the earthly realm within which Christ mediates salvation and as the association through which its fruits are cultivated. Repudiating individualism, the Catholic "finds it congenial and connatural to live and pray as part of a vast worshipping and believing community which through its adherence to its own traditions imparts a unique vision of life both here below and there above."[14]

Martin Luther, in contrast, stood precisely for the openness of every individual to the gospel as communicated by the word of God in Scripture interpreted through the Spirit. A mid-twentieth century Protestant voice, E. Harris Harbison, captures this theme. "This was to be the heart of Protestant belief as it developed later: the Bible and a man's conscience are the channels through which God speaks to human beings, not the Roman Church and its sacraments."[15] Luther, Calvin, and other Reformers did, of course, retain a place for church and sacraments, especially as the locus in which the gospel is preached and heard in the Spirit. But their view of ecclesial authenticity and authority was more centered on the immediate proclamation and its reception in faith than on historic traditions specifying faith's content and the parameters of its lived form. The Reformers implicitly ask by whose authority the medieval edifice is sustained. Their answer is that its authority is not Jesus's own, nor is it confirmed in the existential union with Christ experienced by those who have truly heard and embraced the gospel.

SCRIPTURE AS KEY TO THE REFORMATION

The sixteenth-century reform of Christianity kept the Bible close to the heart of theology and ethics. Both Luther and Calvin believed that all of Scripture is the inspired word of God and the indispensable source of theology. By the principle of *sola scriptura* they held that neither pope nor councils can infallibly interpret Scripture or obviate the need for a

---

13. Robert E. McNally, SJ, "The Reformation: A Catholic Reappraisal," in *Luther, Erasmus and the Reformation: A Catholic Reappraisal,* ed. John C. Olin (New York: Fordham University Press, 1969), 42. After the Second Vatican Council (which concluded in 1965) the inherent sociality of the person and of faith was still a marker of Catholicism, but the church came increasingly to be seen as open to dialogue with the "modern world," including members of other religious traditions, who could also be recipients of the gift of salvation.

14. McNally, "Reformation," 43.

15. Harbison, *Age of Reformation*, 50.

continuing scriptural test. In contrast to the reliance of Augustine and Aquinas on the authority of the church, the patristic "rule of faith," or the authority of theological predecessors to determine Scripture's meaning, the Reformation spirit resisted the authority of tradition. Their spiritual and doctrinal iconoclasm is captured in Luther's famous declaration at the Diet of Worms (1521), as reported by an eyewitness and later by Luther himself:

> Unless I am convinced by the testimony of the Scriptures or by clear reason (for I do not trust either in the pope or in councils alone, since it is well known that they have often erred and contradicted themselves), I am bound by the Scriptures I have quoted and my conscience is captive to the word of God I cannot and I will not retract anything, since it is neither safe nor right to go against conscience. I cannot do otherwise, here I stand, may God help me, Amen.[16]

Reforming theologians did not consider the written text to be beyond subsequent interpretation, every part of Scripture to have equal authority, or the present working of the Holy Spirit to be unnecessary to know God's will, even given its unique expression in Scripture. Both Luther and Calvin acknowledge inconsistencies in the biblical narratives. They will often explain "immoral" deeds performed by biblical heroes and heroines, not via allegory but by presuming a "special command" of God in biblical times. God now speaks primarily through the Bible, which narrows the possibility that such commands might be replicated in contemporary ethics.[17] Yet the Reformers rarely consult the Bible in search of specific moral prescriptions that can be applied simply, literally, and directly to contemporary situations. They are more concerned with the spiritual substance of the gospel than with the details of its prima facie "literal" sense, or with the explanation and harmonization of passages whose surface meanings seem contradictory. The gospel is not what is written as such, but the promises of God in Christ, communicated in the Word of God preached and received in the Holy Spirit. This allows an important role to the interpreter and preacher of scripturally based teaching, one who discerns what in the Bible is essential to the gospel and what is peripheral, superfluous, or even misleading.

The Radical Reformers—for instance, the Anabaptists—are more

16. Nevertheless, the last sentence at least may be apocryphal. See Erik W. Gritsch, *Martin Luther—God's Court Jester: Luther in Retrospect* (Philadelphia: Fortress, 1983), 41, citing from "Luther at the Diet of Worms," trans. Roger A. Hornsby, *Luther's Works*, vol. 32, *Career of the Reformer II* (Philadelphia: Fortress, 1958), 112–13.

17. An exception may be God's commands to secular rulers to order ecclesial affairs in cases of special emergency—to be discussed below.

inclined to a New Testament literalism and to view statements and accounts within the New Testament as less subject to the interpreter's nuance. All Reformers see the New Testament as at least in some sense more authoritative than the Old, which prefigures the coming of Christ and reveals him less clearly. The discrepancy is perhaps greatest for the Anabaptists, though they rely heavily on Old Testament imagery. Their key to the interpretation of all Scripture is Jesus Christ as a sacrificial Lamb. Luther permits Old Testament incidents to have more influence on his normative positions but still sees the New Testament as central. Calvin attempts more thoroughly to integrate the Old Testament into Christian theology, because it supported his hope for a church and state united in a Holy Commonwealth.

Though all were committed to a scriptural test for faith and life, Reformers differed on whether the gospel demands resistance to or even withdrawal from ordinary political life in order to carry out the teachings of Jesus. The separatist Anabaptists and, in the following century, the Quakers did indeed take a more radical route. But mainstream Protestantism, in the sixteenth century and after, sought to approve the use of force as a worldly necessity, a responsibility of the Christian, and even as a support for the flourishing of true religion. This is perhaps ironic, given their emphasis on the authority of Scripture over inherited traditions, on a direct encounter with Jesus through the preaching of the word of God, and on the formation of gospel-based communities that challenged medieval Catholicism's accommodation to imperial rule.

MARTIN LUTHER

The theological pluralism and demands for reform that characterized the fourteenth and fifteenth centuries "came together in the life and teaching of Martin Luther"(1483–1546).[18] Luther, one of eight children, was born in Saxony in the town of Eisleben, and moved with his family to the neighboring town of Mansfeld the following year. His father, Hans Luther (or Luder), was a peasant and former farmer who owned a small copper mining and smelting business. Like Augustine's father, he managed to provide his son a good classical education in the hope of improving his opportunities by preparing him to be a lawyer. At

18. Pelikan, *Reformation*, 127. Biographies of Luther include Roland H. Bainton, *Here I Stand: A Life of Martin Luther* (New York: New American Library, 1950); Bernhard Lohse, *Martin Luther: An Introduction to His Life and Work* (Philadelphia: Fortress, 1986); Eric W. Gritsch, *Martin Luther—God's Court Jester: Luther in Retrospect*; Heiko A. Oberman, *Luther: Man between God and the Devil* (New Haven, CT: Yale University Press, 2006); and Lyndal Roper, *Martin Luther: Renegade and Prophet* (New York: Random House, 2016).

eighteen, Luther went to Erfurt University, where he studied liberal arts and acquired a master's degree. Later he enrolled in the School of Law at Erfurt, specializing in canon law.

In 1505, Luther entered the Augustinian monastery against his father's will, and apparently in fear of unexpected death. Much later, he recounts in his "Table Talk" how he vowed to St. Anne to become a monk if she would intercede to spare him in a thunderstorm on the open road. But sudden death was no extraordinary occurrence in the Middle Ages, playing a significant part in Luther's milieu even if the thunderstorm story is apocryphal. Two of his brothers were among the estimated twenty million who died in Europe of the Black Death. Death was appreciated vividly via a spirituality emphasizing the pains of hell and the dangers of this world, best avoided by a commitment to an ascetic and prayerful life.

In the monastery, Luther continued his education, especially in Scripture. He was educated in the art of disputation and was exposed to scholastic theology, humanism, and nominalism. At Erfurt he became acquainted with a form of late medieval scholasticism, the *via moderna* (a type of nominalism going back to the thought of the fourteenth-century British theologian William of Ockham). This theology, which Luther would oppose most vehemently, was premised upon the idea of a covenant between God and humanity, by which God promises to save or justify all those who try to satisfy God's laws or demands to the best of their ability. To Luther the *via moderna* comes far too close to the "Pelagian" idea that human beings can justify themselves on the basis of their own efforts. To the contrary, Luther came to believe (with Augustine) that saving grace is an entirely free and unmerited gift of God, given despite the fact that humans will always remain unworthy sinners. Luther received his doctorate at the University of Wittenberg and was immediately granted a chair of biblical studies, which he taught for the remainder of his life. Luther's lectures on the Bible, especially the letters of Paul, provided the occasion and a lasting framework for the development of his theology of justification by faith.

Despite his assiduous and by all accounts successful efforts to lead the life of an exemplary monk, Luther was tormented by scrupulosity and doubts of his own salvation. The encouragements of his confessor, Johann von Staupitz, were to no avail. After about a decade of struggle, meditation on Scripture finally led Luther to a breakthrough in the "tower experience" described by him (admittedly with hindsight, at age sixty-two, the year before his death) in the preface to the 1545 Latin edition of his complete works. In the tower room of the monastery at Wittenberg, pondering the meaning of God's "righteousness" in Romans 1:17, Luther was struck by the insight that God's righteousness does not judge but justifies. In his mercy, God imparts the divine righteousness as a gift to those who have faith.

This was the seed of the theology that was to carry Martin Luther through the next three turbulent decades. Neither merits nor good works earn faith and grace, which are given freely by God in Christ. The Christian responds to this gift with trust in God and God's promises and by spontaneously living out works of love toward the neighbor. Luther formulated his ground-breaking Ninety-Five Theses in 1517 in a letter of protest to the archbishop who had sponsored the Dominican monk Johann Tetzel in his indulgence-selling tour. In 1519–20 Luther was incredibly productive, publishing, among other things, his three famed early works: "Treatise on Good Works," "To the Christian Nobility of the German Nation," and "Freedom of the Christian."

Luther might best be described as an exegete whose theology is pre-eminently a theology of the word of God.[19] The heart of the gospel is that "the person is justified and saved, not by works or laws, but by the word of God, that is, by the promise of his grace, and by faith, that the glory may remain God's, who saved us not by works of righteousness which we have done (Titus 3:5), but by virtue of his mercy by the word of his grace when we believed (1 Cor 1:21)."[20] Luther understands the Word of God as the concrete action of God, through which God acts redemptively, conferring the forgiveness of sins. Above all, God acts in the crucifixion and resurrection of Jesus, events that the preaching of the Word of God in the church makes contemporary. Study of the Scriptures sustains preaching of the gospel and tests its content. Although all theology assumes a political context and has social and political consequences, Luther did not primarily envision himself as theological ethicist or a political theologian. He saw himself, rather, "as one who interprets Scripture for the mission of the Church."[21]

Luther's key message or insight—as important for ethics and action as for theology and faith—is that God's promises in Jesus Christ free people from fear and empower them to live in gratitude, trust, joy, and hope, serving the neighbor with love and generosity. True Christians are "Christs to one another. . . . filled by the Holy Spirit. . . . because he

19. Jaroslav Pelikan so describes it in *Luther the Expositor: Introduction to the Reformer's Exegetical Writings* (St. Louis: Concordia, 1959), 48.

20. Martin Luther, *Christian Liberty* (1520), ed. Harold Grimm (Philadelphia: Fortress, 1957), 25–26.

21. William R. Russell, "Introduction," in *Martin Luther's Basic Theological Writings*, 3rd ed., ed. Timothy F. Lull and William R. Russell (Minneapolis: Fortress, 2012), xix.

dwells in us."[22] Obedience to the government and doing "the works of [one's] profession or station" are ways to maintain self-discipline and to serve others, not means of improving one's status in God's eyes, since salvation, freely given, is already the reality out of which every true Christian lives.[23]

Luther distinguishes the gospel from the law. Whereas the gospel is the good news of God's free grace and salvation, the law demands obedience. The law may refer to the natural moral law, the Ten Commandments, or even the gospel misunderstood as placing a burden of compliance and worthiness on the believer. According to Luther, the law thus has two uses: to control the sinner and maintain order in society and government (the civil use); and to condemn sinners and bring them to the point of repentance (the theological use). A third use, for moral guidance (found in Calvin), is on the face of it repudiated by Luther, who expects that works of love toward the neighbor will flow spontaneously from faith. Nonetheless, insofar as Luther retains a pedagogical function for the Ten Commandments in the life of the believer, he recognizes the law's third use. After all, no one is fully a Christian in actuality, and so all need the law for discipline. Moreover, even the Christian is a "Christian-in-relation," striving to serve the neighbor in the world and so relying on the laws and restraints that structure temporal life.[24]

Although Luther later fought against all academic theology, and especially against the *via moderna*, his exposure to nominalism may have influenced his insistence on the sole sufficiency of grace and faith. In contrast to the thought of Thomas Aquinas, the nominalists stressed the distinction or even contradiction between reason and faith. The consequence of this for Luther's political theology was a strong contrast between (though not separation of) discipleship and citizenship, of what is required to be a follower of Christ and what is necessary to order worldly affairs. Similar to Augustine, Luther considered the Christian to live in "two kingdoms," requiring different moral and social expressions—a framework for his politics that will be discussed further below.

Luther remained the active and often contentious father of the reform movement in Germany, constantly risking capture and imprisonment as a heretic. However, the German princes never enforced the imperial edict against him issued at Worms (1521) as a result of Pope Leo's condemnation of his views (in the papal bull *Exsurge Domini*, 1520). In 1525, at age forty-two, he married the twenty-six-year-old former nun,

---

22. Luther, *Christian Liberty*, 30–31.
23. Luther, *Christian Liberty*, 32.
24. Luther, "The Sermon on the Mount," *Luther's Works*, vol. 21 (St. Louis: Concordia, 1956), 109–13.

Catherine von Bora. Six children were born to them, of whom four survived to adulthood. Luther conducted debates with theologians such as John Eck (on indulgences), Carlstadt and Zwingli (on the Eucharist), and Erasmus (on free will and grace), and he became embroiled in attempts to squelch both radical manifestations of the Reformation spirit (Thomas Müntzer) and the peasant rebellion, yet he rejected the theological legitimation of the Crusades as conquest of "the infidel."

LUTHER'S VIEWS OF GOVERNMENT AND POLITICS

Luther's ethics and politics are, like his theology and biblical interpretation, experientially grounded, lending to his political views an ad hoc and pragmatic character.[25] Luther replies to questions as they arise, and his solutions are directed more to immediate duties and outcomes than to long-range interpretations of social life or integrated political programs. He relates positively to Augustine's tensive construal of the political and religious spheres of life, preserving like Augustine a high sense of Christian demand, even while coming to terms with the necessary conditions of maintaining civil order.

Luther's views of the authority of government, and of the relation between Christian faith and politics, have often been rendered in simplistic and stereotypical terms: the government has its place in the world, the place of sin, law, and works; grace establishes a spiritual kingdom, where the Christian lives by the gospel, God's promises, and the freedom of faith. The Christian obeys secular authority because it maintains a minimal kind of social order, but this is an order strictly separate from faith, a temporal realm essentially untouched by the gospel, a world in which the Christian will never be at home.

The intellectual and pastoral framework with which Luther represents this duality of secular and spiritual is his rubric of the "two kingdoms." This framework is set out most explicitly in an early work, *On Temporal Authority* (1522), but reverberates through many of Luther's writings, and is related to companion themes, such and law and gospel, works and faith, sin and grace. In the temporal kingdom are "the law's realm of Satan, the fallen world, sin, death and the temporal sword of Caesar," while in the heavenly or spiritual kingdom are "the gospel's realm of God in Christ, the redeemed church, faith, new life, and the sword of the Spirit." Hence, William Lazareth points out, if taken at face value,

---

25. B. A. Gerrish, *The Old Protestantism and the New: Essays on the Reformation Heritage* (Edinburgh: T&T Clark, 1983), 57: "Experience is necessary for understanding the Word, which must be lived and felt."

Luther's two kingdoms metaphor, like Augustine's two cities, reflects an "eschatological dualism" that seems to divide humanity into two opposed categories.[26]

Yet the picture is actually more complicated. To begin with, Luther does not strictly divide Christians from non-Christians, for he sees the "two kingdoms" opposition as existing even within the Christian life itself. Like Christians before and after him, Luther struggled with the seeming paradox of the kingdom or reign of God, preached by Jesus, as both accessible in our own lives and yet always out of reach, an ideal in light of which human efforts fall radically short. For Luther the ambivalent and even conflicted nature of Christian existence is more than a theological proposition; it is an existential experience that eludes coherent explanation or capture by a theological system. Believers are always *simul iustus et peccator* (in themselves always sinners, though completely accepted in God's eyes). Day-to-day existence certifies that Christians live out of trust and gratitude, yet struggle daily with temptation and sin; are transformed by faith, but need Christian formation and healing; are assured of God's love and mercy, yet confronted by the enigma of human suffering; gather around the Eucharist, yet remain citizens of a larger, harsher, and irrepressibly violent social body.

Moreover, considering the matter from the standpoint of the so-called "worldly" realm, secular authority does seem to have some responsibility for the maintenance of true religion. According to David Little, Luther—despite authorizing theologically a "new populism" resistant to oppressive rule—came to believe that "people are best served by supporting a strong, religiously uniform, unitary government."[27] For example, Luther appeals to the German nobility to defend himself and other Reformers from prosecution by the papacy and the Catholic emperor; and Luther, Calvin, and others expect the civil magistrates to guarantee proper worship and Christian morals in cities that had been converted to the Reformation. On behalf of civil order and the common good, Luther urged the civil authority to forcefully put down the peasants' rebellion that had been inspired by their interpretation of Luther's religious call for Christian freedom. As James Estes instructively notes, Luther's "arguments justifying action in support of religious reformation had a complexity and an inner tension unmatched" in the thought of his contemporaries.[28]

---

26. William H. Lazareth, *Christians in Society: Luther, the Bible, and Social Ethics* (Minneapolis: Fortress, 2001), 139.

27. Little, "Religion, Peace," 67.

28. James M. Estes, "Luther on the Role of Secular Authority in the Reformation," *Lutheran Quarterly* 17, no. 2 (2003): 199.

The tension begins in Luther's explanation of the origin and purpose of government itself. Toward the end of his life, Luther clearly states in his *Lectures on Genesis* (1544–45) that civil government is established due to sin, a view that would be conducive to understanding government as requiring extreme measures to fend off extreme threats. Says Luther, "there was no government of the state before sin," for government is required only because of "our corrupted nature." Laws and government would have been unnecessary had humans remained in the state of blessedness in which they were created; therefore government can be assumed to have only a negative function.[29] But in his earlier treatise, *On Temporal Authority* (1523), there seems to be a margin of ambiguity about the original status of government, for Luther maintains that government was given to Adam (though in anticipation of sin) and is described as God's creation. "If it is God's creation, then it is good, so good that everyone can use it in a Christian and salutary way."[30] Yet, although "this temporal sword has existed from the beginning of the world," Luther first illustrates its use with the punishment of Cain for the murder of his brother—not as the facilitator of harmonious social life for Eve, Adam, and their children.[31]

Another factor in the complexity of Luther's view of government is that Luther is both interpreting biblical texts that are somewhat at odds with one another and is doing so in light of real questions about how, at the practical level, Christians should interpret some of the New Testament's stronger statements about the demands of being a follower of Christ. These questions are urgent for those occupying positions of secular or governmental authority. *On Temporal Authority* is written as a response to Duke John (brother of Frederick the Wise, Luther's protector), who worries that texts such as Matthew 5:38-48 and Romans 12:19 ("Vengeance is mine, I will repay, says the Lord") will make either his Christianity or his public functions impossible. Luther counters with Romans 13:1 ("Let every person be subject to the governing authorities") to establish the temporal sword, even though there "appear to be powerful arguments to the contrary."[32]

Luther deals with the seeming discrepancy between the Sermon on the Mount and government authority by asserting that there are "two classes" of people and "two kingdoms." This view is developed, nuanced,

29. Luther, *Luther's Works*, vol. 1, *Lectures on Genesis, Chapters 1–5*, ed. Jaroslav Pelikan (St. Louis: Concordia, 1955), 104; cf. 115.

30. Luther, "On Temporal Authority," *Luther's Works*, vol. 45, *The Christian in Society II*, ed. Walther I. Brandt (Philadelphia: Fortress, 1962), 99.

31. Luther, "On Temporal Authority," 86.

32. Luther, "On Temporal Authority," 87.

and expounded in many places and contexts.[33] Put most starkly, it means that all true believers belong to the kingdom of God under a spiritual government, whose membership is by grace and faith; whereas nonbelievers belong to the kingdom of this world, whose criterion is works and which is disciplined by the law, under a secular government. Luther's interpretation of Matthew 5, then, is addressed to those among whom the kingdom has already been established. Jesus tells his followers, "you have the kingdom of heaven"; therefore a Christian will not "seek legal redress in the law courts"—unless necessary to fulfill his or her responsibilities to others—nor refuse to "suffer every evil and injustice without avenging himself."[34] If everyone were "real Christians," then law, sword, and government would be superfluous.[35] But everyone is not. Government by law is necessary to restrain unbelievers, to deal with remaining sinfulness even among believers, and to offer structures and means by which Christians serve others in an evil world.

Luther mentions the teaching of unnamed predecessors that it is enough for a Christian "to be ready in his heart to offer the other cheek," but he views this as a false resolution because it obscures the fact that "Christ is addressing His sermon only to His Christians."[36] Luther insists that "the Christians' way is altogether different," for "we have been transferred to another and a higher existence, a divine and an eternal kingdom," where "only mutual love and service should prevail, even toward people . . . who hate us."[37] For this reason, even the negative form of the Fifth Commandment should be given a positive translation. Whenever we cause our neighbor—friend or enemy—harm by omitting a needed service, we "have culpably withheld from him that love and kindness by which his life might have been saved."[38] Roles in the secular world, on the other hand, entail different responsibilities.

Luther's treatment of the way Christians relate to the social and political realms is complex. Luther's presumed division of the spiritual and

33. Luther, "On Temporal Authority," 88, 91–92, 110; "Whether Soldiers, Too, Can Be Saved," *Luther's Works*, vol. 46, *The Christian in Society III*, ed. Robert C. Schultz (Philadelphia: Fortress, 1967), 99; "Sermon on the Mount," 105; "On War against the Turk," *Luther's Works* 46:166, 186; "An Open Letter on the Harsh Book against the Peasants," *Luther's Works* 46:70–71; and *A Treatise on Christian Liberty,* ed. Harold J. Grimm (Philadelphia: Fortress, 1957), also available in *Luther's Works*, vol. 31, *Career of the Reformer*, ed. Harold J. Grimm (Philadelphia: Muhlenberg, 1957), 7–8, 32–36.

34. Luther, "Sermon on the Mount," 11–116; "On Temporal Authority," 100–101.

35. Luther, "On Temporal Authority," 88–89, 92–95; cf. "Sermon on the Mount," 108, but see also 111.

36. Luther, "Sermon on the Mount," 107.

37. Luther, "Sermon on the Mount," 108–9.

38. Luther, *The Large Catechism,* "Fifth Commandment," in *Luther's Catechetical Writings*, ed. John N. Lenker (Minneapolis: The Luther Press, 1907), 77–78.

temporal is modified in at least four ways that are germane to his views of war and peace. At the end of the day, serious questions must be raised about why these modifications do not lead Luther to a more restrained view of the legitimacy of armed force and on the scope of its implementation. These four ways are Luther's idea of worldly vocations or estates; his thesis that Christians may not only fulfill such vocations but should do so in specifically Christian ways; his suggestion that union with Christ sanctifies and transforms Christian action; and his practical efforts to change public political and social structures in areas such as social welfare and educational reform.

First, far from avoiding contamination by the exigencies of public duties, Christians may and should participate in temporal roles or vocations for the sake of good order and the common good. Although Luther rejects what he perceives to be the medieval Catholic confusion of the secular and salvific orders, he wants to distinguish without entirely separating them. He also distances himself from the Reformation "enthusiasts" who wanted Christianity to be a community set apart from the secular order, defined in terms of its mission and witness.[39] Thus Luther conceptualizes specific forms of participation in the larger society, through which Christians unite the expression of their Christian identity with the responsibilities required of them as members of civil society and citizens. Luther calls these variously estates, stations, vocations, offices, or callings, and groups them in the three overarching categories of minister, magistrate, or marriage. Within these three fall a variety of specific roles such as prince, lord, soldier, spouse, parent, or minister (referring to service of the church as a social institution).[40]

Second, when a Christian fulfills these roles or vocations, he or she is a "Christian-in relation" who spans the divide of spiritual and worldly realms.[41] He or she does not abandon Christian identity or its practical expressions, but uses the roles as an occasion to serve the neighbor—within the order of justice but with the motive and effects of love. Thus, although Luther presents the eschatological opposition of the two kingdoms dualistically, their historical relation manifests "the inaugurated but not yet realized, eschatology of the New Testament."[42]

God's rule dialectically interpenetrates both kingdoms, compensating

39. Gerhard Ebeling, *Luther: An Introduction to His Thought* (Philadelphia: Fortress, 1970), 178–82.

40. See for example, Luther, "On Temporal Authority," 99, 100; "Sermon on the Mount," 109; *Lectures on Galatians*, vol. 26, *Lectures on Galatians, Chapters 1–4*, ed. Jaroslav Pelikan (St. Louis: Concordia, 1962), 11–12.

41. Luther, "Sermon on the Mount," 109.

42. Lazareth, *Christians in Society*, 140.

for the still-shadowy vision of Christian faith (1 Cor 13:12) and beginning the promised transformation of the entire creation (Rom 8:19–22).
True, a simple counsel to "turn the other cheek" to a person in public
office "would be ridiculous," but the Christian prince uses his office,
including the sword and coercion, to self-denyingly serve and protect.[43]
He overcomes temptations to misuse authority or neglect responsibilities
and maximizes opportunities to enhance the common good.[44] If Christian princes try to "conduct their office in love toward" their subjects,
giving them "the care and attention required," they will soon discover
that "many a fine dance, hunt, race and game would have to be missed."[45]
Although spiritually they belong to Christ alone, Christians live out of
the gifts of grace and faith in society through their daily occupations and
vocations, the arena of God's continuing gifts to them.[46]

Third, and contrary to many "standard" interpretations of Luther, it
is not necessarily true that Luther's central theological theme of "justification by faith alone" nullifies the concrete, visible, reliable effect of
grace in the life of the believer. In some interpretations, justification
not only trumps sanctification in Luther's theology, it almost eliminates
it. Luther's concern, of course, was to rule out any possibility that the
faithful could rest assurance of salvation anywhere but in the plenitude
of divine grace, and to repudiate any conception that human works
are somehow related causally to it. He particularly wanted to deny the
Thomistic or scholastic idea that grace works an inherent change in the
recipient, infusing new virtues and the equivalent of a new "nature," so
that the Christian is able to perform works of merit, albeit as a result of
grace.

In the past three or four decades, however, a different angle on
Luther's theology of grace has emerged, one that has rediscovered in
Luther's own writings an emphasis on the effect that union with Christ
in faith, or the indwelling of Christ or the Holy Spirit, can have. Beginning in the 1980s with a group of scholars in Finland,[47] this reading
supports a more consistent transformation of the Christian moral life

43. Luther, "Sermon on the Mount," 109–10.
44. Luther, "On Temporal Authority," 118–21.
45. Luther, "On Temporal Authority," 121.
46. Lazareth, *Christians in Society*, 215.
47. See Tuomo Mannerma, *Christ Present in Faith: Luther's View of Justification*, trans. Kirsi I.
Stjerna (Minneapolis: Fortress, 2005); Veli-Matti Kärkkäinen, "'Drinking from the Same Wells
with Orthodox and Catholics': Insights from the Finnish Interpretation of Luther's Theology,"
Currents in Theology and Mission 34, no. 2 (2007): 85–96; Carl E. Braaten and Robert W. Jenson,
eds., *The New Finnish Interpretation of Luther* (Grand Rapids, MI: William B. Eerdmans, 1998);
and Gordon L. Isaac, "The Finnish School of Luther Interpretation: Reponses and Trajectories,"
Concordia Theological Quarterly 76, no. 3 (2012): 251–68.

by virtue of "human participation in Christ through his presence in our faith, within us (*Christus in nobis*), by which we receive the grace and righteousness of God."[48] Rather than an ontological change in the believer, there is a gift of ongoing relationship to God in Christ. As George Hunsinger expresses it, Luther rejects the "more and more" of sanctification to be found in Aquinas and Calvin, but his view can be characterized in terms of the grace of Christ working in the believer "again and again."[49] The union of Christ with the believer is continually renewed, and the believer participates in the activity of Christ without possessing Christ's virtues as his or her own. Consequently, the works of the Christian can and should exhibit greater love and justice because they are really manifestations of Christ. They are signs of Christ's union with or presence within us, of our graced participation in Christ. This same relationship can also be expressed in terms of the gift or indwelling of the Holy Spirit.

A key—though not the only—source for this view in Luther's writings is his 1535 *Lectures on Galatians*. Here Luther does reject Aquinas's infused charity and defends imputed righteousness. Nevertheless, he continues, faith takes "hold of and possesses this treasure, the present Christ," who "lives in the heart."[50] Although sin remains even in the person justified, "Christ lives in me. . . . we become one body in the Spirit," and "Christ is speaking, acting, and performing all actions" in me.[51] Indeed, "the Word of God comes, whenever it comes, to change and renew the world."[52] Our moral condition may require a painful struggle, but it is not static, nor is it barred from the beneficial influence of the Spirit. "Therefore any Christian can and does morally improve (*progressus*) and develop into more responsible service under the vocational dimension of God's twofold rule (2 Cor 3:18)."[53] This permits Luther or the Lutheran theologian to anticipate, expect, and require that those who profess faith in Christ will gain some moral-political traction against worldly forms of domination, exploitation, corruption and violence.

48. Günther Gassman, "Luther in the Worldwide Church Today," in *The Cambridge Companion to Martin Luther*, ed. Donald McKim (Cambridge: Cambridge University Press, 2006), 296.

49. George Hunsinger, "A Tale of Two Simultaneities: Justification and Sanctification in Calvin and Barth," *Zeitschrift für dialektische Theologie* 37 (2001): 316–38.

50. Luther, *Lectures on Galatians*, 129–30. See also *On Christian Liberty*, 25, 30–31, on union with Christ.

51. Luther, *Lectures on Galatians*, 167–71.

52. Carter Lindberg, "Luther's Struggle with Social-Ethical Issues," in *Cambridge Companion to Luther*, 167, citing Luther, "The Bondage of the Will," *Luther's Works*, vol. 33, *Career of the Reformer III*, ed. Philip S. Watson (Philadelphia: Fortress, 1972), 52.

53. Lazareth, *Christians in Society*, 201.

LUTHER'S SOCIAL INITIATIVES

Fourth, then, Luther not only expected or hoped for such changes, he was personally active and successful in advocating for them and bringing them about. A first example is Luther's mobilization of the church and its members to take measures against poverty, measures that eventually assumed social-structural forms not limited to charity or philanthropy. As Carter Lindberg points out, poverty was widespread in early sixteenth-century Europe because the profit economy was growing in the absence of government regulation. In the presence of a medieval Catholic spirituality that saw hierarchies of social class as part of the natural order, this spirituality endowed poverty with religious meaning by idealizing it as conducive to salvation, assuring the rich that almsgiving is of salvific value too. Rich and poor were placed in a "symbiotic" relationship that validated the *status quo*: "almsgiving provided the poor with some charity, enabled the rich to atone for their sins, and blessed the rich with the intercessions of the poor."[54] Luther's theology of justification by faith pulled the rug out from under this scheme by depriving both poverty and almsgiving of saving merit. Poverty could be recognized as a spiritual and social evil that Christians should combat if they are serious about serving the neighbor.

Luther was vehemently opposed to the excesses of capitalism and exploitative entrepreneurship that caused inflation while depressing wages, conditions that he chalked up to mere greed and characterized as murder and robbery. However, his efforts to win social control of business practices and interest rates, or to cancel the debts of the poor, were unsuccessful. Thus "Luther and his colleagues moved in alliance with local governments to establish and legislate government welfare policies."[55] The measures that they instituted eventually spread to multiple cities of the Reformation in Germany.

The Wittenberg Church Order (1522) established a "common chest" of financial resources to be used on behalf of the destitute, poor orphans, citizens in debt who needed to refinance their loans at an affordable interest, the educational and vocational training of boys, young women who required a dowry to marry, and artisans who needed loans to start businesses. The Wittenberg common chest was originally supported by ecclesiastical financing, but grew to include public collections, taxes, sales of grain, and a simple form of banking. As its resources increased, the fund expanded to include care for the sick and elderly in hospi-

54. Lindberg, "Luther's Struggle," 171.
55. Lindberg, "Luther's Struggle," 171–72.

tals, a medical office and doctor for the poor, proactive measures against hunger and inflation, and support for community schools.[56]

The reform in Germany brought a crisis in education, because most education at the time occurred under the auspices of the Roman Catholic Church. Luther was a strong advocate for thorough educational reform, not only because educational opportunity favored the sons of the wealthy, but also because there were no unified educational systems or standards, and Luther was concerned about the future of Christian theology and ministry if education in biblical and classical languages were neglected.[57] He saw local city councilmen as best positioned to take effective action, and he appealed to them on the basis that an educated citizenry is essential to the prosperity of a city. Luther envisioned structural change that would not only ensure high-quality schools, but would invest the entire community in raising the prospects of the poor. Now free of obligatory contributions and fees to the church, he insisted, "every citizen should be influenced . . . to contribute a part of that amount toward schools for the training of poor children."[58]

Lindberg summarizes Luther's approach to anti-poverty programs with words that could be applied to many social initiatives:

> Luther believed that not only was the church called publicly and unequivocally to reject [unjust] economic developments, but also to develop a constructive social ethic in response to them. This social ethic developed social welfare policies and legislation and called for public accountability. . . . It is common to think of Luther as a Pauline theologian; true enough, but he . . . understood the relevance of Matthew 25:31-46.[59]

LUTHER ON POLITICAL AUTHORITY AND WAR

When we turn to Luther's justifications of war and other uses of force by government, this biblically inspired reformist stance falters. One might expect that Matthew 5 would be as important to Luther's social activism as Matthew 25, and that the Christian identity of the prince or citizen would orient his or her public role toward the reduction of violence and

56. Lindberg, "Luther's Struggle," 171–72; see also Carter Lindberg, "Luther on Poverty," in *Harvesting Martin Luther's Reflections on Theology, Ethics, and the Church*, ed. Timothy J. Wengert (Grand Rapids, MI: William B. Eerdmans, 2003), 140–43.

57. Reimer Faber, "Martin Luther on Reformed Education," *Clarion* 47, no. 16 (1998), 376–79.

58. Luther, "To the Councilmen of All Cities in Germany that They Establish and Maintain Christian Schools," in Jarrett A. Carty, *Divine Kingdom, Holy Order: The Political Writings of Martin Luther* (St. Louis: Concordia, 2012), 322, also in *Luther's Works* 45:339–78.

59. Lindberg, "Luther on Poverty," 148.

the increase of reconciliation and mercy. Unfortunately, however, while Luther recognizes that Christians "should love not only those who do us good, but our enemies, too,"[60] he limits this radical demand to the personal sphere and the Christian community.[61] In what concerns his or her own interests and rights, the Christian will not "seek legal redress in the law courts" nor refuse to "suffer every evil and injustice without avenging himself."[62]

While "the rule in the kingdom of Christ is the toleration of everything, forgiveness, and the recompense of evil with good," the rule in the world of politics, even for the Christian, is to maintain order by coercive force whenever necessary, with few if any restraints on means.[63] "At times, war might be a necessary evil. The power of the sword is given to magistrates to limit chaos, crush evil, and promote justice on behalf of the innocent."[64] As far as the use of violence is concerned, church and civil government, spiritual authority and temporal authority, inhabit distinct and separate spheres.

More positively from the standpoint of the evangelical counsels, Luther makes an advance on the tradition by reducing the rationale for the Crusades and by beginning to question (with Aquinas) the legitimacy of unjust regimes. And while he retains the concern of both Augustine and Aquinas to preserve in war a rightful intention, he moves away from Augustine and toward Aquinas by seeing defense of the common good as the primary legitimation of war, not punishment or retribution. Like both his predecessors, he puts a tremendous amount of weight on the right of sovereign authority to declare and wage war,[65] leaving to the individual conscience only a small margin—but still a margin—of freedom for dissent.[66] The sovereign's right to declare war, however, is not unlimited, because it is subject to the criterion or goal of peace and the common good. First we will look at Luther's general view of war, then turn to three exceptional cases where again Luther's views are complex and to some extent inconsistent. These are the Crusades against the Turks, opposition to the reform movement by secular rulers, and the Peasants' War.

60. Luther, "Sermon on the Mount," 129; cf. 116.
61. Luther, "On Temporal Authority," 95, 101–2; "Sermon on the Mount," 113–14, 119–23.
62. Luther, "On Temporal Authority," 100–101.
63. Luther, "Sermon on the Mount," 113.
64. Whitford, "Luther's Political Encounters," 189.
65. See James Turner Johnson, "Aquinas and Luther on War and Peace: Sovereign Authority and the Use of Armed Force," *Journal of Religious Ethics* 31, no. 1 (2003): 3–20.
66. For a comparison of Luther to earlier positions, see Corey, "Luther and the Just-War Tradition"; David D. Corey and J. Daryl Charles, *The Just War Tradition: An Introduction* (Wilmington, DE: ISI, 2012), 85–101.

For Luther, the primary and key justification of war is not punishment of evil for its own sake but the duty of the ruler to maintain social order and restore peace against disruption. He stresses the civil order, the importance of maintaining peace, and legitimate authority to declare war.[67] War and killing "have been instituted by God" in order to punish wrong, and "protect the good and preserve peace." They are a small price to pay to avoid a "universal, worldwide lack of peace which would destroy everyone."[68] Just war assumes that a wrong has been committed; it must be fought in self-defense: "whoever starts a war is in the wrong."[69]

However, no prince or ruler has the right to wage war against someone in a higher position of authority, since this would constitute a fatal assault on the social order.[70] If the antagonist is a social equal or the head of a foreign government, then the aggrieved ruler should pursue peaceful means to resolve the conflict. However, if the entire land is in peril, and war is a last resort, then the duty of "help and protection" toward subjects prevails and war may be undertaken as an act of love toward them. Nevertheless, even this justified decision requires wisdom and prudence, so that injury to the innocent is avoided.[71] Luther insists that the just warmaker should be motivated by a sense of duty to the common good, and love and care for his or her subjects, not by simple revenge or retribution. Like Augustine, he compares the government to a parent and cautions that its anger must be "an anger of love," "sweet and friendly, free of any malice."[72]

The individual soldier is obligated to obey the ruler's declaration of war unless the former is absolutely sure that the command is unjust and a violation of the will of God. Luther insists on the nearly absolute obligation of the soldier to obey,[73] for "those who resist their rulers resist the ordinance of God."[74] Once war is engaged, Luther envisions that love for one's subjects can justify almost any means necessary to prevail: "it is both Christian and an act of love to kill the enemy without hesitation, to plunder and kill and injure him by every method of warfare until he is conquered (except one must beware of sin and not violate wives and

67. Luther, "On Temporal Authority," 99; "Whether Soldiers, Too," 114, 126.
68. Luther, "Whether Soldiers, Too," 95–96.
69. Luther, "Whether Soldiers, Too," 118, 121.
70. Luther, "On Temporal Authority," 124; "Whether Soldiers, Too," 103.
71. Luther, "On Temporal Authority," 123–25.
72. Luther, "Sermon on the Mount," 76.
73. Luther, "On Temporal Authority," 130: "unless you know for sure that he [the authority declaring war] is wrong"; "Whether Soldiers, Too," 114: "unless he is sure that he has a command from God or from God's servants the rulers"; see also "Whether Soldiers, Too," 126, 131.
74. Luther, "Whether Soldiers, Too," 126.

virgins)."[75] The military activity of "stabbing and killing, robbing and burning," can be "godly and right" in a good cause.[76]

One can hope that these are simply intemperate statements by Luther rather than his considered policy, for he also says that princes must treat "evildoers" with "a restrained severity and firmness," and that one should "offer mercy and peace" to those who have surrendered.[77] Certainly the unrestrained and indiscriminate infliction of violence during war is not only sure to injure the innocent and make social reconstruction difficult; it is also inimical to the restoration or achievement of peaceful coexistence between former adversaries after the conflict has concluded. Luther's instructions to princes can be read to imply overall the moral importance of restraint in war and peaceable settlements post-conflict. Yet these implications are short-circuited by Luther's intemperate and repressive reaction to a peasant revolt in favor of greater economic rights.

Turning to the specific occasion of the Peasants' War, we find a plus and a minus, a positive and a negative illustration, of Luther's theory of just war. Positively, he argues that the rebellion can and should be suppressed because the peasants are endangering the common good by their violent and disruptive behavior. Negatively, however, he endorses very extreme measures, with no mercy or accommodation of their demands, though he himself recognizes that they are fundamentally just.

The Peasants' Rebellion of 1525 resulted from the fact that longstanding entitlements to the land they worked and its products were being diminished or abolished by landlords—members of the nobility and often of the episcopacy or religious orders—who were experiencing financial pressures and other threats to their control over their holdings. A group of peasants composed a protest document known as the Twelve Articles, in which they set out their complaints, backed by Scripture and Luther's theology of Christian freedom, and called peacefully for adjudication by theologians and sympathetic civil authorities. They affirmed that government and taxes were necessary, even rejecting revolution.[78] Yet they also demanded the right to call their own pastors, to be relieved of certain tithes, to freely gather wood in the forests and fish from streams, and for the restoration of communal land. These demands quickly became a common rallying point, as a document circulating their content surpassed 25,000 copies.

Luther was initially sympathetic, but when the peasants' complaints went unmet, rioting ensued, and Luther began to call for a swift and

75. Luther, "On Temporal Authority," 125.
76. Luther, "Whether Soldiers, Too," 95.
77. Luther, "On Temporal Authority," 126, 125.
78. Carty, *Divine Kingdom, Holy Order*, 23.

firm government response.[79] In all, he wrote six essays on the matter, including the initial *Admonition to Peace*, followed by the much more adamant *Against the Robbing and Murdering Horde of Peasants*, a "blistering attack."[80] Beyond the question of social order, Luther thought that the peasants were illegitimately using a spiritual rationale (Christian freedom) to back a political agenda (social reform), thus egregiously confusing spheres of authority. The peasants call for mercy, whereas, according to Luther, they have violated the gospel command not only to refrain from inflicting violence on others, but to "endure every kind of suffering—robbery, murder, arson, devil, and hell."[81] The peasants were decisively defeated—or rather massacred—at a battle in Frankenhausen less than two months after their protest began. The 6000 peasants who died that day brought the total of their losses to 100,000.[82]

Despite Luther's legitimate fear of social breakdown and rampant violence, it is hard to argue that his ethics of faith active in love by the "Christian-in-relation" provides genuine grounds for such a disproportionate response with so little respect for the justice of the original protest. As Alister McGrath comments,

> the Peasants' War seemed to show up the tensions in Luther's social ethic: the peasants were supposed to live in accordance with the private ethic of the Sermon on the Mount, turning the other cheek to their oppressors—while the princes were justified in using violent coercive means to reestablish social order.[83]

Luther's endorsement of extreme violence to counter the rebels' violence is the converse of the picture of government authority that he paints to oppose the efforts of Charles V and other Catholic rulers to quash the nascent Reformation. In one of his earliest arguments for the need of reform, Luther appeals directly to the German princes to take action in defiance of Rome.[84] This was of course, in tension with his "persistent

79. Luther, "Against the Heavenly Prophets in the Matter of Images and Sacraments," in Carty, *Divine Kingdom, Holy Order*, 366–68; also in *Luther's Works*, vol. 40, *Church and Ministry II*, ed. Conrad Bergendoff (Philadelphia: Fortress, 1958), 73–223.

80. Whitford, "Luther's Political Encounters," 185. Key sources are the following treatises of spring 1525, all in *Luther's Works* 46: "Admonition to Peace," 3–43; "Against the Robbing and Murdering Hordes of Peasants," 45–55; and "An Open Letter on the Harsh Book Against the Peasants," 57–85.

81. Luther, "Against the Robbing," 70.

82. Luther, "Against the Robbing," 186.

83. McGrath, *Reformation Thought*, 214.

84. Luther, "To the Christian Nobility of the German Nation on the Reform of the Christian Estate," *Luther's Works*, vol. 44, *The Christian in Society I*, ed. James Atkinson (Philadelphia: Fortress, 1966), 123–217.

refusal . . . to attribute to secular authority *as such* any responsibility for the maintenance and support of true religion."[85] Theologically, secular authority has no direct responsibility for or authority over the preaching of the gospel and practice of the faith. Yet when national governing authorities are inclined to support his reforming agenda, he calls on their protection.

Luther sees repression by Catholic rulers backing Rome as a special case, both because the clergy have forfeited their proper spiritual authority through their faithlessness and because many of the abuses committed by people in ecclesiastical roles are in fact also secular crimes, many resulting from greed (robbery, theft, and extortion). Moreover, the earthly church goes beyond spiritual realities because it includes institutions, laws, and ceremonies that exist in and have an effect on "secular" society. Baptism creates a "priesthood of all believers," that in emergency circumstances can validate the responsibility of secular rulers to punish and restrain clerical offenses against the civil law, a responsibility also accruing to them by virtue of their role-related secular duty to protect the common good. In the *Warning to His Dear German People*, Luther departs from the "two kingdoms" division of political and ecclesial authority by urging armed resistance to the anti-reformation laws of the Holy Roman Emperor. Here resistance is characterized not as rebellion but as self-defense, on the grounds that the actions of the emperor and imperial forces are themselves illegal.[86] "The emperor's edicts are contrary to God and justice."[87]

When Luther was censured by a papal bull and excommunicated in 1520–21, he became an imperial outlaw.[88] At the Diet of Worms in 1521, Charles V announced his explicit intention to force the Reformers back into the Catholic Church;[89] but Luther was in fact protected by Fredrick the Wise of Saxony who secluded the fugitive in his castle, the Wartburg. Just as Luther was to blame the peasants for disrupting the social order and precipitating violence, so the emperor no doubt felt that the reform was threatening his precarious control over his territories. It is a fact that the conflicting movements of reformation and counter-reformation were to produce over a century of mayhem and bloodshed in the form of the so-called "wars of religion." Luther however seems to have been blind to the parallels between the peasants' conscientious revolt and his own.

85. Estes, "Luther on Secular Authority," 199.
86. Luther, *Dr. Martin Luther's Warning to His Dear German People* (1531), 467–69.
87. Luther, *Warning*, 473.
88. Luther, *Warning*, 200–205.
89. Corey, "Luther and Just-War Tradition," 307–8.

Toward the end of Luther's life, the Reformation had spread to an increasing number of territories and cities, "with an increasingly well-defined and government-imposed orthodoxy of faith and practice." In commentaries on Psalms 82 (1530) and 101 (1534–35), Luther merged the identities of the prince as Christian and as ruler. Drawing on King David as an example, he portrays the Christian ruler as simply obeying the command of God as far as action in the spiritual realm is concerned, not as acting on his own authority—an argument that has been characterized as "tortuous" and "convoluted."[90]

One potential albeit somewhat hidden asset of Luther's appeal to the German nobility against the emperor is the tacit qualification of his ostensibly rigid and hierarchical notion of the duty of obedience and respect for the rule of law, even unjust laws. Although he blurs the temporal and spiritual reasons for doing so, he does establish a right of resistance to higher authority, based on something like Aquinas's idea that an unjust law is no law at all. David Corey calls the incipient development of a theory of resistance a "monumental development" in Luther's thought. On the other hand, however, he has a remarkably unimaginative approach to the impact of love of enemy on the conduct of war, going so far as to remove practically all restraints, whether against foreign aggressors or civil protestors.[91]

More positively, however, Luther was the first major Christian author to condemn "war fought in the name of 'Christendom' or for the sake of stamping out false [non-Christian] belief."[92] The Crusades (to be discussed in chapter 8) are generally envisioned to have ended at the end of the thirteenth century. While they no longer dreamt of control over Jerusalem, European Christians in Luther's day still feared the incursions of the Ottoman Empire, maintaining a crusading ideology in their battles to fend off Turkish expansion. Charles's predecessor, the emperor Maximillian, and Pope Leo X both advocated a new crusade. Past crusades were used as models for present-day Christians, and eternal salvation was still promised to all who died in battle against the "infidels."[93]

Not all Christians heeded this call, and Sebastian Franck (sounding surprisingly like Karl Rahner) even called for reconciliation in the name of Christ and Christian love: "for whether they outwardly are called

90. Estes, "Luther on Secular Authority," 216–17, 219.

91. Corey, "Luther and Just-War Tradition," 323n55, 326.

92. Corey, "Luther and Just-War Tradition," 317.

93. Gregory J. Miller, "Wars of Religion and Religion in War: Luther and the 16th Century Islamic Advance into Europe," *Seminary Ridge Review* 9, no. 2 (2009): 39, 42–44. See also Gregory J. Miller, "Luther on the Turks and Islam," in Wengert, *Harvesting Martin Luther's Reflections*, 185–203.

heathens, Jews, Turks, or Christians, whoever lives righteously, then let them be a true brother, flesh and blood in Jesus."[94] Luther completely rejected any idea of nonresistance against the Turks. He did however, repudiate the idea that they should be killed on religious grounds, appealing instead to the ideas of just defense and the common good. As he argued elsewhere, the sword can legitimately be used by rulers to protect the common good and serve the people.

Retreating from the confusions besetting Luther's appeal to secular authority in his own defense and against the peasant protests, Luther denounced the Crusades as blasphemous confusions of the earthly and heavenly kingdoms and asserted unequivocally that there could be no such thing as a "Christian" holy war. Muslims could not be attacked simply because they were Muslims, much less forced to convert, but only repelled if they had first attacked Christian territories.[95] In the 1529 treatise *On War against the Turk*, Luther justifies crusades only to the extent they qualify as just wars, since "the Turk certainly has no right or command to begin war and to attack lands that are not his."[96]

Important developments over time in Luther's theory of war are his granting to soldiers a limited right of conscientious objection, his disallowing crusades of religion, and his recognition of a right of resistance against unjust laws as having no real authority. At the same time, he inconsistently separates and confuses the earthly and heavenly kingdoms, seemingly according to his own advantage or proximate political goals.

An underdeveloped resource within Luther's thought on establishing peace is his creative commitment to measures against social ills that precipitate conflict, such as poverty and inferior education. Here he sees Christians as responsible for the social order; enlists the church, civil government, and citizens in favor of structural change; and envisions that concrete steps can be taken locally to reduce social injustice through policies and practices that will serve the common good.

Why were these insights not applied more forcefully in the cause of ending violence and establishing conditions amenable to peace? On the conflict with the "illegal" papists, Luther did attempt dialogue or at least theological interaction with his Catholic adversaries, for example at the Leipzig Disputation, the Diet of Worms, and in exchanges with other

94. Miller, "Wars of Religion," 45, citing Bernhard Capesius, "Sebastian Francks Verdeutchung des 'Tractatus de ritu et moribus Turcorum,'" *Deutsche Forschung im Südosten* 3, no. 1 (1944): 121. For comparison, see Karl Rahner, "Reflections on the Unity of the Love of Neighbour and Love of God," *Theological Investigations* 6 (New York: Crossroad, 1974), 231–49, especially 232.

95. Miller, "Wars of Religion," 51–53.

96. Martin Luther, "On War against the Turk," in Carty, *Divine Kingdom, Holy Order*, 445; also in *Luther's Works* 46.

leaders of reform like Ulrich Zwingli. Although these events (in which Luther participated with his usual pugnacious style) did not bring any of his main interlocutors over to his side, the interactions may have influenced Charles V, who seems never to have pursued Luther's capture aggressively nor explicitly mandated his execution.

It might be hard to envision peacemaking dialogue with the Turkish invaders intent on imperial expansion. But certainly Luther could have taken the moderation he showed as compared to proponents of the crusade ideology, and turned it into a modification of his views of "just war" in Europe as a divinely sanctioned cause permitting virtually unrestrained killing and destruction. Luther opens the possibility that union with Christ in the Spirit can inspire Christians to work successfully for intimations of kingdom life in historical societies, but it remains for later interpreters to develop these suggestions into a peacebuilding ethic.

JOHN CALVIN

John (Jean) Calvin (1509–64), the French Reformer of the Swiss city of Geneva, already represents a second generation of Reformation thought. He straightens out Luther's ambivalence toward the right relation of temporal and religious authority by explicitly endorsing their alliance and cooperation in the governance of Geneva. Calvin *begins* from the idea that government is "religiously infused," not "strictly secular."[97] Government is charged properly and not only on an emergency basis with the protection and fostering of true doctrine, worship, and church order. The kingdom of God cannot be reduced to political life and civil government. But since Christ "begins the heavenly kingdom in us, even now upon earth, and in this mortal and evanescent life commences immortal and incorruptible blessedness," civil government aids human conduct to conform not only to "civil justice," but also to the "true piety" to which Christian "pilgrims" aspire.[98] Magistrates act with divine authority, and "represent the person of God," whose judgments they execute.[99]

Needless to say, this mingling if not merging of civil and ecclesial responsibilities will raise problems of its own, not least of which is the use of violence to coerce religious conformity in the name of Christian love. Not only were heretics and moral delinquents executed in Geneva,

---

97. Corey and Charles, *Just War Tradition*, 12.

98. John Calvin, *Institutes of the Christian Religion*, vol. 2, trans. Henry Beveridge (Grand Rapids, MI: William B. Eerdmans, 1962), 4.20.2.

99. Calvin, *Institutes*, 4.20.4.

but Calvin endorsed the idea of "holy war," including the crusade. More positively, however, government, with its officials and its functions, is embraced as being as natural to human existence as "bread and water, light and air, while its dignity is much more excellent."[100]

Calvin shares with Luther the characteristic emphases of the Reformation: justification by faith, the authority of Scripture, and the Christian life of self-denial that union with Christ's righteousness produces. But Calvin's writing gives a distinctive and very different coloring to these themes, insofar as it is more orderly, more analytical, more indebted to humanism and its scholarly tools, and places more emphasis on the church as the indispensable forum of conversion and discipleship.

The French Reformer's father had come from the artisan classes to become a registrar of the town of Noyon and to serve various offices for the local episcopacy. The young John Calvin was able to associate with the sons of more aristocratic families, with whom he formed lasting ties. In preparation for a theological vocation, he was sent to school in Paris. There he was exposed not only to a classical education, a strict discipline, and a conservative doctrinal orthodoxy, but also to the humanism that was to be a formative influence in his thought.[101] He was attracted to the contemporary and popular humanist intellectual currents both by his masters (Jean Budé, Michel Cop) and through his friendship with other young men (including his cousin, Pierre-Robert Olivétan) who had already been converted to the Reformation.[102]

In 1528, Calvin withdrew from his philosophical and theological pursuits, apparently on the decision of his father, and entered the study of law at Orleans. The paternal motives seem to have been partly financial and partly political, deriving from a dispute with the local clergy in Noyon over the senior Calvin's handling of an estate he had been charged to settle. Upon his father's death two years later, Calvin returned to Paris and began his study of classical literature while continuing studies to complete his law degree. In 1532, he developed some of his humanist insights in a treatise on Seneca's *De clementia*.

---

100. Calvin, *Institutes*, 4.20.3.

101. For Calvin's biography, consult Bruce Gordon, *Calvin* (New Haven, CT: Yale University Press, 2009), published in commemoration of the five-hundredth anniversary of Calvin's birth; François Wendel, *Calvin: The Origins and Development of His Religious Thought* (New York: Harper & Row, 1963); T. H. L. Parker, *John Calvin—A Biography* (Louisville, KY: Westminster John Knox, 1975); B. A. Gerrish, "John Calvin," in *Reformers in Profile: Advocates of Reform, 1300–1600*, ed. B. A. Gerrish (Philadelphia: Fortress, 1967), 142–64; William J. Bouwsma, *John Calvin: A Sixteenth-Century Portrait* (New York: Oxford University Press, 1988).

102. On Calvin's humanism, see Gordon, *Calvin*, 8–14, 18–33; Wendel, *Calvin*, 27–37; and Bouwsma, *John Calvin* (New York: Oxford University Press, 1988), 113–27.

By 1534 Calvin had announced his conversion to the Reformation and his commitment to Scripture by authoring a preface to Olivétan's French translation of the New Testament. For Calvin the unity of both Testaments, their hermeneutical key, is Christ. What should be sought "in the whole of Scripture" is "truly to know Jesus Christ, and the infinite riches that are comprised in him and are offered to us by him from God the Father."[103] Scripture is neither a simple historical record of Jesus's life nor a moral rule-book. It is a medium of a life-transforming relation to Christ. In 1535, at the age of twenty-six, Calvin published the first edition of his major work, the *Institutes of the Christian Religion*, to be revised repeatedly until it reached its final form in 1559.[104] The *Institutes*, which was an immediate success, was intended to provide Scriptural support to true piety and assurance of salvation for those touched by God's grace, brought to faith, and called to live the Christian life in gratitude, love, and self-sacrifice.[105]

As Calvin puts it, the church finds its "strength . . . only in the word of God." No individual nor the church as a whole has a mandate or permission "to coin some new doctrine."[106] Like Luther, Calvin sees the Spirit as the guarantor of authentic interpretation of Scripture and preaching of the Word—that is, of Jesus Christ as the object of faith and the accommodation to human capacity of the divine command and promise.[107] Calvin and Luther were one in rejecting both pope and councils as the indispensable and irrefutable interpreters of the Bible.[108] The "testimony of the Spirit" is "a higher source than human conjectures, judgments or reasons."[109] Yet Calvin did respect the weight of tradition and employed all the methods and disciplines of contemporary scholarship in order to explicate the meaning of the gospel. For Calvin the divine intention in Scripture must be elucidated in conjunction with a careful and educated

103. Calvin, "Preface to Olivetan's New Testament," in *Calvin's Commentaries,* ed. Joseph Haroutunian (Philadelphia: Westminster, 1958), 23:70.

104. On Calvin's conversion, his preface to the New Testament, and the first edition of the *Institutes,* see Gordon, *Calvin,* 33–46, 54–62.

105. Gordon, *Calvin,* 61–62. Calvin's infamous doctrine of double predestination is a derivative of and must be understood in relation to his conviction that people of faith can and must be completely assured of the security of God's love and grace for them (*Institutes,* 3.21.1, 7). See Brian A. Gerrish, "The Place of Calvin in Christian Theology," in *Cambridge Companion to John Calvin,* ed. Donald McKim (Cambridge: Cambridge University Press, 2004), 293.

106. Calvin, *Institutes,* 4.8.9

107. Calvin, *Institutes,* 2.6.1; 3.21.4. Although for Calvin the church is governed by the Spirit, the Spirit has "bound" it to the word of God (Pelikan, *Reformation,* 187; citing Calvin's *Reply to Sadoleto).* See also John Hesselink, "Calvin's Theology," in *Cambridge Companion to Calvin,* 80–81.

108. Calvin, *Institutes,* 1.7.2–3.

109. Calvin, *Institutes,* 1.7.4–5; 2.6.

study of the literal text in its canonical and historical setting. He was familiar with Hebrew and Greek, grammar and rhetoric, medicine and science, geography and history, philosophy and classics, all of which he brought to bear in understanding biblical texts.

Like Luther, but more explicitly and on a different model of the work of grace, Calvin believes that the Holy Spirit empowers the Christian life. According to George Hunsinger, Calvin believed not only that a process of sanctification begins simultaneously with justification, but that it may be described in terms of gradual increase.

> "Christ is not outside us but dwells within us," he wrote. "Not only does he cleave to us by an indivisible bond of fellowship, but with a wonderful communion, day by day, he grows he grows more and more into one body with us, until he becomes completely one with us" (*Institutes* III.2.24). Calvin saw the existential aspect of salvation primarily as a matter of growth, healing and gradual progress by degrees.[110]

With his strong doctrine of regeneration or sanctification, Calvin (unlike Luther) develops a "third use of the law" to guide the conduct of the believer.[111] Calvin does reject any idea that grace changes the human essence or human nature ontologically; saving righteousness is a gift from God and is imputed, not inherent. Nevertheless, the faithful are always united to Christ by the Spirit, and this union enables progress.[112]

The Holy Spirit enables Christians actually to live out "the Christian life as cross and self-denial," difficult though Calvin thinks this is sure to be.[113] According to Calvin, we will be "required to render account of our stewardship," and that especially includes helping the neighbor. One's own advantage should always be subordinated to the other's benefit, since "the only right stewardship is that which is tested by the rule of love."[114] Yet because it is the Holy Spirit who renovates, regenerates and activates the human will, "all the actions which are afterwards done are truly said to be wholly his."[115]

Calvin is more explicit than Luther about the inherently communal nature of salvation and, therefore, the importance of the church. The church is the forum of God's justification, which occurs by means of the

110. Hunsinger, "A Tale of Two Simultaneities," 324.
111. Calvin, *Institutes*, 3.6.12.
112. Calvin, *Institutes*, 3.22.3, 5.
113. Calvin, *Institutes*, 3.7–8.
114. Calvin, *Institutes*, 3.7.5.
115. Calvin, *Institutes*, 2.5.14. For another comparison of Luther's and Calvin's theologies of moral change through the Holy Spirit, see Paul S. Chung, *The Spirit of God Transforming Life: The Reformation and Theology of the Holy Spirit* (New York: Palgrave Macmillan, 2009).

preaching of the Word; the church is the community of worship, cele-
bration of the sacraments, and regeneration. Indeed, although the membership of the visible church includes both the reprobate and the elect,
it is "fatal" to salvation to leave the church.[116] "For unless we are united
with all the other members under Christ our head, no hope of the future
inheritance awaits us."[117]

CHURCH AND SOCIETY

The basis of Calvin's social ethics is his humanistically oriented recognition that despite sin, there is a remnant of God's image in human nature
and in reason. The Christian life implies a moral regeneration conducive to ordered social life under God, but even the unregenerate recognize the basic moral law, including the essentials of true worship. In
an Augustinian vein, Calvin holds that the image of God in the human
person comprehends both the rational nature and its proper orientation
toward God (thankfulness). While the latter is obliterated by sin, the former is not entirely destroyed by human revolt but continues, "by Divine
indulgence," to distinguish "the whole human race from other creatures." Although not sufficient for salvation, this surviving natural ability
to know the good contributes to social order and enables cooperation
between the spheres of Christian discipleship and of citizenship. Public
morality and social concord are made possible by the fact that "in a common nature the grace of God is specially displayed."[118]

Like Augustine and Luther, Calvin understands there to be essentially
two societies at stake in discussion of the social order. "In man government is twofold: the one spiritual, by which the conscience is trained
to piety and divine worship; the other civil, by which the individual is
instructed in those duties which, as men and citizens, we are bound to
perform. We may call the one the spiritual, the other the civil kingdom."[119] Calvin favored a close alliance between civil and religious government, but was also committed to "independence of church from state,
freedom on conscience, new ideas of citizenship, participatory government, special protection for the deprived and vulnerable, and transna-

116. Calvin, *Institutes*, 4.1.4.

117. Calvin, *Institutes*, 4.1.2.

118. Calvin, *Institutes*, 2.2.17; 1.15.3. On Calvin and the Reformed doctrine of "common
grace," see Charles Partee, *The Theology of John Calvin* (Louisville, KY: Westminster John
Knox), 116–19. Calvin associates grace and common human nature under the idea of divine
providence, and he believes God gives special graces even to the reprobate, but he does not
actually use the term "common grace."

119. Calvin, *Institutes*, 3.9.15.

tional obligations."[120] Calvin is careful to state (contra Luther) that not even the inbreaking of the kingdom of God makes the functions of government superfluous, for "perfection . . . can never be found in any community of men."[121] In Calvin's mind, however, historical imperfection does not so much amount to misery (Augustine) as to the need for firm social organization in light of religious ideals.

As previously noted, Calvin claims that the magistrate's office "extends to both tables of the law," which should be protected and enforced on divine authority. The authority of the king or magistrate is immune from rebellion unless there is "a legitimate command from God," as in Old Testament wars; unless the situation involves an inferior magistrate who, in carrying out the duties of office, resists a superior; or unless the king commands acts against God.[122] On the other hand, a moderating influence on the authority of the king or magistrate is the interdependency in Calvin's political outlook of the magistrate, laws, and people, which implies their reciprocal critical relationship.[123] He even anticipates that God may raise up "avengers" to defend the people from tyranny, and that certain public officials may have as their appointed duty watchfulness against abuse of power.[124] In a sermon not long before his death, Calvin "went so far as to condone acts of individual resistance against tyrannical rulers."[125] Calvin undoubtedly believed that legitimate challenges to government would be rare, although his views have been conducive to later theological developments favoring democracy and popular reform.[126]

Committed though Calvin was to at least a partial realization of the kingdom on earth, he was a realist about the perdurance of historical conflict and the need for coercive restraint of crimes and aggression. Still, he thought that in a city formed around the experience of salvation, and constituted by members of the church, ecclesial and political goals could overlap and support one another. Under Christian auspices, political life and government could achieve new heights, envisioned as what is sometimes referred to as Calvin's "theocratic ideal."[127]

The factor that most determined Calvin's mature life—personally, theologically, and politically—was his association with the Reformed church

---

120. Little, "Religion, Peace," 73.
121. Calvin, *Institutes*, 4.20.2.
122. Calvin, *Institutes*, 4.20.23–30; 4.20.32.
123. Calvin, *Institutes*, 4.20, 3, 14.
124. Calvin, *Institutes*, 4.20.30–31.
125. Little, "Religion, Peace," 74, citing Calvin, *Homilies on I and II Samuel*.
126. Corey and Charles, *Just War Tradition*, 116. See Calvin, *Institutes*, 4.20.25.
127. Bainton, *Christian Attitudes*, 147.

in Geneva. Calvin's original excursion there occurred in 1536, as part of a circuitous route (made necessary by political instabilities) from Paris to Basel, where he had taken refuge in exile from France, still a Catholic land. Calvin apparently intended to bring his brother and sister to reside with him and to begin a prolonged period of study and writing. Though Calvin and his party had planned to stay in Geneva only for one night, the French leader of reform there, William Farel, heard of Calvin's arrival. Farel prevailed upon Calvin to remain and help implement reformation in the city by threatening him with God's curse upon his leisure were he to refuse.[128]

A persistent problem in Calvin's relations with Geneva was the precise nature of cooperation between civil and ecclesiastical authorities. While Calvin was determined that the worship and discipline of the church should be in its own hands, the civil authorities were equally adamant about maintaining control. The situation was not helped by Farel's confrontational and divisive tactics to spread the new faith, such as taking over churches and monasteries where the Catholic mass was about to be celebrated, barring the doors, and forcing those present to hear a sermon based on the principles of reform. In his efforts in Geneva Farel had the support of the neighboring city of Bern, which gave financial and military backing to the imposition of the reform by edict in 1536. Friction and factionalism continued nonetheless, with some people remaining steadfast Catholics, and Calvin and Farel resisting Bernese control over specific points of church order. They refused the Bernese communion rites involving unleavened bread and stone cups, and they demanded the right to exclude from communion any who failed to meet their standards.[129] Calvin was evicted from Geneva in 1538 and went to assume a pastorate in Strasbourg, where he married. There he enjoyed a few happy years as pastor and lecturer. In 1541, when he was still only thirty-one, Calvin again succumbed to pressure to return to Geneva, where he was to remain until his death in 1564 at age fifty-four.

Although Calvin regarded the spiritual government as higher than the temporal and thought there was no need for conflict between the two in terms of temporal matters, the Genevan civil authorities had in practice more power over the ecclesial offices than vice versa. Calvin wrote the 1541 *Ecclesiastical Ordinances* as the charter for the reform, ordering the church around the four types of ecclesiastical office that he regarded as scripturally prescribed: pastors (responsible for preaching and sacraments), doctors (who test preaching by Scripture), elders (responsible for

128. Gordon, *Calvin,* 64–65.
129. Gordon, *Calvin,* 64–70, 78–81.

church discipline), and deacons (who minister to the needy). Religious and moral discipline were charged to the Consistory, composed of the pastors and lay elders. But the magistrates selected the elders, and the most powerful institution in the Geneva was the twenty-member Small Council, which made the most important decisions for the city and hired and fired ministers.[130]

Together, the religious and civil authorities, backed by sanctions in both spheres, set upon the improvement of the moral and the spiritual condition of the citizens, vigorously seeking to supervise virtually every area of personal and social conduct. Forbidden by law were indecent songs, dancing, gambling, loitering outside during Sunday sermons, praying in Latin, dining out except in establishments with strict codes of conduct, or speaking ill of the city magistrates. People were excommunicated or expelled from the city for these and other offenses. In 1526 alone, fourteen people were executed in Geneva for rape, homicide, sodomy, theft, witchcraft, and counterfeiting.[131] With Calvin's support, the civil authorities at Geneva took on the protection and even enforcement of the "true" religion, conducting, for instance, the heresy trial and execution of Michael Servetus in 1553. In fact, it was around this time that Calvin grew increasingly skeptical of humanity's natural moral ability and of the idea that the jurisdiction of civil government should be limited to the Second Table of the Decalogue.[132]

Despite draconian measures against religious unorthodoxy and moral turpitude, the institutional structures in place in Geneva also had within their purview the improvement of the lot of the unfortunate, a responsibility headed by the deacons. Geneva had a church court concerned primarily with marital conflicts and domestic abuse, a secondary school, and an academy.[133] The city's social ministry was conducted out of a new hospital established in the former convent of the Poor Clares. The hospital provided for the poor—including orphans, the sick, and the disabled—whether they were housed at home or in the hospital itself. The hospital ovens turned out a weekly dole of bread, and, at Calvin's suggestion, the silk industry was brought to the hospital so the indigent could learn a craft. Women also had a place in the diaconate, as caring for the

130. Gordon, *Calvin*, 69.

131. Philip Benedict, "Calvin and the Transformation of Geneva," in *John Calvin's Impact on Church and Society: 1509–2009*, ed. Martin Ernst Hirzel and Martin Sallman (Grand Rapids, MI: William B. Eerdmans, 2009), 6–8.

132. Little, "Religion, Peace," 76.

133. Jeannine E. Olson, "Calvin and Social-Ethical Issues," in *Cambridge Companion to Calvin*, 154.

poor was thought by Calvin to be the only appropriate and biblically attested ecclesial office for women.

As refugees from Catholic countries poured into Geneva, welfare resources became strained, and various ethnic groups (French, Italian, German) set up additional funds for refugees. The deacons helped with housing and jobs, found wet nurses for infants, and placed orphans in foster homes. They also lent money, especially to enable formerly solvent refugees to acquire tools and start businesses.[134]

These efforts show at the concrete level the possible effect of Calvin's ethics as grounded in the full "drama of human existence" and as confident about "the moral consequences of faith, including the regeneration of human responsibility."[135] In fact, according to Eric Fuchs, the interaction between church and government in Geneva was "a show of social solidarity" and "a powerful driving force for transformation."[136] From Calvin's standpoint, ethics may be seen as a response to God's providence, to God's promise that believers may and must take responsibility for their lives and those of their neighbors with confidence for the future and "without fear of the circumstances they may have to face." To submit to God's will is not to surrender to events or fall into passivity; it is to interpret life in light of the gospel and, in responding to the gospel, "progressively reach Christian, and thus human, wholeness."[137] A Jamaican evangelical theologian, Dieumeme Noelliste, even sees Calvin's advocacy for systemic, structural change as a promising theological-ethical model for the "majority world" (primarily inhabiting the global South). Social action is a sure sign of genuine piety, for "the social validates the reality and genuineness of the vertical."[138]

THE SWORD AND WAR

This positive and transformationist trajectory in Calvin's theology and in Genevan government and civil society falls short when the question of authorized violence arises. Though centering the Christian life on union with Christ and making love of neighbor and service key to the expression of faith, Calvin is convinced that the Bible commands both capital punishment of individuals and war against outside aggression or crime.

---

134. Olson, "Calvin and Social-Ethical Issues," 164–67.

135. Eric Fuchs, "Calvin's Ethics," in *Calvin's Impact on Church and Society*, 145.

136. Fuchs, "Calvin's Ethics," 153.

137. Fuchs, "Calvin's Ethics," 157.

138. Dieumeme Noelliste, "Exploring the Usefulness of Calvin's Sociopolitical Ethics for the Majority World," in *John Calvin and Evangelical Theology: Legacy and Prospect*, ed. Sung Wuk Chung (Louisville, KY: Westminster John Knox, 2009), 225; citing Calvin, *Institutes* 1.8.50.

The assumed recognition of the presence and consequences of evil does not necessarily undermine the Christian commitment to solidarity and justice, for this commitment is one type of response to sin and suffering. However, the fundamental question is how Calvin or any other theologian discerns the proper ethical response.

Calvin's approach is not to concentrate on the building of institutions through which conflicts can be mediated, violent clashes defused, necessary coercion minimized, restorative justice practiced, or perpetrators rehabilitated—all of which might have been instituted to deal with transgression of the laws of Geneva itself, if not at the imperial level. Yet even in this city reformed in the Christian faith, Calvin urges authorities to unleash the righteous anger that wields the sword, to meet violence with violence, and to destroy the aggressor or perpetrator. He seems to harbor a particular rage at those who interpret the gospel differently.

Calvin believes that Scripture makes abundantly clear that individual and social sin have existed both before and after "the coming of Christ," and that the gospel neither changes this fact nor alters the legitimacy of coercion as the appropriate response. In refuting Anabaptist pacifism, he insists that "the Christian man, if according to the order of his country is called to serve his prince, not only does not offend God in taking up arms, but also fulfills a holy vocation, which cannot be reproved without blaspheming God."[139]

Calvin is aware that the Sermon on the Mount presents difficulties for Christian proposals of violence, even (or especially) in pursuit of religious objectives. He reminds readers that Christ came to establish a "spiritual kingdom," not a "civil polity."[140] In coming to terms with the "hard sayings," Calvin does not eliminate the prerogative of self-defense. Commenting on the Lord's command not to dispute with those who "would go to law with thee" (Matt 5:40), Calvin argues that a Christian is "not entirely forbidden recourse to law" and "a fair defence." Certainly "resist not evil" does not exclude "nonviolently deflecting" unfair injury.[141] Beyond nonviolent resistance one may also invoke the help of the magistrate to protect one's goods, and even "with zeal for the public interest, to call for the punishment of the wicked," keeping in mind that some can be reformed by nothing but death.[142]

---

139. John Calvin, *Brief Instruction for Arming All the Good Faithful against the Errors of the Common Sect of the Anabaptists,* in *John Calvin: Treatises against the Anabaptists and against the Libertines,* ed. Benjamin Wirt Farley (Grand Rapids, MI: Baker, 1982), 73.

140. Calvin, *Institutes,* 4.20.12.

141. *Calvin's New Testament Commentaries,* ed. David W. Torrance and Thomas F. Torrance (Grand Rapids, MI: William B. Eerdmans, 1975), 194–95.

142. Calvin, *Institutes,* 4.20.20.

Like Augustine, Calvin claims that the Sermon on the Mount refers primarily to individual intent, not to how that intent is expressed in "external" conduct. Calvin references Augustine's counsel to Marcellinus to bear nonretaliation and love of enemies "in readiness of mind," but not necessarily to act on them. Like Augustine, Calvin thinks that Jesus's precepts refer to "the preparation of the heart" and what is in "the secret of the heart," rather than to that which "may be done openly."[143] And even when they can't themselves repay evil with evil, Christians are allowed to pray that God "takes vengeance on the reprobate."[144]

This emphasis on love as an inner intention, rather than action, continues in Calvin's justification of war. Justifying criteria of war are protection of the common good, last resort, legitimate authority, and right intention. War's justifying conditions and limitations are based on "natural equity and duty," especially the duty to protect subjects who have been "hostilely assailed." Rulers are obligated to defend and protect "the common tranquility of all" and not "allow the whole country to be robbed and devastated with impunity."[145] But even when the cause is just, "all other means must be tried before having recourse to arms." If the criteria of the public good and last resort have been met, then those in authority may wage war "for the good and service of others."[146]

The criterion of right intention demands that those waging war not be driven by "anger, or hatred, or implacable severity," but maintain compassion toward the enemy interiorly, in view of his "common human nature."[147] Calvin does not see love as necessarily animating the warrior's external acts in any discernible way, as long as it is felt "in the secrecy of the soul."[148] Yet he also mentions, in a personal letter and with a felicitous bit of inconsistency, that not even enemies should be denied basic humanitarian services, such as water, food, and fire. Nor can peace treaties once enacted be broken.[149]

Although self-defense (but not humanitarian intervention) is a just cause of war, not all war requires a defensive cause to be just.[150] War is

143. Calvin, *Institutes*, 4.20.20.

144. *Calvin's New Testament Commentaries*, 198.

145. Calvin, *Institutes*, 4.20.11.

146. Calvin, *Institutes*, 4.20.12.

147. Calvin, *Institutes*, 4.20.12.

148. Calvin, *Institutes*, 4.20.20.

149. See Corey and Charles, *Just War Tradition*, 114–15; citing letter to the duchess of Ferrara, January 24, 1564, trans. M. R. Gilchrist, in *The Letters of John Calvin*, ed. Jules Bonnet (New York: B. Franklin, 1975) 4:336–37.

150. Corey and Charles, *Just War Tradition*, 113; citing letter to duchess of Ferrara, 137.

also justified for religious purposes, as holy war.[151] Going back to Augustine's language of "punishment," Calvin cites the account of Moses's rage in Exodus 32 to validate retributive slaughter with no other purpose than vengeance. Calvin characterizes wars led by Moses and David as demonstrations of "their piety, justice, and integrity to God."[152] If what seems to be wanton cruelty in the cause of religious persecution is commanded and demanded by God, then wars of religion are legitimate, just, and holy.

In sixteenth-century Europe, wars of religion were raging on all sides, replete with torture, executions, and the ravaging of whole regions. The Inquisition was still going on. Only the exceptional religious leader was not inured to this slaughter. At the practical and personal level, Calvin was constantly threatened with religious dissension, destabilizing his hard-won hold on the Reformation in Geneva. He almost seems to put more passion into violence as the execution of God's vengeance on or punishment of the faithless than into mass military conflicts between nations and empires. Yet, as John Locke objected already in 1689, it is problematic for any Protestant writer to deem religious persecution a just cause, since this rationale is just as easily turned around on the agents of reform.[153]

Calvin would probably reply that he is assured of his own election, and of the guidance of the Spirit. But, given the importance for Calvin of sanctification and its corporate dimensions, it is still surprising—even shocking—that he can so widely divide loving, compassionate intention and vengeful, violent action. Similar questions may be put to Calvin and Luther as to Augustine: Has it no effect on one's character if one engages in murder and mayhem without scruple or qualm? If one is truly informed by Christ-like and Spirit-empowered dispositions of compassion, mercy, and hope, will this and should this not inevitably color one's actions toward neighbor and enemy, producing practical efforts toward the peaceful and just coexistence of all?

151. Corey and Charles, *Just War Tradition*, 111–12, citing Calvin's 1565 *Commentaries on the Book of Joshua* (10:40, 7:24).

152. Calvin, *Institutes*, 4.20.10.

153. Calvin, *Institutes*, IV420.10. See Corey and Charles, *Just War Tradition*, 110–12.

CONCLUSION

This question is answered in the affirmative by theologians carrying the Reformers' insights into a global context and addressing worldwide issues of justice and peace. Writing in commemoration of the 500th anniversary of the Protestant Reformation, the Lutheran scholar Ulrich Duchrow finds that the rallying cry of the Reformation—the priority of Scripture—offers a key insight for the church's contribution to justice, peace, and creation. (Duchrow specifically targets global capitalism.) Like many ecclesial reform movements before them, the sixteenth-century Reformers, with their slogan *ad fontes* ("back to the sources"), "went back to the radicalism of Jesus" and to "the original biblical sources as critical potential against the tradition (*sola scriptura*)."[154] This warrants a continuing critique of the Reformers themselves, in light of their own deepest commitments. There is no such thing as a guaranteed and permanent reformation, because every reform movement risks the danger of a "Constantinian" cooptation by "secular power" and economic interests. This is even true of Luther himself, as exemplified by his attacks on Jews and Muslims.[155] To this we might add his intemperate war on the peasants and his lack of compassion and mercy for military adversaries. This is a failing shared by Calvin, who moreover mandated the execution of religiously dissenting fellow Christians. The evangelical reform principle that inspired Luther and Calvin provides for a continuing reform of their social views, their policies, and of the church's agency in political society.

Munib Younan, president of the Lutheran World Federation and a Palestinian born in Israel, urges the church to offer the world a prophetic presence and "a word of comfort, a word of strength, and word of empowerment." This is especially important in all regions torn by conflict and violence, and it requires interdenominational and interfaith cooperation.[156] To this end, Luther, followed in these essential respects by Calvin, provides three relevant insights. First, faith liberates the conscience and the community to "seek the Lord's call on the church in today's context" and to respond with appropriate action. Second, Luther's translation of the New Testament into his vernacular German, and Calvin's endorsement of his cousin's French New Testament, teach

154. Ulrich Duchrow, "Radicalising the Reformation," in *Reformation: A Global Perspective*, ed. Marie-Theres Wacker, Felix Wilfred, and Andrés Torres Queiruga (London: SCM, 2017), 67.

155. Duchrow, "Radicalising the Reformation," 68.

156. Munib A. Younan, "Reflections on 'Reformation' Today," in *Reformation: A Global Perspective*, 90.

"the importance of reading in our own languages and interpreting from within our own contexts." Finally, a Christian is subject to none, but servant of all (*On the Freedom of a Christian*). This universalizing vision of Christian service "propels us out of the church . . . and into the world" to offer "the love and dignity gifted to us through the cross"[157]—and, by the power of the Spirit, through our unity with the risen Christ.

157. Younan, "Reflections," 87.

7.

War in God's Name
Crusaders, Joan of Arc, and Puritan Revolutionaries

This chapter focuses on the Crusades, especially the First Crusade, with some comparisons to the life of Joan of Arc and to the English Puritan Revolution of the seventeenth century. The problem of the medieval crusade will receive greater attention, inasmuch as these wars covered a longer historical period than did either the fifteenth-century struggle to regain France from the English, or the English Civil War. The Crusades also involved many more people, not only as military aggressors and victims, but also as part of a massive popular movement that included elements of pilgrimage, penance, self-defense (of Jerusalem as a "Christian" territory), and holy war.[1] Despite the mixed motives and spiritualities that backed the crusading movement, as representing violence instigated by the papacy for religious ends, it is arguable that the Crusades are unparalleled as the nadir of Christian advocacy of violence and bloodshed.

Wars flowing from religious inspiration or fought on behalf of religious causes have existed from the early centuries of Christianity, and they have been legitimized in the writings of just war thinkers from Augustine onward. While violations of the law of nature and natural justice (of "peace" and "the common good") are the primary warrants for armed violence in the mainline Christian tradition, they are not the only ones. While he did not concur in the death penalty frequently imposed on heretics by the civil authorities, Augustine advocated the forcible

---

1. Jill N. Claster argues that the idea of a pilgrimage to liberate Jerusalem defined the First Crusade, and it remained a key factor in defining crusade ideology, even after Jerusalem had been gained. See Claster, *Sacred Violence: The European Crusades to the Middle East, 1095–1396* (Toronto: University of Toronto Press, 2009).

conversion or suppression of the Donatists.[2] Relying on his doctrine of God's predestination of the elect, he held that God could somehow "graft in" even those dragged by force to the body of Christ.[3] During the Reformation, Christians on most sides of any question were willing to use force to quell their opponents. Even wars fought for the sake of public welfare or justice, rather than for properly religious causes, have been given indirect religious justifications. Just war theorists appeal to doctrines of creation, to God's image in human reason and freedom, to God's delegation of authority to temporal rulers, and even to the New Testament love command. Aquinas quotes Augustine's teaching that "the natural order" demands authority "to declare and counsel war," claiming that knowledge of this natural order is a participation in the mind of God.[4]

Yet the crusading movement that gained momentum in the eleventh century was clearly a new phenomenon, even if the First Crusade for Jerusalem was not without precedent.[5] In recent decades scholars have debated the defining characteristics of a crusade, with most agreeing that the question may be hard to settle, and some arguing that the causes and motives behind crusades are so pluralistic as to escape any one definition.[6] The idea of the crusade evolved slowly from the eleventh to the thirteenth centuries. The term "crusade" was a fifteenth-century development, applying to battles against invaders in Europe, and even to battles in later years against heretical Christian groups.[7]

Important in the historical context that allowed the crusading mentality to first emerge was the medieval view of society as an organic, hierarchical, and teleologically ordered whole with God as its creator, lawgiver, and ultimate destiny. Right action or morality consisted primarily in contributing to and defending the common good of the whole under God. At every level of authority, political and religious leaders were to endeavor to conform society on earth to the body of Christ. The places of individuals within this order were defined by their functions or

2. See Phillip M. Thompson, "Augustine and the Death Penalty: Justice as the Balance of Mercy and Judgment," *Augustinian Studies*, 40, no. 2 (2009): 197–99.

3. Brown, *Augustine of Hippo*, 235–36.

4. ST II-II, q. 40, a. 1, citing Augustine, *Against Faustus*, 22.75; ST I-II, q. 91, a. 2.

5. On precedents, as well as a more diffuse starting point than the First Crusade, see Paul E. Chevedden, "Pope Urban II and the Ideology of the Crusades," in *The Crusader World*, ed. Adrian J. Boas (London: Routledge, 2016), 7–10.

6. For general discussions, see Giles Constable, "The Historiography of the Crusades," in *The Crusades from the Perspective of Byzantium and the Muslim World*, ed. Angeliki E. Laiou and Roy Parviz Mottahedeh (Washington, DC: Dumbarton Oaks, 2001), 1–22; Helen Nicholson, *The Crusades* (Westport, CT: Greenwood, 2004), x–xix; Norman Housley, *Contesting the Crusades* (Oxford: Blackwell, 2006), 2–23.

7. Nicholson, *Crusades*, xl.

social roles—whether political, economic, domestic, or ecclesial. Personal morality was conceived primarily as the fulfillment of the duties deriving from one's role in the ordering of the whole. There was little notion of individual rights apart from these duties; social and legal protection was due the individual insofar as his or her ability to fulfill duties so required. The good of the society as a whole took priority over the good of any individual or group within it.

The "infidels" whom the Crusaders battled were outsiders to the order of Christendom and so were perceived as obstacles to the fulfillment of Christian duty toward God, church, and nation. They certainly were not viewed, as in modern terms, as having any intrinsic entitlement to life, liberty, property, or exercise of religion. Richard B. Miller comments that the value of order in the writing of Aquinas had as its underside the "phenomenon of otherness."[8] Violence is more easily countenanced if its potential object is not perceived as a fellow sharer in the good that peaceable order preserves, but rather as a threat to that order's most essential and cherished values. In the twenty-first century, readers can appreciate that the global media conveying images and voices of people in extremely diverse societies offer different and more compassionate imaginative possibilities to their viewers than were available to people in the era of the Crusades. Therefore it might have been even easier than it is today to demonize "infidels" as wicked, fearsome, and unworthy of respect or sympathy.

JUST WAR, RELIGIOUS WAR, HOLY WAR, CRUSADE

Crusade historians tend to use "holy war" as an overarching category and to include the Crusades within it along with other sorts of religiously condoned violence, such as measures taken against heretics and schismatics. This choice of terminology strengthens the impression that the motivations behind and the atrocities perpetrated by the Crusaders were not so different in kind or rationale from other, perhaps less extreme, manifestations of the holy war spirit. Carl Erdmann opens his landmark work, The Origin of the Idea of Crusade, with a definition of holy war as "any war that is regarded as a religious act or is in some way set in a direct relation to religion."[9] Erdmann suggests that the Crusades are different from other holy wars only insofar as "religion itself provided the

8. Richard B. Miller, *Interpretations of Conflict*, 60.
9. Carl Erdmann, *The Origin of the Idea of Crusade* (Princeton, NJ: Princeton University Press, 1977), 3.

specific cause of war." But religion was equally the cause of earlier—and later—suppressions of heretical movements.

Similarly, another important historian, Jonathan Riley-Smith, places crusades in a larger category of holy war, contrasting that category to just war,[10] isolating "the authority of Christ" as the "most characteristic feature of crusading."[11] His definition of what this might mean in practice is broad enough to include wars against local heretics as well as foreign expeditions. "A crusade was a holy war fought against those perceived to be the external or internal foes of Christendom for the recovery of Christian property or in defence of the Church or Christian people."[12]

In *Christian Attitudes toward War and Peace,* Roland Bainton distinguishes the crusade as a third ideal type alongside just war and pacifist outlooks, and he goes further in specifying the distinctive nature of holy wars as entailing extreme convictions of righteousness and of hatred for the foe. He explains, "the crusading idea requires that the cause shall be holy (and no cause is more holy than religion), that the war shall be fought under God and with his help, that the crusaders shall be godly and their enemies ungodly, and that the war shall be prosecuted unsparingly."[13]

James Turner Johnson takes issue with Bainton's strong distinction between just war and holy war, inasmuch as some holy war thinkers saw defense of religion as a just cause for war. He also believes that holy war can have multiple meanings (he enumerates ten), and it can include diverse factors in multiple combinations.[14] Of course, the term "holy war" can be more expansively or more narrowly understood—as more akin to just war, or as a more extreme war ideology, involving aspects not found in Augustine, Aquinas, or the Reformers. Referring to the development of the early modern holy war thinking that culminated in the Puritan revolution, Johnson identifies two characteristics that further refine Bainton's claim about the nature of holy war and can contribute to a better definition of holy war in the narrower (more extreme) sense. They apply both to the Crusades and to the English Puritans.

First, the "fundamental rationale" of the holy war—not true of every war waged against religious adversaries (like the Donatists)—is "the idea that God is 'a man of war' who directs his people into certain battles in

10. Jonathan Riley-Smith, *The Crusades* (New Haven, CT: Yale University Press, 1987), 256.
11. Jonathan Riley-Smith, *The First Crusade and the Idea of Crusading* (Philadelphia: University of Pennsylvania Press, 1986), 17.
12. Riley-Smith, *The First Crusade*, xxxviii.
13. Roland Bainton, *Christian Attitudes*, 148.
14. James Turner Johnson, *The Holy War Idea in Western and Islamic Traditions* (University Park, PA: Pennsylvania State University Press, 1997), 37–44.

the service of their faith."[15] Second, "it is integral to holy war doctrine that one's own side be defined as totally righteous and the other as totally reprobate."[16] Supreme confidence in the merit of one's own cause and in the evil of the opposition is congenial to "the idea that holy war has no limits, but is an unrestrained, all-out struggle of good against evil."[17] These two characteristics—violence as an integral part of God's own way and of the divine will for Christians, and self-righteous abandonment of restraint in war based on a dualism of righteousness and evil—distinctively set off radical holy war ideology against just war theory, and even more they set apart the crusading ideology as a subcategory within holy war. So understood, holy war is fundamentally different from more traditional uses of force in religious conflict (e.g., suppression of heretics), and from wars waged for properly political objectives. During the First Crusade, the crusading mobs reportedly slaughtered "infidels" *en masse*, including children, as though the Eastern inhabitants deserved death whether they presented a danger to any specific Christian interests or not.[18]

It is undoubtedly true that theorists defending both the Crusades and the Puritan Revolution utilized just war terminology, stretching it to meet a new agenda by emphasizing points of contact with standard apologies for the Christian use of violence. This project was facilitated by the fact that just war theorists had themselves not only given religious backing for political wars but also countenanced violent suppression of heresy. Yet differences are substantial.

In standard just war thinking (Augustine and Aquinas, for example), religion is not a primary reason for engagement in armed conflict, nor is war waged entirely without restraint. In fact, in the context of just war

15. James Turner Johnson, *Ideology, Reason, and the Limitation of War: Religious and Secular Concepts, 1200–1740* (Princeton, NJ: Princeton University Press, 1975), 82.

16. Johnson, *Ideology, Reason*, 115.

17. Johnson, *Ideology, Reason*, 104. David Little reinforces the point: "Not only is force undertaken for religious purposes and under direct religious authorization, but opponents in a holy war or crusade tend to regard each other as cosmic enemies with whom compromise is improbable." See Little, "'Holy War' Appeals, and Western Christianity: A Reconsideration of Bainton's Approach," in *Just War and Jihad: Historical and Theological Perspectives on War and Peace in Western and Islamic Traditions*, ed. John Kelsay and James Turner Johnson (New York: Greenwood, 1991), 122.

18. The aim of the Crusades was not conversion and social incorporation—possibly excepting the Jews in Europe whom the Crusaders on their way to the Holy Land either murdered or "converted" at swordpoint—but the recapturing of Christian territories and the liberation of the Eastern churches, as requiring the destruction of the Muslims then in control. See Erdmann, *Origin of the Idea of Crusade*, 97. Jonathan Riley-Smith concurs, but points out one exception: in 1098, when Raymond Pilet led an expedition south of Antioch, where he took a Muslim-occupied fortress and killed all those within it who would not consent to baptism. See Riley-Smith, *The First Crusade*, 1100.

theory, religious coercion tends to be approached with ambivalence if not reserve, as a far less than optimal way to settle religious differences or instill faith. In response to a letter late in life from an old school friend who had become associated with Donatism, Augustine admits that the decision to inflict punishment in spiritual matters is occasion for "trembling" and "darkness."[19]

More importantly, war and killing have never been key to traditional Christian religious self-understanding, whatever compromises with religious identity Christians have made in practice in the political arena. Although Aquinas, a contemporary of the Crusades, speaks in the thirteenth century in acceptance of them, his genre, tone, and subject matter are far from the crusade "preaching" by which popes and theologians converted laity to their mission against the infidels. Aquinas takes up only the specific question of whether the promised papal indulgence is to be applied to the Crusader who "dies before he can take the journey across the sea" and so does not attain his vowed objective.[20] The problem arises as an ad hoc inquiry put to Aquinas during an open forum of questioning and response. Aquinas comments on the preexisting papal decree, but he does not make the Crusades a part of his coverage of the general causes of engagement in war, nor does he address the fundamental moral status of the Crusades.[21]

The crusades represent a change from tradition in that they place violence (and especially killing) at the heart, not the periphery, of Christian faithfulness; they put forward aggressive interpretations of "defensive" violence on behalf of church interests; they involve clergy as real and not merely spiritual knights; and they attach to warring a guarantee of eternal reward. The Crusades were initiated and preached by religious leaders and attracted a transnational following, not dependent on the support of any one civil authority.

The Puritan holy wars represent a similar concept of offensive war for religion, but they differ in that they are directed against other Christians and aim at both national political and religious goals through the specific unification of religious and state leadership in the persons of godly magistrates and rulers. Puritan holy war proponents demand that the soldiers be godly or personally holy, while the Crusaders place more emphasis

---

19. Brown, *Augustine of Hippo*, 243, citing Augustine, Letter 95.

20. Aquinas, *Quodlibetal Questions* 2, q. 8, a. 2. Quodlibetal disputations, held periodically in medieval universities, gave the masters the opportunity to demonstrate their learning by responding to a range of questions from a large and mixed audience including both teaching faculty and students. Questions often had to do with issues then being debated in the church or by theologians.

21. ST II-II, q. 40.

on their own sinfulness and the efficacy of war as penance. It has been argued that at least some Puritan revolutionaries even shifted toward secular just war theory in sanctioning their cause.[22] Some (but not all) of the early modern holy war advocates demand that religious warfare be conducted under limitations similar to those which in just war theory restrain political conflict. But fundamentally, holy war and crusade thinking take root in a Christian version of exclusivist triumphalism that assumes an obligation to extirpate the opposition in the name of Christ.

Both Crusaders and Puritans make use of Old Testament war imagery, and in addition they construe the significance of Christ and of Christian love in violent terms (the latter is particularly true of the Crusaders). Crusaders shared medieval conceptions of a hierarchy of natural and supernatural worlds, conceiving of God's kingdom as a place of delight, comfort, and repose after death. Yet, constantly confronted with the vivid reality of death, they also feared mightily for the fate of their souls. For many Crusaders, the idea of the coming reign of God took on apocalyptic tones: God was about to remake the world by destroying evil. Remission of penalties for sins was promised by crusade preachers, preeminently Pope Urban II, who initiated the First Crusade. Thus, compared to other holy war ideology, the Crusades share another differentiating trait: "what was common to many of these people [the Crusaders], though not necessarily all of them, was the hope of acquiring merit in God's sight by taking part in his war."[23] The Crusaders endured unimaginable hardship—and inflicted unimaginable violence—to ensure their own salvation.

The Puritans were at once more biblical and less susceptible to crass promises of "works righteousness." They sought to make God's reign more present on this earth in the lives of God's elect through the establishment of a religious commonwealth uniting godly living with political control. Though they still rested ultimate hope in a heavenly fulfillment, they, distorting Calvin's vision of a holy commonwealth, sought to actualize in every social sphere a covenanted community of the redeemed.

22. Little, "'Holy War' Appeals," 134.

23. Norman Housley, *Contesting the Crusades* (Oxford: Blackwell, 2006), 22. Housley draws this conclusion after a discussion of types of Crusades, and of theories about how to define crusades.

THE CRUSADES

It was during the era of the First Crusade that preexisting just war ideas, especially those of Augustine, were reshaped into a recognizably different form. It was a time when violence moved from the margins of Christian social ethics into the heart of the Christian calling, as pictured and proclaimed by the pope and as embraced by thousands of his followers. The eleventh century, like the sixteenth, was a time of unrest in Europe. In the former case, the unrest was due to the gradual establishment of feudalism, precipitating the decline of the authority of central government. Loss of imperial or royal protection resulted in general insecurity and the multiplication of private wars, in which churches were sometimes involved. The defense formerly afforded the church by the ruler was now undertaken by circles of knights who became the advocates of bishops and monasteries.[24] Violence was particularly endemic in France, which was to supply the forces for the First Crusade.

French society had long been accustomed to institutionalized violence, first in the expansion of the Carolingian empire, and then in its defense against invasions. When the invasions ceased after 1000, the organization and energy formerly directed at external enemies began to seek internal outlets.[25] The Truce of God and Peace of God movements, which began in France, were attempts to curtail the resultant violence and impose some measure of control on the rampant knighthood. These measures were instigated by the church and ratified with ecclesiastical legislation that required knights and local lords either to forswear war for certain periods or to vow immunity from it for clergy, churches, monasteries, and the poor.[26] Some of these early peace decrees even seemed to promise forgiveness of sins, a precedent to the later crusade indulgence.[27] An ironic outcome of these peace initiatives, however, was the constellation of troops of "enforcers" around the ecclesiastical authorities. The monasteries and bishops themselves had knights committed to take action against breakers of the peace. Hence the church at once condemned the knighthood and its activities and found a positive role for its violence under the church's aegis.[28]

When the First Crusade was preached by Urban II in 1095 at the Council of Clermont, the holy war was in part a solution to problems of

24. Erdmann, *Origin of the Idea of Crusade*, 57–59.

25. Riley-Smith, *First Crusade*, 3.

26. On the Peace of God and Truce of God, see chapter 1 above; Johnson, *Holy War Idea*, 104–9.

27. Erdmann, *Origin of the Idea of Crusade*, 76.

28. Riley-Smith, *First Crusade*, 4; see also Erdmann, *Origin of the Idea of Crusade*, 60–63.

violence at home.[29] Remarking that the French were hemmed in geographically by mountains and sea, and that their land could scarcely provide for them, Urban judges, "Because of this you murder and devour one another, you wage wars, and you frequently wound and kill one another." He then appeals, "Let this mutual hatred stop. . . . Begin the journey to the Holy Sepulcher; conquer that land which the wicked have seized."[30] The conciliar decrees promise an indulgence: "Whoever might set forth to Jerusalem to liberate the church of God, can substitute that journey for all penance."[31]

Exacerbating popular enthusiasm for this proposal, at least in the case of the First Crusade, was the apparent resurgence of an apocalyptic worldview in which Christ was expected to return, violently reclaim the Holy City Jerusalem from the antichrist, and establish God's kingdom on earth—a vision derivative from apocalyptic biblical books like Daniel and Revelation, but one very different from that of the inbreaking reign of God in the gospels. Jay Rubenstein goes so far as to claim that many people across society believed they were living in the Last Days, seeing the Crusade as part of "an ongoing Apocalypse." "Theirs was a shared Apocalypse, a lived Apocalypse, an Apocalypse without end," one "in which their world was being remade" partly through their agency, as instruments of the divine will.[32] This religious worldview or spirituality inspired many to partake in the Crusade not necessarily as warfare, but as pilgrimage or penance, though many never took up arms or traveled as far as the Holy Land. If the journey on which Urban urged them was a pilgrimage—travel to the Holy Land had been going on (more or less peacefully) since Jerusalem was taken by the Muslims in the seventh century—then it was open to the young, the old, members of religious orders, and women.[33]

These developments must also be placed against the background of a

---

29. Steven Runciman, *A History of the Crusades*, vol. 1, *The First Crusade* (Cambridge: Cambridge University Press, 1962), 91.

30. "The Sermon of Pope Urban II at Clermont," an eyewitness account, in *The Crusades: A Documentary Survey*, ed. James A. Brundage (Milwaukee: Marquette University Press, 1962), 19.

31. Jay Rubenstein, *Armies of Heaven: The First Crusade and the Quest for Apocalypse* (New York: Basic, 2011), 24.

32. Rubenstein, *Armies of Heaven*, 319. For a more cautious view of the role of apocalypticism in inspiring a broad social movement, see John France, review of *Armies of Heaven: The First Crusade and the Quest for the Apocalypse*, by Jay Rubenstein, *The Medieval Review* 12.06.05 (2012), accessed August 1, 2017, https://tinyurl.com/y98b66cn.

33. Megan Cassidy-Welch and Anne E. Lester, "Memory and Interpretation: New Approaches to the Study of the Crusades," *Journal of Medieval History* 40, no. 3 (2014): 231–32. Also see Helen Nicholson, "Women's Involvement in the Crusades," in *The Crusader World*, 54–67.

reform movement in the church, undertaken especially by Gregory VII. Gregory's call for armed support set a precedent for sacralization of military forces. In the eleventh century, clergy and laity were considered two distinct orders, with the former dedicated to the spiritual life and divine worship and the latter to worldly affairs. However, many civil rulers and lords were accustomed to wielding considerable influence in the affairs of the local churches, including the appointment of bishops and abbots. There was great concern on the part of the papacy to define the role of the laity positively but more narrowly. The key theme in the reform was to limit civil rulers' authority in church affairs by associating lay roles with monastic values and seeing action in the political order as a God-given vocation of service to the church.

The Investiture Contest shows how difficult it was to curb existing prerogatives of lay elite. Henry IV of Germany (later to become Holy Roman Emperor) resisted the reforms, instigating a prolonged conflict over the relative influence in ecclesiastical appointments of the pope and the Holy Roman Emperor. Gregory asserted the independence of the church from imperial influence by claiming authority as the successor of St. Peter in both the spiritual and the temporal realms, including, if necessary, resort to the secular sword wielded by his allies.[34] The ongoing dispute devolved not only into the excommunication of emperor by pope and the installments of anti-pope and anti-king, but also into outright war.

Gregory made the most of the availability of military men in aid of the church, calling them "soldiers of Christ" and "soldiers of St. Peter" or "vassals of St. Peter," who were called to the "warfare of Christ." This military imagery was already familiar as a description of the monastic life (for example, in the *Rule of St. Benedict*) and even of the secular clergy (in the writings of Gregory the Great). But Gregory VII transformed its function from metaphor for monastic spirituality to exhortation to real military action.[35]

Gregory's creation of a papal army, recruited with offers of forgiveness of sins, did not pass without rebuke from other members of the episcopacy who did not concede the consistency of the Christian ideal of love with the militarization of the church. Gregory's countermove was to gather a number of supporters who sought to justify his concept of Christian warfare with reference to the Bible, tradition, and canon law. At the center of this coterie was Countess Matilda of Tuscany, who con-

34. I. S. Robinson, "Gregory VII and the Soldiers of Christ," *History* 58, no. 193 (June 1973): 170–77.
35. Riley-Smith, *First Crusade,* 6; Robinson, "Gregory VII," 174, 177–80.

tributed invaluable resources, both economic and military, and who harbored the papal theologians in her court.[36] Early on, one of these, John of Mantua, assured Matilda that Scripture endorsed military force in defense of true religion. He admonished her, "Do not ever be ashamed, O Bride of Heaven," to take up the sword against heretics, for "the God still lives who sanctified such action through the arms of David."[37]

One of the most industrious and influential of these Gregorian theologians was Bishop Anselm II of Lucca, who combed the works of Augustine to compile a systematic theory of war that would justify violence against heretics, while reducing Augustine's ambivalence on the subject.[38] Anselm proposes that killing at the behest of church authorities is grounded ultimately in the command of God and should be embraced as a work of Christian love. Drawing from Augustine's anti-Donatist writings, Anselm allegorizes the casting out of the slave Hagar by Sarah (Gen 16:6) to work out a concept of holy or blessed persecution of heretics. Yet Anselm qualifies his program of violence with a reserve that became all but nonexistent during succeeding centuries when the Crusades were in full bloom. He grants both that the individual Christian may not use the sword in self-defense and that use of the sword even for righteousness' sake does not accord with the full perfection of the Christian life. However, he uses a series of biblical references to draw a distinction between Christian perfection and the demands of the church's actual situation. Anselm justifies violence here and now by asserting a vast distance between God's kingdom and the present life. He notes that, although Paul preferred all to be celibate, he allowed that every man might have his own wife, and although the Decalogue prohibits killing, Moses still allowed the Israelites to repay a life with a life.

Similarly, concluded Anselm, "would that Catholics 'wrestled not against flesh and blood' (Eph. 6:12); would that they might live in peace . . . so that there was no need of 'the minister of God, an avenger to execute wrath on evildoers' (Rom 13:4)." But since some members of the church prove refractory and threaten schism, the Gregorians have no choice but to punish them.[39]

Although the birth of the Crusades against the pagans was to await the pontificate of Urban II, Gregory and his partisans provided two conditions that made the Crusades possible. In the first place was what for

36. Robinson, "Gregory VII," 184. See also Erdmann, *Origin of the Idea of Crusade*, 224–25.

37. Robinson, "Gregory VII," 185, citing *Tractatus Iobannis Mantuani in Cantica Canticorum ad semper felicen matildam*, ed. B. Bischoff, 41.

38. Erdmann, *Origin of the Idea of Crusade*, 241–47; Robinson, "Gregory VII," 186–88.

39. Robinson, "Gregory VII," 187, citing Anselm of Lucca, *Liber contra Wibertum*, cap. 6, *M.G.H.*, *Libelli de lite* 1.525.

many medieval people would be an irresistible motivation for undertaking hardship and death: a guaranteed escape from eternal retribution for sins. Second, and more importantly for the career of Christian thinking about peace and war, was an ethos of lay service to the church that soldered professional violence to the highest Christian ideals, especially fraternal charity.

The motive of love for those whom "punishment" might move to repentance was not abandoned totally, but neighbor-love took on a nonuniversal or exclusive meaning: love for and defense of comrades bound by ties of nationality, kinship, or religious affiliation. Even before the First Crusade, Gregory appealed for an expedition—which he proposed to lead personally—to succor Constantinople against pagan invaders. Although his plans never came to fruition, they consolidated the reinterpretation of Christian virtue that the Crusades would require.

> The example of our redeemer and the obligation of brotherly love demand that we lay down our lives for the liberation of our brethren, just as he "laid down his life for us and we ought to lay down our lives for our brethren."
>
> We beseech you, therefore, that you be moved to fitting compassion by the wounds and blood of your brethren and by the peril of the aforesaid Empire and that your strength be brought, in Christ's name . . . to the aid of your brethren.[40]

When Urban II preached the First Crusade in a tour of France (1095–96), he expressed the sentiment in favor of a war of liberation on behalf of the Eastern churches that had been gathering momentum in the West for half a century. Urban actually had two aims in announcing the crusade, the interrelation and priority of which have been the subjects of much scholarly debate. These aims were to free the Eastern churches from the Turks and to make a novel (that is, armed) pilgrimage to the holy sites of Jerusalem with the purpose of recapturing them for Christianity.[41]

The immediate impetus for Urban's initiative was an appeal from the Byzantine emperor for assistance in fending off the Turks who approached Constantinople. In his opening sermon at the Council of Clermont, as remembered by an eyewitness, Urban deplores the fact that "the people of the Persian kingdom, an alien people, a race completely foreign to God . . . has invaded Christian territory" and devastated it "with pillage, fire and the sword." Moreover, he expected his

---

40. Letter addressed "to all those willing to defend the Christian faith," and dated Rome, March 1, 1074, in Brundage, *Crusades,* 9–10.

41. Erdmann, *Origin of the Idea of Crusade,* 330–31.

French audience to be "especially aroused by the fact that the Holy Sepulcher of the Lord our Savior is in the hands of these unclean people." He invokes the gospel, recalling Jesus's promise that whoever leaves house, lands, and family "for my name's sake" shall receive "life everlasting." Promising remissions of sins, he enjoins the Crusader to take up the cross of Christ: "Whoever shall decide to make this holy pilgrimage and shall take a vow to God, offering himself as 'a living sacrifice, consecrated to God and worthy of his acceptance,' shall wear the sign of the Lord's cross, either on his forehead or on his breast."[42]

The imagery of the cross was the symbolic nexus of the crusading movement and was thoroughly effective in stirring up popular fervor on behalf of the "knights of Christ." As the chronicle of a literate but not high-ranking participant in the First Crusade reveals, Christ's nonresistant suffering and death were used to justify slaughtering the infidels with relish rather than scruple and to exalt violence into martyrdom and sainthood:

> When that time had already come, of which the Lord Jesus warns his faithful people every day, especially in the Gospel where he says, "If any man will come after me, let him deny himself, and take up his cross, and follow me," there was a great stirring of heart throughout all the Frankish lands, so that if any man, with all his heart and all his mind, really wanted to follow God and faithfully to bear the cross after him, he could make no delay in taking the road to the Holy Sepulchre as quickly as possible.[43]

An arriving band of French Crusaders is described to the leader Bohemond in a warlike transposition of New Testament sacrifice imagery: "They are well-armed, they wear the badge of Christ's cross on their right arm or between their shoulders, and as a war-cry they shout all together, 'God's will, God's will, God's will.'"[44]

Riley-Smith estimates that perhaps as many as 136,000 people responded to Urban's appeal, including many whom the pontiff had discouraged, such as women, children, and the infirm. Why such a broad response? Many incurred great financial burdens, including debts and mortgages, and were—surely not unexpectedly—in danger of disease, injury, hunger, and death on the way. Yet an overriding motive was fear of punishment after death, a fate to be averted by the tremendous sacrifices to be undertaken voluntarily in the crusade.

That being said, crusading expeditions would not have attracted such

42. "The Sermon of Pope Urban," 18–20.
43. Rosalind Hill, ed., *The Deeds of the Franks and the Other Pilgrims to (Gesta Francorum)* (New York: Thomas Nelson & Sons, 1962), 1.
44. Rosalind Hill, ed., *The Deeds of the Franks*, 7.

a following were there no appeal in the prospect of waging holy warfare. The reinvigorated military theme and the prospect of shedding the blood of aliens drew some of their ideological and emotional resonance from the medieval culture of family vengeance. At a time when ties of kinship provided protection and stability, and landholdings were crucial to survival, vendettas or blood feuds were common. Family members joined together in avenging wrongs.[45] After the Crusaders conquered Jerusalem, they were "maddened by so great a victory after such suffering."[46] Save the general Iftikhar, who surrendered and with his bodyguard was guaranteed safe passage out, the Christians massacred all the Muslim inhabitants, including women and children in houses and mosques, reputedly filling the temple with blood that reached up to one's knees. Jill Claster, a historian who titles her study *Sacred Violence*, conveys the mentality that made such a scene possible: "The intensity of the cruelty that then occurred strained the descriptive powers of the chroniclers who witnessed it." Yet though "they all reported the same degree of horror that ensued," they "were in no doubt about the suitability of what they had done, no doubt at all that God would rejoice with them."[47] The rhetoric of the crusade and the violent social settings that fed its power prepared the killers to see their deeds as just retribution for egregious insults to the dominion of God and the proprietary rights of the church.

As Jonathan Riley-Smith argues, the "idea of the crusade" grew in magnitude during and after the fact. The Crusaders' horrific experiences of deprivation and suffering en route to Jerusalem, combined with their almost miraculous triumph there, led to a recasting of the meaning of crusade as divinely inspired and providential warfare, rising to the heights of monastic spirituality and complete with visions, signs, discoveries of relics, and martyrs—as recounted in accounts of eyewitnesses narrating their adventures some years later.[48] Christianity fully absorbed and was transformed by, rather than transforming, a violent cultural ethos.

Papal preaching and the popular response received further theological development that allowed the outlook of the First Crusaders to be transmitted normatively to their successors. This theological interpretation incorporated suppositions about violence and Christian living that fueled the Crusades. For instance, three French Benedictine monks mediated the ideology of the First Crusade by writing shortly after the assault on Jerusalem: Robert the Monk, Guibert of Nogent, and Baldric of Bour-

45. Riley-Smith, *Crusades*, 7.
46. Runciman, *First Crusade*, 286–87.
47. Claster, *Sacred Violence*, 87.
48. Riley-Smith, *Crusades*, 2, 7–8, 118–19.

gueil. They based their accounts on the *Gesta Francorum,* the anonymous narrative of an Italian Norman knight (the "participant" cited above), refining his rough style into a more convincing apology. Robert even draws a parallel in importance and divine approbation between the success of the crusade and the creation of the world and Jesus's sacrifice on the cross.[49] These writers justify the crusade by announcing the Christians' prior claim to the Muslim-occupied territories, especially the Holy Land. They reinforce a sense of religious privilege and mission through a rhetoric of unity in Christ, validating unrestrained injury to offenders against the church. Laments Baldric:

> Our brothers, members of Christ's body. . . . Your blood-brothers, your comrades-in-arms, those born from the same womb as you, for you are sons of the same Christ and the same Church. . . . Christian blood, which has been redeemed by Christ's blood, is spilled and Christian flesh, flesh of Christ's flesh, is delivered up to execrable abuses and appalling servitude.[50]

Baldric's connotative uses of kinship metaphors (blood, womb, flesh) allow a Christian audience to replace the universal and inclusive thrust of the gospel love command with fierce group loyalty.

Such efforts cast the mold for the enthusiasm with which later church theologians were to take up the cause. In the crusading centuries, the voices calling for peace were few. More representative was one of the medieval church's greatest theologians and preachers, Bernard of Clairvaux. Bernard devoted the energies of his later years to preaching very convincingly the ill-destined Second Crusade (under Pope Innocent II, beginning in 1145). Bernard's surviving letters have been called "the most powerful crusade propaganda of all time."[51] A sample:

> Now is the acceptable time, now is the day of abundant salvation. The earth is shaken because the Lord of Heaven is losing his land, the land in which he appeared to men. . . . And now, for our sins, the enemy of the cross has begun to lift his sacrilegious head there. . . . What are you doing, you mighty men of valor? What are you doing, you servants of the cross . . . ? Gird yourselves therefore like men and take up arms with joy and with zeal for your Christian name, in order to 'take vengeance on the heathen and curb the nations.'[52]

49. Riley-Smith, *First Crusade,* 140.

50. Riley-Smith, *First Crusade,* 145; citing Baldric of Bourgueil, "Historia Jerosolimitana," RHC oc. 4, 12–13.

51. Riley-Smith, *First Crusade,* 95.

52. Bernard of Clairvaux, "Letter to the People of the English Kingdom" (ca. 1146), in Brundage, *Crusades,* 91–92.

Bernard also admonishes his audience to lay aside the sword in their native lands to take it up elsewhere.

More than two centuries later, Catherine of Siena shared Bernard's interest in diverting local disruption and trouble when she urged a crusade that never transpired. She believed that a crusade might repair deep rifts in the church owing to the fact that for seventy years popes had been absent from Rome, ruling instead from the French city of Avignon. Catherine is best known for her impassioned pleading, ultimately successful, that Pope Gregory XI return to Rome from France.

Catherine's lifetime saw the revolt of several Italian states against Gregory XI and the legates through whom he continued to rule in Italy, who even by Catherine's account were often power-hungry and corrupt.[53] Concerned to reconcile the church, she built the need for a crusade into her appeals for unity. She begs Gregory XI to forgive rebels and "by love" restore "the wandering sheep to the fold of Holy Church." Addressing the pope affectionately, she proposes to give a common focus and to turn past differences to cooperation. "And then, sweet my 'Babbo,' you will fulfil your holy desire and the will of God, by making the holy Crusade, which I summon you in His Name to do swiftly and without negligence. They will turn to it with great eagerness; they are ready to give their life for Christ."[54] Later she writes to Gregory's successor, Urban VI, in support of the identical program. She begs him "by the love of Christ crucified" to show mercy to "the little sheep who have strayed from the fold," adding that "once peace is made, you can raise the standard of the most holy cross. As you can plainly see, the infidels have arrived on our shores to challenge you."[55] Catherine's exhortations continue the now-familiar theme: Christian love, reduced to group loyalty, is a sword's edge against perceived adversaries.

A final phenomenon setting crusade theory and practice off from earlier just war thinking is the establishment of religious orders of knights that adopted certain monastic vows and included some members of the ordained clergy. Departing from the traditional exclusion of clergy from violent professions, these orders reflect the inroads made by the conviction that force of arms is appropriate to a Christlike life. The most prominent of the military orders are the Order of Knights Templar and the Order of the Hospital of St. John of Jerusalem. The Hospitalers were founded in 1113, originally with the purely charitable motive of caring

---

53. See Mary Ann Fatula, *Catherine of Siena's Way* (Wilmington, DE: Michael Glazier, 1987).

54. "To Gregory XI" (ca. 1375), in *Saint Catherine of Siena as Seen in Her Letters*, ed. Vida D. Scudder (New York: E. P. Dutton, 1905), 126.

55. J. Kirshner and K. F. Morrison, *Medieval Europe* (Chicago: University of Chicago Press, 1986), 429.

for sick pilgrims to the Holy Sepulchre. Later they took on the role of defending the frontiers of Christian settlements and began accumulating land, while their ministry to the poor became secondary. In 1118–19, a French knight and eight companions took vows of obedience, poverty, and chastity and swore to protect pilgrims on the road to Jerusalem. The order they formed, the Knights Templar, was supported by the king, Baldwin II, and by Bernard of Clairvaux, who drafted their rule. Both orders came directly under the authority of the Holy See, which guaranteed them unusual freedom from the usual civil and ecclesiastical institutions. Eventually they developed into transnational organizations of notable military strength and great wealth, exercising important roles both in defense of the Latin states that had been established in the East and in international finance.[56]

Aquinas later offers the defense that, although members of religious communities should not defend by violence any "worldly purpose," the "religious order directed to soldiering" can accomplish work belonging to the active (versus contemplative) part of a consecrated life of service to God. He continues, "a religious order may be fittingly established for soldiering . . . for the defense of divine worship and public safety, or also of the poor and oppressed."[57]

The capture of Jerusalem that ended the First Crusade brought only temporary satisfaction—the city was recaptured in 1187 by the Muslims under Saladin. Yet the victory was to inspire other initiatives for two centuries, with nearly continual waves of Crusaders departing for the East in between the major contingents. In these Eastern initiatives, success tended to be ephemeral, though the Crusaders sometimes stayed to settle colonies (the states of the "Latin Kingdom of Jerusalem," the last holdout of which fell again to the Muslims in 1291). The final Ninth Crusade (led by Prince Edward of England in 1271–72) was, like most of its predecessors, a failure.

The term "crusade" was extended to campaigns mounted in Europe, both against non-Christian invaders (for example, the Wends in Germany) and against heretical Christian insurrectionists (the Albigensians and Hussites, for example). Political goals could be intertwined with religious ones: the status and privileges of Crusaders were awarded the Teutonic knights who campaigned against the Prussians (1226), and the pope proclaimed a crusade against Holy Roman Emperor Frederick II (1228). Despite their longevity, the high point of the Crusades had really been at their beginning. As Riley-Smith tells it, the movement "died a

56. See Hans Eberhard Meyer, *The Crusades,* 2nd ed. (New York: Oxford University Press, 1988), 77–80; and Riley-Smith, *Crusades,* 56–60.
57. ST II-II, q. 88, a. 4.

lingering death," its popular energy lost by the late fourteenth century. The crusade of Sebastian of Portugal in 1578 "may have been" the last, although various remaining Crusaders still "may well have been found in the late seventeenth or early eighteenth century." The crusading era was definitely brought to a close—in disconcertingly recent history—by the defeat of the last bastion of a military order when Napoleon overtook the Hospitalers on Malta in 1798.[58]

JOAN OF ARC

A figure that casts into relief the crusading mentality and prepares the transition to the Puritan revolution is Joan of Arc—"la Pucelle" or "the Maid" of Orleans, as she designated herself (1412–31). At first look, Joan in many ways seems to fit into the crusade genre, especially its ethos of Christian knighthood and its sense of divinely appointed mission to recapture occupied lands. But there are crucial differences. Most obviously, those against whom she contended were also Christians, not "infidels," and hence not genuine outsiders to her social vision. Moreover, Joan's martial leadership, while supernaturally inspired, was neither yoked to ecclesial aims nor, in fact, put in the service of religion as such at all. She perceived herself as commissioned for a properly political (justice-based) goal: to conclude the Hundred Years' War by saving France from English dominion and to ensconce Charles VII on his rightful throne.

More noteworthy from a theological point of view is that Joan expressed ambivalence about the enterprise of killing, avowing at the end of her career that she had never personally engaged in it. To put anyone to death offended her sense of the mission with which she had been divinely charged (though she hardly discouraged her troops from measures that were to her personally repugnant). Moreover, she repeatedly expressed her hope for peace with her adversaries, in a spirit of forgiveness and reconciliation, not conquest or extermination.

Daughter of a French farmer in Domremy, Joan grew up in a time of conflict between France and England, near the border of the two countries, where frequent "raids and pillaging" taught her "firsthand the horrors of war."[59] She began as a girl of thirteen to hear the "voices" of St. Michael, St. Catherine, and St. Margaret. When she was about sixteen, they exhorted her to come to the aid of Charles the Dauphin. Shortly

58. Riley-Smith, *Crusades*, 255.
59. Larissa Juliet Taylor, *The Virgin Warrior: The Life and Death of Joan of Arc* (New Haven, CT: Yale University Press, 2009), 1.

after news came in 1428 that the English had taken Orleans, she jour-
neyed to see Charles at Chinon Castle. There, in a secret conversation,
she convinced him of her mission to raise the siege of Orleans and have
him crowned at Reims. (One theory is that she reassured him, on God's
authority, of the legitimacy of his birth, a matter in some doubt in his
own mind as well as others. Hence she was able to secure Charles's confidence in his right to the throne and in her ability to lead him to it.)

The appeal of the Maid to the imaginations of so many, from her
contemporaries to the present, is due not only to her reputed ability to
inspire military confidence and hence success, but also to the aura of
mystery and miracle, or at least of inexplicability, with which she has
constantly been surrounded.[60] When the army to march on Orleans was
organized at Tours, Joan put on a suit of white armor and carried a standard, the prerogative of a knight, on which were inscribed "Jesu Maria,"
a depiction of Christ, and the French white fleur-de-lis.[61] She is reputed
to have made an unusual request for a special sword, with five crosses
engraved on it, which she said would be found behind the altar in the
Church of St. Catherine in Fierbois. It was in fact discovered there and
brought to her. Joan is said to have prized her banner even more than
her sword. "'I truly love my sword,' said the Maid, 'because it was found
in the church of St. Catherine whom, too, I love. But I value my standard forty times more highly than my sword.'" When she was asked why
she carried it into battle, she replied, "Because while carrying my banner I could avoid the shedding of blood I have never killed anybody."[62]
Whatever else she may or may not have been, Joan had a natural instinct
for battle and was a formidable foe for the English. Her leadership in

---

60. See Taylor, *Virgin Warrior*, and "Joan of Arc, the Church, and the Papacy, 1429–1920,"
Catholic Historical Review 98, no. 2 (2012): 217–40; Françoise Meltzer, *For Fear of the Fire: Joan
of Arc and the Limits of Subjectivity* (Chicago: University of Chicago Press, 2001); Karen Sul-
livan, *The Interrogation of Joan of Arc* (Ann Arbor: University of Michigan Press, 1999); Deborah A. Fraioli, *Joan of Arc: The Early Debate* (Woodbridge, UK: Boydell, 2000); and Bonnie
Wheeler and Charles T. Wood, eds., *Fresh Verdicts on Joan of Arc* (New York: Psychology,
1996). Among the many earlier biographies and works on Joan's influence are Lucien Fabre,
Joan of Arc (New York: McGraw-Hill, 1954); Ingvald Raknem, *Joan of Arc in History, Legend
and Literature* (Oslo: Universitets-Forlaget, 1971); W. S. Scott, *Jeanne d'Arc* (London: Harrap,
1974); Marina Warner, *Joan of Arc: The Image of Female Heroism* (New York: Alfred A. Knopf,
1981); and Anne Llewellyn Barstow, *Joan of Arc: Heretic, Mystic, Shaman* (Lewiston, NY: Edwin
Mellen, 1986).

61. Warner reports that in December 1429 Joan "and her family and all their issue in the male
and female line were ennobled by Charles in perpetuity." See Warner, *Joan of Arc*, 165.

62. Fabre, *Joan of Arc*, 277, from a transcript of Joan's trial; also see 131. See also Warner, *Joan
of Arc*, 165. Warner cites *Prods de condamnation de Jeanne dArc: Traduction et notes par Pierre Tisset
avec le concours de Yvonne Umbers*, 3 vols. (Paris, 1870).

the battlefield won several decisive victories, and her skill at artillery was notorious.[63]

Other events and circumstances in Joan's life also contributed to the tremendous power she was able to exercise over the imaginations of her followers and even her enemies. One of these was her seeming ability to predict the future or to know contemporaneous events that had not yet come to light. She predicted accurately that she would be wounded, yet not seriously, at the battle of Orleans, and that a man who at Chinon swore at and insulted her was near his death (which came to pass within an hour). Even before her audience with the Dauphin, she had known of an important defeat of the French near Orleans and told of it to the immediate disbelief and later conversion of her hearers. Joan's mystique was enhanced by her anomolous gender identification, manifest most obviously in her refusal to wear women's clothing and her adoption of knightly garb. She not only was a virgin (certified at least three times through examination by officially commissioned groups of matrons), but also apparently was amenorrheic.

After the successful siege on Orleans in 1429, Joan took a place of honor beside Charles VII at his coronation. However, her fortunes were about to turn. The same year, she was unsuccessful in her siege of Paris and was later captured by the Burgundians, who sided with the English, to whom they sold her. Charles, unintelligibly if not reprehensibly, made no attempt to ransom her.[64] She was eventually turned over to the ecclesiastical court at Rouen. There she was tried in "an atmosphere of threats of exile, imprisonment, and drowning," in the heart of English territory in France, and in a castle surrounded by English soldiers.[65] Indeed, "hatred felt by the English for Joan drove the trial."[66]

Pierre Cauchon, bishop of Beauvais, indebted both financially and politically to the Burgundians and the English, tried her personally for heresy and witchcraft. Fear caused her finally to sign a statement disavowing the saints whose voices had led her. But after a three-day period in which the voices rebuked her for her faithlessness, she returned to the steadfastness of her original convictions. She did not waver in her beliefs when she was shortly thereafter burned at the stake as a heretic.

The events of Joan's death evoked wonder and strengthened rather than undermined her reputation. She begged that a crucifix be brought from a local church, so that the sight of it could console and steady her, as she met her death calling upon the names of her saints and of

63. Taylor, "Joan," 221.
64. Taylor, *Virgin Warrior*, 172–73.
65. Taylor, "Joan," 230.
66. Taylor, "Joan," 233.

Jesus Christ. By at least some accounts, her heart did not burn, and was ordered to be cast, along with other potential relics of the execution, into the river Seine.[67] Yet "Joan was not burned by the Church but executed with considerable difficulty by an English-controlled court that had as its foregone conclusion her ultimate conviction and death."[68] In 1456 Joan was "rehabilitated" in a special trial that repudiated the biased partisan proceedings of the first. In 1920 she was canonized.

Whatever else she was, that Joan was an avid patriot who sought French independence through allegiance to God as its true sovereign is clear. She was best known to her contemporaries as a genius at warfare and a terror to the English.[69] Certainly she endorsed and personally led troops to the kill in defense of her political aim, and she embossed her leadership with the popular ideals and emblems of knightly chivalry. What more is known of her attitudes toward violence and toward the role of divine intervention in the political conflicts that she believed she was sent to resolve? Some evidence comes from letters that she sent to the English prior to the campaign against them at Orleans. Addressing herself to the king, the regent of France, and other high-ranking officers, she implores, "I call upon you to make submission to the King of Heaven, and to yield into the hands of the Maid, who has been sent hither by God, the King of Heaven, the keys of all the fair cities which you have seized and ravished in France." Nevertheless, Joan declares herself "willing to make peace with you if you be willing to hearken to her [the Maid's] demands, which are that you shall leave France in tranquility and pay what you owe."[70] She promises that if her plea is heeded, then the Duke of Bedford, Regent, might join with her "and with the men of France in so high an exploit that the like has never been seen in all Christendom."[71] Later, she was to state at her trial that "I first demanded that peace should be made, and was prepared to fight only if that could not be brought about."[72] Lucien Fabre states that Joan's voices had instructed her to warn the English to surrender before resorting to violence against them.[73]

The records of Joan's trials provide her own self-justifications in response to hostile questioning. She firmly refuses to draw either God or her voices into any rhetoric of hatred for the English. In response to

67. See Scott, *Jeanne d'Arc*, 125; Fabre, *Joan of Arc*, 323; Raknem, *Joan of Arc*, 18.
68. Taylor, "Joan," 240.
69. Taylor, "Joan," 237.
70. Quoted in Fabre, *Joan of Arc*, 140.
71. Fabre, *Joan of Arc*, 140. Fabre speculates that the "exploit" is a projected crusade.
72. Fabre, *Joan of Arc*, 293.
73. Fabre, *Joan of Arc*, 140.

the query whether St. Margaret and St. Catherine "hate the English," she replies only that they "love what Our Lord loves, and hate what He hates." When pressed, "Does God hate the English?" her answer is that even if the English "are beaten . . . because of their sins," she still "know[s] nothing of any love or hatred which God may bear to the English," but also "that God will give to the Frenchmen the victory against them."[74]

Joan's responses contrast to Urban's rhetoric at Clermont, urging the "heralds of Christ" to "exterminate this vile race [the Muslims] from the lands of our brethren," the "worshippers of Christ":

> Oh, what a disgrace if a race so despised, degenerate, and slave of the demons, would thus conquer a people fortified with faith in omnipotent God and resplendent with the name of Christ! Oh, how many reproaches will be heaped upon you by the Lord Himself if you do not aid those who like yourselves are counted of the Christian faith![75]

The most overt and easily specifiable difference between Joan and the Crusaders is that she was motivated by what she considered to be just political goals—not by the expansion or defense of the institutional church, and certainly not by its temporal stakes in civil or political affairs. Such ecclesial interests were, in fact, clearly aligned against her in the trials at Rouen. Although Joan invoked a divine mandate, the military objectives backed by that mandate were justified by political criteria, not religious or revealed ones. The similarity between Joan and the Crusaders lies in her confidence in divine guidance in a violent contest over territorial dominion. The guidance is voiced in her case not by the church's institutional representatives, but by divine emissaries who give her independent and compelling counsel.

This similarity is modulated by a second, even more fundamental, difference: Joan refuses to make grandiose assertions about God's final designs in history, or to identify those designs more than provisionally with the "election" of the historical group with which she identifies. Joan justifies armed violence primarily in terms of justice and the common good. She does not urge the ultimacy or righteousness of her cause beyond the limited political objective of restoring a French monarch to the French throne.

Joan in no way identifies her adversaries as the accursed of God, nor

74. Fabre, *Joan of Arc*, 278–79.

75. "Pope Urban II: The Call to the First Crusade, 26 November 1095," from an eyewitness account, in *Readings in Church History*, vol. 1, *From Pentecost to the Protestant Revolt*, ed. Colman J. Barry (Westminster, MD: Newman, 1960), 328.

even suggests that her temporal enmity with them is intrinsic and irre-
mediable. In Joan's attitude the Christian ideal of mercy and forgiveness
toward enemies moderates rather than capitulates to the then-prevailing
ethos of warfare and revenge. However skeptical she may have been of
obtaining it, Joan did not rule out in principle the possibility of English
and French cooperation in securing justice for the French nation. She
rejects the plain injustice of the English position, but she does not project that perception as a cosmic struggle between good and evil. Strongly
convinced as she is of the rightness in God's eyes of the French cause, she
does not lose all perspective on the limits of its historical and religious
importance.

THE PURITAN REVOLUTION

The English Civil War of the mid-1600s was also anchored in a supposed divine mandate to reform the political order, a mandate defining
the covenanted mission of a religious group, called to establish on earth
a society that had its charter in a heavenly contract. The term "Puritan"
originated in the 1560s to describe a growing movement to simplify
and reform the Church of England. Puritans were critics of the settlement with which Elizabeth I had established order in the English church
by making it coterminous with the nation. Repudiating the Roman
Catholicism of her predecessor and sister, Queen Mary Tudor, Elizabeth
established the future contours of Anglicanism by favoring an inclusive
Calvinistic Protestantism, which tried to accommodate as norms both
Bible and tradition, thus leaning away from the more radical continental
reforms. At the same time, the Church of England retained some of the
Roman flavor in its liturgy and episcopal hierarchy.

The Puritans (also Calvinist in general outlook and comprising
Presbyterians, Congregationalists, and Baptists) were unsatisfied by the
compromise. They advocated less reliance on the hierarchy, preferring
local government by counsels or presbyteries. Puritans saw the reliance
on tradition, along with reason and church authority, as a betrayal of the
biblical heart and spirit of Christianity. Moreover, they thought church
organization should reflect that of the early church, as portrayed in the
New Testament—though there was little agreement as to the details of
church polity. In 1604, King James I summoned the Hampton Court
Conference to hear Puritan arguments for change, but no resolution was
reached. Finally, civil war erupted in 1604.

An important theme in Puritan religious thought is religious experience, especially that of election by God to salvation, preeminently

expressed in terms of God's "covenant of grace" with the elect. In Puritan thought, the prominence of an experienced relationship to God was able to disrupt and supersede the medieval ordering of all beings in a natural hierarchy, leading to radical implications for both the ecclesial and the political orders.[76] Leadership of the "saints" was not assigned by rank or class but by personal holiness, talent, and zeal for the Lord's work.

The individual's experience of God broadens into an experience of relationship within the Christian community, which again provides a model for the ordering of relationships in the world. All functions and duties contributing to the good of society are callings in the sight of God. The community as a people both civil and religious is related to God in a covenant modeled on that of the Lord's with Israel. The state and its rulers represent God's kingly authority and impose religious practice as well as civil order. Since no human activity falls outside of responsibility to God, the Puritans hoped to organize all social, political, and economic relationships according to Christian patterns.[77]

> The most pervasive theme of applied ethics in Puritan thought is what the Puritans called "government" but what would most likely today be termed "community." "Government" in Puritan usage meant not only the activities of monarchs, members of Parliament, or local officials; like God's government of the world, it referred to the entire nexus of human relationships, their proper ordering, and the use of the resources of the world by humans. Of course, this term had a special use in referring to the governing persons and associated institutions of the nation; yet it is crucial that this special meaning was implicitly connected to the broader sense of the term.[78]

Puritans were activist in their attitudes toward the world because of—and not in spite of—their belief in predestination. One's experience of salvation is social in nature and leads one to do God's work, to fulfill God's purposes, as the fruits and signs of election. Although it is God who initiates the covenant with the people, the covenant establishes a response through which all is ordered under God's plan and dedicated to God's glory.

The Christian magistrate has a duty "to improve every talent and

76. See Michael Walzer, *The Revolution of the Saints: A Study in the Origins of Radical Politics* (Cambridge, MA: Harvard University Press, 1965).

77. For background, see John Dillenberger and Claude Welch, *Protestant Christianity: Interpreted through Its Development* (New York: Scribner's, 1954), 99–121; David L. Edwards, *Christian England*, vol. 2, *From the Reformation to the 18th Century* (Grand Rapids, MI: William B. Eerdmans, 1983), 144–58; and James T. Johnson, "Puritan Ethics," in *The Westminster Dictionary of Christian Ethics,* ed. James F. Childress and John Macquarrie (Philadelphia: Westminster, 1986), 519–22.

78. Johnson, "Puritan Ethics," 521.

advantage entrusted with him, for the honour of Christ and good of the body," and to this end taking care "to direct even all the common acts and parts of his government." Christian magistrates ought "principally *ex intentione* to direct their whole government to the good of the churches, and the glory of God therein, forasmuch as all things are the churches', and for the churches." Even though the magistracy is "an ordinance of man," "yet it is a most glorious ordinance, and of singular use and service, if rightly applied, to the Church."[79] At the same time, the Puritans hardly saw the covenanted community as the kingdom of God on earth. It was, rather, an anticipation and a guarantee of future salvation. "Haply a shilling or ten shillings [are] given in earnest for the payment of a hundred pounds or more. So are the special gifts and graces of God given here to God's children but a small thing in comparison of that fulness of grace they shall receive in the kingdom of heaven."[80]

Some Puritans represent an interesting development of Reformed thought, carrying on yet intensifying Calvin's validation of killing by the civil government. Like Calvin, they understand Christianity to assimilate worldly institutions, an attitude that lends social and political stability to religion. They see violence as available to the civil authority to defend the will of God, and they portray the legitimacy of violence in biblical terms. To a much greater degree than Calvin, however, Puritans tend to view the political world militaristically and to use elaborate warfare imagery. As Michael Walzer argues, this imagery may have propelled the acceptance and even the promotion of actual war, once Puritan revolutionaries had opportunity to use arms effectively.[81] Calvin himself did not promote holy war, especially in the sense of unrestrained violence. In fact, he said biblical commands to destroy whole populations (such as Deut 20:15–18) do not apply in contemporary times.[82] As for killing combatants who have surrendered, he asks rhetorically, "How

79. "Liberty of Conscience: The Independent Position," from *The Ancient Bounds* (1645), cited in A. S. P. Woodhouse, ed., *Puritanism and Liberty* (Chicago: University of Chicago Press, 1951), 249. The Independents were a centrist Puritan party, which, along with the Presbyterian party, sometimes attained a precarious majority in Parliament. See Woodhouse, introduction to *Puritanism and Liberty*, 16.

80. Edward Elton, *The Triumph of a True Christian* (1623), 528; cited in David Zaret, *The Heavenly Contract; Ideology and Organization in Pre-Revolutionary Puritanism* (Chicago: University of Chicago Press, 1985), 177.

81. Walzer, *Revolution of the Saints*, 277, 290.

82. John Calvin, *Commentaries on the Book of Joshua*, trans. Henry Beveridge (Grand Rapids, MI: Baker, 1979), 4:97. On this point, see Mark J. Larson, "The Holy War Trajectory among the Reformed: From Zurich to England," *Reformation and Renaissance Review* 8, no. 1 (2006): 19–22.

does God, the Father of mercies, give His sanction to indiscriminate bloodshed?"[83]

Because the Puritans' reform movement was repressed in England, they sought other outlets, especially in the seventeenth century. Through migrations to New England, they were to have lasting effects on the social and political systems of the New World. Through civil war at home, their energy for social reorganization was to have an effect that would be of shorter duration but more radical and more violent. Under James I, Elizabeth's successor, and Charles I, his son, the Puritans were persecuted, especially at the hands of Archbishop William Laud. With the support of the king, Laud claimed that Anglican bishops were successors of Peter in the universal church, and he marshaled both religious and political forces behind a strict following of Anglican ritual. The opposition to the Royalists gradually took control of Parliament, leading to several open conflicts with the king, including his dissolution of Parliament in 1629. After eleven years he was forced to reconvene it, in order to seek its financial aid. But by 1640 the Presbyterians, a Puritan party, had gained a majority in Parliament. Laud was impeached and imprisoned, though there was little agreement within Parliament about the direction that Puritan reforms should take.

Civil war was precipitated when Parliament unsuccessfully demanded from the king control over the army and the appointment of royal ministers. Oliver Cromwell, who had served as a member of Parliament, emerged as a Puritan military leader in 1643. Justifying his military endeavors, he insisted "from brethren, in things of the mind, we look for no compulsion, but that of light and reason." However, in "other things, God hath put the sword into the Parliament's hands, for the terror of evil-doers, and the praise of them that do well. If any plead exemption from it he knows not the Gospel." His regiment, the Ironsides, was supposed to be made up of "godly" men who fulfilled their calling with Christian self-discipline. In 1644–45, the parliamentary army was organized into the New Model Army, shaped to the same ideals. Wrote Cromwell of his troops, who obtained their victories by "faith and prayer": "It's their joy that they are instruments to God's glory, and their country's good; it's their honor that God vouchsafes to use them." And of his conquests: "All this is none other than the work of God. He must be a very great atheist who does not acknowledge it."[84] Yet the godly disci-

83. Larson, "Holy War Trajectory," 15, citing *Commentaries on the Last Four Books of Moses Arranged in the Form of a Harmony*, trans. Henry Beveridge (Grand Rapids, MI: Baker, 1979), 3:54.

84. "Letter from Cromwell" (Bristol, September 14, 1645), in *The Puritan Revolution: A Documentary History,* ed. Stuart E. Prall (Garden City, NY: Doubleday, 1968), 125.

pline of Cromwell's army broke down on at least one infamous occasion, at Drogheda (1649).

The Puritan army defeated the king at Naseby in 1645. In 1648, under Cromwell's direction, the army purged from Parliament those members still interested in negotiating some agreement with the king, and it arranged the trial of Charles I for treason. The king, preserving a remnant of his dignity by refusing to justify himself before the court, was condemned and beheaded in 1649. Upon his death, the government of the British republic was entrusted to the Commonwealth, governed by Parliament. In the first year of its rule Cromwell led a punitive campaign into Ireland—regarded like the Crusaders' "infidels" as outsiders to the common cause—and massacred more than three thousand defenders of the Royalist garrison at Drogheda. A month later hundreds of civilians were executed in Wexford. Cromwell then transferred Irish properties to English landlords, a policy for which he assumed divine approval. "'The Lord is pleased still to vouchsafe us his presence and to prosper his work in our hands,' he wrote, and he spoke complacently of the 'righteous judgment of God upon these barbarous wretches.'"[85]

During the years of the Commonwealth (to 1653) and of the ensuing Protectorate under Cromwell's reign (to his death in 1658), comprehensive Puritan reforms in theology, church government, and liturgy were enacted in England. After Cromwell's death and a short rule by his son, Richard, the nation was returned to the Commonwealth, and eventually to Charles II in 1660, who reinstated Anglicanism as the official church.

James Johnson notes that the English transformation of just war categories into the idea of holy war spanned the years from 1560 to 1660. Motivated by England's rivalry with Spain as well as its internal conflicts, it was not limited to Puritans.[86] Indeed, wars of religion proliferated all over Europe during this period, and there was heavy rivalry among Christian nations for expansion and colonization. Johnson describes holy war doctrine as taking its bearings from the idea that "God himself inspires and commands some wars." Unlike the version of just war theory that becomes part of modern international law, holy war doctrine does not seek "the presence of certain naturally defined, politically manifested criteria."[87]

The greatest theological inspiration behind Puritan holy war is not

85. C. V. Wedgwood, *Oliver Cromwell* (London: Gerald Duckworth, 1973), 71. The quotations come from a letter to Parliament, via the Speaker, reporting on the Irish expedition. See also Antonia Fraser, *Cromwell Our Chief of Men* (London: Wiedenfeld & Nicolson, 1973), 338–39; and Bainton, *Christian Attitudes*, 51.

86. Johnson, *Ideology, Reason*, 84.

87. Johnson, *Ideology, Reason*, 81–82.

Calvin but Heinrich Bullinger.[88] Bullinger sees religion as "the highest cause for making war" and builds holy war on the right of defense against attack, correction of error, execution of "incurable" evildoers, including idolators and enemies of the true faith.[89] Puritans enthusiastically depicted God as commander in war. God was a "man of war," Christ a "captain," and the angels an "army." The earth was a "field of war," and the Christian a "soldier" against both spiritual enemies and heretics or persecutors.[90] The Puritans' passionate use of biblical warrants for violence (against other Christians) resembles crusading rhetoric against the Muslims in the Holy Land, but with two important differences. First, the ideal of personal righteousness sometimes grounds restraint of means (as in the writings of Alexander Leighton, but contrasting strongly with Henry Bullinger, William Allen, and Thomas Barnes).[91] Second, Puritan divines like William Gouge have, apparently, enough appreciation of the countercultural thrust of the New Testament love command to realize that defense of holy war is on shaky ground if it takes the lordship of Jesus as its point of departure. The wars of the Israelites are much more amenable prototypes. Moreover, appeals to the Old Testament are a good fit in a theology of community and government shaped around the Israelite covenant. The final objective, however, is to depict war as unambiguously a Christian duty.

Among the Puritans, William Gouge's version of holy war thought stands out as a self-assured and decisive legitimation of violence in service of both political and religious ends. Born in the late sixteenth century, Gouge was the son of a wealthy gentleman and was related on his mother's side to divines and churchmen influential among Puritans. Educated at Eton and King's College, Cambridge, Gouge became an "Arch-Puritan." A powerful and renowned preacher, he was minister of the parish at Blackfriars in London for thirty-five years until his death in 1653. Gouge was a prolific writer, aided the publication of the pious and edifying works of his colleagues, helped to arrange financing for the sending of ministers throughout England, and served among the divines of the Westminster Assembly.[92]

Besides defensive war, Gouge justifies extraordinary wars commanded

88. See Larson, "Holy War Trajectory," 23–24; Johnson, *Holy War Idea*, 57–60; and *Ideology, Reason*, 110–14.

89. Johnson, *Holy War Idea*, 57, citing a sermon "On War," included in Bullinger's collection of sermons, *Decades*, which was mandated reading for English clergy.

90. Walzer, *Revolution of the Saints*, 277–80, 290.

91. Johnson, *Ideology, Reason*, 141; and *Just War Tradition and the Restraint of War: A Moral and Historical Inquiry* (Princeton, NJ: Princeton University Press, 1981), 234.

92. William Haller, *The Rise of Puritanism* (Philadelphia: University of Pennsylvania Press, 1973), 67–69.

by God and offensive wars to assert the rights of true religion, including wars to weaken enemies and subvert their political goals. Gouge's 1631 commentary on Exodus 17:8–16 is an unusually unrestrained example of Puritan holy war thinking.[93] The biblical text is the Israelites' battle with the Amalekites in the wilderness, as the chosen and covenanted people made its way to the Promised Land. Finally Joshua is victorious. The Lord says to Moses, "I will utterly blot out the remembrance of Amalek from under heaven," whereupon Moses builds an altar that he calls "The Lord is my banner" (Exod 17:14–15). Gouge's theme is not the restraint of war, as in traditional just war theory, but the duty of Christians to participate in war. "Warre is a kind of execution of publique justice: and a means of maintaining right. . . . By it a free and quiet profession of the true Faith is maintained: peace is setled: kingdomes and common-wealths are secured . . . all manner of callings freely exercised: good lawes put in execution: due justice executed: ill minded persons kept under: and many evils prevented."[94]

Most importantly, offensive wars are allowed for "Maintenance of Truth, and purity of Religion." Gouge asserts that the wars of the Israelites provide a model for "the warres of the Kings of the earth against Anti-Christ," whom Gouge identifies with "papists," not heathen unbelievers. Gouge elaborates thirteen scripturally derived reasons for war, adding up to his assertions that "Battels are stiled warres of God, and the Lords Battels" and that "God himselfe is stiled A man of warre, and the Lord of hosts." He gives the examples of Abraham, Joshua, and some of the Judges and Kings; God's granting to them assistance in war and receiving spoils from it; and the promise of victory in war as a blessing. Like the Crusaders, Gouge believes that those who die in battle for a good cause are commended into "God's handes," although he adds the proviso that they must sincerely have repented of all their sins.

In this defense of war, Gouge mentions the New Testament only once (Heb 11:33–34), and then only to prove that the conquests of Israelite heroes were by faith. Indeed, "the Lord is the chiefe Captaine and generall" in "gods warres."[95] The cautious and even regretful approach to violence marking mainstream Christian just war theorists has disappeared in

93. On the centrality of the Exodus image for the Puritan revolutionaries, see John Coffey, *Exodus and Liberation: Deliverance Politics from John Calvin to Martin Luther King Jr.* (Oxford: Oxford University Press, 2014), 25–55.

94. Gouge, *Gods Three Arrowes: Plague, Famine, Sword, in Three Treatises. I. A Plaister for the Plague. II. Dearths Death. III. The Churches Conquest over the Sword* (London: George Miller for Edward Brewster, 1631), 213; quoted in Johnson, *Ideology, Reason*, 119. Johnson makes available substantial quotations from early editions of Gouge's writings.

95. Above quotations from *Gods Three Arrowes*, 209–17, 290, in Johnson, *Ideology, Reason*, 120–24.

Gouge's treatise. Restraint of means in war is a subject he ignores. Gouge feels no pressure to bring violent coercion into line with the Sermon on the Mount, via either an understanding of the kingdom as awaiting eschatological fulfillment or an understanding of coercion itself as a form of love.

CONCLUSION

What are the salient features linking the Crusades and the English Puritan revolution as both types of holy war? It may be true, as Johnson argues, that it is more fruitful to consider "holy war" expressions as bearing degrees of relation to an ideal type, rather than requiring all to display every one of a series of possible characteristics. Yet one thing that unites Puritans and Crusaders, and may in the end stand out as the most central feature of a true holy war (narrowly defined), is the elevation and cultivation of violence as a core meaning of faithful following of Christ. It can scarcely be denied that this is a perversion—not just a conflict-driven application—of the gospel as embodied in the life and teaching of Jesus and in his death on the cross. A related feature of crusading and of the Puritan revolution as holy war is the transformation of Christian love into group loyalty, love of fellow warriors. This heightens willingness to use violence against outsiders, especially if they are perceived to threaten the group.

It is this sanctification of violence as an essential meaning of fidelity to Christ and to God's will that, especially in the Crusades, is promoted through Bible-linked warfare imagery. Undergirded by the assurance that the fallen warrior will be granted an eternal reward, the glorification of killing in the name of Christ encourages abandonment of all compassion or moderation toward the enemy. Imitation of Christ can hardly function as a curb on violence once killing is assimilated into the very meaning of Christlike behavior. And unrestrained violence gives the lie to any claim of holy warriors to concur in the just war aim of seeking the peace and common good, because it makes future cooperative relations virtually impossible.[96]

The medieval wars against Muslims in the Holy Land exhibit the worst traits of the crusading ethos, with their alienation of the "infidel," their lack of attention to *jus in bello,* their grants of papal indulgence for sin, and their highly developed ethos of warrior sainthood and martyrdom. But the Puritans, at least in some instances, reflect a central fea-

96. On the effects of means in war to postwar relations, see James Turner Johnson, *Morality and Contemporary Warfare* (New Haven, CT: Yale University Press, 1999), 217–18.

ture of the crusade, in that unrestrained violence against the enemies of church and nation is praised in similar terms of godliness and fidelity to Christ (though they favor biblical proof texts from the Old Testament).

Joan of Arc resembles the Crusaders and the English Puritan revolutionaries in that she claims religious inspiration for war-making. Yet she departs from their ideology in fundamental respects. Her adversaries are Christian and participate in the same basic culture and political institutions as she does. For her, war is neither an apocalyptic judgment against God's enemies nor a privileged form of the Christian life. The difference between war and Christian discipleship as such is accentuated by the fact that she fights in an essentially secular cause, not a religious one. Though she is commanded to make war on her political opponents, the mission of killing is clearly provisional as an expression of fidelity to Christ. Joan's ambivalence about killing in the name of God is shown in her refusal to kill personally.

Christians today rarely if ever directly endorse holy war. Nevertheless, religious rhetoric has been deployed in favor of programs of national defense, expansion, or other military intervention to give a transcendent legitimacy to political aims. Moreover, the insider-outsider mentality is often at the root of political conflict. Thus it remains important to examine the warrants, rhetoric, and outcomes that have been associated historically and normatively with the Crusades' fundamental corruption of Christian social responsibility. Twenty-first century Christians may find it difficult to recapture or even imagine the triumphal ethos for which so much blood was poured in the eleventh century (and even the seventeenth). But consider the fairly recent words of a Roman Catholic author, rendering an account of the Crusades only shortly before the Second Vatican Council was to produce the *Declaration on Religious Liberty*. Henri Daniel-Rops, in his biography of Bernard of Clairvaux, praises the saint's ability "to summon Christianity to a holy war for the empty Tomb."[97] Calling the Second Crusade the "culminating point" in Bernard's "brilliant career," Daniel-Rops, without evident disapproval, describes the Crusade to be, for Bernard, "the total expression of Christianity" and "a testimony to the Communion of Saints."[98] Here is not only a romanticization of war for chauvinistic aims of the church, but also tacit identification of violence with Christian saintliness.

97. Henri Daniel-Rops, *Bernard of Clairvaux* (New York: Hawthorn, 1964), 62.
98. Daniel-Rops, *Bernard of Clairvaux*, 95, 100.

The Crusades and their near relatives represent a low point in Christian ethics precisely because they fail utterly in the mission of the Christian community to challenge the sinful ethos of the culture in which it participates. A gestalt of exclusion, competition, conflict, coercion, and killing is permitted to eat into the very heart of the Christian moral life, betraying its witness and offering to the world "false prophets," wolves in "sheep's clothing" (Matt 7:15) and "whitewashed tombs" (Matt 23:27). These phrases of Jesus's damn religious groups and representatives who eviscerate God's care for human creatures and God's call to be merciful and to forgive. A particularly pernicious rewriting of the Christian mandate to love occurs when Jesus's inclusive and generous compassion for the outcast and outsider is recast as a defensive in-group loyalty.

In the Holocaust (or Shoah), for example, Christian churches for the most part condoned or actively supported the annihilation of millions of Jews. The Jews were refused recognition as fellow human beings, much less as the "neighbors" Jesus urges his followers to love. Going further, many Christians were able to persecute Jews actively out of a perversion of the meaning of Jesus's death. Instead of identifying with the self-sacrificial character of Christ's suffering, or seeing the cross as God's solidarity with other innocent sufferers, they turned the cross into a false accusation of Judaism and into another weapon of destruction.

In the United States in 2017, a study by the Southern Poverty Law Center found that the number of Islamophobic hate groups had risen sharply in the two preceding years, including groups specifically dedicated to white nationalism and/or Christian identity, one called "Knights of the White Disciples."[99] Another called the "Crusaders" schemed to blow up an apartment complex housing mostly Somali-born Muslims and a mosque.[100] Similar trends have occurred in Europe, where the rate of Muslim immigration is greater than in the United States.[101]

Although the New Testament, particularly the Pauline and Johannine writings, encourages members of the body of Christ to love and to bear all things for one another (1 Cor 13) and to be to one another as friends in Christ (John 15:12–15), the love nourished within the community is not self-enclosed, much less expressed as violence toward "the other." Complemented by other texts—for example, the Matthean and Lukan

99. See Melanie Eversley, "Report: Anti-Muslim Groups Triple in U.S. amid Trump Hate Rhetoric," *USA Today*, February 15, 2017, accessed August 7, 2017, https://tinyurl.com/ycul zlw5. See also "Active Hate Groups," *Intelligence Report* (Spring 2017), Southern Poverty Law Center, accessed August 7, 2017, https://tinyurl.com/y9p9wkjp.

100. Steven Piggot, "One More Enemy," *Intelligence Report* (Spring 2017), Southern Poverty Law Center, accessed August 7, 2017, https://tinyurl.com/ycemy7sn.

101. See the annual *European Islamophobia Report*, 2nd ed., 2016, accessed August 7, 2017, https://tinyurl.com/y9dulg5d.

extensions of love from neighbor to outsider and enemy (Matt 5:43–44; Luke 6:35; 10:29–37)—communal love and cohesiveness, as biblically portrayed, bear fruit (Matt 12:33; Luke 6:43–45; John 15:16). The love that edifies and "builds up" (1 Thess 5:11) the Christian community is tested by its capacity to engender and enable outwardly directed movements of empathy, concern, beneficence, and inclusion.

8.

A Witness for the Kingdom
Humanist, Anabaptist, and Quaker Pacifists

The Catholic humanist Erasmus of Rotterdam, as well as the radical Anabaptist and Quaker Reformers, all embrace the compassionate and nonviolent example of Jesus as definitive of Christian identity. Though they accept that the civil government has the responsibility to order the peace and security of society, and while they do not urge that governments on the whole surrender the use of force necessary to fulfill this responsibility, they do see violent coercion as a type of participation in structural sin. This yields different stances among the three toward the state, toward Christian participation in politics, and even toward the exceptional or indirect approval of force. Yet they are confident that their faith demands and makes possible a new way of life embodied personally and communally in the church.

The Anabaptists and Quakers, like Christian teachers of the first three centuries, reject any Christian involvement in killing. Erasmus descries killing as contrary to human nature, and as an egregious offense against the Christian calling, even when Christians are serving in government or other political roles. Yet he is not entirely consistent on this point, for he does not exclude the possibility of armed defense by Christians against non-Christians. Therefore, while the Anabaptist theologian Menno Simons, and the Quaker George Fox, can be termed "pacifists," it might be more accurate to call Erasmus a peacemaker or "irenicist," as some interpreters have done.[1] The thrust of Erasmus's attention, however, is not on justifying wars, but on the evils of war. He pleads repeatedly with warring Christian factions in Europe to cease their bloodshed, in

---

1. For a discussion of some of these, see Nathan Ron, "The Christian Peace of Erasmus," in *The European Legacy* 19, no. 1 (2014): 27–43, accessed October 3, 2016, https://tinyurl.com/ybkdmuqh.

the name of Christian and human values. For this reason, he is included in this discussion of early modern pacifists.

Christian pacifists build both on the commands of Jesus to love neighbors and enemies and on an empathetic insight into the common humanity of all persons and their potential unity in Christ. The latter insight flows from practical experiences of Christian conversion and community that instill attitudes of compassion, inclusion, forgiveness, and reconciliation. Christians (and others) tend more often to reject violence as a means of attaining their ends when their religious symbols and self-descriptions enable them to identify empathetically with dissenters, opponents, and persecutors; in short, when they are able practically and, in some sense, affectively to "love their enemies." Differences exist, however. While the Anabaptists ground nonresistance more in emulation of Jesus than in any identification with the inhabitants of what they see as the "kingdom of Satan," Erasmus appeals directly to a sense of common humanity as well as to the inclusive thrust of Christian charity. The Quakers respond on religious grounds to "that of God in every man," and their founder George Fox frequently expresses a near-mystical sense of the unity of all things and persons in Christ.

Therefore, at least two strands within Christianity's developing pacifist trajectory can be identified: compassionate pacifism and obediential pacifism. While empathetic identification with "the other" (friend, stranger, or foe) is key to the first, that theme is subsumed in the second under obediential imitation of Christ's sacrifice.[2] In the first category may be placed Erasmus, the social gospel movement, Dorothy Day,

2. James Childress distinguishes four kinds of pacifism: legalist-expressive; consequentialist pragmatic-utilitarian; redemptive witness; and technological, especially nuclear, pacifism. The first holds that pacifism is right religiously, even though it is not effective; the second that pacifism is right morally because it is effective; the third that pacifism is both religiously right and that it will be effective; and the fourth that just war criteria themselves lead to the exclusion of certain measures of war, or even modern war itself so long as it entails such means. My response is that the fourth variety is not really pacifism, but an application of just war theory. Moreover, *Christian* pacifism is never based solely on consequentialist grounds, apart from any idea of union with God in Christ. That leaves Childress's first and third varieties as points of comparison with my two. I am distinguishing types based not on whether they view pacifism as effective or not but rather on how they ground pacifism as an aspect of Christian identity and community. The point of similarity between Childress's categories and my own is perhaps this: obediential imitation of Christ sees effects of action on fellow humanity as a secondary and derivative consideration, while compassionate pacifism does begin with a transformed relation to other persons as well as to God. But even in Christian compassionate pacifism, the starting point is not political and social effectiveness, but a change in relationships, which pacifism does not "bring about," but of which it is *the expression.* In other words, while "nuclear pacifism" is not really pacifism, "effectiveness pacifism" is not really Christian, if utility is its only motive or warrant. Christian conversion is fundamental to Christian pacifism and is expressed in the primary mode either of fidelity or of compassion. See James F. Childress, "Contemporary Pacifism: Its Major Types and Possible Contributions to Discourse about War," in *The American Search*

Thomas Merton, and the Quakers; in the second are Tertullian and Origen, the Anabaptists, John Howard Yoder, and H. Richard Niebuhr. These examples certainly do not exhaust the Christian pacifist tradition, yet their reasons for pacifism are representative of the two forms.

Among the three primary pacifist examples in this chapter, the Anabaptists (represented especially by their great theologian Menno Simons) are most radically biblical, while Erasmus is the least so. As a humanist, the latter finds wisdom in classical sources and also sees the patristic period as a crucial resource for theological interpretation of the biblical models of Christian life. Erasmus does reject violence, but he accepts the congeniality of Christian life and politics. He wants to change society through rather traditional means (by appeals to rulers, to patrons, and influential people—by using the power network). Again, Erasmus never absolutely rejected the possibility that even the Christian ruler might be justified in using armed force. Yet his main goal is to persuade rulers and other leaders that violence is not necessary as a tool of statecraft, and that government can proceed on more peaceable terms.[3] The Quakers also hope to change society, but work through the spread of a largely working-class movement. They see everyone as a potential peacemaker, because all can respond to the presence of God as "the Light within."

The Anabaptists (or Mennonites) and the Friends (or Quakers), along with the Church of the Brethren, are called the historic peace churches precisely because, since their institution, they have represented opposition to warfare on the basis of the Sermon on the Mount. The Anabaptists stake everything on Scripture itself and on radical imitation of Christ. They have little interest in influencing social life. Menno Simons and his community see government as necessary to keep order, but they do not participate in it or other worldly institutions that bring potential for conflict with God's commands. The Quakers (and their founder George Fox), in contrast, make both Scripture and traditions relative to the present working of the Holy Spirit ("the Light within") as a guide to what biblical religion demands now. As a grassroots and working-class movement, Quakerism's social power lies in conversion of people to the

---

for Peace: Moral Reasoning, Religious Hope, and National Security, ed. George Weigel and John P. Langan, SJ (Washington, DC: Georgetown University Press, 1991), 114–20.

3. On this point, see James T. Johnson, "Two Kinds of Pacifism: Opposition to the Political Use of Force in the Renaissance-Reformation Period," *Journal of Religious Ethics* 12, no. 1 (1984): 39–60. Johnson argues that, while the Anabaptists saw violence as both sinful and inevitable, Erasmus hopes for "a totally peaceful world society." This attitude or conviction (that nonviolence is generalizable as a mode of government) typifies an increasingly large number of pacifist authors and activists in the twentieth century, especially but not exclusively Roman Catholics.

cause. The Friends hope that by living in the kingdom they will broaden its base and give it progressive transformative power in the world.

Grappling with the challenge of the kingdom made present in Jesus is constitutive of the Christian ethical tradition, especially since the kingdom will not be fully present until the *eschaton.* Minority pacifist groups throughout the history of the Christian church have taken the eschatological or kingdom trajectory of the gospel seriously by setting an agenda of radical practice and witness for the church. This seriousness characterizes the Anabaptists and Quakers more decidedly than Erasmus, but it is true of the latter also, to the extent that he refused to divide Christians into higher and lower states of life and expected all to strive to attain the perfection Jesus urges as a real goal in their lives. As in the early church, all three run into difficulties and quandaries in determining how to live their pacifist ideals at the level of practical, political life. Yet all are resolutely faithful to the promise of God's inbreaking reign.

ERASMUS

The Dutch humanist Desiderius Erasmus (ca. 1466–1536) embodies the confidence in reason and privileging of classical sources typical of the Renaissance and, at the same time, the return to Scripture and commitment to purifying the church definitive of the Reformation.[4] Erasmus was the illegitimate son of a priest, who contributed to the support of Erasmus and his older brother. After the death of his parents during the plague, Erasmus joined the Augustinians in order to continue his education. His early schooling was in the spirit of the *Devotio Moderna,* the "modern piety" of the Brethren of the Common Life, who were committed both to contemplation and to an active life serving the sick and poor, and educating children. Erasmus looked back with repugnance on their pedagogy of rote learning as boring, constricting, and antiintellectual; but there is a similarity between their social commitment and his own empathetic pacifism.

In the Augustinian monastery, Erasmus attracted a sizable peer following and stimulated controversy through his independent inquiries into the Latin classics, as well as into Scripture and Christian authors. After

---

4. Bainton's biography of Erasmus gives an overview of his theology and politics: Roland H. Bainton, *Erasmus of Christendom* (New York: Scribner's, 1969). For a discussion of Erasmus's influence on later early modern authors, see Peter G. Bietenholz, *A Radical Erasmus: Erasmus' Work as a Source of Radical Thought in Early Modern Europe* (Toronto: University of Toronto Press, 2009). For an argument that Erasmus's interpretation of the Great Commission influenced later Anabaptist theology and mission activity, see Abraham Friesen, *Erasmus, the Anabaptists, and the Great Commission* (Grand Rapids, MI: William B. Eerdmans, 1998).

his ordination in 1492, his prior allowed him to become a bishop's secretary, a position that enhanced Erasmus's access to ecclesiastical, political, and academic worlds of influence. He spent some years at the University of Paris, where the influence of nominalism was strong. Erasmus traveled to England and to Italy as tutor to the sons of royalty and their associates, eventually teaching at Cambridge University. He made lasting friendships with great humanists such as John Colet and Thomas More. Having gained a wide European reputation, Erasmus moved in 1514 to Basel, a center of Reformed Protestantism, where he spent most of his remaining years.

Erasmus is noted for his publication of the New Testament based on Greek manuscripts, which he used to correct the Latin Vulgate, and for his controversy with Martin Luther over the freedom of the will. Both involvements reflect his humanist convictions. His reconstruction of the New Testament evinces the humanists' interest in the return to classic sources. For centuries, scholars had commented on the Bible without ever reading it in the original Greek. The humanists were confident that if they could pass over the accumulation of arid commentary and return to the original texts, using the study of languages as a tool, they would succeed in turning Christian leaders and rulers to the true and the good.[5] It was the humanist in Erasmus who could not allow Luther's strong doctrine of "justification by faith" to imply that God's grace makes the human person an automaton. Yet for his part, Luther detected in Erasmus a strain of the Pelagian "justification by works" against which the former had fought so fiercely—although the two men appear not to have disagreed over what either considered essentials of the faith.

According to E. Harris Harbison, Erasmus represented Christian humanism's "faith in man's reason and fundamental goodness, its confidence in education, its tolerance and sense of proportion," as well as its exaggerated trust that scholarship and reasonableness could change the world and eradicate human sinfulness.[6] At the same time, humanists had a "grasp of history" inaccessible to the scholastics. In medieval universities history was not taught as a subject, and little accurate information was available about heroes of the past, their exploits, and the cultures out of which they rose.[7] War, for instance, is a problem Erasmus tries to put in historical context, showing that its just causes are exceedingly difficult to determine and that its consequences are almost without exception disastrous. Both as a Christian and as a Renaissance humanist, Erasmus was

---

5. See Harbison, *Age of Reformation*, 44.

6. Harbison, *Age of Reformation*, 45–46.

7. George Faludy, *Erasmus of Rotterdam* (London: Eyre & Spottiswoode, 1970), 18.

a reformer, drawing on the critical resources appropriate to both: Scripture, the church Fathers, and classical antiquity. Erasmus's vocation was "to apply the best humanistic scholarship of his day to the key doctrines of the Christian faith with a view to cleansing and purifying the whole religious tradition."[8]

As biblical interpreter, Erasmus adopted the basic medieval scheme of meanings: the literal (grammatical and historical), the tropological (moral), the allegorical (figurative or christological), and the anagogical (eschatological). For Erasmus, the moral was the most important. He curbed runaway allegorization by insisting that the grammatical sense be derived on the basis of careful linguistic study, and that the spiritual sense be expounded in close reliance on grammatical study. Although Erasmus's writings on the Old Testament are few, he nonetheless resolved some difficulties there via an allegorizing approach to the Hebrew Bible. On war, for instance, he argues that what is meant by calling the Hebrew God a "god of vengeance" is that God destroys vice, and that the slaughter of enemies in the Hebrew Bible refers to "the driving away of wicked affections out of the breast and mind of man."[9]

Advocating a return to New Testament sources, Erasmus acknowledged that they demand interpretation, and that interpretation must rely on extrabiblical tools: the original languages, the classics, the church fathers, and a sense of *pietas* or piety to ground and guide the process.[10] In his debate with Luther, he agreed that the most weight must be given to the Scriptures. But Erasmus insisted that the traditions of the fathers should be taken into account in reading Scripture. Who could leave aside such "a body of most learned men . . . whom not only their skill in divine studies but also godliness of life commend"? If Scripture were "crystal clear," there would not have been confusion among so many respected interpreters, for so many centuries, about matters of such great importance.[11]

On the subject of war, Erasmus seems to transcend centuries of circuitous just war theory that justified what the New Testament hardly envisions as part of following Christ. He expects all Christians to emulate Christ's example, refusing to accept that only a few of the elite are called to live fully the ideals of the gospel. Erasmus also reproaches humanity's

---

8. E. Harris Harbison, *The Christian Scholar in the Age of Reformation* (New York: Scribner's, 1956), 78.

9. *The Complaint of Peace*, 19; see n. 13 below.

10. See Albert Rabil Jr., *Erasmus and the New Testament: The Mind of a Christian Humanist* (San Antonio, TX: Trinity University Press, 1972), 109.

11. Erasmus, "On the Freedom of the Will," in *Luther and Erasmus: Free Will and Salvation,* ed. E. Gordon Rupp and Philip S. Watson (Philadelphia: Westminster, 1969), 43, 44.

penchant for armed conflict because it is a transgression of what ought to be the species' natural sociability. He especially objects to the involvement of the Vatican and of clergy in power politics and war. He notes that the reasons for which secular rulers engage in armed conflict are usually self-seeking and disingenuously presented, and that the consequences of war for the populations involved are scarcely worth the suffering and bloodshed—observations that still apply five centuries later.

In Erasmus's own age, the breakup of the papal states prepared the way for decentralization of authority and for competitive politics. His approach to the avoidance of war was to seek the ear of rulers and their advisers, advocating negotiation and arbitration. Erasmus's most extensive discourses on war are *An Essay on War* (*Bellum,* published originally as a commentary on the adage "War is sweet to those who know it not"),[12] and *The Complaint of Peace* (*Querela Pacis*).[13] Other treatments of the subject appear in *Handbook of the Militant Christian* (*Enchiridion militis Christiani*)[14] and *Education of a Christian Prince* (*Institutio principis Christiani*).[15] The latter, his most famous political treatise, commended Christian ideals to princes and was dedicated to the young man who would become Emperor Charles V.

Although Erasmus's views carried influence in nearly every court of Europe, they never were translated into policies to guide relationships of states. His champions were ignored, speculates John P. Dolan, because "they advocated compromise in an age of growing intolerance. . . . Few movements in history have suffered a greater disillusionment than the irenicists of the sixteenth century."[16] The religious and political crises

---

12. This essay is included in *Bellum: Two Statements on the Nature of War,* with an introduction by William R. Tyler (Barre, MA: Imprint Society, 1972), 11–37. (Students of Erasmus frequently refer to his works by their Latin titles, such as *Bellum* and *Enchiridion;* therefore they will be given here, along with English titles.) As Tyler states, "The first publication of *Bellum* was as *Adagium 3001,* under the title *Dulce bellum inespertis,* in the Froben edition of 1515. However, its origins go back to a letter which Erasmus wrote in March 1514 to Antonius van Bergen (abbot of the monastery of St Bertin at St. Omer), brother of the benefactor of Erasmus, Hendrick van Bergen. It was first published as an independent work by Froben in April 1517."

13. In *The Complaint of Peace by Erasmus,* with an introduction by William James Hirten (New York: Scholars' Facsimiles and Reprints, 1946). First published in 1517 by Froben, this work was translated into French, German, Spanish, and English.

14. In *Erasmus: Handbook of the Militant Christian,* trans. John P. Dolan (Notre Dame, IN: Fides, 1962). The *Enchiridion* appeared in Latin in 1514 and had been translated into nine other languages by 1585.

15. Erasmus, *The Education of a Christian Prince,* trans. Lester K. Born (New York: Columbia University Press, 1936). This work was first published in 1516 by Froben and within a few years went into several editions.

16. Dolan, "Introduction," in *Erasmus: Handbook,* 11.

provoked by the Reformation were simply too deep, too polarized, and too vitriolic to permit successful mediation by moderate voices.

The argument of *Bellum* is governed by three favorite themes that recur in other works of Erasmus. First, war is naturally wrong. Not even the beasts war against members of their own species, much less with weapons designed to increase natural destructive capacity. How much more, then, should humans respect one another's lives. Humanity was created for cooperation and to develop "the attachments of friendship and love."[17] Second, Christianity forbids war. Sophistry has distorted the gospel message. "Christian disinterestedness" has been rationalized away in favor of self-interest, money, and power.[18] Christ teaches love; all are called actually to live the life Christ presents. "Our Lord did not come to tell the world what enormity was permitted, how far we might deviate from the laws of rectitude, but to show us the point of perfection at which we were to aim with the utmost of our ability."[19] Third, "just cause" in war will be claimed by both sides and will be next to impossible to determine fairly.[20] Hence, the traditional criteria of the just war are nonfunctional.

Erasmus's rhetoric contrasts sharply to that of the Crusaders. He builds his ethical critique precisely on common humanity, although he also sees Christians as having among themselves still closer and more morally demanding bonds.

> Man has arrived at such a degree of insanity, that war seems to be the grand business of human life. We are always at war, either in preparation, or in action. Nation rises against nation; and, what the heathens would have reprobated as unnatural, relatives against their nearest kindred, brother against brother, son against father!—more atrocious still!—a Christian against a man! and worst of all, a Christian against a Christian![21]

According to Erasmus, it is impossible to ignore the gospel's many exhortations to peace, or the clear fact that Jesus claimed only one law as his own, and that was "the law of love or charity. What practice among

---

17. Dolan, *Erasmus*, 13.

18. Dolan, *Erasmus*, 28.

19. Dolan, *Erasmus*, 32. The gospel teaches "in decisive words" that "we must do good to them who use us ill." Further, not only the apostles, but "all Christian people," "the whole body," should be "entire and perfect" (33).

20. Dolan, *Erasmus*, 34.

21. Dolan, *Erasmus*, 18. See also "If a brother murder his brother, the crime is called fratricide: but a Christian is more closely allied to a Christian as such, than a brother by the ties of consanguinity. . . . How absurd then is it, that they should be constantly at war with each other; who but form one family, the church of Christ" (23).

mankind violates this law so grossly as war?"[22] Erasmus has no patience with proof-texting where isolated biblical incidents are taken to provide exceptions to the law of love. Every biblical reference must be put in the context of Jesus's whole life and teaching. If Christ approved war, "as some most absurdly infer," then why is it that "the uniform tenor of his whole life and doctrine teaches nothing else but forbearance?"[23] This is a criterion of biblical meaning that has withstood the test of time.

In the *Querela Pacis,* a lament by Peace personified, Erasmus reiterates several of these objections and concludes to the moral superiority of arbitration as a means of settling disputes. Addressing Christian princes primarily, Peace advises them to seek the common good, avoiding wars for petty and self-interested causes. "There is scarcely any peace so evil but that it is better than the most equal [*just*] war."[24]

Erasmus is particularly horrified by armed struggles among Christian nations, whose rulers even go so far as to claim that they are serving the common good of Christendom.[25] He specifically excoriates clergy and prelates who become involved in wars:

> Cardinals and the vicars of Christ are not ashamed to be the authors and firebrands of that thing the which Christ so greatly hath detested. . . . What hath a crosier or a sheephook to do with a sword? What hath the Gospel book to do with a shield . . . ? Dost thou with the selfsame mouth wherewith thou preachest peaceable Christ laud and praise war?[26]

Little could be more offensive than the custom of bearing the cross as a standard in war, carried by mercenaries "hired for money to tear and murder men." "O thou wicked soldier! What hast thou to do with the cross?"[27]

Erasmus's focus is the special egregiousness of wars among Christians in God's name and with the encouragement of the church, because he writes from the midst of the internecine conflicts then tearing Europe apart. Unfortunately, the recurrent theme of a common human nature that precludes violence even against non-Christians is muted and even broken in some of Erasmus's writings. Peace exclaims that "this world is the common country of all men,"[28] yet her repudiation of war exempts

22. Dolan, *Erasmus,* 24.
23. Dolan, *Erasmus,* 32.
24. Dolan, *Erasmus,* 39.
25. Erasmus, *Complaint of Peace,* 31–32.
26. Erasmus, *Complaint of Peace,* 33–34.
27. Erasmus, *Complaint of Peace,* 36.
28. Erasmus, *Complaint of Peace,* 46.

those who "repel the violent incursions of the barbarians and . . . defend the public and common tranquility."[29]

The *Enchiridion* was written to edify a manufacturer of armaments whose wife had approached Erasmus for assistance in the reform of her husband's rowdy ways. Bainton points out that the title involves a double entendre; "enchiridion," indicating something held in the hand, can be taken to mean either a dagger or a handbook.[30] Like some early Christian thinkers and like the Puritan revolutionaries, Erasmus here styles the Christian life as warfare, but he clearly demarcates spiritual from temporal war. Perhaps most notable in this work is the emphasis he gives the seriousness of dedication to Christ's kingdom. The perfection of the Christian life consists essentially in charity, realized in the following of Christ and the sharing of his cross. "Even though all of us cannot reach this goal, cannot attain the perfect imitation of the Head, all of us must aim for this goal with all our efforts."[31] And again, "We are weak human beings and cannot attain fully to these ideals. This does not mean we should stop trying, but, on the contrary, it means that we should come as close to them as we possibly can."[32]

In summary, Erasmus was a man both of and against his time. His investment in the power relationships of the European heads of state prevented his pacifist Christianity from repudiating all those political institutions that arise from, depend upon, and perpetuate armed violence. At the same time, he was able to combine Renaissance humanism's confidence in reasonableness and justice with Reformation Christianity's candid critique of distorting political and ecclesial traditions that undermine the social implications of the gospel. Insisting lucidly that Jesus meant what he said and did, Erasmus sought within political and governing structures to transform social relationships in light of Christian values.

ANABAPTISTS

George Hunston Williams refers to Erasmus as "a patron of the Radical Reformation."[33] Despite the fact that his own commitment to peace was implemented with a dose of political pragmatism, Erasmus did prepare the way for the adamant biblical nonviolence of the Anabaptists, with his straightforward approach to the Bible and with his campaign in favor

29. Erasmus, *Complaint of Peace*, 44.

30. Bainton, *Erasmus of Christendom*, 36.

31. Bainton, *Erasmus of Christendom*, 95.

32. Bainton, *Erasmus of Christendom*, 157.

33. George Hunston Williams, *The Radical Reformation* (Philadelphia: Westminster Press, 1962), 8–9.

of the uncompromising emulation of its ideals in the life of every individual.

First emerging as a real movement in Zurich in 1524 under the leadership of Conrad Grebel and Felix Manz, the Anabaptists repudiated not only Roman Catholicism, but also the Lutheran ("evangelical") and Calvinist ("Reformed") movements. They were in search of a more radical return to biblical discipleship. Their sense of eschatological possibility was strong, though directed to a relatively small circle of the converted. The Radical Reformers wanted a full restitution of the New Testament way of life and saw persecution and suffering as marks of the true church. Although they preferred the name "Christian Brethren," their opponents called them Anabaptists ("rebaptizers") because they accepted only adult baptism as reflective of early Christian practice. The concrete and practical aspects of discipleship were crucial to them, especially the formation of voluntary and disciplined communities, the integral relation of faith and works, and rejection of violence and "the sword." They were critical of Christian participation in government, though there was diversity on this point. The convictions that "Christians were entirely separated from the old and new churches of the Reformation era and all temporal power, and that the latter was an ordinance of God outside 'the perfection of Christ,' arose quite naturally from the early Anabaptists' modeling themselves on the New Testament."[34]

James Stayer connects some of the developments within Anabaptism, as well as the violently hostile reactions against them to the fact that the movement arose simultaneously with the Peasants' War and, like the Peasants' War, was a radical social movement "from below," in which some urged the forceful overthrow of power (an exception among the Anabaptists), and that was perceived to have destabilizing effects.[35] Under Ulrich Zwingli's influence, the city council of Zurich had "decreed the Reformation" in 1523, but the Protestant movements in the city were multivocal. Through a close study of the Bible, which Zwingli encouraged, some groups came to diverge on certain points of practice, especially infant baptism. For Grebel, adult baptism signified a certain view of the church: the church does not belong to "Christians" of lukewarm commitment; it is a fellowship of those who truly believe and live rightly. The first clear profession of nonresistance appears in a letter from Grebel to Thomas Müntzer in 1524:

---

34. James Stayer, "The Anabaptist Revolt and Political and Religious Power," in *Power, Authority, and the Anabaptist Tradition*, ed. Benjamin W. Redekop and Calvin W. Redekop (Baltimore: John Hopkins University Press, 2001), 70.

35. Stayer, "Anabaptist Revolt," 52.

> The gospel and its adherents are not to be protected by the sword, nor are they thus to protect themselves. . . . True Christian believers are sheep among wolves, sheep for the slaughter. . . . Neither do they use worldly sword or war, since all killing has ceased with them—unless, indeed, we would still be of the old law.[36]

The dissenters met almost immediately with the persecution that was to make them "a hunted minority."[37] Fearing the entire reform movement might be discredited by "extremists," Zwingli tried to persuade them to recant, then tortured them, and finally had some executed by drowning. One among hundreds of eventual casualties was Michael Sattler, author of the Swiss Brethren's Schleitheim Confession, who was executed in 1527. A notorious decree of the imperial Diet of Spiers (1529) pronounced, with the concurrence of both Catholics and Lutherans, the death sentence for all Anabaptists. Luther and Melanchthon personally endorsed severe measures against them.

As far as the sixteenth-century Radical Reformers were concerned (with few exceptions[38]), the way of Jesus Christ so contradicts the sinfulness of the world that to participate in its institutions at all is to compromise the gospel. They portrayed the love and life of the kingdom, as contrasted to the ethic of the world and of political institutions, in sharply dualistic terms. The magistracy is ordained to punish the wicked and protect the innocent, because it is necessary in the present to maintain good order.[39] However, the Christian cannot participate in this office, although he or she must obey the civil authorities to the extent

---

36. As cited by Peter Brock, from George Hunston Williams's revision of a 1905 translation by Walter Rauschenbusch, in *Pacifism in Europe to 1914* (Princeton, NJ: Princeton University Press, 1972), 60. The doctrine of nonresistance was further ratified in the Schleitheim Confession of 1527 and was an established Anabaptist tenet by the early 1530s (Brock, *Pacifism in Europe*, 87). On the emergence of Anabaptism, see Werner O. Packull, "An Introduction to Anabaptist Theology," in *The Cambridge Companion to Reformation Theology*, ed. David Bagchi and David C. Steinmetz (Cambridge: Cambridge University Press, 2004), 194–219; Stayer, "Anabaptist Revolt"; Fritz Blanke, "Anabaptism and the Reformation," in *The Recovery of the Anabaptist Vision: A Sixtieth Anniversary Tribute to Harold S. Bender*, ed. Guy F. Hershberger, Dissent and Nonconformity 22 (Scottdale, PA: Herald, 1957). See also William Klassen, "Anabaptist Ethics," in *The Westminster Dictionary of Christian Ethics,* ed. James F. Childress and John Macquarrie (Philadelphia: Westminster, 1986), 20–21.

37. Packull, "Introduction," 196.

38. Peter Brock believes that even within the Dutch Anabaptist community united by Menno there was some diversity, especially from 1557 onward. Separate sects developed out of disputes over application of principles; for example, over the strictness of the ban, or whether to sanction the holding of offices. See Brock, *Pacifism in Europe*, 162–63.

39. See Robert Kreider,"Anabaptists and the State," in *Recovery of the Anabaptist Vision*, 180–93.

that their commands do not conflict with the commands of God (as based on Romans 13).[40]

In preaching a return to the primitive church, the Anapabtists see the Christian community as perfectionist, separatist, and pacifist. The essence of Christianity is not faith as such, but a way of life captured as "following Christ" *(nachfolge Christi)*. Membership in the church through adult conversion and baptism is followed by rigorous conformity to the example of Christ and his kingdom. The true church consists only of those who are committed to holy living. The inner experience of faith produces transformed behavior, newness of life is as important a criterion as conversion. Discernment of the proper moral shape of that life takes place within a gathered community that places its trust in biblical guidance. The membership of the church was expanded by preaching and example, for the Anabaptists took with utmost seriousness the Great Commission to "go and baptize all nations" (Matt 28:16–20).

Most characteristic of the Anabaptist way of life were sharing of goods in common and nonresistance. Some groups, such as the Hutterites, translated brotherly love into complete community of property, but, for all Anabaptists, brotherly love meant at least a willingness to yield one's own possessions to the brother or sister in need. The Anabaptists also took the "hard sayings" of Jesus literally and did not try to accommodate them to survival in the world. As anticipated by the biblical accounts of martyrdom, nonconformity leads to persecution. But Christians must neither use the sword nor engage in war. They must not take oaths nor make any other compromises, such as bringing a suit in a court of law.

Even according to their most rabid critics, the morality of the Anabaptists was exemplary. Harold Bender cites the testimony of the Catholic theologian Franz Agricola, offered in his 1582 treatise *Against the Terrible Errors of the Anabaptists:*

> Among the existing heretical sects there is none which in appearance leads a more modest or pious life than the Anabaptists. As concerns their outward public life they are irreproachable. No lying, deception, swearing, strife, harsh language, no intemperate eating and drinking, no outward personal

40. A primary source for Anabaptist views of government is the Schleitheim Confession prepared by the Swiss Brethren in 1527. This document sees the restraint of evil by force as necessary but "outside the perfection of Christ" An edited version is available in John C. Wenger, "The Schleitheim Confession of Faith," *Mennonite Quarterly Review* 19, no. 4 (1945): 243–53. Excerpts are included in George W. Forell, *Christian Social Teachings* (Minneapolis: Augsburg, 1971), 184–88. However, James Stayer recognizes this as the position of the Schleitheim Confession ("Anabaptist Authority," 56), but also presents the attempt of Balthasar Hubmaier, a refugee from violence into Moravia, to legitimize government as necessary to order the world, and to counsel deference to Christian rulers (59).

display, is found among them, but humility, patience, uprightness, neatness, honesty, temperance, straightforwardness in such measure one would suppose they had the Holy Spirit of God.[41]

Another contemporary, Sebastian Franck, writes that they gained a huge following because "they taught nothing but love, faith, and the cross. . . . They helped each other faithfully, and called each other brothers. . . . They died as martyrs, patiently and humbly enduring all persecution."[42]

The radical nature of the Anabaptist commitment to Christ, to a close community of sanctified believers, and to the kingdom made present in the religious and moral conduct of Christians is illustrated in their use of excommunication as a last resort. The "ban" and "shunning" require a complete ostracism of unrepentant sinners from all social fellowship, including that of the immediate family. This practice was based on Matthew 18:15–17, with its injunction to warn repeatedly brethren who have sinned, then finally to let the obdurate "be to you as a Gentile and a tax collector." Since the reign of God in Christian fellowship is sharply opposed to the kingdom of Satan in the world, spiritual government can be maintained only by excluding from Christian community those under Satan's influence. Anabaptists had no delusion that the ethic of the kingdom would become accepted in the world at large.

Nevertheless, the political impact of Anabaptist beliefs and forms of community was significant, even "revolutionizing." They offered a vision of limited government, voluntary participation in politics and civil society, and freedom of conscience, including the right of conscientious objection for ordinary citizens. They aspired to community of property and to greater gender equality, though these ideals were not uniformly realized or sustained over time. Speaking to Christian peacebuilding, David Little even believes it is

> reasonable to attribute to Anabaptists the early practice of what has come to be called 'restorative justice.' Forsaking retributive, usually coercive, punishment associated with the earthly magistrate, Anabaptists emphasized consensual acts of forgiveness and mercy aimed at overcoming estrangement and restoring right relations among offender, victim, and community. Expelling a resolutely unrepentant offender from the group was the closest they came to practicing retributive justice, and even that was nonviolent in character.[43]

41. Harold Bender, "The Anabaptist Vision," in *Recovery of the Anabaptist Vision*, 45.
42. Bender, "Anabaptist Vision," 46.
43. Little, "Religion, Peace," 72.

ANABAPTIST REVOUTIONARIES

A lamentable exception to the Anabaptist theology of voluntary commitment and ethic of nonresistance occurred in Germany in 1534 in the town of Münster, where a group of extremists succeeded briefly in taking over the municipal government by force. Their inspiration, Melchior Hoffman (1495–1543), was a millenarian preacher who was attracted to the reform through Lutheranism and associated with early Anabaptist reformers in Strasbourg. Hoffman taught his followers to await the New Age, and he even predicted that in 1533 his own imprisonment would be followed by the coming of the Lord. Hoffman expected an apocalyptic siege of the city by the emperor, believing the city's godly rulers should defend it by the sword, while the members of his sect preached the gospel of grace. (Instead the Strasbourg authorities threw him into the dungeon, and he spent the rest of his life in prison.)

Both the influences behind and the actual events at Münster are complex.[44] Evidently, the same social dissatisfaction that led to the Peasants' War of 1524–25 combined with years of religious persecution to set the stage for further radical experimentation.

> Those who had lived under the continual shadow of death in caves and desolate places of the earth began . . . to dream dreams of the birds of heaven coming to devour the carcasses of the oppressors, of the return of the Lord to vindicate the saints, of the New Jerusalem from which the 144,000 of the redeemed should go out to slaughter the ungodly, whether the Lord should accomplish all this by Himself, or whether men should assist, was not altogether clear.[45]

Some of a revolutionary frame of mind located the New Jerusalem in Münster. Unlike other Anapabtist communities, the Münsterite leaders used the Old Testament as a practical model for restoration, alluding to the covenant of the Exodus from Egypt.[46] Intolerant of the reluctant or rebellious, the leaders at Münster combined the agenda of the theocracy with the ideology of the crusade.

The Dutch Melchiorite prophet Jan Mathijs arrived in the city in 1534, claiming to have received direct revelations about the fulfillment of time and the establishment of Zion in the city of Münster. He asserted the right of true believers to destroy dissenters. Although the city council tried to stem the insurgency, its power had already been undermined by

44. For an overview, see Packull, "Introduction," 196–98.
45. Roland Bainton, *Reformation of the Sixteenth Century* (Boston: Beacon, 1952), 105.
46. Williams, *Radical Reformation*, 363.

the citizens' support for the radicals, and Mathijs was in control. With the city beleaguered by episcopal troops, Mathijs confiscated all property, money, and food and instituted communism of property. Even household goods theoretically belonged to all.

When Mathijs was killed in a confrontation with the bishop's forces, he was succeeded by his assistant Jan Beukels, who enforced harsh penalties against a variety of moral and social infractions, including blasphemy, disrespect to parents or master, lewdness, adultery, and complaining. Beukels's attempted restitution of the Davidic kingdom as tyrannical rule, along with a "harem of sixteen concubines and Matthijs' beautiful widow as royal queen, remains difficult to reconcile with sober, moral Anabaptist practices elsewhere. Obviously, desperate circumstances in the besieged city were partly to blame for the aberrations."[47] Following further victories over the troops outside the city, Beukels had himself ceremoniously crowned king. But his "religious fanaticism and maniacal wickedness,"[48] along with famine and continued siege, sapped the energy and morale of his constituents. Two deserters finally betrayed one of the gates of the town, and the bishop's forces overtook it in 1535, slaughtering most of the inhabitants.

For centuries, the debacle at Münster was associated with the Anabaptist theologian Thomas Müntzer (ca. 1488–1525), owing to a biography by a contemporary (possibly Luther's associate Melanchthon) that aimed to discredit him. Müntzer was a fellow German priest who took his original bearings from Luther but eventually turned vociferously against him. Unlike both the humanists and the "sola scriptura" reformers, Müntzer's spirituality was nourished by medieval mysticism, and the necessity of suffering in obedience to God's will. He was also an advocate of the common people, one who encouraged revolt.[49] Later scholarship has shown that Müntzer had no direct influence on the events constituting the Münster disaster; in fact, he died eight years before the eschatological experiment there began. However, Müntzer's fierce prophecies and warnings illustrate the flavor of those Anabaptist fringe movements that had lost their moorings in pacifist witness and become violently revolutionary. By 1524, Müntzer was advocating insurrection against rulers and against the more conservative leaders of reform. During the peasant uprising in Thuringia, he sided with and preached to the peasants, writing letters to rulers above the name "Thomas Müntzer with the Sword

47. Packull, "Introduction," 197.
48. Williams, *Radical Reformation*, 380.
49. Hans-Joergen Goetz, *Thomas Müntzer: Apocalyptic, Mystic, and Revolutionary*, trans. Jocelyn Jaquiery (London: T&T Clark, 2000).

of Gideon."[50] Toward the end of those bloody events, Müntzer was captured, tortured, and beheaded.

Müntzer believed in a Spirit-inspired community of avowed believers who come to faith through personal suffering and who confirm that faith with practical results. God calls the elect to rise against the godless and will ensure their triumph even in this world. "God will strike to pieces all your adversaries who undertake to persecute you." Although Müntzer often relied upon Israelite examples of war—for instance, the destruction of the Canaanite people when "the Chosen were bent on entering the Promised Land"—he also discovered the occasional supporting text in the life of Jesus. Because Christ's enemies are ruining the government of his church, "Christ our Lord says (Matt 18:6): Whosoever shall offend one of these little ones, it is better for him that a millstone be hung about his neck and that he be thrown in the depth of the sea." The "true governors" of Christ's church must "drive his enemies from the elect." "The sword is necessary to wipe out the godless (Rom 13:4)," for "the godless have no right to live except as the elect wish to grant it to them." This extermination should be accomplished by the princes, but if they are remiss, "the sword will be taken from them (Dan 7:26f.)."

The rabid preaching and extremist social plans of the Münsterites and of Thomas Müntzer clearly resemble the crusading ideals surveyed in the previous chapter. They just as clearly represent a sharp departure from the form of radical Christianity preached, for instance, by Menno Simons. What elements of Christianity, retained in what way under what circumstances, seem most likely to lead to such ignominious distortions? One thing to be learned is that militaristic twists of Christianity can be spawned not only by imperialistic elites or power-hungry revolutionaries, but also within groups experiencing extreme deprivation. A massive social revolt in God's name can appear to offer hope of emancipation and victory, and even a justification to trample their oppressors in a frenzy of revenge. Suffering past the point of endurance can lead either to martyrdom or fanatical delusion. The paradigmatic response of the early Christians, as a persecuted social minority, was to die proclaiming their faith and their trust in a spiritual victory and reward. But once Christians divide the world into the righteous and the godless, locate themselves confidently among the former, and—especially—arrogate a mission to exterminate God's enemies, the guiding ideal "kingdom" becomes a blueprint for religious and social mayhem. The kingdom as a coherent way of life is lost, replaced by a crazed and myopic literalism

50. Hans J. Hillerbrand, "Thomas Muentzer," in *Reformers in Profile*, ed. Brian A. Gerrish (Philadelphia: Fortress, 1967), 219. This essay, along with Williams's chapter on Müntzer, provides the backbone of the biography here.

that makes biblical events and injunctions subservient to social and political tyranny or vendettas.

MENNO SIMONS

The greatest theologian of the Reformation's characteristically nonresistant left wing, Menno Simons (ca. 1496–1561), was born in Friesland, a Dutch province, and was ordained a Catholic priest. The radical reform movement had been brought to the Netherlands in the early 1530s and was nurtured under the leadership of the brothers Obbe and Dirk Philips. Menno (Simons is a patronymic) did not become familiar with the Bible until after his ordination, when he opened it to verify the doctrine of transubstantiation against the challenges of Protestants. In the end, he was led not only to reject that doctrine, but also the baptism of infants and the authority of the pope.

Personal example contributed to his decision. As a young priest, Menno was disconcerted by reports of the execution of a godly man who had accepted rebaptism. A few years later, Menno felt both judged and inspired by the example of his own brother, killed in 1535 after having been caught up in a revolutionary religious movement. Menno was ashamed that he had not had the courage to stand up for his beliefs. In 1536 he was rebaptized into the brotherhood of Obbe Philips, who stressed one's inner relationship to God (Dirk emphasized communal discipline). Menno became an evangelical pastor, married, and was ordained a bishop or overseer in 1537.[51] His leadership and writings did much to establish the Anabaptist fellowship as a disciplined congregation with a distinctive, separatist, and, above all, scriptural way of life. Real transformation of life by those baptized in Christ is key to Menno's theology. God's grace affects all areas of life, so that Christians can already be "citizens of the New Jerusalem," because Jesus Christ is already Lord over all of life.[52] "Menno makes the doctrine of sanctification the very

51. On Menno's life, see Harold S. Bender, "A Brief Biography of Menno Simons," in *The Complete Writings of Menno Simons*, ed. John C. Wenger (Scottdale, PA: Herald, 1955), 3–29; Harold S. Bender, *Menno Simons' Life and Writings: A Quadricentennial Tribute, 1536–1936* (Eugene, OR: Wipf & Stock, 2003), 1–50; and J. C .Wenger, "Menno Simons," in *Reformers in Profile*, 194–212. See also Sjouke Voolstra, "Menno Simons (1496–1561)," in *The Reformation Theologians: An Introduction to Theology in the Early Modern Period*, ed. Carter Lindberg (Oxford: Blackwell, 2002), 363–77, which concentrates on the sources of Menno's theology; and Lydia Harder, "Power and Authority in Mennonite Theological Development," in Redekop and Redekop, *Power, Authority*, 73–94, which presents Menno's theological contributions and highlights their ethical-political significance.
52. Harder, "Mennonite Theological Development," 75.

heart of his theology, in line with the entire Anabaptist movement."[53] Completely rejecting violence either as a way of safeguarding the purity of this way or of fending off persecutors, Menno gave eloquent expression to a strain of pacifist thinking that continues to inspire contemporary Christian countercultural movements.

For the Anabaptists, the Bible defines the Christian life. They embrace the Reformation principle of *sola scriptura* and mandate every Christian to read the Bible as a source of instruction, admonition, and correction. The word of God is found in the written text of Scripture, of whose right interpretation they are confident. However, the Bible is interpreted in what Werner Packull calls a "hermeneutic community" with a "congregational hermeneutic." This was (at least in principle) an "egalitarian, church-centered hermeneutic," based on the priesthood of all believers, and a lack of distinction between clerical and lay.[54] Both Old and New Testaments are authoritative, but both are read through Jesus Christ, and the New takes precedence over the Old.[55] It was assumed that communal discernment would lead to a correct interpretation, although debates that erupted within and between Anabaptist communities demonstrate that this was not always borne out in practice.

Menno introduces his most influential treatise, *Foundation of Christian Doctrine*, with a call to discipleship premised on the kingdom's accessibility: "Now is the time to arise with Christ in a new, righteous, and penitent existence, even as Christ says, The time is fulfilled, and the Kingdom of God is at hand: repent and believe in the gospel." Christ leaves and proclaims "an example of pure love, and a perfect life."[56] Unless conversion, repentance, and baptism are followed by regeneration from "this wicked, immoral and shameful life, . . . it will not help a fig to be called Christians." Of the "spiritual strength" the Christian receives, baptism is the "outward sign."[57]

The Lord's Supper is important in the radical fellowship insofar as it signifies the unity and love of the community: "by the Lord's Supper Christian unity, love, and peace are signified and enjoined."[58] By the same token and because of the absolute expectation that conversion brings sanctification, sinners are to be excluded from this fellowship. Any

53. Voolstra, "Menno Simons," 369.

54. Packull, 199–200.

55. Menno, *Foundation of Christian Doctrine*, 159–60; *Why I Do Not Cease Teaching and Writing*, 312, both in Wenger, ed., *Complete Writings*, from which all subsequent citations of Menno's writings will be taken. For a more literalist reading of Menno's approach, see John C. Wenger, "The Biblicism of the Anabaptist," in *Recovery of the Anabaptist Vision*, 67–93.

56. Menno, *Foundation*, 108.

57. Menno, *Foundation*, 110–11.

58. Menno, *Foundation*, 145.

who would "sit at the Lord's table . . . must be sound in the faith and unblameable in conduct and life. None is excepted, neither emperor nor king, prince nor earl, knight nor nobleman."[59] It was because of the near impossibility of reconciling worldly offices such as these with Christianity that most pacifist radicals rejected the magistracy for their members, even while recognizing that civil authority and the sword have a use outside the Christian fellowship.[60] On the other hand, seeming to depart from the separatist mentality of the Schleitheim Confession, Menno calls lords and princes to fulfill their responsibilities "in the true fear of God with fairness and Christian discretion." In fact, he promises that if they

> believe Christ's Word, fear God's wrath, love righteousness, do justice to widows and orphans, judge rightly between a man and his neighbor, fear no man's highness, despise no man's littleness, hate all avarice, punish with reason, allow the Word of God to be taught freely, hinder no one from walking in the truth, bow to the scepter of him who called you to this high service. Then shall your throne stand firm forever.[61]

It is doubtful that Menno envisioned that any members of his congregation would take up public governance roles. It may be simply that he took the fact of "Christian" rulers for granted, calling them to account more in a spirit of prophetic critique than with any expectation that Christian governance would or even could be successfully carried out.

This seems particularly likely, given the high standards to which he and other Anabaptists held church members and the care they took to prevent offenders from endangering the rest of the flock. Menno devotes extensive attention to the exclusion of sinful and recalcitrant congregants.[62] His stringent expectations are a direct outcome of his ecclesiology and, particularly, his view of the church as presently realizing kingdom life. In the *Instruction on Excommunication,* he defines Christ's church as "a congregation of saints."[63] Since the devil can work evil from within the community, the exclusion of any who may serve as Satan's weapons must be absolute.[64]

However, Menno's tool for purifying the community is not violent but social. The "ban" can even part marriages and families, though in

59. Menno, *Foundation*, 150.

60. See Robert Kreider, "The Anabaptists and the State," in *Recovery of the Anabaptist Vision*, 180–93. For a discussion of differences on this point, see Stayer, "Anabaptist Power," 59–64.

61. Menno, *Foundation*, 193.

62. Menno, *A Kind Admonition on Church Discipline*; *A Clear Account of Excommunication*; and *Final Instruction on Marital Avoidance*; as well as letters and other references.

63. Menno, *Instruction on Excommunication*, 962.

64. Menno, *Instruction on Excommunication*, 963.

cases of hardship, Menno makes some exceptions.[65] Unlike excommunication in modern churches, the Anabaptist ban is not a merely juridical matter, a decision of the temporal church; as long as it is in effect, it actually excludes the sinner from the eternal kingdom.[66] Yet it does have as one purpose the conversion and readmittance of the sinner.[67] The ban should be seen relative to the weapons resorted to at that time by other Christian groups trying to induce conformity among their members, such as imprisonment, torture, and death, in which they sought the backing of the civil government. For typical Anabaptists, the voluntary nature of the church precludes physical force even as it demands total religious and moral conformity.

A dominant theme in Menno's writings is the "persecution of the Lamb" in whose cross, sufferings, and blessings the Christian shares. The kingdom of God, present to believers in their sufferings, is begun but never completed on earth. "The Lamb is slain"; he enters into glory through the cross and death, and his children and servants must do likewise.[68] As both Testaments demonstrate, persecution will continue as long as the righteous and the unrighteous remain on the earth together.[69] The Anabaptists do not embrace suffering simply for its own sake, nor even for the sake of imitation alone. Suffering and taking up the cross have a pedagogical function that fits the radicals' emphasis on sanctification. To "pick up and bear daily" the cross is "profitable and advantageous."[70] The Lord Jesus "teaches, admonishes, rebukes, threatens, and chastises, in order that we should deny ungodliness and worldly lusts, die entirely unto the world, the flesh, and the devil, and seek our treasure, our portion, and our inheritance in heaven."[71]

Somewhat paradoxically, Menno cites Israelite paradigms of faith at least as frequently as Christian ones. Menno does not hesitate to mention wars and killings by Abraham, Moses, and David, while praising their obedience and righteousness.[72] David "did great works in the name of the Lord: he slew the terribly great Goliath; he got him two hundred foreskins of the Philistines."[73] Menno lauds the faith and humility of the Roman centurion without taking up the implications of his profession.

---

65. For instance, when there are young children, or when one or both parties refuse to give up sexual relations (Menno, *Final Instruction on Marital Avoidance*, 1059).

66. Menno, *Instruction on Excommunication*, 966–67.

67. Menno, *Instruction on Excommunication*, 966–67.

68. Menno, *Foundation*, 109.

69. Menno, *Cross of the Saints*, 582; for Old Testament examples, see 589–90.

70. Menno, *Cross of the Saints*, 620.

71. Menno, *Cross of the Saints*, 616.

72. Menno, *The True Christian Faith*, 346–47; *Cross of the Saints*, 589.

73. Menno, *Cross of the Saints*, 589.

He also makes use of warfare imagery in exhorting the faithful to fervent cross-bearing, calling them "soldiers and conquerors in Christ," and referring to the cross as "an armor and a shield."[74]

Certainly, Menno intends the followers of Jesus to rely on the "sword of the Spirit" in self-defense and the reproof of wickedness,[75] but he still appeals to the civil authorities for relief, arguing as Tertullian and Origen had before him that separatist Christians are not seditious.[76] Yet, although Menno himself escaped a martyr's end, his followers were subjected to the most extreme hatred, torture, and death at the hands of the civil authorities and at the behest of Catholics, evangelicals, and Calvinists. While never a dominant thread in the Christian tradition, the pacifist churches have made an indispensable contribution to its vitality. Significant aspects of the Anabaptists' life and faith continue today among the Mennonites, Amish, and Hutterite Brethren—for instance, a shared way of life set aside from the world and a commitment to biblical nonviolence.

The theology and example of the Anabaptists and their heirs suggest some challenging questions for later Christians. Is genuinely redeemed life in Christ best expressed in a small community of faith and witness that shares not only a common creed but also a specific set of radical ecclesial and moral practices? If so what is that community's relationship to larger social and political institutions that make such community possible by providing for basic needs and security? Is a countercultural community within a culture complicit in its "rejected" practices by relying on their benefits? What can or should a countercultural church do to alleviate this dilemma or tension?

In the twentieth century and subsequently, Mennonites have increasingly turned toward the possibilities for social transformation of society through Christian influence, and they have sought constructive ways to participate in society and politics, at which Menno may have hinted in his advice to lords and princes. John Howard Yoder, who indefatigably advocated a countercultural church, also debated the proper application of just war theory to avoid conflicts as far as possible. After his death, Yoder's interest in and contributions to public discourse were highlighted and promoted by his colleagues.[77] Lydia Harder maintains that Menno's theology contains an incarnational dimension that makes

74. Menno, *Cross of the Saints*, 621.

75. Menno, *Cross of the Saints*, 603–4.

76. Menno, *A Pathetic Supplication to All Magistrates*, 523–31; *Foundations of Christian Doctrine*, 117–20; *Cross of the Saints*, 602–5.

77. John Howard Yoder, *When War Is Unjust: Being Honest in Just War Thinking*, 2nd ed. (Maryknoll, NY: Orbis, 1996); John Howard Yoder, with Glen Harold Stassen, Mark Thiessen

it possible to see the gospel and the kingdom as incarnate and transformative in society as well as the church, especially as that theme has been developed by contemporary Mennonites.[78] James Reimer has developed an Anabaptist-Mennonite political theology in which he proposes a more positive role of the state and other civil institutions than did Yoder, argues that no one can escape the public sphere altogether, and sees constructive political participation as a mandate for Christians.[79]

This survey of the premodern pacifist circle will close with the profound religious experience of mercy and forgiveness in Christ, which inspires the Quakers' nonviolent ethic.

QUAKERS

The seventeenth-century English and eighteenth-century American members of the Religious Society of Friends were in agreement with the Reformation pacifists that the presence of the kingdom makes possible a life in the gospel of which violence has no part. The movement of Friends—or Quakers, the more common term today—began in the northwest of England.[80] George Fox (1624–91), who was from a radical Puritan family, is usually regarded as its founder. The movement carries on the Reformers' call for reform of the church, and the Puritans' desire that the reforms in England go further.

The Society of Friends grew out of Puritan radicalism and can be connected to the theology of the Anabaptists and English Baptists, many of whose working-class members joined the early Quaker movement during the English Civil War (1642–49). The Puritans' Calvinist faith in the sovereignty and power of God in this world led them to expect that those elected to receive God's irresistible grace would transfigure church and state in the Holy Commonwealth. The Quakers shared the Puritans'

Nation, and Matt Hamsher, eds., *The War of the Lamb: The Ethics of Nonviolence and Peacemaking* (Grand Rapids, MI: Brazos, 2009).

78. Harder, "Mennonite Theological Development," 79–80, 90–94.

79. A. James Reimer, "An Anabaptist-Mennonite Political Theology: Theological Presuppositions," *Direction* 38, no. 1 (2009), 29–44, accessed August 7, 2017, https://tinyurl.com/y774s5ow; *Mennonite and Classical Theology: Dogmatic Foundations for Christian Ethics* (Kitchener, ON: Pandora, 2009); *Toward an Anabaptist Political Theology: Law, Order, and Civil Society*, ed. Paul G. Doerksen (Eugene, OR: Cascade, 2014); and *Christians and War: A History of Practices and Teachings* (Minneapolis: Fortress, 2010).

80. "Quaker" fitted the violent trembling that overtook those experiencing a confrontation and struggle with the inner Light or Spirit. See Hugh Barbour and J. William Frost, *The Quakers* (Westport, CT: Greenwood, 1988), 28; and *The Journal of George Fox*, ed. Rufus M. Jones (New York: Capricorn, 1963), 125, where Fox says that in 1650 a judge first gave them the name, "because I bade them tremble at the name of the Lord."

aim to accomplish a worldwide victory over evil, but at the same time they were radically skeptical of the institutional church and reluctant to participate directly in institutions of government. Thus the Quaker challenge to the Puritan theocracy; Quakers stressed a direct relationship of the individual to God, which was shared in community but was not dependent on ecclesiastical mediation. Nor were they amenable to a program of violent conquest, especially on religious grounds.

George Fox saw the Friends "as the fruit of the renewal of the conquest of the world by the Spirit or Light of Christ, the climax of God's plan for world history that had begun with Paul the Apostle, had halted for a thousand years of Catholic apostasy, and had begun again as incomplete renewal in the Protestant Reformation and Puritan Revolution."[81] Quakers rejected the Calvinist and Puritan beliefs in predestination, infant baptism, and national churches; in common with the Anabaptists, they believed in moral perfectibility, adult faith commitment, and the church as a gathered body of professed believers willing and able to practice stringent discipleship and simplicity of life. Though less formal and widespread than Anabaptist excommunication, the Quakers used "disownment" as a means of separating the committed from the wayward.

Although the Quakers did not withdraw from all involvement with government and the state and did not at first demand nonviolence (many were members of Cromwell's army), they did root religion in personal experience and in the shared faith of the immediate community, as confirmed by Scripture. By 1611, every church had an English Bible, driving new interpretations of spirituality, theology, ecclesiology, and liturgy. As Christians waiting for the Second Coming of Christ, the Quakers saw Christ and his kingdom as present now, through the direct inward encounter of God with the individual.[82] This was to have political ramifications opposed to the revolutionary Puritans.

The most essential characteristic of the Quaker movement is the presence and revelation of God in Jesus Christ experientially ("experimentally") in the heart, a revelation open to every person (not only the predestined "elect"). In the early years, Quaker beliefs and practices were both fairly unsystematic and diverse.[83] Yet there are some uniting factors. First is the direct inward experience of God, then, derived from this, the belief in radical spiritual equality (which opened the door to

---

81. Barbour and Frost, *Quakers*, 28. Cf. *The Journal of George Fox*, 11.

82. On the history, theology, and development of Quakerism, see Ben Pink Dandelion, *The Quakers: A Very Short Introduction* (Oxford: Oxford University Press, 2008), 1–18, 55–71; and *An Introduction to Quakerism* (New York: Cambridge University Press, 2007).

83. Meredith Baldwin Weddle, *Walking in the Way of Peace: Quaker Pacifism in the Seventeenth Century* (Oxford: Oxford University Press, 2001), 4–11.

greater leadership of women).[84] Quaker worship was simple, with no formal liturgy or clergy; it was common for them to choose relatively untrained ministers who also earned their livelihood by some other craft or trade. Preaching was interspersed with periods of silence that encouraged experience of God's inward presence. When God grants the Light of Christ within one's soul, one's consciousness is transformed and sin abandoned.

An early attempt to systematically capture Quaker theology is Robert Barclay's *Catechism and Confession of Faith* (1673), which states succinctly the Quaker view of renewal in Christ.[85] Jesus's command to "be perfect" (Matt 5:48) exerts a serious practical demand. The power of Christ's death allows all Christians who persevere "in this life to be freed from the dominion of sin."[86] This experience and conviction become a mission to the word, through the witness of plain worship, speech, and dress, nonviolence, and various attempts to inspire political and social change in view of Quaker principles, especially work for peace and against slavery.

GEORGE FOX

George Fox was born in Leicestershire, England. His father, a weaver, had a local reputation for piety. George's mother, a woman of more than average education, encouraged her son in his reflective and religious pursuits. In his *Journal,* Fox tells of his early formation: "When I came to eleven years of age I knew pureness and righteousness; for while a child I was taught how to walk to be kept pure."[87] Educated in the local primary school, George was apprenticed to a cobbler and a shepherd and began early to seek a better religious understanding than that offered him in his intense conversations with his father, his pastor, and a local squire who supported the Puritan reform. By all accounts, George Fox was a singular person who at an early age came to enjoy what might almost be termed a mystical consciousness of the all-encompassing presence of God in Christ.

The period of searching and spiritual travail Fox endured in his youth led him to leave home in 1643, hoping to discover some religious teaching or leadership that could answer his doubts and anxieties. About four years later, the Lord "opened" Fox to faith while he was returning from

---

84. See Margaret Hope Bacon, *Mothers of Feminism: The Story of Quaker Women in America* (San Francisco: Harper & Row, 1986).

85. Robert Barclay, *Catechism and Confession of Faith* 7, in *Early Quaker Writings,* ed. Hugh Barbour and Arthur O. Roberts (Grand Rapids, MI: William B. Eerdmans, 1973).

86. Barclay, *Catechism and Confession of Faith* 7.

87. *Journal of George Fox,* 66.

a walk alone. "I was taken up in the love of God, so that I could not but admire the greatness of his love; and while I was in that condition, it was opened unto me by the eternal light and power, and I therein clearly saw that all was done and to be done in and by Christ, and how He conquers."[88] In his redeemed state, George came to appreciate "the greatness and infinitude of the love of God, which cannot be expressed by words."[89]

All those enlightened by Christ are restored to Adam's original state. "I knew nothing but pureness and innocency, and righteousness; being renewed into the image of God by Christ Jesus to the state of Adam, which he was in before he fell." Moreover, "the Lord showed" Fox "that such as were faithful to Him, in the power and light of Christ, should come up into that state," in which they too might know and do "the admirable works of the creation, and the virtues thereof."[90] For Fox, two primitive periods were normative: the first days of creation before sin marred the world and human nature, and the years of early Christianity, before the apostasy of the Catholic Church.[91] Renewed in the Spirit of Christ that dwells within, the believer returns to a pristine spiritual consciousness and moral purity.

By 1648, Fox had begun his own ministry in complete assurance that he was called to serve as an instrument of God. Of imposing appearance, Fox wore his hair long and, according to his contemporaries, had piercing eyes capable of summing up in a glance one's spiritual state.[92] Like Joan of Arc, he seemed to have a telepathic knowledge of events transpiring elsewhere.[93] At once assured in his beliefs and generous to his companions, as well as quick to attribute his enemies' misfortunes to God's judgment, Fox had a magnetic and commanding effect on his followers. Many wrote to Fox or addressed him in terms full of enough adulation to cause him alarm and embarrassment. In his preface to Fox's autobiography, William Penn—first instructed by Fox as a young man, and destined to give Quaker universalism a humanistic retouching in the New World—remembers the Quaker leader this way:

88. *Journal of George Fox*, 84.
89. *Journal of George Fox*, 88.
90. *Journal of George Fox*, 97.
91. See James F. Childress, "'Answering That of God in Every Man': An Interpretation of George Fox's Ethics," *Quaker Religious Thought* 15, no. 1 (1974): 2–41.
92. See, for example, *Journal of George Fox*, 344.
93. In his autobiography, Fox tells of feeling in his own body, while in prison in England, the death by hanging of some Friends in New England, after the colonies had enacted laws against Quakers. See *Journal of George Fox*, 374.

So meek, contented, modest, easy, steady, tender, it was a pleasure to be in his company. He exercised no authority but over evil, and that everywhere and in all; but with love, compassion, and long-suffering. A most merciful man, as ready to forgive as unapt to take or give offence . . . the most excellent spirits loved him with an unfeigned and unfading love.[94]

George Fox taught others in the movement to rely on religious experience rather than ecclesiastical or doctrinal knowledge of God. Fox claims he "knew experimentally," and "in the pure knowledge of God, and of Christ alone, without the help of any man, book, or writing," that only in Jesus Christ would he find the answers to unbelief and sin. Fox speaks of himself as having been enlightened by Christ; Christ, he says, "gave me His light" and "His Spirit and grace."[95] Even though Fox had read the Scriptures, he still knew neither Christ nor God until "the Father of Life drew me to His Son by His Spirit."[96] It is only by the power of the Light that the Scriptures' meaning is clear.[97] One must be inspired by the same Spirit that moved the prophets and the apostles who wrote the Scriptures.[98]

Because of the Quaker reliance on experimental knowledge of God and their custom of inspired preaching during meetings, they needed some way to test the genuineness of the "leadings" they received and to convince outsiders that they were not anarchists. Initial indications of validity were moral purity and patient waiting and testing of inspirations to eliminate self-will. More important is the self-consistency of the Spirit, both historically and in comparison with biblical conduct, and among members of the group gathered in faith or for worship. After 1656, the custom developed of testing any one member's leading by submitting it to the group's "sense of the Meeting."[99]

The Quakers, and particularly George Fox, seem less concerned about ethics or moral purity for their own sake than are Menno and the pacifist Anabaptists. The key for the Friends is the inner experience of joy and light in Christ, of which mercy, forgiveness, and innocence are a result. Notable in Fox's writings is a relative disinterest in expending much attention on morality, except for his disavowal of force. He also commends detachment from family in favor of the gospel. Other dis-

94. "The Testimony of William Penn Concerning That Faithful Servant George Fox," in *The Journal of George Fox*, 58–59.
95. *Journal of George Fox*, 83.
96. *Journal of George Fox*, 82–83.
97. *Journal of George Fox*, 102.
98. *Journal of George Fox*, 176–77.
99. Hugh Barbour, *The Quakers in Puritan England* (New Haven, CT: Yale University Press, 1964), 119–21; Frost and Barbour, *Quakers*, 40.

tinctively Quaker behaviors—such as the custom of marriage without a priest; the worship form of egalitarian response to the Light via spontaneous preaching; and, to an extent, the refusal to swear—have more a religious basis than a properly moral one.

George Fox had an unusual approach to gender, for a man of his time. He argued that in Christ men and women are returned to their prelapsarian state, overcoming the hierarchy and division that entered their relationship in Genesis 3. He appeals to the prophetesses of the Hebrew Bible and to New Testament examples such as Mary Magdalene, sent by Jesus to preach the resurrection, as well as to leaders of the Pauline churches, such as Priscilla and Phoebe.[100] A remarkable feature of the Quaker communities from their inception was the participation of women in leadership roles and in preaching and prophesying in religious services. Such practices had already begun to appear in other sects that sprang from Puritanism. Although it would be anachronistic to call Fox a feminist, he wrote two tracts in which he defended women's activity against literalist readings of the later pastoral epistles that prescribe submissiveness for women and their silence in church (for example, 1 Tim 2). Women's preaching was upheld on the basis of the freedom of the Spirit of God to inspire and speak through whom it will.

The first person in England to preach Fox's message was Elizabeth Hooten, already a local Baptist teacher. Even as an elderly woman (her four children were grown when she converted to Quakerism), she suffered brutal beatings and imprisonments but remained undeterred in her missionary work.[101] Even more important to the shape of Fox's life and ministry was Margaret Fell, whom he converted in 1652. The wife of Judge Thomas Fell and mother of eight, she presided over a large country home and was in a position to offer considerable protection and support to the Quakers. Though her husband never became a Quaker, he sympathetically used his influence on their behalf. Eleven years after Judge Fell's death, George Fox and Margaret Fell married. (Margaret, at fifty-five, was a decade George's senior and was to survive him for eleven

---

100. See Bacon, *Mothers of Feminism*, 10–13; and Barbour, *Quakers in Puritan England*, 132–33. The titles of the two treatises are *The Woman learning in Silence; or, the Mysterie of the womans Subjection to her Husband, as also, the Daughter prophesying, wherein the Lord hath, and is fulfilling that he spake by the Prophet Joel, I will pour out my Spirit unto all Flesh* and *Concerning Sons and Daughters, and Prophetesses speaking and Prophesying in the Law and the Gospel*. At the behest of Quaker women, Fox eventually endorsed separate men's and women's meetings to allow women a sphere in which they would be able to speak freely of women's religious concerns.

101. Phyllis Mack, "Gender and Spirituality in Early English Quakerism, 1650–1665," in *Witnesses for Change: Quaker Women over Three Centuries*, ed. Elisabeth Potts Brown and Susan Mosher Stuard (New Brunswick, NJ: Rutgers University Press, 1989), 31–32.

years.) Fox left his own family of birth to pursue his religious quest, but he was welcomed into a large and supportive stepfamily through his marriage. He and his wife continued to travel frequently and to spend long periods apart, whether in missionary outreach (Margaret was called by other Quakers the "nursing mother" of the movement) or in jail. Margaret too was an avid proponent of women's preaching, writing from prison her own treatise on it.[102]

Fox had begun to attract large numbers of followers by 1652 and was especially successful in the north of England. He wrote and traveled extensively, venturing through the British Isles and to Holland, Germany, and America, where he spent two years. He was brought to court sixty times and served a total of six years' imprisonment on eight convictions for blasphemy or heresy, for example, for his claim that Christ's spirit dwells in the believer so fully that sin is eradicated.[103] A more radical claim about kingdom presence is hardly imaginable. To an inquiry as to whether he was "sanctified," Fox replied, "Yes; for I am in the paradise of God" and "Christ my Saviour has taken away my sin; and in Him there is no sin."[104] In many instances, crowds in towns where Fox arrived to preach beat him unmercifully, subjecting him to serious physical harm. He attributed his seemingly miraculous recoveries to the healing power of the Lord in him. Persecution of the Quakers continued until the passage of the Toleration Act in 1689.

PEACE TESTIMONY AND POLITICS

Openness to Christ and regeneration lead to the Quakers' commitments to love of enemies, nonviolence, and pacifism, known as the "Quaker peace testimony." Despite its radicality, Fox's conception of the kingdom is neither exclusivist nor separatist; its inclusiveness is the major support of Quaker pacifism. God revealed to Fox that "every man" is enlightened by Christ, although some will "believe in" the Light and others will "hate" it.[105] In certain of his letters concerning Quaker work in the New World, Fox expresses his belief that the Light is in people of all races, and that the missionary must recognize that Light and evoke a response on the basis of it. "Let your light shine among the Indians, the blacks

102. Bacon, *Mothers of Feminism*, 13–17. The work of Margaret Fell is entitled *Women's Speaking Justified, Proved and Allowed by the Scriptures, all such as speak by the Spirit and Power of the Lord Jesus*.

103. T. Canby Jones, *George Fox's Attitude toward War* (Annapolis, MD: Academic Fellowship, 1972), 6–8. These incidents are also related in Fox's *Journal*.

104. Barbour, *Quakers in Puritan England*, 120–21.

105. Barbour, *Quakers in Puritan England*, 102, 444.

and the whites, that ye may answer the truth in them and *bring them to . . . Jesus Christ.*" James Childress argues that "answering that of God in every man," a phrase central in later Quaker religious thought, may be equally key to Fox's own writings.[106] Particularly in the early days of the movement, when hopes of converting the world were still high, there was no sectarian double standard for belief or action. God calls to the moral agent through each and every other person, as well as through Scripture, Christ, and the Spirit; and each person the Quaker meets is to be invited through his or her witness to recognize the Light of Christ within both.[107] All persons "in all Towns, Countries and Nations" have "something of God in them" that enables them to answer and observe the "Royal Law of God."[108]

For Quakers, to wage the "Lamb's War" means to demonstrate that the kingdom has begun by engaging in nonviolent acts that challenge human pride, violate social expectations (especially those tied to political and class hierarchies), and are aimed at conversion. Among their iconoclastic and egalitarian efforts were the disruption of public worship by challenging the priests, the refusal to pay tithes to support the parish clergy of the Church of England, the refusal to give common forms of respectful greeting to acquaintances or to address social superiors with "you" rather than "thee," and—of dubious practical effect—walking through the streets naked "for a sign."[109]

The main source of the Quaker peace testimony is the actions and sayings of Jesus. Hebrew belligerency is unequivocally rejected, for Jesus introduces a new dispensation and a new law that is in discontinuity with the old. Quaker leaders such as Fox and theologian Robert Barclay are not rigorously literal or legalist in their reading of the Bible, claiming as they do the direct moving of the Spirit, the "Inner Light" or "Light Within," which provides an "experimental" knowledge of God.[110] Apparently inconsistent teachings of Jesus about the "sword" are sometimes explained figuratively on the grounds that they contravene the central and overriding message of the gospel, which is one of repentance, mercy, peace, and nonresistance.[111]

Quaker opposition to war and violence was not absolute and universal

106. Childress, "That of God."

107. Childress, "That of God," 7, 30.

108. Childress, "That of God," 30, citing *The Royal Law of God Revived* (1671–72).

109. James F. Childress, *Moral Responsibility in Conflict: Essays on Nonviolence, War, and Conscience* (Baton Rouge: Louisiana State University Press, 1982), 17.

110. Beyond Fox, see Robert Barclay's "Turn Thy Mind to the Light," in *The Quaker Reader*, ed. Jessamyn West (New York: Viking, 1962), 226–30.

111. Howard H. Brinton, *Sources of the Quaker Peace Testimony* (Wallingford, PA: Pendle Hill Historical Studies, 1941), 10–11.

from the beginning. It originated in Fox's personal experience of the presence of the kingdom in his own life and extended gradually to others as conversion was followed by a progressive shaping of Christian fellowship in interaction with external events and challenges. For instance, Fox was imprisoned in 1650 for six months for "blasphemy," and, having had some success in converting officers in Cromwell's army, was offered a captaincy upon his release. He refused, telling the soldiers that he "was come into the covenant of peace, which was before wars and strifes were"—thus earning himself an additional and equal jail term.[112] In a subsequent letter to Cromwell, who demanded written assurance that Fox would never bear arms for the king and against Cromwell, Fox identified himself as "the son of God sent to stand a witness against all violence," avowing that his "weapons are not carnal but spiritual."[113] In two 1659 letters advising Friends, Fox insists that all wars and fighting belong to the fall, that fighting for Christ is a deception, and that in Christ's kingdom are only peace, light, unity, and love, which "take away the occasion of wars" (a phrase he repeated often).[114]

Like the Anabaptists, the Friends taught their members to expect persecution and to suffer it patiently. Violence, "defensive war," and even swearing explicitly contradict Christ's sayings. The rule for the Christian is love of enemies and forgiveness of hatred, after Christ's example. A primary difference between Anabaptists and Quakers is that the latter trust nonviolence to evoke a similar response from others. At least in the beginning, they hoped to convert the world, expecting the eventual rule of Christ on earth. Yet the implications of the kingdom for civil society were less important to them than the real presence of the kingdom in the community of "the Children of the Light," as they originally called themselves.

Although some early members of the movement served as soldiers, the peace testimony became clear and adamant in 1660, when Charles II was restored to the throne and any hope for a Puritan Commonwealth destroyed. In that year, Fox wrote a letter to the king reiterating the themes of love of enemies and repudiation of weapons.[115] In the "Declaration of 1660" (sent to Charles II in January 1661), the Quakers publicized their peace testimony in a classic statement repudiating violence, conspiracies, and plotting. This declaration dissociated Quakers from the violent uprisings that took place after the beheading of Charles I and the death of Cromwell, and during the restoration of Charles II to the

112. *Journal of George Fox*, 128–29; cf. Jones, *Fox's Attitude toward War*, 24–25.
113. Jones, *Fox's Attitude toward War*, 25–26.
114. Jones, *Fox's Attitude toward War*, 27–29.
115. *Journal of George Fox*, 347n51; cf. Jones, *Fox's Attitude toward War*, 30–32.

throne. Revenge, weapons, and wars are "contrary to the spirit of Christ, his doctrine, and the practice of his apostles."[116] While there may not have been "ideological homogeneity" behind these principles, they were not simply a political response to dangerous times either. The peace principles expressed religious convictions born from spiritual and communal experience and transformation.[117]

Yet Fox accepted that the sword can be exercised legitimately as part of the police function of the state, and even that when properly used, it responds to the Light of Christ that the criminal violates within himself or herself. "The Magistrate of Christ . . . is in the light and power of Christ, and he is to subject all under the power of Christ. . . . And his laws here are agreeable and answerable to that of God in every man; when men act contrary to it, they do evil: so he is a terror to the evil doers."[118] In 1654, Fox admonished King Charles to use the "sword of magistracy" to banish the "wickedness" then "at liberty." "Our prayers are for them that are in authority, that under them we may live a godly life in peace."[119]

Not willing, as the Puritans did, to unite church and government, the Quakers did have a more positive view of the magistracy's function than the Anabaptists. Anabaptists accused all historical churches of fatal deviation from the apostolic church; usually refused to compromise with the demands of the state, much less to adopt them; and expected the apocalyptic return and conquest of the Lamb to crown the suffering of his saints. Mistrusting the state, they rejected all coercive measures in matters of faith and preached patience toward enemies. Quakers, on the other hand, did not withdraw from society nor necessarily require refusal of public office; they believed that rulers have authority from God, though secondary to God's. Still, Quakers did not see participation in structures of violence as appropriate for those in whom Christ dwells. Instead, they expected total regeneration of life through God's grace, and took as seriously as the Anabaptists the Christian mission to convert the world and so transform it.

This created uncertainty and tension for those still serving in governing or political roles. Meredith Weddle illustrates this point in a book developing the example of colonial Rhode Island, where Quakers were

116. As cited in Jones, *Fox's Attitude toward War*, 36; excerpts from the *Declaration of 1660* are included in Douglas V. Steere, ed., *Quaker Spirituality: Selected Writings*, Classics of Western Spirituality (Mahwah, NJ: Paulist, 1982), 105–7.

117. Weddle, *Walking in the Way of Peace*, 7-8, 10.

118. Childress, "Answering That of God in Every Man," 25; quoting Fox's *The Great Mystery of the Great Whore Unfolded.*

119. *Journal of George Fox*, 355.

dominant in government. They had to discern how to reconcile their peace principles with defense in 1675, when armed conflict erupted between Native American inhabitants of present-day New England, led by the Wampanoag sachem (chief) Metacom, and English colonists and their Indian allies ("King Philips War"). The Rhode Island government, led by Friends, maneuvered to avoid killing or commanding others to kill, while still taking part in defensive preparations. There was a continuum of adaptations among individual Quakers, as many apparently were "freed up" to "a broader interpretation of requirements" entailed by their peace testimony.[120] Meanwhile, other Friends not serving in government issued a statement severely criticizing these war-supporting activities. In different parts of New England, Friends faced similar choices: whether to collect or pay taxes to support war, whether to carry a gun when working in one's fields, whether to fortify one's house, or whether to nurse the wounded on both sides. Weddle concludes that

> it is not at all self-evident what behavior flows from pacifist belief. The choices foist themselves anew upon the conscientious in every changing circumstance . . . because there is a line beyond which consequences and meaning are difficult and ambiguous. . . . the very location of that line may be disputable.[121]

Thomas Hamm exposes similar divisions and uncertainty among Quakers in America during the American Civil War, during which many Quakers joined the Union army, while others persevered in the Quaker principle that evil cannot be met with evil.[122]

Despite the practical ambiguities that result from dual responsibilities to Christ and to government, the Quaker attitude to war is summed up in Fox's declaration that he "lived in the virtue of that life and power that took away the occasion of all wars."[123] Centuries later, H. Richard Niebuhr was to characterize the qualities of the Protestant view of the kingdom of God as vividness, absoluteness, and temporal immediacy.[124] The Quakers certainly bear out Niebuhr's description. Important to them and other pacifists is a sense of closeness to Jesus and his community. The Scriptures are not just a promise, but they bring disciples into

---

120. Weddle, *Walking in the Way of Peace*, 130. This war is analyzed at length in the seven chapters of part III.

121. Weddle, *Walking in the Way of Peace*, 6–7.

122. Thomas Hamm, *The Transformation of American Quakerism* (Bloomington, IN: Indiana University Press, 1988), 66–71.

123. *Journal of George Fox*, 128.

124. H. Richard Niebuhr, *The Kingdom of God in America* (New York: Harper, 1937), 25.

the reality out of which the Scriptures communicate God's Word. This reality is one in which killing has no place.

The Rules of Discipline, compiled annually at regional Friends' meetings since the seventeenth century, continue to reiterate their witness, its basis in the realized kingdom, and its hope for the conversion of Christian states. One representative expression comes from the London conference of 1883, which recapitulated and revised Quaker teachings since 1672:

> We dare not believe that our Lord and Saviour, in enjoining the love of enemies and the forgiveness of injuries, has prescribed for man a series of precepts which are incapable of being carried into practice or of which the practice is to be postponed till all shall be persuaded to act upon them. We cannot doubt that they are incumbent upon the Christian now . . . and upon nations also. Wherefore, we entreat all who profess themselves members of our Society to be faithful to that ancient testimony . . . that, by a conduct agreeable to our profession, we may demonstrate ourselves to be real followers of the Messiah, the peaceable Saviour, of the increase of whose government and peace there shall be no end.[125]

CONCLUSION

Pacifist Christianity correlates with neither a strictly literalist reading of the Bible nor the isolation of commands like "Love your enemies" (Matt 5:44) from their contexts as direct and specific norms for conduct. Erasmus was an irenicist, if not a pacifist, even while insisting on the complexity of biblical interpretation, and the more strongly pacifist Friends make a true reading of Scripture dependent on inspiration by the Spirit. Their "experimental knowledge" of God implies in practice the relevance of the many founts of awareness and identity that make up the consciousness of the person the Spirit touches. The pacifist Anabaptists, in their total rejection of violence, are no more fundamentalist than the Münster Anabaptists, though the former privilege New Testament texts over Old Testament ones.

Yet even though pacifism does not equate with biblicism, it does seem to correlate with an experience of Christ's immediacy, known in the Spirit through the reading or preaching of Scripture, and confirmed in a community of mutual support and *nachfolge Christi*. Physical force and

125. *Book of Discipline of the Religious Society of Friends in Great Britain* (London: Samuel Harris, 1883), 153–55. Virtually all versions and editions of the Rules of Discipline, both English and American, contain such examples. Another is given in George W. Forell, ed., *Christian Social Teachings: A Reader in Christian Social Ethics from the Bible to the Present* (Minneapolis: Augsburg, 1971), 239–40.

especially war drive against Christ's cross, salvation, mercy, charity, and the church's service of the vulnerable. They could never be direct expressions of salvation in Christ or Christian identity.

Christian pacifists are formed by Jesus's moral demands as both radical and necessary—or better, by his life as putting within reach in the present a new life for us, out of which flows conduct often indicated in the language of demand, but actually constituting a spontaneous and characteristic mode of being for those united to Christ. The disciple of Christ, the member of his body, responds to neighbor and enemy alike with the mercy and forgiveness commanded in Luke 6:36 ("Be merciful, just as your Father is merciful") and even with the "perfection" of Matthew 5:48 ("Be perfect, therefore, as your heavenly Father is perfect"). To harm the other any more than God harms God's children is impossible even for a just cause—which is why Fox can envision use of the sword only in a disciplinary response to "that of God" in the wrongdoer. No doubt this is also why Fox tends to speak of force in terms of restraint and peace rather than of killing and never speaks approvingly of war. God's reign or kingdom "takes away the occasion of all wars."

Menno Simons is rigorous in his expectation that Christian persons will actually accomplish a sanctified life and realize the kingdom now, albeit in conflict with the world. Cross-bearing is a requirement of faith and the substance of discipleship, an inherent result of Christ's provocation of Satan and his world. More than those of Erasmus and Fox, Menno's writings capture readiness for martyrdom. The circumference of Erasmus's interests encircles the humanist values of rationality, sociability, and cooperation, and he keeps a tight enough grip on their practical conditions to permit him to retain violence as a marginal recourse to save the social order. But he, like the Quakers and Anabaptists, is confident in the God-given power of human beings to live rightly as Christians; asserts the reality of the kingdom in its beginnings on earth; elaborates both the natural and the religious bonds among persons and communities; and is appalled that Christianity does not erase proclivities toward violent behavior.

The figures and movements discussed in this chapter demonstrate how likely it is that the Christian pacifist will read the New Testament witness in favor of peace and against nonviolence in the clear light of a practical or "experimental" knowledge of God's forgiving love and of the generosity toward others that being loved and forgiven engenders. To live truly in the body of Christ is not merely to reject, but to be incapable of, violence and killing. Erasmus reveals less in his writings about his own inner experiences of God than Menno and certainly less than Fox. Yet in exhorting Christians to aim at the perfection of Christ's kingdom and to live the life of love, he holds up the unity of persons in their shared nature and especially in Christ. The Anabaptists may have fallen short of genuine concern for the welfare of the enemy when they divided the world into the godless and the godly. Even so, they still respected the potential salvation and holiness of all through the central place they gave to missionary activity and to the freedom of all to choose a commitment to Christ and to live a life of moral perfection. (The danger inherent in making that first division, however, is evident in the errors of the violent Anabaptist extremists.) For George Fox, the key to Christian pacifism is not obedience, duty, or even imitation *of* Christ as such but an inner transformation of life *in* Christ. The ideals of the kingdom do not demand or compel as rules from without. The joy and mercy of God's reign become present within the person and community, through the presence of Christ's Spirit. That which the "hard sayings" depict, then, is not only commended or possible, but real and inevitable.

9.

From Just War and Pacifism to Peacebuilding

In the twenty-first century, debates over the meaning, viability, and development of just war theory continue unabated. New categories, such as *jus ante bellum*, *jus post bellum*, and just policing have emerged to make just war theory more effective in limiting, restraining, and preventing war. The Christian pacifist witness and way of life continue to be vital, biblically inspired counterweights to just war thinking, urging religious believers and wider societies to reconsider the morality and effectiveness of violence as a solution to conflicts and of just war principles in accomplishing their purported aims. Yet, as in past eras, the ideologies and actions of "holy warriors," both religious and secular, threaten to undercut the reasoning of the just war theorist and the ideals of the pacifist.

Just war theory was originally conceived to govern the decisions of rulers and their surrogates: emperors, monarchs, and (later) heads of nation-states. In the early centuries of Christianity, in the early modern period, and for most of the twentieth century, pacifists did not expect their witness to have a significant effect on government. In fact, Christian pacifism was often a counterculture with an intentional minority status, outside the mainstream of politics. In the twenty-first century, the situation has changed in at least three important ways. First, although the danger of nuclear weapons remains high and unsettling, wars between nation-states have decreased drastically since World War II. But the world is still wracked by politically motivated violence and atrocities, from repressive government to civil wars, cross-border ethnic and religious conflicts, transnational terror networks, and proxy wars.[1] Civil

1. See Mauro F. Guillén, "Wars between States Are Down, but Civil Wars Are Up, *New York*

war or "intrastate" war has increased since the 1950s, so that today it is the major form of warfare. According to the International Institute for Strategic Studies, twenty-first century warfare (e.g., in Syria, Iraq, Afghanistan, and Yemen) has seen "an inexorable intensification of violence," such that more than three times as many people (180,000) died in conflicts in 2014 than in 2008.[2] At least 75 percent of those killed in war are civilians, compared to 5 percent during the First World War.[3] Second, and derivatively, the control of heads of state over the use of armed force is even more limited than in the past. Although in the age of globalization, both government and armed force have assumed new transnational forms, the capacity of regional, international, or global authorities to control armed violence is often no match for its virulent extralegal expressions.[4]

Third, Christians (and others) committed to nonviolence are less willing to accept that their stance and way of life are largely politically irrelevant. Instead, they seek a political voice and urge expansive, collaborative social practices with a shared vision of societal peace with justice. Exposed by new communications media to vivid and almost instantaneous images of the concrete realities of violence and human suffering worldwide, Christians are increasingly convinced that moral responsibility is political responsibility—and that the gospel implies networked social action connecting local churches and their members to neighbors near and far.

This is why a movement toward peacebuilding from just war theory and pacifism, at least as traditionally conceived, is essential and indeed underway. The next chapter will look at religious peacebuilding that seeks to avoid and resolve conflict. First, some important twentieth-century figures will illustrate evolutions in just war theory and pacifism that prepare the way for the Christian and political priority of peacebuilding. These figures are Reinhold Niebuhr, Dietrich Bonhoeffer, Dorothy Day, and recent Roman Catholic popes, especially after the Second Vatican Council. Certainly, these are not the only voices that have contributed to this trajectory. They are selected because they confront the historical reality of armed violence in different contexts and

Times, September 6, 2016, accessed August 17, 2017, https://tinyurl.com/yar8bu9c. See also Center for Systemic Peace, INSCR Data Page, accessed August 17, 2017, https://tinyurl.com/y8e5sxc8.

2. Richard Norton-Taylor, "Global Armed Conflicts Becoming More Deadly, Major Study Finds," *The Guardian*, May 20, 2015, accessed February 14, 2018, https://tinyurl.com/ycw2staq.

3. "The World at War," Global Security, accessed August 21, 2017, https://tinyurl.com/yddwycx4.

4. See Anne-Marie Slaughter, *A New World Order* (Princeton, NJ: Princeton University Press, 2004).

from different theological perspectives. They represent different yet representative ways of addressing armed force and peacebuilding based on a commitment both to the gospel and to justice, allow us to consider further what it means to designate both killing in war and pacifism as irreducible moral dilemmas, and point the way to a commitment to peacebuilding.

Reinhold Niebuhr was a US theologian in the Augustinian tradition. According to the peace theorist David Cortright, "no modern theologian has exerted more influence on the debate about war and peace than Reinhold Niebuhr,"[5] evoking engagement from thinkers as diverse as Hans Morgenthau, John Courtney Murray, Martin Luther King Jr., and John Howard Yoder. Niebuhr recognizes more directly than most the inherent dilemmas posed by Christian decisions about force, bringing into conflict as they do the norm of Christian love and the responsibility to defend the common good from mortal evils. Although other important twentieth-century just war thinkers, especially Paul Ramsey, could be referenced in relation to the recent development of Augustinian thought, Niebuhr is here chosen because he directly confronts and appropriates the ambiguity in Augustine's attitude toward war.[6] He also follows this to its logical conclusion: war and killing in war not only cannot be fully justified from a Christian perspective, they also always involve some degree of guilt. Niebuhr's validation of the indiscriminate killing of civilians for proportionate reason, however, shows the danger of letting the fact of true dilemmas marginalize all absolutes. Paul Ramsey once worried, against pacifism, that if more things than necessary are seen as wicked, then the ability to judge the truly wicked will vanish. In turn, if wickedness cannot be avoided in any event, then "no limits will be set on it."[7] Ramsey himself saw noncombatant immunity as such an absolute, but Niebuhr hesitated to back this criterion of a just war as a nonnegotiable. Ramsey's concern should haunt anyone who maintains that irreducible moral dilemmas with their attendant guilt and remorse are inevitable. How will limits be set on the level of wickedness for which an agent should accept responsibility? This is a question Niebuhr does not answer.

5. David Cortright, *Peace: A History of Movements and Ideas* (Cambridge: Cambridge University Press, 2008), 203.

6. See Alan J. Watt, "Which Approach? Late Twentieth-Century Interpretations of Augustine's Views on War," *Journal of Church and State* 46, no. 1 (2004): 99–113; James Turner Johnson, "Just War in the Thought of Paul Ramsey," *Journal of Religious Ethics* 19, no. 2 (1991): 183–207. For an important Catholic thinker of the same era as Niebuhr, see John Courtney Murray, "Remarks on the Moral Problem of War."

7. Paul Ramsey, *The Just War: Force and Political Responsibility* (New York: Scribner, 1968), 364.

Dietrich Bonhoeffer, a German Lutheran who had gradually become committed to pacifism as an authentically Christian way of life, similarly faced a moral dilemma when confronted with the opportunity to assassinate Adolf Hitler. After a failed plot to do so, Bonhoeffer was hanged by the Third Reich just as the Second World War was ending. Bonhoeffer is someone who, from the pacifist side, took extremely seriously the Christian obligation and opportunity to embody new life in Christ, but also encountered the profound moral conflict that can shadow Christian discipleship in a sinful world. Dorothy Day, a Catholic pacifist from the United States, shows the importance of a committed and communal way of life as the basis for Christian advocacy of nonviolence. She foreshadows the evolution of contemporary Christian pacifism into a political movement aiming at broad cultural, political, and interreligious participation. Yet, in at least one case, she considered whether different circumstances could call for a different stance on violent resistance to tyranny. Finally, the recent Roman Catholic popes, culminating in Pope Francis, have not definitively rejected all justifications of armed force. Yet they embody the peacebuilding ethos and agenda as they denounce war, proclaim peace, and take symbolic actions to inspire international and interreligious commitment, from local communities to international leaders.

Taken together, these authors show the vital importance of political responsibility to Christian identity. They bring home the reality that any Christian decision to use or *not* use mortal force, as a last resort to defend innocent lives, involves an irreducible moral dilemma. The dilemma consists in the clash of the duty to save and protect the innocent and the common good, as well as the duty to respect the value and dignity of every human life, including that of the perpetrator and of those who suffer the collateral damage of war. In prioritizing one of these values or duties, the agent (individual or collective) cannot avoid some level of moral responsibility for the concomitant violation of the dignity and welfare of other human beings, even when the choice of priorities is justifiable. The thinkers chosen and the dilemmas they confront help raise the question whether, even within an irreducible dilemma, some rules must still obtain, and if so, what their function will be. They also underwrite the peacebuilding trajectory of recent Christian political ethics as accomplishing three goals: embodying salvation by the risen Christ in the power of the Spirit; alleviating the conditions and effects of ongoing political violence without resorting to violence; and making visible the universal reality of God's reign in the world.

REINHOLD NIEBUHR (1892–1972)

Reinhold Niebuhr's father emigrated to America from Germany in 1881, raising his family in Missouri and Illinois, where he served German-language churches of the German Evangelical Synod of North America. The Evangelical Synod emphasized religious experience over doctrine, heartily resisted rationalism, and was ecumenical in spirit both toward other denominations and toward American culture.[8] Reinhold Niebuhr's younger brother H. Richard was also to become a theologian. Both engaged energetically with major movements in Continental and North American theology, and both addressed the social and political problems of their time, including war and peace.

Reinhold was, like his father, educated at Eden Theological Seminary in St. Louis, and subsequently studied at Yale Divinity School. Partly because of his father's early death and the need to contribute to the support of mother and siblings, he left Yale to accept an assignment at Bethel Evangelical Church, a Detroit mission. His firsthand encounter with the effects of industrialization propelled the social concern that colored all Niebuhr's later writings. One biographer, Richard Fox, points out that a key formative influence upon Niebuhr was the rapid growth of the city's black population in the 1920s, primarily in the overcrowded "colored" neighborhoods where rents were exorbitant. With the Ku Klux Klan on the rise during this time, Niebuhr became deeply involved in fighting the manifestations of racism in Detroit and worked with politicians and philanthropists on a citywide basis. Niebuhr later stated that his life in Detroit "determined my development more than any books which I may have read."[9] In 1928 Reinhold Niebuhr became Professor of Applied Christianity at New York's Union Theological Seminary, where he spent the remainder of his career.

Important intellectual and religious landmarks in the background of Niebuhr's social ethics are the theology of the social gospel and the neoorthodox theology of Karl Barth. The American social gospel of the late nineteenth and early twentieth centuries was part of a wider movement in Western countries to come to terms with the effects of industrialization and immigration, especially vast wealth inequality. Theologians of the social gospel, most notably Walter Rauschenbusch, rejected individualistic interpretations of faith and salvation. They used emergent historical-critical methods to rediscover the power of the gospel

8. Richard Wightman Fox, *Reinhold Niebuhr: A Biography* (New York: Pantheon, 1985), 3–5.

9. Reinhold Niebuhr, "Intellectual Autobiography," in *Reinhold Niebuhr: His Religious, Social, and Political Thought*, ed. Charles W. Kegley and Robert W. Bretall (New York: Macmillan, 1956), 5.

message against economic exploitation.[10] The proclaimers of the social gospel saw that sin is perpetrated through social institutions and not only by individual selfishness. They trusted that human response to God's initiative in Jesus could not only challenge those institutions and begin a process of social change, but even lead to greater social equality, cooperation, and harmony—indeed, even to a real initiation of the kingdom of God in history. Much social gospel thought was pacifist. Although the social gospelers may have had unrealistically high hopes for moral education and for the historical power of Christian virtue, it is not true, as some critics have charged, that they either ignored the reality of original sin or reduced the eschatological kingdom and salvation to historical social progress and universal brotherhood. Instead, they took Jesus's kingdom preaching as a serious mandate for social reform, in the face of and against the power of evil.

After the devastations of World War I, the social gospel seemed exceedingly optimistic, while what came to be known as "neoorthodox" theology emerged explosively on the Continent. Karl Barth, one of the most powerful proponents of this new theology, repudiated the social gospel's program of reform, insisting on the transcendence of God, sinfulness of humanity, and absoluteness of revelation that overrides all human moral knowledge. The Barthian themes represented a return to the Reformation, especially Calvin's keynote of the sovereignty of God, although Barth's creative theology, sensitive to the challenges of his own context, was no simple return to the Reformers.[11] Barth crystallized the reaction against the humanism and liberalism of the social gospel and its analogues in Europe. Barth's challenge to renew theology in a new, more sober mode was met by Reinhold Niebuhr, who saw neoorthodox theology as endangering the political dimensions of theology and the social responsibilities of Christians.[12] Niebuhr also rejected the idea that the teachings of Jesus could be applied in a simple, direct way to the complexities and particulars of historical situa-

---

10. See Robert T. Handy, "Introduction," in *The Social Gospel in America, 1870–1920*, ed. Robert T. Handy (New York: Oxford University Press, 1966), 3–16; and "Social Gospel," in *The Westminster Dictionary of Christian Ethics*, ed. James F. Childress and John Macquarrie (Philadelphia: Westminster, 1987), 593–94.

11. Barth rejects the label "neoorthodox" in *Church Dogmatics*, vol. 3, *The Doctrine of Creation*, part 3, *The Creator and His Creature* (London: T&T Clark, 1961), xii. Bruce McCormack argues that the characterization originated in Anglo-American readings of Barth's work that were influenced by their own theological context. See Bruce L. McCormack, *Karl Barth's Critically Realistic Dialectical Theology: Its Genesis and Development, 1909–1936* (Oxford: Oxford University Press, 1995), 1–28.

12. Reinhold Niebuhr, *The Nature and Destiny of Man*, vol. 2, *Human Destiny* (New York: Scribner's, 1943), 278–79.

tions in which God's kingdom can have only a relative presence. Barth would have agreed with that, but for the reason that God's claims and commands must always be heard anew on every occasion of decision. Still, Niebuhr saw Barth as not pragmatic or realistic enough in the face of contemporary social trouble, seemingly abandoning it to its own inevitable bad outcome. Moreover, the immunity of revelation and faith in the Barthian scheme to validation by any extrinsic criteria made them seem dogmatic and even fundamentalist to Niebuhr,[13] an impression shared by Bonhoeffer. The retreat into awe before divine transcendence threatened, if not to enervate Christianity, then at least to disconnect its social dimensions from political realities and make them seem arbitrary.

Niebuhr's Detroit experience had imbued him with a passion for social change reminiscent of the social gospel, but which the war gave a more pragmatic character. In his characteristic approach to theological ethics, termed "Christian Realism," the dialectical relation of justice and love is foundational. In his major and most systematically theological work, Niebuhr writes that love is the "end term" of any moral system, both fulfilling and transcending any scheme of justice. At the same time, real love "is no simple possibility" and depends on the love of God, even while it points to God as its final realization. "Love is the law of freedom; but man is not completely free; and such freedom as he has is corrupted by sin. There is, therefore, no historic structure of justice which can either fulfill the law of love or rest content in its inability to do so."[14]

Niebuhr judges that "modern liberal Protestant interpretations of human nature and human destiny stand in . . . obvious contradiction to the tragic facts of human history."[15] While all structures of justice have the potential to embody "an indeterminate approximation" of love, they still always retain some contradictory and sinful elements.[16] Mutual love, with its reciprocal response, is the only love justified in historical terms, and even mutual love depends on some element of disinterestedness or sacrificial love for its initiation and renewal.

Transcending self-interest and meeting the standard of justice, let alone mutual or sacrificial love, is difficult for historical individuals and virtually impossible for groups. "Collective egoism" is a familiar theme in Reinhold Niebuhr's writings, especially *Moral Man and Immoral Society*. There he notes, "Every effort to transfer a pure morality of disinterested-

---

13. See Fox, *Reinhold Niebuhr*, 117.

14. Niebuhr, *The Nature and Destiny of Man,* vol. 1. *Human Nature* (New York: Scribners, 1941), 294–96. See also *Nature and Destiny* 2:247.

15. Niebuhr, *Nature and Destiny* 1:298–99.

16. Niebuhr, *Nature and Destiny* 2:236.

ness to group relations has resulted in failure."[17] Hence, "all social cooperation on a larger scale than the most intimate social group requires a
measure of coercion," and "conflict between the national units remains
as a permanent rather than a passing characteristic of their relations to
each other."[18] As Niebuhr noted regarding the civil rights movement in
the United States, power imbalances will never be corrected simply by
appeal to the moral sentiments of those in power; self-interest guarantees
that those with much to lose will play hard in order to win. Hence, "politics will, to the end of history, be an area where conscience and power
meet, where the ethical and coercive factors of human life will interpen-
etrate and work out their tentative and uneasy compromises."[19]

In his later and more comprehensive work, *The Nature and Destiny of
Man*, Niebuhr makes it clear that history holds some possibility of "systems and principles of justice" and of "structures of brotherhood" that
reflect in some degree the kingdom of God.[20] In a late work, *Man's
Nature and His Communities*, he insisted that "a realist conception of
human nature should be made the servant of an ethic of progressive justice," that the "unity and common humanity of men" is obvious, and that
there is a "common grace" that allows selves to relate unselfishly to others.[21] But he remained convinced that self-concern is a stronger human
drive, and that the defeat of evil in history will not be simple, direct, or
decisive.[22] Although Niebuhr thought Augustine exaggerated the degree
to which society is "constantly threatened" by conflict and tyranny, he
found Augustine "a more reliable guide than any known thinker."[23] For
Niebuhr, all political choices in history stand under God's judgment;
making a responsible choice demands that goods be weighed repeatedly
in different situations, and some goods might be incommensurable or
irreconcilable.[24]

17. Reinhold Niebuhr, *Moral Man and Immoral Society: A Study in Ethics and Politics* (New
York: Scribners, 1932), 268. See also *Nature and Destiny* 1:212–13.

18. Niebuhr, *Moral Man*, 3.

19. Niebuhr, *Moral Man*, 4.

20. Niebuhr, *Nature and Destiny* 2:248, 254, 265, 308n.

21. Reinhold Niebuhr, *Man's Nature and His Communities: Essays on the Dynamics and Enig-
mas of Man's Personal and Social Existence* (New York: Scribner's, 1965) 24, 90, 107–8, respectively.

22. Niebuhr, *Man's Nature and His Communities*, 39, 125.

23. Niebuhr, *Nature and Destiny* 2:273; "Augustine's Political Realism," in *Christian Realism
and Political Problems* (New York: Scribner's, 1953), 146.

24. Robin Lovin, "Christian Realism for the Twenty-First Century," *Journal of Religious
Ethics* 37, no. 4 (2009): 676. See also John D. Carlson, "Is There a Christian Realist Theory of
War and Peace? Reinhold Niebuhr and Just War Thought," *Journal of the Society of Christian
Ethics* 28, no. 1 (2008): 133–61; and "The Morality, Politics and Irony of War: Recovering
Reinhold Niebuhr's Ethical Realism," *Journal of Religious Ethics* 36, no. 4 (2008): 619–51.

Niebuhr questioned too firm a distinction between violent and non-violent coercion, referring to the latter as "covert violence," not a way to assure moral security.[25] Impatient with those who rejected violence but participated in or benefited from other forms of coercion—like, he said, the Quakers—Niebuhr thought "pure religious idealism" had to result both in total nonresistance and in renunciation of any aspiration to be socially efficacious or politically responsible.[26] Such idealism or perfectionism might have a valid function as a stimulant to greater justice, but must always accept as its end "the Cross" and not social change.[27]

Robin Lovin offers an interpretation of Niebuhr's Christian realism that highlights Augustinian themes, surfacing the role of moral conflict in the way Niebuhr sees Christian political responsibility. First, God does provide "a reality in which a comprehensive unity of moral meanings is conceivable," meaning that ultimately love, not self-interest or a balance of risks and benefits, is "the law of life."[28] However, the "God's eye point of view" is not available to human moral agents.[29] Even more problematically, the imperfect and sinful conditions of history mean that the law of love can rarely if ever be fully realized in the concrete. In fact, some situations present only resolutions that involve an ultimate moral ambiguity. Yet moral-political abstention is not an option: "we are responsible for making choices between greater and lesser evils, even when our Christian faith, illuminating the human scene, makes it quite apparent that there is no pure good in human history; and probably no pure evil either."[30] Options must be measured against the demands of the gospel, yet the agent must still be "prepared to make the real choices, even though all the options are less than what love requires."[31] Niebuhr grants more forthrightly than Augustine that some obligatory moral choices are irreducibly conflicted, ambiguous, and even culpable, a premise that pervades his ethics of war.

Reinhold Niebuhr's occasional writings throughout the war years,

25. Niebuhr, "Why I Leave the F.O.R.," *Christian Century* (January 3,1934), in *Love and Justice: Selections from the Shorter Writings of Reinhold Niebuhr*, ed. D. B. Robertson (Gloucester, MA: Peter Smith, 1976), 257.

26. Niebuhr, *Moral Man*, 264.

27. Reinhold Niebuhr, "Perfectionism and Historical Reality," *Christian Century* (December 14, 1940), in *Love and Justice*, 217.

28. Robin W. Lovin, *Reinhold Niebuhr and Christian Realism* (Cambridge: Cambridge University Press, 1995), 67.

29. Lovin, *Reinhold Niebuhr*, 68.

30. Reinhold Niebuhr, "Theology and Political Thought in the Western World," in *Faith and Politics*, ed. Ronald Stone (New York: George Braziller, 1968), 56. See Lovin, *Reinhold Niebuhr*, 72–74.

31. Lovin, *Reinhold Niebuhr*, 93.

in publications such as *The Christian Century, Christianity and Crisis,* and *Christianity and Society,* offer bold examples of his results-oriented approach to ethics. He did not repudiate just war theory, but he was skeptical that its principles could be applied casuistically or with certainty and universality.[32] He was very conscious of the "political" conditions of and constraints on "just war" decisions, realizing that considerations of national interest and advantage would be significant determinants of the outcome. James Childress maintains that principles or values like love and justice, justice and order, equality and freedom did have an important place in Niebuhr's thought about war, but they were dialectically related in concrete situations, not systematically prioritized. The problem is that no criteria can specify in advance, apart from consideration of consequences, which particular policies or actions best balance the goods at stake in a given situation.[33]

In effect, argues Childress, Niebuhr reduces the principles of just war to proportionality—what will serve the greater good? Proportionality is the main limit on the evils of war, not any principles of inherent morality, such as noncombatant immunity. But calculations of proportion not only are context-dependent and insecure, they can involve agents in decisions to deny or destroy important goods that are judged to have a lesser claim in a given situation. Moreover, considerations of national interest or of the political advantage of decision-makers, may not be of morally equal weight with justice, order, equality, or love; but at the practical level they are surely part of the evaluation of proportionate use of force.

Reinhold Niebuhr publicly clashed with his brother H. Richard's quite different theological views only once, and that was on the issue of a pacifist Christianity—specifically, on the nature, wisdom, and viability of a pacifist response to the Japanese invasion of Manchuria in 1931.[34] Since Japan had violated clear nonaggression agreements and went on to bomb civilians in 1932, many pacifists were willing to advocate coercive eco-

32. For an extensive discussion of the evolution of or variation in Niebuhr's views of war, especially nuclear war, see John D. Carlson, "The Morality, Politics and Irony of War."

33. James F. Childress, "Niebuhr's Realistic-Pragmatic Approach to War and 'the Nuclear Dilemma,'" in *Reinhold Niebuhr and the Issues of Our Time,* ed. Richard Harries (Grand Rapids, MI: William B. Eerdmans, 1986), 126.

34. H. Richard Niebuhr, "The Grace of Doing Nothing," *The Christian Century,* March 23, 1932, also available on the website of the United Church of Christ, accessed August 20, 2017, https://tinyurl.com/ybnebft4; Reinhold Niebuhr, "Must We Do Nothing?," *The Christian Century,* March 30, 1932, https://tinyurl.com/y7d66zh8; H. Richard Niebuhr, "The Only Way into the Kingdom of God," April 6, 1932, https://tinyurl.com/ybn6nryg. For a discussion, see John D. Barbour, "Niebuhr vs. Niebuhr: The Tragic Nature of History, *The Christian Century* (November 21, 1984), 1096–99, accessed August 20, 2017, https://tinyurl.com/yczdsxv5.

nomic measures against Japan by the League of Nations and the United States. Reinhold Niebuhr supported these. An economic embargo or a consumer boycott of Japanese products, however, would harm the civilian population at least as much as its military leaders. The resultant moral impasse in Western opinion was seen by Niebuhr as proof of the inadequacy of absolute pacifism as Christian social policy.

It is not difficult to see why Reinhold Niebuhr, who had himself been a pacifist in World War I, eventually rejected pacifism, both because of its political idealism and its moral absolutism.[35] Niebuhr begins his major treatise against pacifism by urging that "the failure of the Church to espouse pacifism is not apostasy, but is derived from an understanding of the Christian gospel which refuses simply to equate the Gospel with the 'law of love.'" Beyond love, the Christian has to deal with sin "realistically,"[36] especially because "the conflict between love and self-love is in every soul."[37]

H. Richard Niebuhr decried the arrogance involved in contemplating that US intervention could control the situation, and thus he proclaimed "the grace of doing nothing." The issue for Reinhold Niebuhr was not whether to resort to coercion at all, but how to find the least destructive form of doing so. Any purely just and noncoercive alternative would surely be ineffective in deterring what was generally seen as Japan's bold-faced imperialism.[38] For Reinhold Niebuhr, deterrence was a commanding moral objective, and the morality of means to achieve it was determined by whether they were likely to attain that goal. He rejected what he sees as his brother's "ethical perfectionism," insisted that international and economic relations cannot be made subservient to "pure love," and concluded that it is important to "try in every social situation to maximize the ethical forces and yet not sacrifice the possibility of achieving an ethical goal because we are afraid to use any but purely ethical means."[39]

Niebuhr supported the area bombing of Germany during World War II because he saw it as the only alternative to capitulation to a less scrupulous foe, even though it involved the indiscriminate killing of civilians.

35. See Niebuhr, "Why I Leave the F.O.R.," 254–59. For a discussion of Niebuhr's relation to pacifism, see Richard Harries, "Reinhold Niebuhr's Critique of Pacifism and His Pacifist Critics," in Harries, *Reinhold Niebuhr and the Issues of Our Time*, 105–21.

36. Niebuhr, *Christianity and Power Politics* (New York: Scribner's, 1940), 1–3. For Niebuhr's general view of the necessity of war, see his "A Critique of Pacifism," *Atlantic Monthly* (May 1927), in *Love and Justice*, 241–47; and "Pacifism and the Use of Force," *The World Tomorrow* (May 1928), in *Love and Justice*, 247–53.

37. Niebuhr, "Augustine's Political Realism," 138.

38. Fox, *Reinhold Niebuhr*, 152.

39. Niebuhr, "Must We Do Nothing?"

He described it as "a vivid revelation of the whole moral ambiguity of warfare. It is not possible to engage in any act of collective opposition to collective guilt without involving the innocent with the guilty. It is not possible to move in history without becoming tainted with guilt," in all its "antecedent, concomitant, and consequent" manifestations.[40] As Childress sums up Niebuhr's position, "such indiscriminate violations of the rules of war as indiscriminate bombing are justified only by necessity, involve guilt, and should be occasions for repentance."[41]

But Niebuhr's moral outlook seemed to shift when confronted later with the horrifying nuclear assaults on Japanese cities near the end of World War II. He writes that "critics of the bomb have rightly pointed out that we reached the level of Nazi morality in justifying the use of the bomb on the grounds that it shortened the war."[42] Niebuhr grants that the threat that the enemy might have perfected nuclear weapons first made it impossible for the Allies to refrain from seeking to reach that goal earlier. But since nuclear weapons can *only* be used indiscriminately, their use is inherently immoral, unless in a policy of deterrence, the purpose of which is to avoid actual use by either side.[43]

In his assessment of the use of nuclear weapons in Japan, Niebuhr seems to suggest that indiscriminate killing of civilians is a wrong-making characteristic, *even if* proportionately more lives will be saved, a position that would be inconsistent with, or a revision of, his position on area bombing. At the same time, the existence of nuclear weapons brings home for Niebuhr the reality that moral agents are not always able to avoid being implicated in courses of action that carry a moral cost. He seems to apply to nuclear deterrence the same analysis he had applied to area bombing: "it is not possible to disavow its use" unequivocally, because that would mean "capitulating to the foe." "No man has the moral freedom to escape from these hard and cruel necessities of history."[44]

Niebuhr later rejected a preemptive use of nuclear weapons against the Soviet Union, but accepted the US policy of "mutual assured destruction," which meant in essence preparing and even guaranteeing that, were the Soviets to strike first, the United States would retaliate in

40. Niebuhr, "The Bombing of Germany," *Christianity and Society* (Summer 1943), in *Love and Justice*, 222.

41. Childress, "Realistic-Pragmatic Approach," 137–38. Childress compares Niebuhr's position here to Michael Walzer's concept of "supreme emergency" in *Just and Unjust Wars*, 251–68.

42. Niebuhr, "The Atomic Bomb," *Christianity and Society* (Fall 1945), in *Love and Justice*, 233.

43. Niebuhr, "The Atomic Bomb."

44. Niebuhr, "The Bombing of Germany," 223.

kind.[45] Despite the analysis that he had already made of nuclear attacks as immoral, Niebuhr still held that "readiness to retaliate" was "the final step that a democracy and a civilization with any kind of moral standards can allow itself into the moral ambiguities of a nuclear age."[46] In a lecture at Union Theological Seminary, Niebuhr confessed that he was unable to imagine that the United States would refrain from using a nuclear weapon if it had been attacked with one first, and added that "the moral ambiguity" is "tremendous."[47]

Even in the face of moral dilemmas in which every choice brings culpable evils, are there still a few moral nonnegotiables that set a line against evils for which guilt should not be accepted, and that can thereby rule out some choices? Killing massive numbers of people who are innocent, in the sense of not posing a proximate danger to anyone else, would seem to be an excellent candidate. Ultimately, Niebuhr does not hold this line in a clear and definite way. This failure poses an important question or challenge for others who support the idea that irreducible moral dilemmas exist, unavoidably implicating agents in wronging others, even if a proportionate reason makes the action or policy on the whole justified.[48] Is it enough to say simply that such dilemmas exist, and that they call for remorse and restitution? Or is it necessary to maintain further that some duties, principles, or goods are inviolable even in the midst of moral dilemmas, that they exclude some ways of dealing with dilemmas, or that they constitute guides through dilemmas, even those to which any solution will involve the agent in wrong? For example, noncombatant immunity might be an inviolable duty or principle; killing the innocent as a goal and not only as a means of self-defense is excluded; and preferential rescue of the especially oppressed or

45. For Niebuhr's views on this policy (a policy with which the US Catholic bishops also agreed in *The Challenge of Peace*, 1983), see Robert E. Williams, "Christian Realism and 'The Bomb': Reinhold Niebuhr on the Dilemmas of the Nuclear Age," *Journal of Church and State* 28, no. 2 (1986): 300–304.

46. Niebuhr, "The Nuclear Dilemma—A Discussion," in *Christianity and Crisis*, 21 (November 13, 1961), 202. For a discussion of the history of Niebuhr's attitudes to nuclear war, see Williams, "Christian Realism and 'The Bomb,'" 289–304.

47. Carlson, "Christian Realist Theory of War," 144. Carlson discusses at length an audiotape of this lecture given on March 29, 1960.

48. As set out in chapter 4, an action or decision can be justified on the whole, or as considered in all its dimensions, even though there is a dimension included that makes it a moral dilemma. The latter dimension involves the agent in an intention, decision, and action that cause injustice (and not merely a regrettable unfortunate outcome), even though on the whole the course taken is justifiable. In the context of war and violence, that subsidiary injustice is often of a grave nature, involving loss of life to another human person, or other violations of rights. In the case of an irreducible moral dilemma, however, the course chosen is not on the whole immoral or blameworthy, though the agent properly experiences remorse for causing what he or she considers morally necessary injustice to another human being.

vulnerable is a guide that permits wronging others. Just war criteria can be understood as an attempt to identify duties, exclusions, and guides applicable to the irreducible moral dilemma of killing in war. Niebuhr is right that they are no guarantee of moral clarity or purity. Yet, as John Courtney Murray maintained, they can function as a moral and not merely political framework to restrain the evils of war. Even when they are met, war is still an irreducible moral dilemma involving wrong and guilt and calling for remorse and reparations, a fact recognized rarely by just war theorists.

Without naming names, John Courtney Murray attacked the "Protestant" demolition of rational moral analysis in no uncertain terms. This "new American morality" is "consciously pragmatist" and "sees things as so complicated that moral judgment becomes practically impossible. The final category of moral judgment is not 'right' or 'wrong' but 'ambiguous.' . . . Finally . . . the new theory teaches that to act is to sin."[49] But Murray rejects that there is an "unresolvable dichotomy between moral man and immoral society" or that life must be lived in the single dimension of "ambiguity."[50] The only resources that can distinguish between force and violence, and thus rescue the human community from barbarism, are "the resources of reason, made operative chiefly through the processes of reasonable law, prudent public policies, and a discriminatingly apt use of force."[51] Setting his own position off from what he views as indefensible Protestant pragmatism, Murray adds that "it is justice that links the use of force with the moral order."[52]

Yet Murray offers essentially the same analysis of nuclear weapons as Niebuhr. At first this analysis is in terms of reason and principle. Defensive warfare is certainly just, says Murray, but there is "no indication" in the just war tradition as transmitted by Catholicism that this principle extends only to "so-called conventional arms." One cannot state simply that "atomic warfare as such . . . is morally unjustifiable."[53] Although there is a moral distinction between combatant and noncombatant, it does not follow that the rights of innocent life are absolute. Ultimately, though, Murray concedes that "the whole Catholic doctrine of war is hardly more than a *Grenzmoral*, an effort to establish on a minimal basis of reason a form of human action, the making of war, that remains always fundamentally irrational."[54] Yet in the very next chapter, he takes

---

49. John Courtney Murray, *We Hold These Truths*, 265.
50. Murray, *We Hold These Truths*, 271.
51. Murray, *We Hold These Truths*, 275.
52. Murray, *We Hold These Truths*, 245.
53. Murray, *We Hold These Truths*, 248. Here Murray draws on the teaching of Pius XII.
54. Murray, *We Hold These Truths*, 251.

up the assault on "ambiguists" who talk of 'ironies,' 'dilemmas,' and 'paradox.'" Murray contradicts himself and effectively cedes the argument to Niebuhr. Is it better to propose that civilians may be targeted unambiguously and rationally for proportionate results; or to admit that justifying such policies to save a greater number of lives entangles agents in irreducible conflicts of obligation? Neither Murray nor Niebuhr set any moral line that pragmatic cost-benefit calculations must never cross, nor any moral value that they must always respect and embody.

DIETRICH BONHOEFFER (1906–45)

Dietrich Bonhoeffer is a Christian theologian and political activist who further explores and exemplifies the morally ambiguous character of killing, even for a just cause. He proposes that, for Christians, a necessary guide through the irreducible dilemma of killing is the priority of human suffering, especially the suffering of the oppressed. In addition, he envisions that the agent who accepts the responsibility and guilt of killing on behalf of the powerless must be willing to take on suffering personally, thereby sharing in the suffering of Christ. Bonhoeffer was born in Breslau, Germany, one of eight children in a successful and well-educated family.[55] His father Karl, an agnostic, was a well-known psychiatrist and (from 1912) chair of the Department of Psychiatry and Neurology at Kaiser Wilhelm University in Berlin. His mother Paula was the daughter of a professor of practical theology and the granddaughter of the renowned church historian Karl August von Hase. To the surprise of family members, Dietrich, as a young teenager, declared his determination to become a theologian and pastor. After studies in Tübingen and Berlin, he completed his doctoral studies at age twenty-one, with a dissertation on the church titled *Communion of Saints*. Bonhoeffer spent a year in Barcelona (1928–29) as the assistant pastor of a German-speaking congregation and did postdoctoral work at Union Theological Seminary in New York (1930), where he studied with Reinhold Niebuhr.

Bonhoeffer returned to Berlin to become a university professor in 1930, where he remained (with some breaks) until forbidden to teach by the National-Socialist government in 1936. He was ordained to the Lutheran ministry in 1931. During this same year, he spent three weeks in Bonn, where he audited a seminar with Karl Barth, whose writings had made a deep impression on Bonhoeffer during his doctoral studies.

55. See the account by Bonhoeffer's close friend, Eberhard Bethge, *Dietrich Bonhoeffer: A Biography*, ed. Victoria J. Barnett (Minneapolis: Fortress, 2000); Larry L. Rasmussen, *Dietrich Bonhoeffer: Reality and Resistance* (Louisville, KY: Westminster John Knox, 2005).

Yet, though he was inspired by Barth's theology of the claim and command of God, he was dissatisfied with the emphasis Barth put on God's absolute transcendence of the world. Deeply imbued with the theology of Martin Luther, Bonhoeffer believed that in Jesus Christ God definitively enters time and the human situation, as represented by the real presence of Christ in the bread and wine of the Eucharist. More strongly than Luther himself, Bonhoeffer insisted that God in Christ changes time and finite human being.[56] In fact, Barth and Bonhoeffer were to become collaborators in a very real and historical expression of faith: opposition of the German Confessing Church to the Third Reich. Their ongoing theological influence was mutual.[57]

Bonhoeffer was a leader of ecclesial resistance to National Socialism, helping to form the Pastors' Emergency League, which eventually won over seven thousand members and was the forerunner of the openly dissenting Confessing Church. Because of his well-known opposition to the regime, his rejection of a German church position under Nazi control, his refusal to be drafted into Hitler's army, and his frustration with the early reticence of the Confessing Church to take a clear stand against Hitler, Bonhoeffer accepted a ministerial post in London (1933–35). While there he established ecumenical contacts and, in light of his social-activist pacifist convictions, prepared to visit Gandhi. Meanwhile, Barth was working to galvanize the Confessing Church, which finally in 1934 issued the Barmen Declaration, establishing the basis of an illegal anti-Nazi Church. Barth did not hold back his reaction to what he saw as Bonhoeffer's desertion: "Get back to your post in Berlin straightaway! . . . you need to be here with all guns blazing! . . . standing up to these brethren along with me. . . . Why weren't you there pulling on the rope that I, virtually alone, could hardly budge?"[58]

Bonhoeffer did return, answering a call from the Confessing Church to take up a position at a new seminary of the Christian resistance in Pomerania. Bonhoeffer was on the faculty there from 1935 to 1937, when it was shut down by the Nazis. It was in Pomerania that he met Eberhard Bethge, a student who was to become his close friend and addressee of most of the letters he wrote later from prison. Bethge married Bonhoeffer's niece Renate and became his posthumous editor. It was during these same years that Bonhoeffer wrote *The Cost of Disciple-*

---

56. Heinz Edouard Tödt, *Authentic Faith: Bonhoeffer's Theological Ethics in Context*, ed. Glen Harold Stassen (Grand Rapids, MI: William B. Eerdmans, 2007), 4.

57. Matthew Puffer, "Dietrich Bonhoeffer in the Theology of Karl Barth," in *Karl Barth in Conversation*, ed. W. Travis McMaken and David W. Congdon (Eugene, OR: Pickwick, 2014), 46–62.

58. Puffer, "Dietrich Bonhoeffer," 49.

ship (1937), a manifesto on the demands of the Sermon on the Mount, the courage needed to follow Jesus, and the fact that grace is "costly" because the incarnation leads to the cross.[59] Only grace saves, according to the theology of Luther, but grace without true conversion of life is "cheap grace." Saving grace is "costly grace," a grace that requires absolute obedience to Christ, and costs one's own life.[60] A corollary is the renunciation of violence. "'Blessed are the peacemakers: for they shall be called the children of God.' . . . But now they are told that they must not only *have* peace but *make* it." Nothing is to be gained by "violence and tumult" in the cause of Christ; followers of Christ create fellowship where it has been broken, choosing to endure suffering rather than inflict it on others.[61]

From early on, Bonhoeffer opposed National Socialism not only because it interfered in the freedom of the churches or because the so-called "German Christians" were acquiescent but because of its unjust and unacceptable Aryan, nationalist, and racist policies, especially its persecution of the Jews. In fact, when Barth read the biography of Bonhoeffer by Eberhard Bethge, Barth acknowledged,

> What was most especially new to me was the fact that from 1933 on Bonhoeffer was the first, indeed almost the only one, who focused so centrally on the Jewish question and attacked it directly. I have felt for a long time that I was guilty of not having made it of decisive importance in the church struggle (for example in both of my drafts of the Barmen Declaration of 1934).[62]

After the emergency seminary was closed, and because the authorities no longer allowed him to teach in Berlin, Bonhoeffer assumed a position with a national intelligence agency where he was not directly involved in the immoral policies of National Socialism. Through his brother-in-law Hans von Dohnányi, Bonhoeffer made connections at the agency with a network of resisters who were planning a coup against Hitler. Although this was clearly one factor precipitating Bonhoeffer's eventual arrest and execution (after the failure of the plot on July 20, 1945), the details of his involvement in the assassination plan remain unknown. The crime for which he was actually convicted was draft avoidance, also a capital offense. Bonhoeffer's own theological-ethical assessment of the

59. Dietrich Bonhoeffer, *The Cost of Discipleship*, 45–49.
60. Bonhoeffer, *Cost of Discipleship*, 53.
61. Bonhoeffer, *Cost of Discipleship*, 126.
62. Karl Barth, *Letters: 1961-1968*, ed. and trans. Geoffrey W. Bromiley (Grand Rapids, MI: William B. Eerdmans, 1981), 250–52; as cited by Glen Harold Stassen, *A Thicker Jesus: Incarnational Discipleship in a Secular Age*, 22.

justifiability of assassinating Hitler cannot be known directly, since the secrecy of the plot and of his involvement in it (especially after his arrest and imprisonment) prohibited his making any written record.

We do know, however, that Bonhoeffer not only saw the persecution of the Jews as a pressing issue for the Christian churches but also interpreted Christian responsibility in terms of fidelity to the demands of God in Christ in the present moment, and that he believed responsibility requires risk and reliance on God's grace. According to a widely accepted framework proposed by Bethge, Bonhoeffer's thought is deeply embedded in the social location and specific challenges of his life, and it exhibits some significant changes within a trajectory that is in other ways continuous. Bonhoeffer's three abiding commitments were biblical spirituality, the ecclesial nature of Christian identity, and a witness to Christ in the world.[63] But his theology can also be seen in terms of three phases, prioritizing "discipleship and community, then the struggle for justice and peace, and finally, faith in a secular age."[64]

Bonhoeffer's major, most mature, and most systematic work is his *Ethics*, but this work, drafted between 1940 and 1943, was never completed. He continued to work on it throughout his imprisonment, asking his mother to send him various books and new materials. Interpreting Lutheran ideas such as the power of grace, Christian freedom, the mandates that structure responsibility in the world, and the role of the law in a way that resonates with Barth,[65] Bonhoeffer's *Ethics* presents a complex theological elaboration of the practical realities of responsibility and guilt that Bonhoeffer faced in his own life. Christians, like Jesus, are to be both obedient and free (Luther's "bound and free"). The primary use of the law, in light of the gospel, is that it "sets the believer in a situation of worldly responsibility."[66] For Bonhoeffer, relationship to God is always both social and thoroughly "this-worldly." "There is one world and it is already in God," already redeemed in Christ, who defines what "reality" is.[67]

Responsible human action is thus characterized by "correspondence to reality," so understood.[68] The specific requirements of Christian action

63. For a discussion of Bethge's thesis and its reception, see John W. de Gruchy, "The Reception of Bonhoeffer's Theology," in *The Cambridge Companion to Dietrich Bonhoeffer*, ed. John W. de Gruchy (Cambridge: Cambridge University Press, 1999), 97–99.

64. De Gruchy, "Reception," 103.

65. Bonhoeffer was able to read a portion of Barth's *Church Dogmatics*, vol. 2, part two, in draft.

66. Bonhoeffer, *Ethics*, ed. Eberhard Bethge (New York: Macmillan, 1955), 316.

67. Larry Rasmussen, "The Ethics of Responsible Action," *Cambridge Companion to Bonhoeffer*, 218.

68. Bonhoeffer, *Ethics*, 316.

are defined "realistically" and in social relationship. For Bonhoeffer, love of God and neighbor is the origin of all responsible action and also its overriding norm.[69] "The responsible man is dependent on the man who is concretely his neighbor in his concrete possibility. His conduct is not established in advance, once and for all, that is to say, as a matter of principle, but it arises in the given situation."[70] This means that "human beings are called to live and act before God and the neighbor within the confines of our limited human judgement and knowledge." In the end, "those who act responsibly place their action into the hands of God and live by God's grace and judgment."[71]

To understand how this perspective played out regarding Bonhoeffer's participation in the plan to kill Hitler, it is important to appreciate how his earlier experience in New York surely enhanced his empathy for Germany's persecuted Jews. While Bonhoeffer was in New York, he not only had studied with Reinhold Niebuhr, but, just as importantly, if not more so, he was introduced to the Abyssinian Baptist Church in Harlem by an African American seminary friend, Franklin Fisher, who was assigned to the church for his field work.[72] There Bonhoeffer heard Adam Clayton Powell and others preach about justice and the social gospel from within African American experience. He saw Powell's congregants, themselves struggling economically, respond with alacrity and generosity to his call to offer relief to destitute and forgotten black people in the midst of the Great Depression. At a deeper religious and theological level, Bonhoeffer was greatly moved by and attracted to black spirituals that captured the suffering, solidarity, and hope of a people. He became convinced that Jesus Christ can be known only through the struggles of those who suffer. Bonhoeffer became personally engaged with this community while teaching Sunday school in Harlem. His experience there thoroughly subverted whatever may have been left of his German nationalist, *Volk*-centered formation. It was a different

---

69. Bonhoeffer, "History and the Good," the second of two incomplete drafts for *Ethics*, in *The Bonhoeffer Reader*, ed. Clifford J. Green and Michael DeJonge (Minneapolis: Fortress, 2013), 645.

70. Bonhoeffer, *Ethics*, 227. "In Christ we are offered the possibility of partaking in the reality of God and in the reality of the world, but not in the one without the other. The reality of God discloses itself only by setting me entirely in the reality of the world, and when I encounter the reality of the world it is always already sustained, accepted and reconciled in the reality of God" (195).

71. Bonhoeffer, "History and the Good," 644.

72. On the significance of this period in Bonhoeffer's life, see Reggie L. Williams, *Bonhoeffer's Black Jesus: Harlem Renaissance Theology and an Ethic of Resistance* (Waco, TX: Baylor University Press, 2014).

Bonhoeffer who returned home to Germany to speak out against Nazi racism.[73]

Bonhoeffer was convinced that Christians as individuals and as church are called to share in Christ's own sufferings by taking up the suffering of other human beings just as Christ did. In "After Ten Years," a reflection written just a few months before he was arrested, Bonhoeffer wrote:

> We are not Christ, but if we want to be Christians, we must have some share in Christ's large heartedness by acting with responsibility and in freedom when the hour of danger comes, and by showing a real sympathy that springs, not from fear, but from the liberating and redeeming love of Christ for all who suffer.[74]

To Eberhard Bethge he later wrote from Tegel prison, "the bible directs man to God's powerlessness and suffering; only a suffering God can help."[75] "Man is summoned to share in God's sufferings at the hands of a godless world."[76] This lends an important nuance or criterion to the resolution of irreducible moral dilemmas, especially those that inevitably entail destruction of human life or other grave assaults on human personhood: the priority of the most poor, powerless, and vulnerable stakeholders in a situation of decision.

Some Mennonite interpreters have argued that there is no direct evidence that Bonhoeffer ever acted against his pacifist convictions.[77] A contrary view is that Bonhoeffer was a Lutheran, not an Anabaptist, and so he believed with Luther that although peace defines the kingdom and the church, the world and the (legitimate) state require the use of force to maintain order and provide an anticipatory peace.[78] Others, like Glen Stassen (and perhaps the majority of Bonhoeffer's readers), appreciate and draw from Bonhoeffer's theology, his commitment to the costly gospel, and his personal courage and example in the face of injustice—without needing to analyze closely what we can know about his

73. Williams, *Bonhoeffer's Black Jesus*, 105–6.

74. Bonhoeffer, "After Ten Years," in *Letters and Papers from Prison*, new and greatly enlarged edition, ed. Eberhard Bethge (New York: Simon & Schuster, 1971), 14.

75. Bonhoeffer, letter of July 16, *Letters and Papers*, 361.

76. Bonhoeffer, letter of July 18, *Letters and Papers*, 361.

77. Ted Grimsrud, "What Do We Make of Dietrich Bonhoeffer?," Thinking Pacifism blog, February 27, 2011, accessed May 24, 2017, https://tinyurl.com/y98fgkng; Mark Thiessen Nation and Anthony G. Siegrist, *Bonhoeffer the Assassin? Challenging the Myth, Recovering His Call to Peacemaking* (Grand Rapids, MI: Baker Academic, 2013).

78. Michael DeJonge, "How to Read Bonhoeffer's Peace Statements: Or, Bonhoeffer Was a Lutheran and Not an Anabaptist," *Theology* 118, no. 3 (2015): 162–71.

consent to killing Hitler, his motives, or whether his decision was consistent with his overall convictions.[79]

Eberhard Bethge, Bonhoeffer's closest confidante both during this time and after his arrest, knew him exceedingly well and exchanged with him multiple soul-searching theological reflections. Bethge was eventually taken prisoner for implication in the same scheme, but was rescued by Soviet troops before the Nazis had a chance to put him on trial and execute him. Bethge has this to say about the period when Bonhoeffer came to learn of plans to overthrow the Nazi government, written in a short biographical forward to the first edition of *Letters and Papers from Prison*, published less than a decade after Bonhoeffer's death:

> Hitherto Bonhoeffer, under the influence of his English and American experiences, had been very near to absolute pacifism—an unheard-of position in the Germany of that time. Now he began to see pacifism as an illegitimate escape, especially if he was tempted to withdraw from his increasing contacts with the political and military leaders of the resistance. He no longer saw any way of escape into some region of piety.[80]

While in prison, Bonhoeffer developed a "new theology," a theology *in extremis*, that looked unflinchingly at what Christians are called to do in a "world come of age." The answer is not "restricting God to the so-called ultimate questions as a *deus ex machina*," as "the answer to life's problems."[81] For Bonhoeffer, the genocidal plans of the Third Reich called for a new confrontation with "reality," one in which reconciliation in Christ demands identification with the suffering of the Jews, and active responsibility on their behalf, to the extent of accepting the possible guilt involved in taking a life. He placed that action in the hands of God, willing to "live by God's grace and judgment." His implication in the conspiracy recalls a warning note from his *Ethics:* "The confession of guilt is the re-attainment of the form of Jesus Christ, who bore the sin of the world." And only by partaking in the "form of Christ" are the church and its members justified.[82]

Glen Stassen, the evangelical just-peacemaking theorist discussed in

---

79. Stassen discusses Bonhoeffer repeatedly and at length in *A Thicker Jesus*, to be discussed further below.

80. Eberhard Bethge, "Editor's Foreword," in Bonhoeffer, *Letters and Papers from Prison* (New York: Macmillan, 1953), 9. While in the United States, Bonhoeffer was in conversation with French pastor Jean Lasserre, a pacifist. Bonhoeffer attributed *The Cost of Discipleship* partly to Lasserre's influence. See letter of July 2, 1944, *Letters and Papers*, enlarged edition, 369.

81. Bonhoeffer, letter of June 30, 1944, *Letters and Papers*, 341. His letter of April 30, 1944, marked a turning point toward this theology.

82. Bonhoeffer, *Ethics*, 116.

chapters 1 and 2, underlines that Bonhoeffer's main theological conviction was the possibility and necessity of making the incarnation and resurrection real under the conditions of history. The primary form this takes is the transformation of division and violence. Yet Niebuhr's influence appears in Bonhoeffer via the seriousness with which he faces the reality of sin, the magnitude of the obstacles it poses to social reform, and the complexity of situations in which Christians are called to act.

Stassen reminds us that for Bonhoeffer (like Niebuhr) abdicating responsibility for the transformation of social evil is itself a sin.[83] Therefore, he says of the fact that Bonhoeffer laid his own life on the line (without explicitly defending Bonhoeffer's apparent justification of killing), Bonhoeffer's actions were done "courageously, truthfully, and sacrificially on behalf of his church and his nation." Bonhoeffer acted in solidarity with the suffering of the Nazis' victims, yet he also identified with all Germans, with and for whom he acted "in corporate solidarity."[84] He was willing to share their guilt and make restitution on their behalf, while remaining in solidarity with their victims, to whose suffering he gave priority. Like Christ on the cross, Bonhoeffer was a vicarious representative, accepting guilt along with freedom.[85]

In his first letter to Bethge after the coup failed, Bonhoeffer explains that he had come to recognize more clearly the danger in trying to live "a holy life" in contrast to the world. What is called for is "a profound this-worldliness, characterized by discipline and the constant knowledge of death and resurrection. . . . By this-worldliness, I mean living unreservedly in life's duties, problems, successes and failures, experiences and perplexities. In doing so we throw ourselves unreservedly into the arms of God, taking seriously, not our own sufferings, but those of God in the world—watching with Christ in Gethsemane."[86]

Like Barth—and for that matter Augustine and Luther—Bonhoeffer was a dialectical theologian. For all of these thinkers, the key to clarity

83. Bonhoeffer, *Ethics*, 136.

84. Bonhoeffer, *Ethics*, 153. A similar perspective is offered by Lori Brandt Hale and Reggie L. Williams, in "Is This a Bonhoeffer Moment? Lessons for American Christians from the Confessing Church in Germany," *Sojourners*, February 2018, accessed January 29, 2018, https://tinyurl.com/y95w9ytm. While believing that "violence is not the answer," the authors hold Bonhoeffer up as a model for his refusal to be a "bystander" in the face of white nationalism.

85. Bonhoeffer, *Ethics*, 241.

86. Bonhoeffer, letter of July 21, 1944, *Letters and Papers*, 369–70. Lisa E. Dahill comments specifically on this passage that, while such an other-directed Christology is true as a Christian affirmation, it must be interpreted critically and cautiously (as must the similar call of Reinhold Niebuhr for sacrificial love) as it applies to people, such as abused women, who are already in a position of exploited powerlessness. See Dahill, "Jesus for You: A Feminist Reading of Bonhoeffer's Christology," *Currents in Theology and Mission* 34, no. 4 (2007): 250.

of purpose in the midst of dialectic is a vivid relation to Christ. Like Niebuhr, ethics and politics are essential dimensions of Christian belief and theology for Bonhoeffer. Like Niebuhr, he believes that political responsibility entails guilt, but unlike Niebuhr he does not think of this in moral categories but in terms of Christ's vicarious sacrifice. Rather than lamenting the burden of culpability and remorse that accompany necessary moral decisions, as comes through in Niebuhr's war ethics, Bonhoeffer (with Barth) proclaims and is consoled by the Christian freedom that comes with faith.

The ethicist will not be slow to realize that convictions about God-given responsibilities transgressing ordinary moral laws may be mistaken or may themselves be forms of self-deception. This is a problem Barth himself tacitly recognizes in reflecting on the failure of Bonhoeffer's coconspirators to realize their goal.[87] But Bonhoeffer put trust in his intense and immediate relation to God in Christ. Faith is the total reliance on Christ that brings assurance of forgiveness and salvation. An English fellow prisoner, Payne Best, remembers Bonhoeffer's parting words as he was led off to execution at Flossenberg: "This is the end. For me the beginning of life."[88]

DOROTHY DAY (1897–1980)

A contemporary of Reinhold Niebuhr and Karl Barth, Dorothy Day also saw the two World Wars, as well as the Korean and the Vietnamese-American Wars, but from a country that inflicted devastation from afar rather than suffer it on home soil. Day was a young adult during the Great Depression, another formative social disaster. She was an outspoken critic of US militarism, but her fundamental concern was society's homeless, hungry, and forgotten. For Dorothy Day, pacifism was part of a total way of life in imitation of Jesus Christ and in service of the poor.

The daughter of a newspaper sportswriter, she and her three siblings grew up in New York, San Francisco, and Chicago. Although the Day family occasionally faced financial difficulties, it provided a loving and

---

87. Barth believed an attack was planned and could have been carried out, but for the fact that no one was prepared to go through with it "in absolute disregard of his own life." Yet Barth does not believe the conspirators should be blamed either for their decision or their failure to act upon it. "The only lesson to be learned is that they had no clear and categorical command from God to do it." Yet, "in such a situation it might well have been the command of God. For all we know, perhaps it was, and they failed to hear it." See Karl Barth, *Church Dogmatics*, vol. 3, *The Doctrine of Creation*, part 4 (Edinburgh: T&T Clark, 1961), 449.

88. Bethge, "Editor's Foreword," 14. Best recorded these words in his 1950 book about the circumstances under which he was captured, *The Venlo Incident*.

protective middle-class environment, where reading of literary classics and philosophy was encouraged. From childhood, Dorothy loved books, determined to become a writer, and was sensitive to the fact that many neighborhood families were considerably less comfortable than hers. Just before World War I, she ended two years of study at the University of Illinois and went to New York City. There, her commitment to social action was galvanized by a young, countercultural intellectual community centered in Greenwich Village.[89] Day found a practically oriented expression for her talents and ideals in journalism, writing for papers with a socialist, activist, and radical bent. Yet she spent her young adulthood in a prolonged anguish of personal searching. For many years, direction and identity seemed to elude her. Unstable romantic liaisons, including an abortion and a brief marriage, culminated in her relationship with Forster Batterham, an avowed socialist and atheist, with whom she nonetheless experienced a deep bond. After the birth of their daughter, Tamar, Day finally took the step of seeking baptism for her child and herself; her religious conversion proved too great an affront to Batterham's own dearly held convictions, and the relationship ended traumatically for both.

For the remainder of her long life, Day devoted her considerable energies to developing practical expressions of Catholicism's social critique. As a convert, she was largely unfamiliar with papal social teaching. Motivated by the same social issues that prompted the Protestant social gospel, Day and her colleagues cultivated a traditional Catholic piety—including, for instance, Marian devotions—in service of leftist ideals and solutions. A primary vehicle for these programs was *The Catholic Worker*, a paper that she and Peter Maurin began in 1933. It advocated social change by publishing stories on, for example, migrant workers, labor organization, schools, housing, food relief, child care, race relations, militarism, and the draft. Day and Maurin founded soup kitchens called Houses of Hospitality to serve the unemployed and established a series of farming communes in the hope that they could unite religiously committed coworkers in communities of mutual love, worship, and labor and offer some solution to the crises of urban life for the disadvantaged

89. Mel Piehl, *Breaking Bread: The Catholic Worker and the Origin of Catholic Radicalism in America* (Philadelphia: Temple University Press, 1982), 9. For more on Day's life and work, see the biography by her granddaughter, Kate Hennessy, *The World Will Be Saved by Beauty: An Intimate Portrait of My Grandmother* (New York: Scribner, 2017); Jim Forest, *All Is Grace: A Biography of Dorothy Day* (Maryknoll, NY: Orbis, 2011); and Stephen J. Pope, *A Step along the Way: Models of Christian Service* (Maryknoll, NY: Orbis, 2015), 109–27. For a treatment that highlights Day's pacifism and its historical importance, see Sara Ann Mehltretter, "Dorothy Day, Union Square Speech (6 November 1965)," *Voices of Democracy* 1 (2006): 165–86, accessed August 10, 2017, https://tinyurl.com/y9e2az4z.

guests whom they would welcome. Since the farms never turned away would-be residents, they never succeeded in achieving economic viability.

Peter Maurin brought the influence of European Catholicism and its intellectual traditions into the Catholic Worker movement, and his ideas, though often abstractly expressed, motivated much of its work. Impractical, temperamental, and even autocratic though he may have been, his love of the poor and hatred of violence had a sincere and obvious religious foundation. It was typical of Day in turn, who admitted that she had little talent for rigorous intellectual analysis and that she found her inspiration in a person rather than in a body of writings or set of ideas. Though she was conservative in theological and moral outlook, inclined to accept Catholic teaching unquestioningly, she had little use for the worldliness and clericalism of the institutional church. In her autobiography, *The Long Loneliness,* she wryly quotes a remark that "the Church is the Cross on which Christ was crucified."[90]

Day invokes the Sermon on the Mount to explain the Catholic Worker policy of never evicting troublemaking guests. Workers were "trying to follow the dear Lord's teachings," including the sayings "Give to him that asks of you and from him that would borrow, turn not away," and "love your enemies, do good to them that hate you."[91] In this, too, they followed Maurin's example, according to Day, for "he took the Gospel counsel literally" and would give away his own coat to the needy, then take another pauper to a friend to beg an additional one.[92] Stephen Pope notes that while Day and Maurin "took hospitality to the 'least' as a central feature of the Christian life," it is a practice that must also take institutional and political forms to reduce the conditions causing exclusion.[93] Pope uses hostility to immigrants as an example. In Day's generation, it was industrialism, capitalism, unfair labor practices, and poverty, factors that she addressed and are of course still in play today.

Day was single-minded in her rejection of any form of violence, especially of war.[94] She called the shooting of striking workers "Pearl Harbor incidents." She described a recent lynching in Missouri and asked, "Are the Negroes supposed to 'Remember Pearl Harbor' and take to arms to avenge this cruel wrong?" She wrote in 1952, "We had been pacifist in

90. Dorothy Day, *The Long Loneliness: The Autobiography of Dorothy Day* (New York: Harper & Row, 1981), 150.

91. Day, *The Long Loneliness,* 261.

92. Day, *The Long Loneliness,* 179.

93. Pope, *A Step along the Way,* 116.

94. On Day's pacifism, see Eileen Egan, *Peace Be with You: Justified Warfare or the Way of Nonviolence* (Maryknoll, NY: Orbis, 1998).

class war, race war, in the Ethiopian war, in the Spanish Civil War, all through World War II, as we are now during the Korean War. We had spoken in terms of the Sermon on the Mount." To the frequent query as to what she would do to protect a loved one from harm, she replied that an "armed maniac" might be restrained but not killed, for "perfect love casts out fear and love overcomes hatred. All this sounds trite but experience is not trite."

Against taking sides in the Spanish Civil War, Day maintained, "Our side should be a side that follows the teachings of Jesus. We are Christians, which means we take our Lord's words and His example as the most important message in the entire world."[95] When the United States entered World War II, she reminded readers of *The Catholic Worker* of "the words of Christ, who is always with us, even to the end of the world. 'Love your enemies, do good to those who hate you.'"[96] At the same time Day, like Erasmus, saw the horror and immorality of war as contrary to reason and human nature. Biblical nonviolence confirms and motivates what should already be evident to any reasonable person.[97]

Day's opposition to war was nuanced to her context as a US citizen during an era in which military might assured the success of America's political goals, its growing economic power, and its influence abroad. Day professed love for her country, as "the only country in the world" that had welcomed refugees fleeing from oppression.[98] Yet she was a vehement critic of government policies that she believed contributed to unemployment, poverty, hunger, and homelessness. In 1942, she questioned how far the Catholic Worker could cooperate with a government that had declared war with Germany, Japan, and Italy. "Speaking for many of our conscientious objectors, we will not participate in armed warfare or in making munitions, or by buying government bonds to prosecute the war, or in urging others to these efforts."[99] The Catholic Worker houses also advocated nonpayment of federal income taxes, an action for which it was eventually prosecuted by the Internal Revenue Service in the 1970s (the case was eventually dropped). Yet Day realized that as an American citizen, she could not step entirely outside the system sustained by the government, and in fact she benefitted from it. At the start of World War II, she wrote that "we must all admit our guilt,

95. As interviewed by Robert Coles, *Dorothy Day: A Radical Devotion* (Reading, MA: Addison-Wesley, 1987), 79.

96. Dorothy Day, *Dorothy Day: Selected Writings*, ed. Robert Ellsberg (Maryknoll, NY: Orbis, 1983), 261.

97. Day, *The Long Loneliness*, 269–70.

98. Day, *Dorothy Day: Selected Writings*, 262.

99. Day, *Dorothy Day: Selected Writings*, 262.

our participation in the social order which has resulted in this monstrous crime of war."[100]

Day's insistence that *The Catholic Worker* stick to pacifism in the face of American patriotism before and during the Second World War caused a sizable rift in the movement, reducing the financial support on which it depended and even prompting the closing of some of the Houses of Hospitality in which the leadership refused to yield. Mel Piehl reports that "in 1939 and 1940 the thirty or so Worker Houses were torn by debate over pacifism and the draft, specifically over the radical anti-war propaganda appearing in the New York *Catholic Worker*." Day's 1940 open letter to all Catholic Workers had a dramatic and divisive impact, leading some within the movement to accuse her of authoritarianism in attempting to close discussion and impose her viewpoint on all. Although she denied that she required orthodoxy on the subject, she persisted in her plan to distribute the paper with her letter. "By the end of 1942 only sixteen Houses remained in operation. By January 1945, just ten were left."[101] Nevertheless, from this point on pacifism was a clear mark of the movement.

Another cause of crisis for supporters of Day and the Catholic Worker was her sympathetic response to the Cuban revolution (1953–59). By 1961, there was consternation, anger, and rejection of Day's support for Fidel Castro. "Were not the Communists in power avowed atheists? Had they not already expropriated extensive Church property and placed restrictions on religious education? Furthermore, how could the Catholic Worker reconcile its pacifism with a movement which attained its aims through violence?"[102] Day responded that Castro had tried to coexist with the Catholic Church, but most priests had left the country, and that socialism "has many meanings."[103] She saw in Castro a defender of the poor and a resister of foreign domination and capitalist exploitation. "We are on the side of the revolution. . . . God bless Castro and all those who are seeing Christ in the poor." In the face of injustice, she was convinced that Christian resistance is nonviolent resistance, carried out in a spirit of love.[104] Nevertheless, she asserted, "we do believe that it is better to revolt, to fight, as Castro did with his handful of men, than to do nothing."[105]

This is an isolated statement and Day did not personally face the

100. Day, *Dorothy Day: Selected Writings*, 266.
101. Piehl, *Breaking Bread*, 197.
102. Day, *Dorothy Day: Selected Writings*, 298.
103. Day, *Dorothy Day: Selected Writings*, 301.
104. Day, *Dorothy Day: Selected Writings*, 304.
105. Day, *Dorothy Day: Selected Writings*, 302.

dilemma of use of force to save the lives of the poor. Her mission was to resist from within what she saw as the domestically and internationally violent behavior of the United States, its policies, and its elites, and to name the entrenched evils of the entire violent system in which its beneficiaries, however unwilling, inevitably participate. However, it is clear that Day recognized both that even gospel-based pacifism does not offer a secure refuge for the Christian conscience and that the meaning and demands of gospel commitment might change with different contexts. It is also clear that her most fundamental and absolute moral standard is one shared with Bonhoeffer: risk-taking compassion for and service to "the poor," to all who suffer unjustly and powerlessly. Both of them especially targeted their own governments, heads of state, and national policies that caused such suffering.

Twenty years after World War II ended, Dorothy Day gave a speech at Union Square in New York that was a "defining moment" for the US Catholic peace movement. It marked the connection of Day's movement of relatively small, service-oriented Christian communities to larger conditions and causes and contributed to institutional change, both ecclesial and public. Day and her adamant peace witness gave momentum to the acceptance of pacifism as an option in Catholic social teaching, and to the Catholic peacebuilding trajectory today. Delivered amid growing public opposition to the Vietnam war and as part of a large antiwar protest, the speech asserted pacifism to be obligatory for all Christians and urged the illegal burning of draft cards.[106]

Since World War II, Catholic Worker activism against war, the arms race, and nuclear weapons had grown more radical and more central to its agenda. In the same year as the Union Square speech, the Second Vatican Council accepted pacifism as a legitimate Christian option but did not repudiate just war theory. Day directly challenged just war teaching, as endorsed by the US Bishops Conference, the majority of whom supported the Vietnam War and the US-backed Catholic president of Vietnam. Day protested that war is inherently evil because it takes the lives of combatants and civilians, steals billions of funding from the poor, and destroys crops and other requirements of human survival.[107]

By 1965, Day, at age sixty-eight, was a well-known cultural and ecclesial authority figure. Inspired by Day, Catholic antiwar leaders such Daniel and Philip Berrigan took up the protest and engaged in nonviolent illegal activities, such as the invasion of and symbolic actions within nuclear facilities. Arrest and imprisonment drew attention to

---

106. Mehltretter, "Dorothy Day, Union Square Speech."
107. Day, *Dorothy Day: Selected Writings*, 174–75.

their cause. As Sara Ann Mehltretter points out, the fact that Day, the Catholic Workers, and the Catholic peace movement always maintained links with the institutional church reduced divisiveness and enabled a greater long-term impact. "Solidarity" was a concept that connoted for them unity in fighting injustice, in Christ, in a common faith, and in the church.[108] Day empowered lay Catholics to critique and resist their church's policies on war, while reforming those policies from within, contributing finally to the decisive shift that has occurred in official Catholic teaching: to an extreme skepticism about the justifiability of specific wars, and to the priority of peacebuilding over war.

Yet neither Day nor the Catholic Workers made pacifism the governing concern of their movement; "pacifism was no more the whole of the 'Catholic worker' idea than soup lines or unionization had been in the thirties."[109] Day herself suggested later that the practice of nonviolence grew integrally out of the movement's effort to respond as Jesus would to the immediate situation. It was not a matter of systematic moral analysis, nor of any theory of war and peace. "We haven't figured out what we should do down to the punctuation marks. In fact, we haven't written a lot of the sentences. We are responding to a life, to Jesus and how He chose to live; we believe that choice says something, even now, to us who live so many centuries later . . . it is in our everyday lives that God judges us, not in the positions we take on issues."[110] In George Fox's words, they "lived in the virtue of that life and power that took away the occasion of all wars." For Dorothy Day, the Christian life consists in a community of love and hospitality to the poor, and militating for institutional change as a political extension of Christian service. This may require personal sacrifice, even of one's most dearly held bonds. Yet it is an *imitatio Christi* in which humanity's own deepest fulfillment is found.

Dorothy Day was not a theologian and certainly no expert on Catholic social thought. Her impact as a Roman Catholic figure lies in the way she turned her evangelical convictions into a countercultural community that aimed to—and did—influence national politics from within the Catholic tradition, eventually shaping the direction of that tradition itself. As Eileen Egan, an associate of Day, captures her significance, "Dorothy did turn the Church around," in that she "found a church where just war thinking reigned, and she helped dispel the

108. Sara Ann Mehltretter, "Dorothy Day, the Catholic Workers, and Moderation in Religious Protest during the Vietnam War," *Journal of Communication and Religion* 32, no. 1 (2009): 1–32. See also Anne Klejment and Nancy L. Roberts, *American Catholic Pacifism: The Influence of Dorothy Day and the Catholic Worker Movement* (Westport, CT: Praeger, 1996).

109. Piehl, *Breaking Bread,* 198.

110. As interviewed by Coles, *Dorothy Day,* 101.

great myth by which Christians can kill other human beings in good conscience."[111] Day's work is part of a larger picture of the developing Roman Catholic view of war and peace, in which the justifiability of war has come to seem more dubious, and the pursuit of nonviolent strategies more realistic and obligatory, than at the time of the two World Wars.

THE PEACEBUILDING TRAJECTORY IN CATHOLIC SOCIAL TEACHING

Day's peace witness has precedents and companions in the tradition itself. The modern social encyclical tradition began to develop around the time of the social gospel, and it replied to some of the same phenomena of social inequality and unrest. As industrialization increased economic inequities, Enlightenment respect for the individual and its confidence in rationality combined with the Marxist critiques of capitalist exploitation to create an explosive situation in many European countries as well as in North America. In 1891, Leo XIII published *Rerum Novarum* (On the Condition of Labor). *Rerum Novarum* was an attempt to preserve social harmony by adapting what remained an essentially medieval view of society, organic and hierarchical. It was a reformist effort to respond to some of the workers' pressure, while still protecting private property and a qualified capitalism.

Just as this tradition responded to labor questions out of a characteristically Catholic framework grounded in natural law and the common good and inclined to political conservatism, so too it originally handled the just war discussion. John Courtney Murray captures the Roman Catholic ethos about war when he describes the "single inner attitude" of the "traditional doctrine" as "a will to peace, which, in the extremity, bears within itself a will to enforce the precept of peace by arms. But this will to arms is a moral will; for it is identically a will to justice." It is inconceivable to such a will that reason would contemplate "surrender to injustice," for that would be an extremity even beyond war itself.[112] In the modern tradition, until the middle of the last century, national governments were given almost unlimited authority to determine just cause for war. There may be a prima facie presumption against war, but it is

111. Egan, *Peace Be with You*, 304.

112. Murray, "Remarks on the Moral Problem of War," 56. Toward the end of the essay, Murray acknowledges that there is a paradox in using war to establish justice, and an even greater one in trying to justify war "at the interior of the Christian religion of love" (57). However, this does not substantively affect his formulation of just war theory.

qualified by the expectation that there will be necessary and inevitable exceptions that reason and justice demand.

However, just as later social encyclicals—from Pius XI's *Quadragesimo Anno* (1931) through John XXIII's *Mater et Magistra* (1961) and *Pacem in Terris* (1963) and Paul VI's *Populorum Progressio* (1967)—were to gradually expand the responsibilities of government from the nation-state to the "world community" and "universal common good,"[113] so the teaching on war and peace has moved beyond the sovereignty of states to include the common cause of peace under the leadership of a world government.[114] While the idea that the United Nations or any similar body would have the capacity and political will to control and eventually eliminate war may be unrealistic, the important point is that the Catholic Church now prioritizes international cooperation for peace to a far greater degree than the right to go to war.

Kenneth Himes points out that longstanding Catholic social tradition carries resources for the peacebuilding efforts that have now emerged, in that it has always been communitarian. It has since its inception sought justice, development, and solidarity; seen true peace as a just peace (not merely the absence of conflict); and envisioned just peace as a genuine historical possibility, inspired by the eschatological reign of God.[115] Phillip Rossi confirms that contemporary Catholic just war theory has been theologically reoriented by an eschatologically informed "anthropology of solidarity and mutuality" that evaluates uses of force in light of "the institutional ordering" of "an increasingly globalized world."[116]

Providing historical perspective on more recent developments, Bryan Hehir identifies the specific link between the just war tradition as formulated by the time of the seventeenth-century Spanish scholastics, and its modern Catholic version, as the teachings of Pope Pius XII in the 1940s and 1950s.[117] John Courtney Murray usefully analyzes the ways

113. For Vatican II uses of the phrase "universal common good," see Vatican Council II, *Gaudium et spes*, Pastoral Constitution on the Church in the Modern World, December 7, 1965, 68, 82, https://tinyurl.com/y7w78qfc.

114. In *Pacem in Terris*, 140, John XXIII endorses "the public authority of the world community," and in nos. 142–45 delineates the responsibilities of the United Nations. For historical and analytical essays on each of the aforementioned encyclicals and other important documents and ideas in Catholic social teaching, see Kenneth R. Himes, ed., *Modern Catholic Social Teaching: Commentaries and Interpretations* (Washington, DC: Georgetown University Press, 2005).

115. Kenneth R. Himes, "Peacebuilding and Catholic Social Teaching," in *Peacebuilding: Catholic Theology, Ethics, and Praxis*, ed. Robert J. Schreiter, R. Scott Appleby, and Gerard Powers (Maryknoll, NY: Orbis, 2010), 265–99.

116. Phillip J. Rossi, "Reframing Catholic Theories of Just War," *Journal of Catholic Social Thought* 11, no. 1 (2014): 236.

117. J. Bryan Hehir, "The Just-War Ethic and Catholic Theology: Dynamics of Change and

in which that tradition was specifically received and revised by Pius.[118] Like the social gospel writers and the Niebuhr brothers, Pius struggles with the new specter of nuclear war. He and subsequent popes decry the immense suffering and chaos that modern war brings in its wake. They sound increasingly clearer notes of caution and reserve about embarking on military solutions to political problems or even defense against aggression. They also consider and eventually reinterpret the problem of the conscientious objector, moving gradually to the contemporary magisterium's recognition of pacifism as a valid Catholic commitment.

Although Pius XII crystalizes the central midcentury heritage of Catholic just war theory, this is not to say that papal exhortations to peace and nonviolence were lacking even then. Modern popes, most notably Benedict XV, an Italian who was elected just as World War I was beginning, have made personal efforts to help mediate international conflicts nonviolently.[119] In Italy, the episcopacy supported the war. Yet Catholics and their bishops around the world were divided. Benedict thought that just war theory merely excuses war and that, even at that time, modern weapons exceeded the bounds of what just war criteria can validate. He devoted his first encyclical to the horrors of modern war. He called for a Christmas truce in 1914, established a Vatican office to reunite prisoners of war and their families, and dedicated Vatican funds to relief efforts, despite the church's financial difficulties.

During World War II, Christians and Catholics among them, participated in anti-Semitic attitudes and activities, and the clergy and bishops were no exception. Pius XII has been criticized for not directly and courageously denouncing the persecution of the Jews.[120] Yet he taught that Christian spirituality and charity, as well as justice, require dedication to the ideal of peace. However, in his 1944, 1948, and 1956 Christmas messages, he alluded to just war criteria in asserting the right of nations to defend themselves from attack. He warns that "a Catholic citizen cannot invoke his own conscience in order to refuse to serve and fulfil those duties the law imposes" in the case of a just war, nor does he support the independent right of individuals to make an evaluation

Continuity," in *War or Peace? The Search for New Answers*, ed. Thomas A. Shannon (Maryknoll, NY: Orbis, 1982), 15–39.

118. Hehir, "Just-War Ethic," 45–53.

119. John F. Pollard, *Benedict XV (1912–1922) and the Pursuit for Peace* (London: Bloomsbury, 2000).

120. For a critique, see Pierre Blet, *Pius XII and the Second World War: According to the Archives of the Vatican* (New York: Paulist, 1997). For a defense, see Margherita Marchione, *Pope Pius XII: Architect for Peace* (Mahwah, NJ: Paulist, 2000). See also John P. Langan, "The Christmas Messages of Pius XII (1939–1945): Catholic Social Teaching in a Time of Extreme Crisis," in *Modern Catholic Social Teaching*, 183–98.

of justice.[121] Yet he goes further than restraints on war in past tradition, by disallowing to individual states the right to resort to arms in order to vindicate wrongs or redress violations of legal rights. He also called for international conventions to renounce research on and use of nuclear weapons and establish general arms control.[122]

During the pontificates of John XXIII, Paul VI, and John Paul II, the visibility of pacifism within Catholicism grew, and skepticism about any moral use of nuclear weapons increased virtually to the point of repudiation.[123] John's *Pacem in terris* (1963) faults the arms race for the climate of fear it produces, the mistrust among nations it perpetuates, and the grave economic injustices it wreaks on less developed nations. Because of "the terrible destructive force of modern arms . . . it is hardly possible to imagine that in the atomic era war could be used as an instrument of justice."[124] "Justice, then, right reason and humanity urgently demand that the arms race should cease," that nuclear stockpiles should be dismantled through progressive disarmament, and that nuclear weapons eventually should be banned. The "true and solid peace of nations" can rest "on mutual trust alone," not on equality in war-making capacity, nor on fear.[125]

The explicit acceptance of pacifism as a Catholic alternative, however, had to await the Second Vatican Council. The Pastoral Constitution on the Church in the Modern World (*Gaudium et spes*) asserts the right of nations to "legitimate defense once every means of peaceful settlement has been exhausted." Yet, it continues, laws should make "humane provisions for the case of those who refuse to bear arms, provided however that they accept some other form of service to the human community."[126] The same document moves unequivocally to exclude nuclear attacks on civilians, even while retaining a right to war in general. "Any act of war aimed indiscriminately at the destruction of entire cities or of extensive areas along with their population is a crime against God and man himself. It merits unequivocal and unhesitating condemnation."[127] The Council also calls for progressive disarmament under the supervision

---

121. Pius XII, Christmas Radio Message, December 23, 1956, quoted in Thomas J. Massaro, SJ, and Thomas A. Shannon, *Catholic Perspectives on Peace and War* (Lanham, MD: Rowman & Littlefield, 2003), 21.

122. Pius XII, Christmas Message, Rome, December 24, 1955, https://tinyurl.com/y8774qqt.

123. Hehir traces this development through the writings of these popes and the documents of Vatican II in "Just-War Ethic," 20–29.

124. John XXIII, *Pacem in terris* (Peace on Earth), encyclical letter, April 11, 1963, 127, https://tinyurl.com/ydx2tneq.

125. John XXIII, *Pacem in terris*, 112, 113.

126. Vatican Council II, *Gaudium et spes*, 79.

127. Vatican Council II, *Gaudium et spes*, 80.

of an international authority with "effective power" to safeguard peace, since true peace "must be born of mutual trust among nations."[128] The expense and danger of weapons and their corrosion of international relations was reiterated by Paul VI to the United Nations in 1965.[129]

Since the time of John XXIII, Paul VI, and the Second Vatican Council, the Catholic Church, and especially the Catholic popes, have moved closer to pacifism by continually rejecting violence, holding up peace as achievable political goal, and embracing nonviolent strategies to realize peace with justice. No pope since the Council has ever approved a specific war or military intervention, or even elaborated a defense of the justice of war in principle, although the use of force for humanitarian purposes has been affirmed—for the first time by John Paul II in 2002.[130] The 1990s had witnessed humanitarian disasters met by international apathy or inefficacy in the former Yugoslavia, Rwanda, and Somalia. Yet the modern popes and Catholic social teaching are not pacifist, or even "functionally pacifist," in that they have not rejected any and all potential instances of armed force.[131] As John Paul II warned regarding Bosnia, when "populations are succumbing to the attacks of an unjust aggressor, States no longer have a 'right to indifference.' It seems clear that their duty is to disarm this aggressor, if all other means have proved ineffective."[132]

Again responding to recent international events, John Paul II upholds a nation's right of defense against terrorism, even while counseling forgiveness and interreligious cooperation as better alternatives.[133] Yet when specific military initiatives such as the Gulf War and the US-led invasion of Iraq were contemplated prospectively, the pope always gave a negative response, rejecting war as "a decline for all humanity" and "a

128. Vatican Council II, *Gaudium et spes*, 82.

129. Paul VI, Address to the United Nations Organization, New York, October 4, 1965, https://tinyurl.com/y96uobut.

130. John Paul II, "No Peace without Justice, No Justice without Forgiveness," World Day of Peace Message, Rome, January 1, 2002, https://tinyurl.com/ycdv837y. For a history and critical discussion of humanitarian intervention, and of its relation to the Catholic tradition on war and peace, see Kenneth R. Himes, "Humanitarian Intervention and Catholic Political Thought: Moral and Legal Perspectives," *Journal of Catholic Social Thought* 15, no. 1 (2018): 139–69.

131. See Kristopher Norris, "'Never Again War': Recent Shifts in the Roman Catholic Just War Tradition and the Question of 'Functional Pacifism,'" in *Journal of Religious Ethics* 42, no. 1 (2014): 108–36. Norris's thesis on the trend in Catholic social teaching, which is substantiated in detail, is essentially the same as mine, as is that of John Langan in an earlier analysis. See John Langan, "The Just-War Theory after the Gulf War," *Theological Studies* 53, no. 1 (1991): 95–112.

132. John Paul II, Address to the Diplomatic Corps, Rome, January 16, 1993, https://tinyurl.com/y7rzjdsr.

133. John Paul II, World Day of Peace Message, Rome, January 1, 2002.

defeat for humanity."[134] In his view, war is not inevitable, and it should be avoided through dialogue and diplomacy in accord with international law.

Benedict XVI agrees that the war against Iraq was unjust, noting that modern weapons inevitably harm civilians.[135] Indeed, Jesus's command to love our enemies, which is the "magna carta" of Christian nonviolence, "is realistic (not merely idealistic), because it takes into account that in the world there is too much violence, too much injustice, and that this situation cannot be overcome without positing more love, more kindness." Christian love of enemies can be the basis of a social "revolution."[136] On a visit to Cameroon and Angola, Benedict asserted that all genuine religion rejects violence in any form, and that beyond nonviolence, the causes and consequences of conflict must be relieved. "In the face of suffering or violence, poverty or hunger, corruption or abuse of power, a Christian can never remain silent. The saving message of the Gospel needs to be proclaimed loud and clear."[137]

Like his predecessor, Benedict endorses intervention under the rubric "responsibility to protect," established by the United Nations in 2004. "Recognition of the unity of the human family, and attention to the innate dignity of every man and woman, today find renewed emphasis in the principle of the responsibility to protect."[138] Yet, perhaps sharing John Paul's skepticism about whether violence can end cycles of violence, Benedict warns in his 2009 encyclical *Caritas in veritate* that the responsibility to protect must be implemented "in innovative ways."[139] Benedict follows both Paul VI and John Paul II in urging "development" as a solution to social problems, and in fact makes this a centerpiece of *Caritas in veritate*, which was written to commemorate Paul VI's 1967 *Populorum progressio* (On the Development of Peoples).

It will come as no surprise that Pope Francis reaffirms these themes, summoning international adversaries to seek peace by dialogue, recon-

134. John Paul II, Address to Diplomatic Corps, Rome, January 12, 1991, https://tinyurl.com/y9j6fm4x; and Address to the Diplomatic Corps, Rome, January 13, 2003, https://tinyurl.com/y8ccebe4, respectively.

135. "Cardinal Ratzinger on the Abridged Version of the Catechism," May 3, 2003, Zenit News Service, accessed August 24, 2017, https://tinyurl.com/yawexyjv. This statement was given the year before Joseph Ratzinger became pope.

136. Benedict XVI, Angelus Address, St. Peter's Square, February 18, 2007, https://tinyurl.com/y92y5ym3.

137. Benedict XVI, Welcome Ceremony Address, Nsimalen International Airport of Yaoundé, March 17, 2009, https://tinyurl.com/yac8bekw.

138. Benedict XVI, Meeting with the Members of the General Assembly of the United Nations Organization, New York, April 18, 2008, https://tinyurl.com/yaczdbcv.

139. Benedict XVI, *Caritas in veritate* (Charity in Truth), encyclical letter, June 29, 2009, 7, https://tinyurl.com/ybnvv5gm.

ciliation, negotiation, and compromise.[140] Praying for peace in Egypt, Francis proclaims "the true force of the Christian is the force of truth and love, which means rejecting all violence. Faith and violence are incompatible!" The way of Jesus is the way of peace, reconciliation, "living for God and for others." The strength of the Christian is "the force of meekness, the force of love."[141]

When Francis is confronted by the prospect of a military intervention in Syria by US and French "superpower," he responds similarly to John Paul and Benedict, insisting that "War brings on war! Violence brings on violence."[142] Reaching out to partners of all cultures and faiths, he adds:

> in the silence of the Cross, the uproar of weapons ceases and the language of reconciliation, forgiveness, dialogue, and peace is spoken. This evening, I ask the Lord that we Christians, and our brothers and sisters of other religions, and every man and woman of good will, cry out forcefully: violence and war are never the way to peace! . . . War always marks the failure of peace, it is always a defeat for humanity. . . . "war never again, never again war!" "Peace expresses itself only in peace, a peace which is not separate from the demands of justice but which is fostered by personal sacrifice, clemency, mercy and love." Forgiveness, dialogue, reconciliation—these are the words of peace, in beloved Syria, in the Middle East, in all the world![143]

There may be a margin of ambiguity in Pope Francis's position on using force for humanitarian purposes, due to some comments on defeating the international terrorist organization, the so-called Islamic State (IS or ISIS). In August 2014, he remarked informally to reporters that dialogue even with ISIS should not be considered a "lost cause," adding that, "I can only say that it is licit to stop the unjust aggressor. I underscore the verb 'stop'; I don't say bomb, make war—stop him. The means by which he may be stopped should be evaluated."[144]

Does the pope envision more limited and carefully targeted uses of

140. For an overview of Pope Francis's views of war and peace, see Christian Nikolaus Braun, "Pope Francis on War and Peace," *Journal of Catholic Social Thought* 15, no. 1 (2018): 63–87. The author argues that Francis is a "prophetic" voice on peace who remains essentially within the just war framework. I believe the peace and peacebuilding aspect of Francis's thought dominates over the just war aspect, and that the two ultimately exist in tension rather than being reconciled into one framework. At the same time, it is plausible to argue that, because Francis never completely rejects armed force, his view is a very "restrictive" version of just war theory. Yet I am not persuaded that this captures his emphasis; it is more plausible to argue that the Catholic magisterial tradition as a whole has evolved to a stance of restrictive just war theory.

141. Pope Francis, Angelus Address, St. Peter's Square, August 18, 2013, https://tinyurl.com/ybjddj7p.

142. Pope Francis, Angelus Address, September 1, 2013, https://tinyurl.com/y7r76oqa.

143. Pope Francis, "Vigil of Prayer for Peace" [in Syria], September 7, 2013.

144. Kathryn Jean Lopez, "Pope Francis on Iraq," *National Review*, August 18, 2014, accessed August 24, 2017, https://tinyurl.com/y8lw6e2o.

violence as a last resort? Or does he mean to limit intervention to nonviolent peacekeeping, civil society acts of nonviolent resistance and protest, or initiatives by Islamic religious leaders and faith communities to deter membership in ISIS? Kenneth Himes surmises that "one reason for the papal hesitancy" about armed force, beyond the fact that it very probably might not be effective or the last resort, is that use of force, particularly unilateral force, "can too easily slide into national interest" and away from humanitarian motives. In fact, any "decision for armed intervention is fraught with difficult judgments," so that there is far from a clear line from a prima facie duty to help to a justified and effective practical action.[145]

The threat of nuclear weapons is perhaps the most acute example of an area in which national interest, uncertainty of the adversary's intentions, and fearful, precipitous decision-making could combine to create a catastrophic international disaster. Pope Francis has amplified calls from every one of his predecessors since Pius XII for nuclear disarmament. This appeal and warning sounded especially clearly in John XXIII's *Pacem in terris,* which decreed that even before the immoral use of nuclear weapons to kill civilians, the dangerous gamble of "deterrence" and the arms race in general do violence to the poor by commandeering egregious amounts of economic resources.[146] In the early years of the administration of US president Donald J. Trump, North Korea was improving its nuclear weapons capacity, apparently afraid that the United States' attacks on Japan could be repeated on the Korean peninsula. Trump and the North Korean "supreme leader" Kim Jong-un exchanged several verbal threats and taunts over the escalating nuclear competition, but eventually met in Singapore, defusing a volatile situation at least temporarily. During this time, Pope Francis took an increasingly firm stand against nuclear weapons. In 2017 a Vatican conference (sponsored by the Dicastery for Promoting Integral Human Development) convened Nobel laureates, government and United Nations officials, theologians and peace activists to strategize paths to nuclear disarmament.[147] On this occasion, Francis insisted that not only the use of

145. Kenneth R. Himes, "Humanitarian Intervention and the Just War Tradition," in *Can War Be Just in the 21st Century? Ethicists Engage the Tradition,* ed. Tobias Winright and Laurie Johnston (Maryknoll, NY: Orbis, 2015), 60–61.

146. John XXIII, *Pacem in terris,* 112: "Justice, then, right reason and consideration for human dignity and life urgently demand that the arms race should cease; that the stockpiles which exist in various countries should be reduced equally and simultaneously by the parties concerned; that nuclear weapons should be banned; and finally that all come to an agreement on a fitting program of disarmament, employing mutual and effective controls."

147. Cindy Wooden, "Consistently Anti-Nuke: Pope Continues Papal Pleas for Disarmament," Catholic News Service, October 31, 2017, accessed February 21, 2018,

nuclear weapons but also the threat of their use, and indeed their very possession, are to be "firmly condemned." Weapons of mass destruction serve "a mentality of fear," create "a false sense of security," and can never be "the basis for peaceful coexistence."[148]

Sometimes episcopal conferences in regions where excessive and predatory violence is being used against local populations reassert the permissibility and even obligatory nature of armed intervention. In 2014, a regional bishops' meeting reported on the "horrible" conditions and levels of suffering in Syria and Iraq. Reflecting some of the tension in the papal voice on this situation, they asserted that "without true reconciliation based on justice and mutual forgiveness there will be no peace," yet they upheld "the right of the oppressed to self-defense." Moreover, they urged "the international community" to use "proportionate force to stop aggression and injustice against ethnic and religious minorities."[149]

An African theologian and scholar of peacebuilding, Elias Omondo Opongo, reiterates just how difficult this is to accomplish morally and successfully. Regional prevention, negotiation, and intervention by force if necessary is far preferable to action by outsiders, whose worldviews, values, and interests are unlikely to mesh with those of their ostensible beneficiaries. Although "in situations of extreme violations of human rights, it is permissible to intervene to stop human suffering," it is difficult to meet the criteria of last resort and reasonable hope of success. Moreover, "a sustainable peace" requires much more than stopping the violence, and, as the popes have repeatedly warned, peace bought with violence is rarely durable and just.[150]

During a 2015 visit to the United States, Pope Francis kept his focus on development and just peace through negotiation. He urged the

https://tinyurl.com /yc9elc6y. This article reviews statements of previous popes against nuclear weapons.

148. Pope Francis, "Prospects for a World Free of Nuclear Weapons and for Integral Disarmament," November 10, 2017, accessed February 22, 2018, https://tinyurl.com/ybsm5qxf. This statement constitutes a condemnation of the position accepting the morality of deterrence in the US bishops' 1983 pastoral letter, *The Challenge of Peace*. This moral condemnation, which in my view is not only principled but persuasive, returns us to the question posed by Reinhold Niebuhr: What is a politically feasible alternative? What should be and can be a path to that alternative? For a debate on the merits of the pope's statement, see Michael C. Desch and Gerard F. Powers, "No More Nukes An Exchange," *Commonweal*, February 9, 2018, accessed February 22, 2018, https://tinyurl.com/y7wdzssd.

149. Statement of the Latin Bishops of the Arab Regions (CELRA), October 4, 2014, accessed August 24, 2017, https://tinyurl.com/ybltu9ta.

150. Elias O. Opongo, "Just War and Its Implications for African Conflicts," in Winright and Johnston, *Can War Be Just?*, 155. See also Anne-Marie Slaughter, "A Regional Responsibility to Protect," in *Lessons from Intervention in the 21st Century: Legality, Legitimacy, and Feasibility*, ed. David Held and Kyle McNally, *Global Policy* ebook (2014), accessed August 25, 2017, https://tinyurl.com/y7hbh52g.

United Nations in New York to support sustainable development, end the hypocrisy of talking about peace while manufacturing arms, and exercise better leadership to find peaceful solutions to global conflicts, especially in the Middle East.[151] Pope Francis brought together religious leaders from multiple traditions in Assisi in 2016, commemorating the thirtieth anniversary of a similar gathering sponsored by John Paul II. There Francis prayed, "May we carry out our responsibility of building an authentic peace, attentive to the real needs of individuals and peoples, capable of preventing conflicts through a cooperation that triumphs over hate and overcomes barriers through encounter and dialogue. . . . Everyone can be an artisan of peace."[152]

In 2017, following a 2016 meeting on nonviolence and just peace convened in Rome by Pax Christi International and the Pontifical Council for Justice and Peace,[153] Pope Francis chose nonviolence as the theme of the annual papal World Day of Peace Message.[154] Diagnosing the present situation as a "horrifying *world war fought piecemeal*," and perhaps outlining themes for a future encyclical, the pope questions whether violence can produce anything more than "a cycle of deadly conflicts that benefit only a few 'warlords.'" Recognizing that lasting peace depends on

151. Pope Francis, Address to the General Assembly of the United Nations, September 25, 2015.

152. Pope Francis, "Appeal for Peace," Assisi, September 20, 2016, accessed February 22, 2018, https://tinyurl.com/y9bne3gv.

153. This conference issued a final consensus statement calling for an end to any teaching of just war theory under Catholic auspices and urging the Catholic Church as a whole to recommit to "gospel nonviolence." Extensive information about this conference, including its preparatory documents, final statement, and follow-up (including the 2017 World Day of Peace Message) can be found at the website of the Catholic Nonviolence Initiative, accessed August 24, 2017, https://tinyurl.com/y7yx93qt. For follow-up debate, see Mark J. Allman and Tobias Winright, "Protect Thy Neighbor: Why the Just-War Tradition Is Still Indispensable," *Commonweal*, June 17, 2016, 7–9, https://tinyurl.com/y8ercw3b; Lisa Sowle Cahill, "'A Church for Peace': Why Just-War Theory Isn't Enough," *Commonweal*, July 11, 2016, https://tinyurl.com/y9435y4h; Marie Dennis and Eli McCarthy, "Jesus and 'Just War'? Time to Focus on Just Peace and Gospel Nonviolence," *Huffington Post*, October 1, 2016, https://tinyurl.com/yb7hozka; Drew Christiansen, SJ, "Pope Francis Calls for a 'Politics of Nonviolence' in Annual World Day of Peace Message," *America*, December 12, 2016, https://tinyurl.com/y8lwgu3t; Gerald Schlabach, "Just War?," *Commonweal*, May 31, 2017, https://tinyurl.com/ybopcaj6; and Peter Steinfels, "The War against Just War," *Commonweal*, June 5, 2017, https://tinyurl.com/y7q4voxf; all accessed August 21, 2018. For an overview of this debate from a just-war perspective, see "Theological Roundtable: Must Just Peace and Just War Be Mutually Exclusive?," *Horizons* 45, no. 1 (2018), including Mark Allman, Drew Christiansen, Laurie Johnston, and Tobias Winright, "Must Just Peace and Just War Be Mutually Exclusive?," 105–8; Drew Christiansen, "The Nonviolence–Just War Nexus," 108–14; Tobias Winright, "Just War and Imagination Are Not Mutually Exclusive," 114–19; Laurie Johnston, "Talking about War," 119–23; and Mark J. Allman, "Practical Implications of Abandoning Just War," 123–27.

154. Pope Francis, "Nonviolence, a Style of Politics for Peace," World Day of Peace Message, January 1, 2017.

security, restorative justice, and reconciliation in local communities, he identifies survivors of violence as "the most credible promotors of non-violent peacemaking.[155] Offering the examples of Mother Teresa, Martin Luther King Jr., Mahatma Gandhi, and Khan Abdul Ghaffar Khan, he makes it clear that peacebuilding through "active nonviolence" is an international and interreligious vocation, as well as "the necessary complement to the Church's continuing efforts to limit the use of force by the application of moral norms" (just war norms?).[156] Finally, peacebuilding is an inclusive and holistic social program. It never loses sight of economic and political justice, including "the care of creation" and action for migrants, the poor, the sick, the imprisoned, the unemployed, victims of armed conflict, natural disasters, all forms of slavery and torture, and all those unjustly excluded or marginalized.[157]

The distinctive contribution of Catholic theology and social teaching to the Christian tradition of nonviolence is to put the emphasis not on refraining from violence as such, nor even on a countercultural church, but on the church's mission to embody Christ's peace, extending to political peace, and to work toward the conditions of peace in partnership with other social entities, religious and nonreligious. In the words of Paul VI, "If you want peace, work for justice."[158]

Since a lack of political will often prevents the success of high-level peace negotiations or impedes their implementation at the local level, it is key to the success of peacebuilding that there be momentum across society. In fact, the most effective teachers of gospel nonviolence and just peace are often local bishops, clergy, women and men religious, pastoral ministers, catechists, educators, community workers, and other members of local communities, as well as national and international Catholic nongovernmental organizations with a strong local presence. To connect with a broad spectrum of society, recent popes engage in symbolic actions that go beyond "teaching" in the sense of pronouncements and documents. Public actions and events can reach out to those of many faiths and span social differences and divisions. One example is the well-publicized prayer vigil for peace in Syria that Francis held in St. Peter's Square in September 2013. He was joined by 100,000 peace advocates, even as international leaders debated the possibility of military action. Another is the 1986 and 2016 gathering of religious leaders in Assisi to pray for peace, mentioned above. A further example is the prayer of

155. Francis, "Nonviolence," 2.
156. Francis, "Nonviolence," 4, 6.
157. Francis, "Nonviolence," 6
158. Paul VI, "If You Want Peace, Work for Justice," World Day of Peace Message, January 1, 1972.

three successive popes—John Paul, Benedict, and Francis—at the Western Wall or "Wailing Wall" in Jerusalem, the remnants of a platform on which the Second Temple was built.

International Catholic peacebuilding organizations such as Caritas Internationalis, Catholic Relief Services, the Catholic Peacebuilding Network, the Community of Sant' Egidio, Maryknoll, Franciscans International, the International Federation of Superiors General, Jesuit Relief Services, Pax Christi International, RENEW International, and Peacebuilders Initiative all carry the message of nonviolent peacebuilding toward a just peace. They are committed to resourceful and practical ways of transforming conflicts, frequently working amid ongoing violence. They often take great risks in the name of the gospel, seeking to bridge ethnic, racial, and religious divisions. These efforts are all embodiments of Catholic social tradition and action, and they are vital aspects of the future of Catholic peacebuilding.

Looking back over the recent past and the present history of Catholic teaching on war and peace, a striking paradox stands out. War and violence are condemned in no uncertain terms, because they destroy human life, human dignity, and human societies—and because they violate the Christian vocation to live in imitation of Christ. Nonviolence and peacebuilding toward just social living are not only commended but they are also seen as mandatory for all people, religions, and cultures. Yet at the same time, armed force in self-defense and, especially, in humanitarian intervention is still accepted, though never defended or exhorted at length, nor are specific proposed uses of force explicitly approved.

Perhaps this seemingly inconsistent message is a tacit recognition that decisions about nonviolence and force involve true moral dilemmas, that is, cases in which, to paraphrase Bonhoeffer, whatever one does, that which is omitted will give one no peace. The "downside" of force in cost to human life is obvious, but the renunciation of violence is not without its own human and moral price. Nonviolence can be politically successful more often than is usually recognized.[159] But when it is not, its price can be torture, rape, killing, and the bombing and burning of villages, cities, fields, natural resources, and material infrastructure. On the one hand, intervention or defense is never politically neutral and disinterested; in practice, it brings new forms of violence and devastation in its wake. On the other hand, the renunciation of all armed intervention by those with the power to limit atrocities could also amount to the "clean

159. See Erika Chenoweth and Maria Stephan, *Why Civil Resistance Works* (New York: Columbia University Press, 2011); and the website of the Nonviolent Peace Force, which works in conflict zones such as Sri Lanka, the Philippines, Myanmar, and South Sudan, accessed August 25, 2017, https://tinyurl.com/y8j3zfqz.

hands" of the privileged, a false righteousness above the fray of human suffering.

The popes may perceive that it is impossible to defend, yet difficult to exclude, any and all potential uses of armed force. Their collective choice, at least to date, is to put their energy and the moral voice of the church behind nonviolence. Perhaps they perceive that the role of Christian teachers and pastors is not to justify violence but to empower nonviolent peace with justice as far as possible, embodying God's reign and seeding Pope Francis's "social revolution." If and when violence is justified, others will ably furnish the reasons—and, one hopes, the "just war" limits.

In fact, Catholic just war thinkers use the theory primarily to critique and reject specific uses of armed force. Noting that recent popes and bishops have expressed extreme skepticism about justifying even humanitarian intervention, Gerard Powers proposes that just war theory can aid peacebuilding if it is used restrictively, and stresses that interventions should take primarily multilateral forms of conflict prevention and management, accompanied by postconflict reconciliation.[160] Whether or not one sees the use of armed force as ever just, there is no doubt that the ecclesial role is to tame and control justifications of mortal force in light of gospel ideals and practices, trusting that nonviolent strategies not only can bring peace but will do so more successfully than violence.[161]

---

160. Gerard F. Powers, "From an Ethic of War to an Ethics of Peacebuilding," in *From Just War to Modern Peace Ethics*, 292–96.

161. David Carroll Cochran reviews these developments with an analysis similar to that given here and discusses and critiques neoconservative dissenters, such as George Weigel and Richard John Neuhaus. See Cochran, "War and the Surprising Realism of Catholicism's Peace-Making Agenda," *Journal of Catholic Social Thought* 11, no. 1 (2014): 105–25. Powers, "From an Ethic of War," 287–89, discusses Weigel and Michael Novak.

10.

Peacebuilding
A Practical Strategy of Hope

An introduction to the theology and practice of Christian peacebuilding was provided in the first chapter.[1][2] Christian peacebuilders embrace

1. Parts of this chapter are based on "Peacebuilding: A Practical Strategy of Hope," *Journal of Catholic Social Thought* 11, no. 1 (2014): 47–66.

2. See Schreiter, Appleby, and Powers, eds., *Peacebuilding: Catholic Theology, Ethics, and Praxis* (Maryknoll, NY: Orbis, 2010) for a collection representing the theory and theology of peacebuilding, as well as practical examples from different regions. Prepared under the auspices of the Catholic Peacebuilding Network, both this book and the initiative as a whole are ecumenical and interreligious in orientation. In addition to work cited earlier (primarily in chapter 1), works by other Christian theorists of peacebuilding and just peace include Ronald J. Sider, *Nonviolent Action: What Christian Ethics Demands but Most Christians Have Never Really Tried* (Grand Rapids, MI: Brazos, 2015); David P. Gushee, ed., *Evangelical Peacemakers: Gospel Engagement in a War-Torn World* (Eugene, OR: Wipf & Stock, 2013); Jarem Sawatsky, *Justpeace Ethics: A Guide to Restorative Justice and Peacebuilding* (Eugene, OR: Wipf & Stock, 2008); and John Paul Lederach, *Building Peace: Sustainable Reconciliation in Divided Societies* (Washington, DC: United States Institute of Peace, 1997). The first two are Protestant, and the latter two Mennonite. Glen Stassen's just peacemaking practices are applied in an interreligious context in Susan Brooks Thistlethwaite, ed., *Interfaith Just Peacemaking: Jewish, Christian, and Muslim Perspectives on the New Paradigm of Peace and War* (New York: Palgrave Macmillan, 2012); and in Susan Thistlethwaite and Glen Stassen, *Abrahamic Alternatives to War: Jewish, Christian, and Muslim Perspectives on Just Peacemaking* (Washington, DC: United States Institute of Peace, 2008). A Special Report from the US Institute of Peace shows how important religious traditions and communities are to peacebuilding internationally, and the increasing attention they are being given by governments, nongovernmental organizations, and academia: Susan Hayward, *Religion and Peacebuilding: Reflections on Current Challenges and Future Prospects* (Washington, DC: United States Institute of Peace, 2012). As a scholar and practitioner of religious peacebuilding, Gerard F. Powers elaborates on the positive contributions and concrete strategies religion brings, especially in terms of integrating local, national, and international efforts ("Religion and Peacebuilding," in *Strategies of Peace: Transforming Conflict in a Violent World*, ed. Daniel Philpott and Gerard F. Powers (New York: Oxford University Press, 2010), 317–52. As a whole, this book displays the strengths and challenges of religious strategies of peacebuilding. See also *The Oxford Handbook of Religion, Conflict, and Peacebuilding*, ed. Atalia Omer, R. Scott Appleby, and David Little (New York: Oxford University Press, 2015).

gospel nonviolence as part of their active commitment to transform conflict and make the reign of God more visible under historically imperfect conditions. They do not all reject violence in every conceivable circumstance, but they do appreciate that use of violence always presents a moral dilemma or conflict, especially from a Christian standpoint. They focus not on possible justifications of violence, but on promising strategies of building just and peaceful societies in difficult circumstances. Peacebuilding goes beyond ending direct violent conflict. It "overlaps with development and good governance" and refers to "the broad, complex, and sustained process of creating, securing, protecting, and consolidating a peaceful order."[3]

This chapter will further highlight important dimensions of peacebuilding. These are the underappreciated effectiveness of nonviolent resistance to violent power; the reality that conflict and violence create long-lasting barriers to peace, creating dilemmas and conflicts within peacebuilding processes themselves; the importance of a broad view of restorative justice, and with it the importance of changing worldviews and imaginations across society; the crucial yet rarely recognized role of women peacebuilders in conflict zones; the important role of social and ecclesial practices in re-forming identities and dispositions; and the need to work interreligiously and interculturally to overcome exclusive identities and build sustainable structures of peace. The second half of this chapter will turn the peacebuilding lens back on the United States. US policies contribute to violence internationally. In addition, violence exists at home. Changing these realities requires broad social momentum toward restorative justice and reconciliation. What do we learn from US peacebuilders combatting racially motivated violence? How do they resemble peacebuilders globally? At least six shared dimensions of peacebuilding can be identified. These will initially be illustrated with international examples and, in conclusion, invoked to illumine the work of peacebuilders in the United States.

Nonviolent resistance works. Historically, Christian pacifism was the practice of a minority with little ambition or claim to political influence. It wasn't really until the middle of the last century that this stereotype of powerlessness began to erode. However, pacifism and nonviolence are still seen as more idealistic than realistic political stances, despite the fact that peacebuilding and religious peacebuilding have been actively and creatively alleviating conflict for decades. In fact, Martin Luther King

3. Susan Hayward and Katherine Marshall, "Religious Women's Invisibility: Obstacles and Opportunities," in *Women, Religion, and Peacebuilding: Illuminating the Unseen*, ed. Susan Hayward and Katherine Marshall (Washington, DC: United States Institute of Peace, 2015), 3.

from the 1960s and the Filipino People Power Movement in the 1980s are precedents. One way in which peacebuilders work is through dialogue, bringing members of communities together around goals and constructing shared social initiatives. But direct nonviolent resistance can also be very successful. When political violence is the problem, the first line of defense tends to be military. But could the results be dramatically different if comparable resources were poured into nonviolent action? Nonviolence does not always work—consider what happened to unarmed protesters in East Timor and Tiananmen Square. That being said, the power of nonviolence to resist and defeat adversaries is underestimated.

In their award-winning *Why Civil Resistance Works,* social scientists Erika Chenoweth and Maria Stephan make an evidence-based case that resisters can defeat an opponent by working through noninstitutional or even illegal channels, mobilizing diverse publics, and ultimately depriving oppressors of legitimacy and therefore of power by eroding the commitment and resource contribution of their support base.[4] They studied thousands of cases worldwide since 1900. In most cases or to a large extent, the power of even a state with resource and military capacity depends on the consent of the civilian population.[5] Hence two factors are key to the success of a nonviolent revolution: "mass mobilization that withdraws the regime's economic, political, social and even military support" and alienation of the adversary from its most important constituencies and providers of resources.[6] A "movement mindset" does not necessarily require a high degree of organization or intensely dedicated membership, but it does require funding, nonmonetary support, and "convening spaces" (physical or virtual), all of which could be supplied or enhanced by donors, nongovernmental, and governmental organizations.[7]

To give a concrete example, Maria Stephan discusses what it might take to defeat ISIS through civil resistance.[8] Technology could be an essential tool, given crackdowns and reprisals against assembly of

---

4. Hayward and Marshall, "Religious Women's Invisibility," 12.

5. Hayward and Marshall, "Religious Women's Invisibility," 25.

6. Hayward and Marshall, "Religious Women's Invisibility," 44.

7. Maria Stephan, Sadaf Lakhani, and Nadia Naviwala, "Aid to Civil Society: A Movement Mindset," USIP Special Report (Washington, DC: United States Institute for Peace, 2015). This and other USIP publications are available online at the USIP website, https://tinyurl.com/y9yq4poz.

8. Maria J. Stephan, "Civil Resistance vs. ISIS," *Journal of Resistance Studies* 1, no. 2 (2015): 127–50. A shorter version is "Defeating ISIS through Civil Resistance? Striking Nonviolently at Sources of Power Could Support Effective Solutions," USIP Olive Branch Blog, July 11, 2016, accessed August 25, 2017, https://tinyurl.com/y76qb6sn.

dissenters, and public resistance.[9] "Hacktivists" from outside support groups are already subverting ISIS's online social media recruiting mechanisms. Humor and satire, part of a long Arab tradition going back to ancient poetry, can also undermine authority and credibility. Testimonies by defectors can counter ISIS's claim to provide an honorable Muslim lifestyle; rebuttals by Muslim religious scholars would also erode support. Outsiders could support these forms of resistance and noncooperation by providing educational materials, by supporting alternative media and communication, and by strengthening the cybersecurity of resisters while undermining that of ISIS members. According to Stephan, organized nonviolent resistance was already going on in Syria, prior to any prospect of military intervention from outside; but instead of funding nonviolent resistance, the United States and potential collaborators turned to the feasibility of military options.

Maria Stephan's advice to the Catholic Church, for example, is that it "take its work on 'just peace' to the next, practical level," by prioritizing teaching and training that brings together the dialogical and the civil-resistance modes of nonviolence. "Catholic universities and peace-building organizations like Pax Christi, Mercy Corps, Caritas Internationalis, and Catholic Relief Services are well-placed to integrate dialogue with nonviolent collective action approaches in their education and field operations."[10] A historical example of religiously inspired, successful, nonviolent resistance is the campaign waged during the Second Liberian Civil War (1999–2003) by a coalition of Christian and Muslim women to pressure president Charles Taylor to attend peace talks in Ghana and finally to go into exile, preparing the way for the election of Liberia's first woman president, Ellen Johnson Sirleaf.[11] Led by Leymah Gbowee, the women used a combination of nonviolent mass protests that drew increasing numbers of women, tactics like a "sex strike" that drew media attention, and direct confrontation with Taylor and his supporters, even following them to Ghana and demonstrating outside the negotiation room. The women managed to alienate portions of Taylor's high-level support, first drawing sympathy and funds from an official in Taylor's government, Grace Minor; then winning the cooperation of the

9. See Kelly McKone, Maria J. Stephan, and Noel Dickover, "Using Technology in Nonviolent Activism against Repression," USIP Special Report (Washington, DC: United States Institute of Peace, 2015).

10. Maria J. Stephan, "What Happens When Your Replace a Just war with a Just Peace," *Foreign Policy,* May 16, 2016, accessed August 25, 2017, https://tinyurl.com/y7d73czf.

11. Gbowee and Sirleaf won the Nobel Peace Prize in 2011. On the story of Gbowee and her sister peacebuilders, see *Pray the Devil Back to Hell,* directed by Gini Reticker, produced by Abigail E. Disney (New York: Fork Films, 2008), 72 minutes, accessed 6/13/2012, https://tinyurl.com/yagmpvbo.

head mediator in Accra, former Nigerian president General Abubakar. While the mediation mode of nonviolence meshes better with inclusive gospel values like reconciliation, the resistance mode can sometimes be more effective in aiding and empowering the oppressed. Perhaps both are necessary and justified from the standpoint of Christian social ethics.

Violent conflict leaves deep wounds and requires a comprehensive response. When one thinks of the extreme and protracted killing and human rights abuses suffered in Syria or Liberia, or at the hands of ISIS, it is easy to recognize that the wounds of war in the body politic are deep. While Maria Stephan and colleagues argue that nonviolent conflicts and revolutions have better long-term success than violent ones, other evidence shows that when violent conflicts are settled by negotiations rather than by the victory of one side, they actually are more likely to break out again into violence.[12] This may seem counterintuitive. But upon reflection, some reasons surface. A negotiated peace will cede some institutionalized power to competing sides, meaning that power is shared among greater and lesser perpetrators and possibly that no one authority has firm control. Further, no matter who settles a conflict, or under what peace arrangements, not everyone in the society will participate or consent to the same degree, nor benefit equally, nor have the same interest either in ending conflict or prolonging it in lower-level or behind-the-scenes ways.

A good example is the fate of United Nations Resolution 1325, adopted by the UN Security Council in 2000 to protect women from gender-based violence after peace accords have been agreed. The magnitude of wounds made by violence varies according to social status, and it especially affects those who exist at the intersection of multiple disadvantages, such as gender, sexual orientation, race, ethnicity, class or caste, religious affiliation, and poverty. Even in countries that are signatories to this Resolution 1325, rape and other types of violence against women often continue with impunity after a conflict has supposedly ended, because buy-in is lacking in the culture as a whole, or by local communities and authorities. When former adversaries coexist on more or less equal terms, it is that much easier for remaining tensions to regain political traction.

Moreover, even when or to the extent that a postconflict society is solidly on the way to reconstruction and the rule of law, past wrongs continue to have deep present effects. Daniel Philpott calls these "the wounds of political injustice."[13] He distinguishes between primary

---

12. Daniel Philpott, "Introduction," *Strategies of Peace*, 7.
13. Daniel J. Philpott, *Just and Unjust Peace: An Ethic of Political Reconciliation* (New York:

wounds like denial of human rights and secondary wounds like memory, which can impede healing and political cooperation. The primary wounds are human rights violations; physical damage with lasting effects on victims, especially torture; traumatic uncertainty about who is responsible for harms like the death of a loved one, why the harm occurred, and its circumstances; lack of public acknowledgment, or acknowledgment by perpetrators, of the suffering of victims, making them feel "invisible"; the "standing victory" of the perpetrator's injustice in a "culture of impunity"; and harm to the persons of wrongdoers, who in perpetrating evil "diminish themselves." Secondary wounds include memories and emotions arising from traumatic events and wrongs suffered (or perpetrated). They also include derivative judgments about justice and responsibility and the actions that should be taken in the future. These judgments can apply to groups and states, not just to individuals. Finally, actions follow from judgments, as individuals, states, and international bodies determine whether and how to bring ostensible perpetrators to justice and make (or not make) reparations to supposed victims. Memories, emotions, and judgments can lead to resentment, hatred, and a desire for acts of vengeful retaliation.

Peacebuilding is multidimensional, consists in a gradual and fallible process, and involves moral dilemmas. While the restoration of right relationships among individuals is an important and worthy goal, the primary goal of political reconciliation is the constitution or reconstitution of a society in which all can trust that their basic needs are met and human rights protected.[14] This is the primary political meaning of just peace. To build a just peace requires that violations or attempted violations of human rights generally will be met with the effective, fair and transparent rule of law within just and participatory institutions. A supporting category is "restorative justice," which does not dispense with just punishment, but aims ultimately to bring those who have committed violence and those who have suffered it into new relationships of mutual respect, based on compensation for harm, and the ability to contribute to the common good of society going forward.[15] Both political reconciliation and restorative justice as a dimension within it require a holistic approach,[16]

Oxford University Press, 2012), 30–47. See also Daniel J. Philpott, ed., *The Politics of Past Evil: Religion, Reconciliation, and the Dilemmas of Transitional Justice* (Notre Dame, IN: University of Notre Dame Press, 2006).

14. On political reconciliation, see Philpott, *Just and Unjust Peace*, 54–58.

15. Stephen J. Pope, "Restorative Justice as a Prophetic Path to Peace," *CTSA Proceedings* 65 (2010): 19–34. See also John W. De Gruchy, *Reconciliation: Restoring Justice* (Minneapolis: Fortress, 2003).

16. Philpott, *Just and Unjust Peace*, 4.

as is widely recognized by peacebuilding theorists. In fact, the need for a holistic, comprehensive and multidimensional political response to violence is a key point of peacebuilding and perhaps especially of religious peacebuilding.[17]

The processes of peacebuilding, restorative justice, and political reconciliation are necessarily complicated and imperfect. In fact, speaking of South Africa, Charles Villa-Vicenzio says that the process of working toward "better understanding, respect, and trust building" is "inevitably uneven," sometimes "counterproductive," and "even violent."[18] Of course reconciliation and peacebuilding processes can fail and break down; but the ambiguous nature of peacebuilding is deeper than that. An example often raised, including by Philpott and Villa-Vicenzio, is that just peace requires trust, and trust cannot coexist with impunity. Peacebuilders indefatigably try to bring former adversaries together in mutual commitment to the common good going forward. However, in the inevitable case that some perpetrators refuse this effort, the rule of law will sometimes require coercive force, up to and including weapons. Moreover, the very project of bringing ongoing perpetrators to justice can play into and exacerbate social divisions that remain, even inciting reprisals. And in the larger picture, bringing adversaries to the negotiating table may have already required compromises and concessions regarding culpability, punishment, and reparations, if not total amnesty for past crimes. As Villa-Vicenzio states, if past perpetrators of gross human rights violations now want "to contribute to transforming the country, then we need where necessary to 'strike a deal.'"[19]

For this reason, Todd Whitmore maintains that peacebuilding, especially Catholic peacebuilding, needs a much more robust and operative concept of sin.[20] Sin can make even peacebuilding a morally conflicted and ambiguous enterprise. Peacebuilding unites partners with different levels of commitment to the justice and integrity of the process. Agents are inevitably entangled in decisions and policies that enable the wounds of past injustice to continue as part of the cost of building a more just but not entirely just peace. Philpott perceives that peacebuilding involves a "predicament" because practices are "suffused with blemish. . . . If the practices were ineffectual, the ethic would be futile; if they

---

17. See, for example, the essays in *Strategies of Peace*, especially John Paul Lederach and R. Scott Appleby, "Strategic Peacebuilding: An Overview," 19–44.

18. Charles Villa-Vicenzio, *Walk with Us and Listen: Political Reconciliation in Africa* (Washington, DC: Georgetown University Press, 2009), 170.

19. Villa-Vicenzio, *Walk with Us and Listen*, x.

20. Todd D. Whitmore, "Peacebuilding and Its Challenging Partners: Justice, Human Rights, Development, and Solidarity," in Schreiter, Appleby, and Powers, *Peacebuilding*, 175.

did not involve partiality, compromise, and intractable dilemmas, the ethic would be pointless."[21]

For the peacebuilder and the peacebuilding ethic, this underscores the importance of maximizing all efforts toward broad social conversion, and to enhancing the integration of peacebuilding at all levels, from local communities (and their churches, mosques or temples) to midlevel entities in the national context, to regional and international social initiatives, policies, and laws. Religious institutions can be especially useful and effective in that they have a presence at all these levels. The Mennonite John Paul Lederach, who works with the Catholic Peacebuilding Network, has noted that the Roman Catholic Church has an almost unparalleled local, regional, and international networked presence and can use its transnational nongovernmental relief and service organizations to do the work of peacebuilding in a coordinated way.

Lederach himself has developed a widely referenced model of peacebuilding, emphasizing, for example, that it requires leaders at the top (high visibility leaders, high-level negotiations and actions like cease fire), middle range (ethnic and religious leaders, academics, staff of aid organizations, and actions like workshops and conflict resolution training, peace commissions), and grassroots (community leaders and activists, local health officials, refugee camp leaders, doing grassroots dialogue, training, psychosocial assistance), all of whose activities can form an integrated network of change agents.[22] Lederach stresses the necessity of building a "peace constituency" of people who can be resources for peacebuilding within a conflict setting itself, using cultural resources.[23] Ultimately what is required for successful peacebuilding—for reducing situations where wounds continue, and enhancing those in which both political and personal reconciliation are accomplished—is a transformation of imaginations and worldviews so that a different reality is grasped as truly possible.[24]

This is an essential part of the hope of survivors, but it is equally and perhaps even more necessary to the reintegration of perpetrators. Song, story, art, and ritual can be powerful vehicles of conversion and change in which the participants re-envision not only their relation to their former adversary, but also their own identity. In a coauthored study, Leder-

21. Philpott, *Just and Unjust Peace*, 5.
22. Lederach, *Building Peace*, chart on 39.
23. Lederach, *Building Peace*, 94–97.
24. See John Paul Lederach, *The Moral Imagination: The Art and Soul of Building Peace* (New York: Oxford University Press, 2010).

ach and his daughter Angela Jill Lederach provide many moving cases.[25] Angela Lederach writes of her experiences in West Africa, including Liberia, where after the war child soldiers and child mothers, many of whom had been abducted a decade ago, streamed out of the forest with literally nowhere to go. In many cases their villages, homes. and families had been destroyed by their own hands or those of their fellow abductees. In all cases, they were crushed down by the stigma of the life they had endured and the atrocities they had been forced to commit. Outside one village a small band of ragged, dirty, hungry, and unarmed boys and young men gathered and subsisted around the trunk of a large kum tree they called the Tree of Frustration. They felt unable to enter the village; that was as far as they would go.

The men of the village skirted the path that led by the tree. The women began to approach a few at a time, sometimes leaving food and engaging the boys in conversation—talking about the ancestors, the community, telling folktales, singing, and praying. They built a palava hut near the tree, the traditional place for resolving conflicts. As Lederach puts it, they "surrounded" the boys and the tree, making a "shared space" in which their identities could be recreated. When their relationship was strong enough for the boys to agree to enter the village, the "mothers" demanded that they first clean up and cut their long, matted hair. This turned into a daylong haircutting ritual by the tree, enacting a traditional form of intimacy between mothers and children; in effect, the young men were symbolically reborn.[26] If celebrated in similarly context-specific forms, Christian rituals like baptism and Eucharist, as well as nonsacramental liturgies, carry rich possibilities for the constitution or reconstitution of community and of just peace after division and violence.[27]

Women are essential peacebuilders. As the previous incident reveals, women are not only targets of violence, they are often key to rebuilding broken community relations, encouraging others to acknowledge and

25. John Paul Lederach and Angela Jill Lederach, *When Blood and Bones Cry Out* (New York: Oxford University Press, 2010).

26. Lederach and Lederach, *When Blood and Bones Cry Out*, 147–49, chapter written by Angela Lederach.

27. See Robert J. Schreiter, "The Catholic Social Imaginary and Peacebuilding: Ritual, Sacrament, and Spirituality," in Schreiter, Appleby, and Powers, *Peacebuilding*, 221–39. Tobias Winright invokes liturgical formation as a resource for Christians in the United States and other nations whose neocolonial policies and military actions often exacerbate the conditions leading to conflict in the global South. See Tobias Winright, "The Liturgy as a Basis for Catholic Identity, Just War Theory, and the Presumption against War," in *Catholic Identity and the Laity*, ed. Timothy P. Muldoon, College Theology Society Annual 54 (Maryknoll, NY: Orbis, 2009), 134–51.

overcome the wounds of war. They take initiative to set aside divisions and harms of the past, while men consider it unjustified or pointless. Yet there are few globally recognized women peacebuilders, and where religious communities or organizations are active in bringing peace, it is exceedingly rare that women's role is highlighted. Women are often denied access to political spaces where men dominate. Women are usually marginalized from formal peacebuilding activities and negotiations, and they lack access to institutional support, funding, and policy-setting.[28] Moreover, men have more control over the processes by which policy is (or is not) implemented. For peacebuilding to succeed more fully in its reconciling and restorative roles, the presence and voices of women must be appreciated, amplified, and brought into peace and development negotiations, policies, and implementation at all levels.[29]

When previously excluded women gain power, they sometimes imitate traditional models of power as dominance and control. Yet women typically bring specific assets to peacebuilding, especially inclusivity and a commitment to justice informed by compassion and forgiveness. Perhaps women's disadvantaged role in patriarchal societies helps them to recognize the effects of structural violence. Religious women frequently stand up for all people's inherent dignity, including perpetrators. Women seek democratic participation, and "are keenly aware of how external power dynamics, including between urban elite and rural poor, majority and minority communities, or among identity groups, can seep into peacebuilding programs and processes."[30] Women are especially engaged in citizen advocacy, drawing together disempowered or minority groups, or other women—on behalf of "those suffering the brunt of war."[31]

Rightly, men who are religious peacebuilders are recognized for the valuable work they do and the risks they courageously take. In the drug wars in Colombia, for example, Roman Catholic bishops have been

28. Hayward and Marshall, "Religious Women's Invisibility," 1–2.

29. See Sanam Naraghi Anderlini, *Women Building Peace, What They Do, Why It Matters* (Boulder, CO: Lynne Rienner, 2007); and Emiko Noma, Aker, and Freeman, "Heeding Women's Voices: Breaking Cycles of Conflict and Deepening the Concept of Peacebuilding," *Journal of Peacebuilding and Development* 7, no. 1 (2012): 7–32.

30. Noma, Dee Aker, and Jennifer Freeman, "Heeding Women's Voices," 20. Speaking specifically about Catholic women, Maryann Cusimano Love confirms this same picture in "Catholic Women Building Peace: Invisibility, Ideas, Institutions Expand Participation," in Hayward and Marshall, *Women, Religion, and Peacebuilding*, 41–69. She highlights that while Catholic women share the values of Catholic social teaching, such as participation, restoration, right relationship, and reconciliation, women are often excluded from formal leadership, even though their presence is essential to the day-to-day activities of the Catholic Church, which is hardly alone in this regard.

31. Hayward and Marshall, "Women's Invisibility," 22.

among the few mediators trusted by adversaries on all sides. The episcopal conference's National Conciliation Commission worked tirelessly to resolve the violence among competing factions in their country in a peace settlement, which was reached in 2017. Individual priests and bishops have ventured into very dangerous situations among armed combatants to negotiate or to offer sacraments in the hope of converting hearts.[32]

Yet clergy also often receive credit for the women working in allied ministries, or they receive appreciation for more visible gestures while women's day-to-day persistence in local community-building and problem-solving stays under the surface of public attention. One reason for this, no doubt, is that women frequently operate by creating relationships of mutual support and networks that enable community survival. For women, strength is often found in collective empowerment. Women often mobilize solidarity, support, and volunteers by organizing through their religious communities or institutions. Funders and intermediary organizations in the global North and South (such as the Catholic Peacebuilding Network, the women Peacebuilders Progam at the Kroc Institute at the University of San Diego, the international Network of Engaged Buddhists, and Action Asia) can provide resources to these networks. They can increase capacity and infrastructure, facilitate the sharing of experiences and best practices at the international level, and provide educational opportunities for network leaders.[33]

When I had the privilege to travel to Colombia with the CPN as a theological advisor in 2007, we not only visited the bishops' conference but also made "site visits" to witness local peacebuilding activities. In a barrio near Bogotá, the inhabitants had been displaced from their rural villages by the rampant violence caused by the three warring groups: the leftist Revolutionary Armed Forces (FARC), the National Liberation Army (ELN), and paramilitary forces. The name of a group of women working in the barrio captures eloquently the way they envision their teamwork: "Hormiguitas de la Paz" (Little Ants of Peace). Although the slum dwellers were threatened with eviction as illegal squatters, they were still being charged for water and electricity, and their children were in constant danger of conscription by armed groups. But the women banded together to accompany children to school, to build a one-room community center by digging out a hillside, and to use microgrants to produce income for their families. These efforts were supported by a

---

32. See John Paul Lederach, "The Long Journey Back to Humanity," in Schreiter, Appleby, and Powers, *Peacebuilding*, 33–38.

33. Jacqueline Ogega and Katherine Marshall, "Strengthening Religious Women's Work for Peace," in Hayward and Marshall, *Women, Religion, and Peacebuilding*, 292–93.

small Catholic foundation, Codo a Codo (Elbow to Elbow), whose guide and mentor is a Catholic nun, Sr. Inez.[34]

Theologians working on peace tend to focus similarly on formal religious leadership, male theologians, and male organizational representatives. In some ways, the marginalization of women in Catholic institutions and in public representation has freed them from constraints on their activity so that they can work more creatively and effectively behind the scenes to build peace, including work with members of different religious traditions. Women's willingness to "reach across lines of difference in tense environments," to "mobilize communities," and to challenge dominant theological constructions of gender roles when working for peace, "holds the promise to change discourse and preconceptions about how religious organizations can be involved in peacebuilding work."[35]

Women can often exploit traditional roles (especially motherhood) to advance the cause of just peace, but reinforcing stereotypes and with them limits is always a danger. Women can be "locked into" grassroots activities such as trauma healing, education, community services, or parish outreach programs, while the far-reaching consequences of gender inequities, and the ways they contribute to violence, are overlooked or denied.[36] Therefore women in general and religious women in particular (including members of women's religious congregations) have a tough challenge in building bridges for peace, while also advocating for and claiming their own dignity, rights, and authority. To be sure, in Liberia, Ellen Johnson Sirleaf became president, and she and Leymah Gbowee won a Nobel Prize. But they are the exceptions. The women reconcilers at the Tree of Frustration were denied any further role by village men, after the former child soldiers had been accepted back into the community. It was only when the young men themselves insisted on the "mothers'" participation, that their presence and voice were acknowledged by village leaders.

Yet a different case from Burundi, in the Great Lakes region of Africa, shows how one woman courageously and in the spirit of Christ converted her mothering role into a multipronged social intervention that set a different example for leadership in church and society. Like its

34. See further examples in an essay by a colleague, David Hollenbach, SJ, who was present for the barrio visit I describe, "Lessons from the Wounded Edge," *The Tablet,* (August 11, 2007), 8–9.

35. Hollenbach, "Lessons from the Wounded Edge," 3.

36. On gender stereotypes and peacebuilding, see Susan Hayward and Katherine Marshall, "Religious Women's Invisibility," 4–6, and "Women Peacebuilders," 31–33; Maryann Cusimano Love, "Catholic Women Building Peace," 58–59; and Susan Hayward and Katherine Marshall, "Conclusion," in Hayward and Marshall, *Women, Religion and Peacebuilding.*

neighbor, Rwanda, where a 1994 genocide led to the deaths of over 800,000 people, Burundi has suffered politically motivated conflict over Hutu and Tutsi "ethnic" identities that were in fact imposed by colonial rulers. "The 'Divide and Rule' policy practiced in the colonies was aimed at creating differences among the people and favoring one group, which enabled the colonial officials to consolidate their rule."[37] These identities were later manipulated to serve political parties and ideologies after Africa was divided into nation states in the postcolonial era. Burundi saw ethnic violence similar to that experienced by Rwanda during a civil war beginning in 1993.

Although a significant number of members of the Catholic Church, including priests and nuns, participated in the ruthless murder of their coworkers, neighbors, and even family members, some did resist the tremendous evils occurring.[38] Emmanuel Katongole, a Catholic priest and former student of Stanley Hauerwas, recounts the witness of a Catholic woman, Maggy Barankitse. Despite rising danger, Maggy adopted seven homeless Hutu and Tutsi children. After the killings began, many Hutus took shelter at the bishop's residence, where she worked. One Sunday Tutsi assailants invaded the residence, tied up Maggy, and murdered seventy-two Hutus, although her own children escaped by hiding in the sacristy. Maggy saved twenty-five more children from the burning building and secured shelter for them with the assistance of a German aid worker. Maggy recalls that God's call and an incredible strength came to her on that day, along with a powerful, even mystical, experience of God's love.

Thousands of children and former child soldiers eventually came to Maggy. She founded Maison Shalom to care for them, which expanded into four children's villages and a children's center, then into shelters for over 20,000 children in Burundi, the Democratic Republic of Congo, and Rwanda. The children are given an education and job training, but most importantly they learn to grow beyond hatred and bitterness to rediscover their identities as children of God. After the government of Burundi shut down Maison Shalom's operations in retaliation for Maggy's human rights advocacy, she moved to neighboring Rwanda

37. Bernard Noel Rutikanga, "Rwanda: Struggle for Healing at the Grassroots," in *Artisans of Peace: Grassroots Peacemaking among Christian Communities*, ed. Mary Ann Cjeka and Tom Bamat (Maryknoll, NY: Orbis, 2003), 135.

38. Four Catholic priests were indicted for their role in the genocide by the UN International Criminal Tribunal for Rwanda, and the Rwandan bishops apologized for the role of the Catholic Church in 2016. See Deborah Bloom and Brianna Duggan, "Rwanda's Catholic Church Says Sorry for Its Role in 1994 Genocide," CNN, November 21, 2016, accessed February 22, 2018, https://tinyurl.com/ycq7v6af. Pope Francis apologized on behalf of the Roman Catholic Church in 2017.

and continued her work with refugee children. Sustained by prayer and the Eucharist, as well as by a large community of supporters inside and outside the church, Maggy sees her real call as proclaiming the gospel through her life, the "good news" of God's love, revealed to her especially as God's presence and power on the cross.[39] She is one of what Katongole calls "ambassadors of reconciliation" (2 Cor 5:18–20), living a "kingdom realism" in the face of violence—standing up to violence, renewing Christian communities of faith and life, and beginning a transformation of the societies around them.[40]

To build a lasting peace, it is essential to engage structurally with injustices that cause tension, and to reach the root causes of conflict, furthering development.[41] This brings the Christian peace mission into partnership with other religious traditions, as well as with other entities in civil society and government. Here women are also vital targets and agents. To take just one illustration, Catholic Relief Services has initiated a project with the Catholic dioceses at the borders of the DRC, Rwanda, and Burundi to bring together sixty women cross-border traders, who distrust one another due to different ethnic or religious backgrounds and nationalities. This project builds informal networks of trust and solidarity, while improving skills, businesses, and long-term financial security, thus increasing the women's status in families and communities. While overcoming prejudices and building friendships along with economic assets, the women traders become "agents for peaceful change" in their communities.[42]

Formative or re-formative social practices are key to lasting and just peace. It is not easy for people who have been bitter adversaries to see one another in a new light, as members of the same community, who contribute to and share in the common good together. Contemporary social sciences make it clear that individual identity is strongly shaped by social context and by the cultures, practices, and institutions in which individuals participate. This does not mean human freedom and self-determination do

---

39. Emmanuel Katongole, *The Sacrifice of Africa* (Grand Rapids, MI: William B. Eerdmans, 2011), 169–97. See also Emmanuel Katongole, *Born from Lament: The Theology and Politics of Hope in Africa* (Grand Rapids, MI: William B. Eerdmans, 2017), 229–33.

40. Emmanuel Katongole, *Mirror to the Church: Resurrecting Faith after Genocide in Rwanda* (Grand Rapids, MI: Zondervan, 2009), 110–11.

41. Elias Omondi Opongo, "Strategies and Approaches in the Catholic Theology of Peacebuilding in Africa: What Have We Learned?," presentation at *Peace From the Ground Up: Post Conflict Socialization, Religion, and Reconciliation in Africa*, Capetown, South Africa, June 5–7, 2013, sponsored by Kroc Institute for International Peace Studies and Institute for Justice and Reconciliation.

42. Catholic Relief Services, "Strengthening Trade, Building Peace," July 13, 2016, accessed August 30, 2017, https://tinyurl.com/yd5ljqh6.

not exist, but that they arise within a shaping environment. Institutions and practices are not "external" to individuals, because identity arises in and through participation. It is the intentions and actions of individuals that sustain cultures, practices, and institutions; institutions and social structures are simply the social organization of individual agency, which, when collectively coordinated and encouraged, takes on direction and efficacy greater than that of an individual alone, or of an unorganized or loosely organized group of individuals.

This is why peacebuilding movements or movements of nonviolent civil resistance can be such powerful forces for good and for transformation, both of social practices and institutions, and of individual and group worldviews. Yet it is also why patterns of injustice are intransigent, conscripting the identities, social perceptions, and habitual behavior of participants, so that the possibilities of mutual respect, political reconciliation, and just peace fail to penetrate the status quo.[43] "Because resistance entails a price, most people most of the time make decisions that avoid significant costs and provide significant benefits. They 'go along' and sustain the existing social structure by their compliance."[44] Importantly, such patterns of behavior also come with sustaining symbols systems that help connect them to the value systems and worldviews of which they are a part. These symbols give force to the significance of the pattern or structure for the participants, often connecting it to religious, ethnic, or national identities that it serves. The worldview and the structure, as well as the identities of participants can be formed around a just and peaceful, or a violent and exclusionary, set of symbols. These are often given transcendent or religious meaning, which can become a vehicle either for solidarity and altruism or for the kind of "collective egotism" that Reinhold Niebuhr saw as the social manifestation of sin. This explains the depth of wounds of war, the persistence of sexism even in peacebuilding movements, the dependence of lasting peace on the mitigation of root causes, and Whitmore's observation that peacebuilding requires a robust concept of social sin.[45]

43. For an illustration and critical theological-ethical discussion, see Kristin Heyer, "Social Sin and Immigration: Good Fences Make Bad Neighbors," *Theological Studies* 71, no. 2 (2010): 410–36. Heyer argues that structures are both the cause and the consequence of the moral quality of individual participation. Thus individuals bear responsibility for situations and ongoing practices in which they participate, even if they are not the single, primary, or independent cause.

44. Daniel K. Finn, "What Is a Sinful Social Structure?," *Theological Studies* 77, no. 1 (2016): 153.

45. See Mark O'Keefe, *What Are They Saying about Social Sin?* (New York: Paulist, 1990). O'Keefe recognizes that sin is not an "external" force or reality that "shapes" individual consciousness, it is both internal and external to individuals as participating in a social environment. Catholic social teaching recognizes the barrier of structural sin, but not always how interde-

As the above case of the women traders demonstrates, profound changes in worldviews and attitudes do not occur unless there is the kind of practical validation of social trust that occurs when people share in activities together around shared goals. To move from a sinful, exclusionary, and violent worldview to a just, inclusive, and peaceful one, with its attendant set of practices, institutions, and symbols, requires new patterns of action, not just verbal persuasion or preaching. An extremely clear example of the importance of social identity formation for the values of peace and justice is the story of Maggy Barankitse, who, inspired by love, created villages in Burundi where children could grow up without hatred and bitterness in their hearts. Maggy created a gracious environment within but not of the murderously divisive surrounding culture that had taken the children's parents and families. She interrupted the cycle of violence to form a new generation whose identities were different. This also describes the patient work of the village women at the Tree of Frustration; it describes the Hormiguitas de la Paz, who were empowering women to recognize their own collective agency for peace; it describes the work of Myla Leguro, a Catholic Relief Services staff member in the Philippines, who runs the Mindanao Peacebuilding Institute, where Muslims, Christians, and indigenous peoples with a conflicted history can learn a different way to see one another and become partners for peace.[46]

Taking social re-formation to the necessary next level, Myla knows that if the community goes forward structured by continuing injustices, then respectful coexistence is superficial and not lasting. She coauthored a report for CRS on land reform, since marginalization of indigenous peoples and Muslims from rights to their ancestral land, by colonial and postcolonial governments, is an ongoing cause of conflict. Not waiting for national reforms, CRS is implementing a plan to use traditional processes and authorities to resolve land disputes. As a "traditional leader" and "village councilor" commented, "Now, people listen to each

---

pendent it is with individual and group identities. John Paul II sees that sinful structures are "difficult to remove," but depicts them as "rooted in personal sin" and "the concrete acts of individuals" (*Sollicitudo rei socialist* 36). While this is true, personal sin and action are also rooted in sinful structures.

46. See Myla Leguro's biography, accessed August 31, 2017, https://tinyurl.com /y8fgovnm; and Myla Leguro, "The Many Dimensions of Catholic Peacebuilding: Mindanao Experience," Catholic Peacebuilding Network, 2008, accessed August 31, 2017, https://tinyurl.com/ y9hmmtpf.

other."[47] Social practices that form identity must be social justice practices as well as spiritual and interpersonal practices.

Forming people differently for a different life together is necessary to every illustration of peacebuilding treated in this book. Core dispositions (virtues and vices), personal behavior, and patterns of social life are interdependent. Social life is no mere product or result of virtues and vices; it instills and enables them too, for the social relationships in which we participate are coconstitutive of our identities and self-understandings.

Interreligious and intercultural cooperation is necessary to expand and revise personal and social identities and create the worldviews, symbols, and structures that sustain and express them. The need for communication and practical action across boundaries of identity has been amply illustrated by many of the foregoing peacebuilders, especially Myla Leguro. Yet pluralistic cooperation is worth lifting up more explicitly. A final example, that of Zilka Spahić Šiljak, a Muslim woman from Bosnia and Herzegovina, will bring into view some concrete dimensions of structural sin, the need for re-formative practices, and the resistance of personal and communal identity-formations that make recurrent violence more likely.

The former Yugoslavia was formed against the background and in a continuing history of contested territories, religiously exacerbated violence, and political turmoil going back to the sixth century. From 1463 to 1878, the region was ruled by the Ottoman Turks. The large numbers of Bosnians who converted to Islam became the privileged class, whereas the Christian Serbs and Croats were mostly peasants. In 1878, Ottoman control was supplanted by the Austro-Hungarian Empire. The event catalyzing World War I was the 1914 assassination in Sarajevo of the Austro-Hungarian archduke Franz Ferdinand by a Serb nationalist. After the war, the territories and ethnic groups were united and named the Kingdom of Yugoslavia in 1929. In 1945, the dictator Marshall Tito consolidated control of the region, which he maintained for thirty-five years. The federation of Yugoslavia comprised three major ethnic groups: the Serbs (primarily Orthodox Christians), the Croats (Roman Catholics), and the Bosniaks (Muslims).

In 1991, the eruption of violence in Croatia began the disintegration of the country, due largely to a struggling economy, continuing ethnic-religious tensions, and the absence of a line of succession after Tito. Slobodon Milošević, a Croat Serbian nationalist, exploited the power vacuum and attempted to maintain by force a united country, under his

---

47. Nell Bolton and Myla Leguro, *Local Solutions to Land Conflict in Mindanao: Policy Lessons from Catholic Relief Services' Applying the 3 Bs (Binding, Bonding, Bridging) to Land Conflict Project*, Catholic Relief Services, 2015, accessed June 20, 2017, https://tinyurl.com/ycsk2bp9.

control. By the end of 1992, Slovenia, Croatia, Macedonia, and Bosnia and Herzegovina had all seceded from Yugoslavia. When Serb paramilitary forces set up barricades and snipers in the streets of Sarajevo, thousands of Sarajevo residents demonstrated, at first successfully. However, the Serbian paramilitary soon began a campaign of ethnic cleansing of Bosniaks and Croats, laying siege to Mostar and Sarajevo. Ultimately Croats and Bosniaks also took up arms, and atrocities were committed on all sides. International peace initiatives failed in 1993 and 1994. In 1995, NATO attacked Serb forces in response to a massacre of 8,000 Muslim Bosniaks at Srebrenica. In 1995 the Dayton Peace Accords were signed, with Bosnia and Herzegovina emerging as an independent state.[48] Between 1993 and 2017, the International Criminal Court for the Former Yugoslavia convicted and sentenced ninety people for crimes against humanity, genocide, and other war crimes, including the former Serbian and subsequently Yugoslavian president Slobodan Milošević.

This series of events has resulted in a "classic" case of an uneasy "peace" established by outside forces, lacking the consent of the governed and disturbed by remaining ethnic resentments, prejudicial historical "memories" of injuries and insults, and religious alignment with factional politics. It illustrates the many moral ambiguities of using armed force, and specifically of humanitarian intervention, to accomplish political goals and establish human security, even when it is justified in the name of protecting the innocent. Religion has played a major role in fomenting divisions and violence and continues to do so, validating the ideology of each group as fighting for ancestral lands against centuries-old demonic enemies. All the main religious constituencies were in some way complicit in the war; accused other groups without admitting responsibility or guilt; and, even after the peace accords, have legitimized ethnic fears and ambitions, which have been manipulated by politicians.[49] Bosnia and Herzegovina remains a volatile region, in danger of slipping back into the violence and death that is so recent a memory.

According to a 2015–16 survey of the Pew Research Center, most people in Bosnia, Croatia, and Serbia are reconciled to, if not entirely accepting of, a multiethnic society. Yet "underlying signs of tension and distrust remain."[50] For example, while 95 percent of Bosnians accept members of other religious groups as citizens of their country, and 90

---

48. David Little, *Peacemakers in Action: Profiles of Religion in Conflict Resolution* (Cambridge: Cambridge University Press, 2007), 98–106.

49. Little, *Peacemakers in Action*, 106.

50. Scott Gardner, "Most in Former Yugoslavia Favor Multicultural Society, Although Some Rensions Temain," Pew Research Center, May 22, 2017, accessed February 24, 2018, https://tinyurl.com/yddmmarw.

percent accept them as neighbors, only 42 percent would accept them as members of their family. This is most true of adults with less than a secondary education. Correlatively, 68 percent of Bosnians believe "our culture is superior to theirs." Unsurprisingly, then, public trust is low across the region, with only 6 percent of Bosnians agreeing that "most people can be trusted."

Owing to resettlement after the war, many more areas of Bosnia and Herzegovina are ethnically homogenous than before the conflict. No nationwide reconciliation process has been implemented; instead, "religious symbols and narratives are habitually put in service of ethnopolitical point scoring," and the construal of religious others as a danger to one's own well-being and survival.[51] A prime barrier to political reconciliation in Bosnia-Herzegovina is the postwar construction of an educational system in which youth are segregated by ethno-religious background and taught the heritage and values of their own religion, contrasted positively with others. Those working on youth interfaith education "testify that the levels of religious knowledge of other communities is at an all-time low."[52]

Zilka Spahić Šiljak is a Bosnian academic and activist whose work focuses on gender studies, human rights, Islamic tradition, and religion and politics. She has taught at several universities in her home country and abroad and is the author of *Shining Humanity: Life Stories of Women Peacebuilders in Bosnia and Herzegovina*.[53] As she states in the introduction, the purpose of the book is to counter the narrative of the country's past and present, as dominated by violence, destruction, crimes, corruption, and ethno-nationalist rhetoric, raising up the stories of women who worked as peacebuilders during the war and now continue to build networks of connection and mutual support to reduce hostilities and enhance solidarity. This is despite the fact that, subsequent to the war, the retrenchment of each religious-ethnic group involved reassertion of traditional patriarchal roles. In order to work across identity boundaries, these women did not emphasize their religious affiliation, especially at first, yet most were inspired by religious visions of common humanity, compassion, and care.

51. Gorazd Andrejc, "Small Steps: Youth Interfaith Work in Post-Conflict Bosnia-Herzegovina," *Perspectives*, Woolf Institute, Westminster College, Cambridge (Winter 2014/15), 10.

52. Andrejc, "Small Steps."

53. Zilka Spahić Šiljak, *Shining Humanity: Life Stories of Women Peacebuilders in Bosnia and Herzegovina* (Newcastle-upon-Tyne: Cambridge Scholars, 2014), xiii. See also Zilka Spahić Šiljak. "Women Citizens and Believers as Agents of Peace in Bosnia and Herzegovina," in Hayward and Marshall, *Women, Religion and Peacebuilding*, 231–44.

Spahić Šiljak is currently the director of the TPO Foundation, Sarajevo, a nongovernmental organization supported by a Dutch foundation.[54] TPO is dedicated to the development of democratic civil society and gender equality. One of its primary missions is intercultural, multireligious, and civic education, including the introduction in schools of programs fostering a sense of common humanity, "universal" human ethical values, and greater appreciation of the values and points of contact among different religious traditions. Through an initiative called "Promotion and Integration of a Global Ethic in Education and Politics BiH," the TPO Foundation is implementing programs for elementary and secondary school teachers, both in schools and online. The content of this program emphasizes that all people share certain basic, humanistic values that transcend religious divisions. Its aim is to "build a new mindset," which can form the basis for the cooperation of people of different worldviews in the public sphere. The trainings both expand the outlooks of teachers and equip teachers with language and program materials to communicate to children the importance of mutual understanding, to overcome trauma and move toward an inclusive, democratic society. Educators are convened from divided educational institutions and encouraged to collaborate going forward. The TPO Foundation supplements and supports its education projects with efforts aimed at adults, for example, invitation to intercultural dialogue both through public venues and by bringing together members of divided groups in small communities.

Postconflict conditions and challenges in Bosnia and Herzegovina illustrate, perhaps more acutely, problems that beset virtually every situation of peacebuilding and political reconciliation. A first step is to empower victims of violence so that they become survivors and resisters. A second step is to change the mindset and behavior of perpetrators, so that they recognize the humanity of their former targets and see themselves as sharing in a common enterprise. A third step is to engage multiple social groups at the practical level in constructive civic, economic, governance, and religious activity. Even in relative "success stories" like South Africa, Rwanda, and Colombia, ambiguities, tensions, and complaints will remain, for example, about the proper political role of forgiveness (South Africa), the fairness of traditional systems of trial and judgement (Rwanda), and just punishment and/or reintegration of former combatants (Colombia). In all these cases, cooperation across religious, ethnic, and ideological boundaries is both necessary and difficult.

54. See the TPO Foundation website, accessed February 25, 2018, https://tinyurl.com/ydg blzcg.

It cannot happen successfully unless adversaries have the opportunity and will to engage together in socially reconstructive programs and institutions, for the good of all.

VIOLENCE AND PEACEBUILDING IN THE UNITED STATES

Most of the peacebuilders showcased in this chapter have been from parts of the world, usually the global South, in which conflict has ravaged society generally and in which stable and accountable government has completely broken down. Yet relatively safe and secure regions and countries are no strangers to violence, including my home country, the United States of America. In the first place, the economic, military, and environmental activities and policies of the United States have been historically and continue to be contributors to violence elsewhere. According to a 1995 report from the Berlin-based Berghof Foundation for Conflict Studies, the most important factor disposing to intrastate armed conflict is poor economic conditions (e.g., the 2008 global financial crisis, which began with poorly regulated mortgage lending in the United States), followed by repressive political systems (which have received support by the United States, e.g., Saudi Arabia), and degradation of renewable resources (as of this writing, the United States is not a signatory to the 2015 UN Paris Climate Agreement to control greenhouse gas emissions, and US corporations are involved in pollution and the extraction of mineral and other resources from countries in the global South). In addition, US military interventions in Iraq, Afghanistan, and Syria have contributed to long-term violence, instability, and displacement and fueled the rise of the so-called Islamic State (ISIS).

In the second place, the United States suffers violence within its borders, including gender-based violence and violence against ethnic, religious, and racial "minorities," intensified by rhetoric defending and promoting white Christian culture and identity as the national norm. The discussion to follow on US peacebuilders will focus on racist, white nationalist violence within the United States. But first it is important to see how these two types of American violence, internally and externally directed, are connected in a political culture that produces the kind of leadership that validates violence at home while breeding it abroad.

To state the obvious, perhaps oversimply, United States economic, military, and environmental policies depend to a great degree (even if not absolutely) on the political parties in control of the presidency, the two houses of Congress, and the appointment of members of the Supreme Court. The power of political parties depends in turn on the electorate, within a democratic process that is subject to significant economic influence through campaign donations. A major factor determining the future of US policies that affect international conflict is the direction of voter support for federal and congressional candidates and the level of voter participation in the electoral process.

In 2016, American voters elected[55] as president Donald J. Trump, a politically inexperienced businessman who ran on a platform of "America First," used racially toned campaign rhetoric, denounced the North American Free Trade Agreement and the Trans-Pacific Partnership, criticized NATO as unfair to US interests, and promised to build "a wall" barricading the country from immigrants from Latin America. As a commentator on Trump's first year in office phrased it, Trump represented a trend toward "populist isolationism" and his inaugural address portrayed "the world in darkly narrow zero-sum terms."[56]

The electoral process that produced President Trump revealed an American public that was deeply polarized, with a very significant number of citizens experiencing some mixture of resentment of political elites, personal economic stagnation if not loss of ground, a tendency to blame other racial-ethnic groups and immigrants for their adversity, and a general cultural anxiety about societal change. The latter was strong both among Trump voters who were white working class (but not among the poor, the majority of whom voted for Clinton), and those who were college-educated, white middle-class suburbanites. Majorities of the white working class say that American culture has gotten worse since the 1950s, the United States is losing its identity, and immigrants threaten the culture. Seventy-one percent of white working-class Americans are Christian, and they are significantly more likely than the general population to identify as evangelical.[57] And white Protestants in the United States are quickly moving from majority to minority status (54 percent in 2009, 45 percent in 2016), a reality that most are slow to acknowledge and accept.[58] "Besides partisan affiliation, it was cultural anxiety—feeling like a stranger in America, supporting the deportation

55. Trump's opponent, Hillary Clinton, won the popular vote. However, the electoral college, which directly elects the president on the basis of majority votes in the districts its members represent, voted for Donald Trump.

56. Eliot A. Cohen, "Trump's Lucky Year: Why the Chaos Can't Last," *Foreign Affairs* (March/April 2018), 2.

57. Daniel Cox, Rachel Lienesch, and Robert P. Jones, "Beyond Economics: Fears of Cultural Displacement Pushed the White Working Class to Trump," *PRRI/The Atlantic Report*, May 9, 2017, accessed February 23, 2018, https://tinyurl.com/yac535rd.

58. See Robert P. Jones, *The End of White Christian America* (New York: Simon & Schuster, 2016).

of immigrants, and hesitating about educational investment—that best predicted support for Trump."[59]

In an essay on immigration and Christian ethics in the Trump era, Kristin Heyer captures the consequences of these dynamics. "The administration has connected economic anxieties with anxieties over cultural shifts," provoking "the demonization of racial, ethnic, and religious minorities. Bias-related hate crimes surged following the election."[60] Within ten days of Donald Trump's election, the Southern Poverty Law Center tracked 900 bias-related incidents against minorities. The elevated rates continued in 2017, culminating in an August white nationalist rally in Charlottesville, Virginia.[61] After one year in office, Trump had lost ground in the opinion polls. Yet while 46 percent of whites disapproved of his performance, that paled in comparison to 76 percent of blacks. White evangelical Protestants gave the biggest share of religious support to Trump (72 percent), while 60 percent of Catholics and 76 percent of black Protestants disapproved.[62] Toward the end of Trump's second year, the number of Americans who recognized racism to be a national problem grew, but the increase was almost entirely among Democrats, with Republicans in agreement declining slightly from 2015. This difference was symptomatic of the partisan divide in America.[63] Party polarization made it highly unlikely that Congress would be able to work together to solve the country's problems, including racism, immigration, and gun violence.

Both before and after Trump, America struggled with its legacies of slavery, racism, and white privilege. African Americans have never enjoyed equity with white Americans in education, employment, housing, medical care, or standing before the law—regardless of the Civil Rights Act of 1964 or their individual social class or income level. African Americans have always been subject to physical attack and killing on the basis of their race, have always suffered extrajudicial violence from law

59. Emma Green, "It Was Cultural Anxiety that Drove White, Working-Class Voters to Trump," *The Atlantic*, May 9, 2017, accessed February 23, 2018, https://tinyurl.com/ybpfs7rq. See also Cox, Lienesch, and Jones, *Beyond Economics*. For data, analysis, and personal stories from a former coal-mining town in Pennsylvania, see Michele Norris, "As America Changes, Some Anxious Whites Feel Left Behind," *National Geographic*, April 2018, accessed March 21, 2018, https://tinyurl.com/y855482b.

60. Kristin E. Heyer, "Internalized Borders: Immigration Ethics in the Age of Trump," *Theological Studies* 79, no. 1 (2018): 152.

61. See "Post-election Spike in Hate Crimes Persists in 2017," *PBS NewsHour,* August 13, 2017, accessed March 2, 2018, https://tinyurl.com/ybfslzom.

62. Pew Research Center, "Trump at One Year: Job Approval, Confidence on Issues, Job Performance," accessed February 27, 2018, https://tinyurl.com/y87xcqf7.

63. Samantha Neal, "Views of Racism as a Major Problem Increase Sharply, Especially among Democrats," accessed February 28, 2018, https://tinyurl.com/y7skk2jb.

enforcement authorities, and have been subject to disproportionate and unfair rates of arrest, conviction, and incarceration for crimes.[64] According to FBI data, black people accounted for 31 percent of those killed by police, despite constituting 13 percent of the population. A 2014 report by the *Baltimore Sun* found that the city had paid about $5.7 million in settlements to over 100 people who claimed to have been beaten by the police, and the majority were black. In 2015, a black man named Freddie Gray was assaulted and pinned to the ground by Baltimore police for allegedly carrying a switchblade knife, a charge the state prosecutor later said was false. Begging for medical attention, he was restrained and driven away in a police van, later to die of spinal cord injuries suffered while in police custody. Charges were brought against six police officers, but none were ultimately convicted. In fact, police are rarely prosecuted and convicted for use of violent force.[65]

But in the second decade of the twenty-first century, police violence against unarmed black men and boys achieved unprecedented notoriety, due in large part to the ability of witnesses to capture images of police assaults on cell phone video cameras and circulate them widely via social media. Witness videos publicized the Gray case, among many others in which unarmed black men were killed by police, including Michael Brown, Erik Garner, Walter Scott, Philando Castile, and Stephon Clark. In the wake of an earlier shooting, of seventeen-year-old Trayvon Martin (unarmed and carrying snacks from a convenience store), the Florida neighborhood watch volunteer who fatally shot him was likewise acquitted.

On news of the 2013 Trayvon Martin verdict, three black community organizers from California working in immigration and prison reform, Alicia Garza, Patrice Cullors, and Opal Tometi, began to strategize a campaign, circulating the hashtag #BlackLivesMatter on Facebook and other social media.[66] In the next few years, the initiative grew to a decentralized network of over thirty local chapters, working primarily through social media, and attained a high national and international profile. This twenty-first century civil rights movement is inclusive, local, and democratic, contrasting to earlier movements that emanated from a single charismatic leader. From the beginning, the leadership of women

---

64. Michelle Alexander, *The New Jim Crow: Mass Incarceration in the Age of Colorblindness* (New York: The New Press, 2010).

65. Jewel Samad, "Police Shootings and Brutality in the US: 9 Things You Should Know," Vox, May 6, 2017, accessed February 23, 2018, https://tinyurl.com/y7a87alc. This article is the source for the data in this paragraph that follows the previous note.

66. Elizabeth Day, "#BlackLivesMatter: The Birth of a New Civil Rights Movement," *The Guardian*, July 19, 2015, accessed February 28, 2018, https://tinyurl.com/y75muy37.

and LGBTQ activists has been basic and contagious. Theologian Shawn Copeland captures the importance of Black Lives Matter founders and activists:

> the critical interruptive performances they inspire have engaged the moral imagination and courage of women and men across the country, *especially* young people of *all* races, of *differing* economic classes, cultural-ethnic backgrounds, sexual orientations, physical-ableness, religious beliefs, education and work experience. The principles of BlackLivesMatter resonate with political theology's efforts to interrogate and repair, reweave and restore the fraying webs of relations that comprise the U.S. cultural and social (i.e., the political, economic, technological) matrices.[67]

While a majority of Americans (55 percent) came to support the Black Lives Matter movement, the support remained much stronger among blacks (82 percent) and Democrats (80 percent) than among whites (52 percent) and Republicans (23 percent).[68]

Many churches and religious leaders became leaders in seeking justice for African Americans and a just peace for our racially divided and violent society. In August 2017, a white nationalist "Unite the Right" rally invaded Charlottesville, Virginia, the home of the University of Virginia. In violent clashes of rally supporters with counter-protesters and police, dozens were injured and three were killed, including two police officers and one woman who was intentionally hit by a rally-goer who ran his car into a crowd of protesters. Many Christian leaders condemned the racist violence in no uncertain terms, including Cardinal Daniel DiNardo, president of the United States Conference of Catholic Bishops; Cardinal Blase Cupich of Chicago; Russell Moore, head of political action for the Southern Baptist Convention; and Traci Blackmon, who leads the justice ministries of the United Church of Christ. As one Protestant pastor in New Jersey told his congregation, "To see American streets with people walking down doing the 'Heil Hitler' salute is just disturbing. . . . We live in a pretty politically divided country, but as followers of Jesus, we need to make sure that . . . we clearly and loudly condemn any ideology that espouses bigotry, hatred, discrimination, and violence."[69]

That being said, US Christian churches remain segregated along ethnic and racial lines. Not all pastors spoke out against the violence, or

67. M. Shawn Copeland, "Memory, #BlackLivesMatter, and Theologians," *Political Theology* 17, no. 1 (March 17, 2016), accessed March 19, 2018, https://tinyurl.com/ydh2rfxy.

68. Neal, "Views of Racism."

69. Emma Green, "How Will the Church Reckon with Charlottesville?," *The Atlantic*, August 13, 2017, accessed February 23, 2018, https://tinyurl.com/y9vuntgy.

linked it with its specific cause, racism. The majority of white evangelicals voted for Trump, and in lesser proportions, so did other Protestants, Mormons, and white non-Hispanic Catholics.[70] Some believe his election empowered white supremacist hate groups like those who rallied in Charlottesville. They represent neither the American majority nor traditional Republican values like personal liberty, small government, fiscal conservatism, and support for business. But will the majority of Americans be committed enough at the practical level to eradicate racial divisions and institutional racism in this country? Will we overcome the sense of entitlement and apathy about racism that is rooted in the fact that what is (for now) a white majority benefits from unacknowledged and unchallenged privilege? Theologian Elisabeth Vasko contends that "unethical passivity (apathy) is manifested by whites in the form of systemic unknowing, permission to escape, and ineffective guilt."[71] In an essay that, like this chapter, applies just peacebuilding norms to US racism, Alex Mikulich insists that white people must be actively accountable for white racism and privilege, and they must begin with humility, truthfulness, and solidarity to change racial attitudes among fellow whites.[72] To be a white ally in a movement for racial equality requires more than personally repudiating biased beliefs and attitudes, and it cannot be accomplished by any one person alone. The social and systemic tentacles of privilege and oppression call for collective and individual action that changes working attitudes, ingrained practices, and standing institutions by beginning to enact a different way of life.

The challenge is steep, but some religious leaders and communities are taking initiative. The Moral Monday protests in North Carolina, and the Forward Together coalition of which they are a part, are led by an African American pastor, the Reverend William J. Barber III, who is a former president of the state NAACP. Every Monday, protesters peacefully enter the state legislature, and some are arrested. The demonstrations began in 2013 as an effort by religious progressives to mobilize public opinion and motivation against the policies of a recently elected

70. Antonia Blumberg, "New Analysis Finds Clinton, Not Trump, Narrowly Won the Catholic Vote in 2016," *Huffington Post*, April 6, 2017, accessed March 1, 2018, https://tinyurl.com/y9aejwvo; and Michael J. O'Loughlin, "New Data Suggest Clinton, Not Trump, Won Catholic Vote," *America*, April 6, 2017, accessed March 1, 2018, https://tinyurl.com/ydgdv9oy.

71. Elisabeth T. Vasko, *Beyond Apathy: A Theology for Bystanders* (Minneapolis: Fortress, 2015), 73.

72. Alex Mikulich, "Becoming Authentically Catholic and Truly Black: On the Condition of the Possibility of a Just Peace Approach to Anti-Black Violence," in *Just Peace Ethic: Virtue-Based and Case Refined*, ed. Eli S. McCarthy (Washington, DC: Georgetown University Press, forthcoming).

Republican governor who, together with Republicans newly in control of both state houses, was rolling back civil rights and social welfare legislation, including benefits of the Affordable Care Act. In 2016, the governor was defeated for reelection, and Democrats regained control of the state Supreme Court and Attorney General's office.

Barber's political vision is oriented theologically and pastorally by the fact that the Bible is far more focused on how "the least of these" are treated (Matthew 25) than on abortion, same-sex marriage, and prayer in schools. Barber and the Moral Monday movement are most centrally concerned with the multifarious manifestations of racism, but their portfolio is not limited, extending to the environment, tax cuts, abortion rights, public education, cuts to unemployment benefits, and voting rights. Barber's movement has since its inception drawn participation from many races, professional walks of life, religious traditions, and even political parties. The marches have grown into a multiracial and multireligious effort, involving thousands, and inspiring similar action in other states. Barber explains that Forward Together and Moral Mondays exist and thrive "so preachers can fight for fifteen and workers can say 'black lives matter,' and a white woman can stand with her black sister for voting rights, and a black man can stand for a woman's right to health care, and LGBTQ folk can stand for religious liberty, and straight people can stand up for . . . queer people, and a Muslim imam can stand with an undocumented worker."[73]

Deep and sustainable change requires a coalition that is broad-based and ready to act. In Barber's analysis, political divisions in the United States in the era of Trump are just another iteration of a reliable American political strategy: bar a politics of solidarity by dividing working and middle class by race, stir up nativism and animosity toward immigrants, and distract from the economic advantages that accrue to the winners.[74] The 2017 annual march drew the largest crowd ever, 80,000 people; and in May 2017, Barber resigned the presidency of the NAACP to focus his efforts on building a national movement.[75]

73. Jedediah Purdy, "North Carolina's Long Moral March and Its Lessons for the Trump Resistance," *The New Yorker*, February 17, 2017, accessed February 28, 2018, https://tinyurl.com/yaxpgtfc. See also Cleve R. Wootson, "Rev. William Barber Builds a Moral Movement," *Washington Post*, June 29, 2017, accessed February 28, 2018, https://tinyurl.com/y8cs2ryt.

74. Wootson, "Rev. William Barber."

75. Paul Blest, "Over 80,000 People Joined the Biggest-Ever Moral March in North Carolina," *The Nation*, February 13, 2017, accessed February 28, 2018, https://tinyurl.com/y8zetyu7; Jelani Cobb, "William Barber Takes On Poverty and Race in the Age of Trump," *The New Yorker*, May 14, 2018, accessed May 14, 2018, https://tinyurl.com/ybwy7oez.

William Barber has a white Catholic counterpart in the north, Cardinal Blase Cupich of Chicago. Following Pope Francis's World Day of Peace Message on nonviolence, and in the midst of an epidemic of gun violence primarily afflicting Chicago's black communities,[76] the Archdiocese of Chicago established an Anti-Violence Initiative directed to interreligious and interracial peacebuilding in its own streets and neighborhoods. The Initiative's mandate covers not only actions against guns, but also programs proven effective in lifting people out of poverty. The $250,000 funding for the new foundation was provided by the cardinal's discretionary charitable fund, money to be used in part to expand mentoring, educational, and job programs under Catholic auspices and to partner with non-Catholic agencies.

In a news conference to launch the program, Cardinal Cupich implored civic, education, and religious leaders and "all people of good will" to make nonviolence a practical and local strategy for peace. "The causes of the violence we are seeing in our city are complex and deep seated, but I have a strong belief, based on the good will and the many dedicated efforts of our civic and religious leaders, that these causes can be addressed and the suffering can end if we all work together." Thus proclaimed Cardinal Cupich at a press conference in a church-sponsored community center dedicated to safety from gang violence and drugs, and providing social services.[77] At the event, he read a supporting letter from Pope Francis linking violence to discrimination and indifference, proclaiming that "nonviolence is not an unattainable dream, but a path that has produced decisive results," and commending the example and words of Martin Luther King Jr. Ten days later the cardinal led a Good Friday "Peace Walk" to commemorate the city's murder victims. In early 2018, Cardinal Cupich appointed Phil Andrew, former director of the Illinois Council Against Handgun Violence and FBI veteran with experience in Chicago, as the Archdiocese's director of violence prevention.

An important lesson from Chicago is that visionary leaders often build on the efforts of others and rely on extensive support for the implementation of their ideals. These others do not always get the credit and publicity they deserve. Two years before the cardinal established the archdiocesan anti-violence foundation, Chicago's black Catholic deacons dedicated a Sunday to preaching against violence in African Amer-

76. Over 3,500 people were shot in Chicago in 2017, 664 fatally, including seven killed by on-duty police officers. See Mitchell Armentrout, "Chicago Homicides Down Sharply in 2017, Still over 650 Slain," *Chicago Sun-Times*, December 31, 2017, accessed March 1, 2018, https://tinyurl.com/yaepre6b.

77. David Gibson, "Cardinal Cupich Unveils Anti-Violence Initiative," *National Catholic Reporter*, April 4, 2017, accessed March 1, 2018, https://tinyurl.com/y77966bt.

ican parishes across the city. At the end of Mass they revealed T-shirts reading "All Lives Matter," and led prayer and protests in the streets outside the churches. A letter signed by LeRoy Gill, chair of the Black Catholic Deacons of Chicago, called the newly appointed Archbishop Cupich to join the Black Catholic Deacons in addressing "violence, distrust, and prejudice."[78]

The success of the cardinal's efforts in that direction are interdependent with those of many working in Catholic parishes and educational institutions. One example is St. Sabina's, a primarily African American parish pastored by the Reverend Michael Pfleger, who gained public attention for his support for the presidential candidacy of Barack Obama. Also key to the parish's leadership and its public role is St. Sabina's full-time pastoral associate (since 2000), Dr. Kimberly M. Lymore, who also directs the Tolton Scholars Program at the Catholic Theological Union. The Tolton Program partners with the archdiocese to prepare black Catholic women and men for lay ministry among black Catholics. According to Dr. Lymore, "Racism is in the DNA of America, so therefore it is in the Roman Catholic Church," and it is being expressed more overtly since Trump's election. "We get a lot of hate calls in our office [at St. Sabina]. The callers usually identify themselves as a 'devout Catholic.' We have a lot of work to do in the church in order to dismantle the racism that is present."[79] She—along with many other black Catholic lay women and men in Chicago—is on the front lines of nonviolent but active, determined, and prophetic resistance.[80]

Of course, to produce significant and sustainable social change, it will be necessary not only to condemn and resist direct violence and killing (including better regulation of gun availability), but also the attitudes that lead some "devout Catholics" to condemn antiracism activism and lead others to disengage from the issue, or engage in only a peripheral or impersonal way. For that, it will be necessary to approach, communicate, and even empathize with those individuals and the circles to which they belong. Just as in Bosnia and Herzegovina (and numerous other places), people who enact, defend, or simply ignore violence in the United States

78. Heidi Schlumpf, "Chicago's Black Catholic Deacons 'Lift Each Other Up,'" *National Catholic Reporter*, January 24, 2015, accessed February 23, 2018, https://tinyurl.com/ybrh4zs2.

79. Gordon Nary, "Profiles in Catholicism: An Interview of Kimberly M. Lymore, M.Div., D.Min.," *CatholicProfiles.net*, accessed February 23, 2018, https://tinyurl.com/y7c9w3a2.

80. For leads and insights concerning the activism of black Catholics in Chicago, I thank Dr. C. Vanessa White, a Catholic Theological Union faculty member, scholar, administrator, and spiritual and pastoral worker who preceded Dr. Lymore as director of the Tolton Program. She received the Juan Diego Award for Distinguished Service in the Church from the National Association of Lay Ministry in 2015 as well as the Augustus Tolton Award for Ministerial Service in the Archdiocese of Chicago in 2002.

are working out of a worldview, symbol system, and set of social practices that are part of identity formation. While not necessarily impervious to challenge on the basis of logic and data, they have a hold that extends to loyalties, emotions, imagination, and a basic sense of belonging and security. The prophetic voice of resistance is necessary, and the recognition and empowerment of those who are violence's targets is essential, as we see with the community action of black lay Catholics in Chicago. But an equally important step is to convert those who have the interest in and power to maintain the status quo—and who also may have fears and anxieties about displacement from the social environment that until now has been familiar, secure, and taken-for-granted. For this reason, Rev. Barber, Cardinal Cupich, and the members of their movements are working across multiple sectors of society.

One religious leader who is a longstanding advocate for racial equality in the United States but is not a Pope Francis appointed bishop like Cupich, and who is not like Cupich and Barber readily identified with "progressive" causes, is Archbishop William Lori, of Baltimore, another racially divided city torn by gun violence and riots. Mark Gray, a polling expert who interprets data on Catholics and voting, observes that Catholics, like other Americans, are attracted to partisan causes, "so if you're a Democrat and a Catholic, you may strongly emphasize Pope Francis' statements about climate change or the preferential option for the poor. . . . If you are a Republican and a Catholic, life issues may be the most important to you."[81] It can reasonably be inferred then, that while Cupich's advocacy for nonviolent resistance to racism might appeal to Democrats, who already see racism as a national problem, Catholic Republicans, who are much less sympathetic to Black Lives Matter and the need for a new conversation about race, might see his message as outside of their zone of identity, concern, and comfort.

Lori, however, who serves as the Supreme Chaplain of the Knights of Columbus, has a track record on the more typically "Catholic Republican" side of the ledger. Appealing to all, one hopes, he has taken swift action in clerical sex abuse cases, and he was one of the first US prelates to establish a local review board. He also joined many other bishop's in denouncing President Trump's plan to terminate DACA (Deferred Action for Childhood Arrivals). Yet he publicly and actively opposed provisions in the Affordable Care Act that would require private health insurance plans to cover contraception and abortion, opposed similar services for trafficking victims receiving protection under Catholic auspices, opposed requirements that Catholic agencies receiving federal

81. O'Loughlin, "New Data."

funding provide contraception and condoms as prophylactics against AIDS, and supported the Defense of Marriage Act that would have barred same-sex couples from civil marriage. Given this profile, Lori's leadership on race has the potential to attract a hearing from those who might feel threatened by Black Lives Matter, or at least not see themselves as active participants in the cause of racial justice.

As a young priest, Lori asked to be assigned to an African American parish to learn more about a Catholic culture and its challenges that was outside his own experience. During the 2015 explosion of violence in Baltimore, Lori visited one of the affected neighborhoods, and saw a priest in the street with a broom, cleaning up the debris—not the steps of his church, but the neighborhood space. Soon others joined him with brooms and rakes, and in this Lori found an important lesson about addressing racial tensions. He shared with other Baltimore faith leaders in a 2017 panel on "violence, faith, and policing," describing their "partnership" as helping the community move forward.[82]

In his 2018 pastoral letter, issued in commemoration of the fiftieth anniversary of the death of Martin Luther King, Lori thanks members of the archdiocesan Office of Black Catholic Ministries for their efforts to educate young people about the accomplishments and legacy of Dr. King, and he recognizes the efforts and support of many in local government, faith communities, education and nonprofits, and well as in the neighborhoods, to birth hope through creative action. Speaking for and to other white people, Lori names "the sin of racism" that "has tarnished the soul of our society for so long that racist attitudes can be deeply embedded in our subconscious, such that we may hardly know they are there." He repudiates coarse and vitriolic public rhetoric. He calls for action on "deep and systemic" problems spawning despair and violence, such as lack of education, housing, and employment; easily available illegal weapons; drug abuse and gangs; and "disintegration of the family."[83] He then develops the contemporary relevance of King's six principles of nonviolent action, concluding with the reconciliation of "opposing parties" in US political and racial debates: "we should not be competing with one another . . . but rather cooperating, networking and pooling our wisdom and resources for the good of others." Realizing this goal in Baltimore are organizations like Catholic Charities' Safe Steps, the grass-

82. Rhina Guidos, "Panel: When Community Tensions Erupt, Faith Can Help Diffuse Violence," *National Catholic Reporter*, May 4, 2017, accessed February 14, 2018, https://tinyurl.com/yae8c5ag.

83. Archbishop William E. Lori, "The Enduring Power of Dr. Martin Luther King Jr.'s Principles of Nonviolence: A Pastoral Reflection," February 2018, accessed February 14, 2018, https://tinyurl.com/yczraffa.

roots thinktank Leaders of a Beautiful Struggle, Showing Up for Racial Justice, which organizes white people, and the Harriet Tubman House, which revitalizes local communities through projects including artistic opportunities and neighborhood gardens.

Martin Luther King Jr. was an advocate and example of nonviolent resistance to injustice. He was convinced that "the arc of the moral universe is long, but it bends toward justice."[84] He did not believe that outcome was to be left entirely in the hands of God or fate, however. He took decisive public action that forced a confrontation between a segregationist culture that tacitly promoted physical violence against African Americans and a rising tide of black confidence and empowerment that, accompanied by some white allies, was intervening decisively in US history. Yet King is sometimes remembered more for his legacy of nonviolence than for that of effective confrontation.

In *Racial Justice and the Catholic Church*, Bryan Massingale delineates in detail the difficulty of eradicating racism ingrained in the mental furniture, language, and daily behavior of white Christians (even in church), showing how it retains its grip and force, even long after it is flatly contradictory to clear Church teaching about human equality and respect.[85] The teaching fails to hit the ground. In his 2010 Presidential address to the Catholic Theological Society of America, Massingale questioned whether a necessary conversation partner for Christian theology and ethics is Malcolm X.[86] Christianity, according to Malcom, has with its white imagery of God and segregationist practices, brainwashed both whites and blacks into a false consciousness of white superiority. "Little wonder, then, that many white Christians regard 'white,' 'Christian,' and 'American' as interchangeable and even equivalent identities."[87]

It is not adequate, according to Massingale, to see Christian compassion, solidarity, and work for the oppressed as smoothly convergent values, since the arena in which they must be actualized is one of social conflict. Echoing not only Malcolm X but implicitly Reinhold Niebuhr, he insists that "authentic transformation cannot evade social conflict, resistance and recalcitrance if it is to be of genuine service in the quest for social transformation." It should factor in not only the conversion of

84. This line, quoted from the nineteenth-century clergyman Theodore Parker, was written by King in a 1958 article in *The Gospel Messenger*, a publication of the Church of the Brethren, and delivered in a 1964 baccalaureate sermon at Wesleyan College in Middletown, CT. See "The Arc of the Moral Universe Is Long, but It Bends toward Justice," *The Quote Investigator*, accessed March 1, 2018, https://tinyurl.com/yabnqr64.

85. Bryan Massingale, *Racial Justice and the Catholic Church* (Maryknoll, NY: Orbis, 2010).

86. Bryan Massingale, "*Vox Victimarum Vox Dei*: Malcom X as Neglected 'Classic' for Catholic Theological Reflection," *CTSA Proceedings* 65 (2010): 63–88.

87. Massingale, "*Vox Victimarum Vox Dei*," 76, 78, respectively.

the powerful, but also "the potential power of the dispossessed."[88] Yet, concludes Massingale, the lamentable and sinful conditions that marked America during the lifetimes of Martin and Malcom still exist. He names several. Most people (or at least most white people) would probably regard "racial violence and hate crimes" as the most frightening and urgent. But Massingale concludes with the heartbreaking example of an experiment in which small black children were asked to say whether white dolls or black dolls were the ones they most "liked" or were "nice" (white dolls were chosen by a majority), then selected a black doll as the one that was most like them.

Reaffirming the difficult realities portrayed by Bryan Massingale, Kelly Brown Douglas reflects personally and theologically on the reality that—over half a century after King's 1963 "I Have a Dream" speech, which she saw televised as a six-year-old child—racism in America is strong enough to make her worry and lament what the death of Trayvon Martin means for her own black son, Desmond.[89] Reaching to the roots of current events, Douglas documents a myth of white Anglo-Saxon exceptionalism that has infected America's identity since before the days of the "founding fathers."[90] But black life is not circumscribed by this culture; it defies the culture by living in a different and prophetic way, by living as "embodied prophetic testimony" to the resurrection.[91] To overcome its racist narrative, America must forge an honest moral memory of its past, let go of present white presumptions of superiority, affirm at a practical and not just notional level the humanity of all, and most importantly, recognize that faith is not about ideas, but about "commitment to a certain way of 'living and moving and having our being' in the world."[92] That requires a moral imagination "driven by the future," an imagination with which "one is able to live proleptically, that is, as if the new heaven and new earth were already here."[93]

US PEACEBUILDERS IN GLOBAL PERSPECTIVE

Comparing the situation in the United States to the international contexts discussed in the first part of this chapter, some important differences stand out. The most important is that we have a *relatively* functional

88. Massingale, "*Vox Victimarum Vox Dei*," 83.

89. Kelly Brown Douglas, *Stand Your Ground: Black Bodies and the Justice of God* (Maryknoll, NY: Orbis, 2015), 207–9.

90. Douglas, *Stand Your Ground*, 117.

91. Douglas, *Stand Your Ground*, 220.

92. Douglas, *Stand Your Ground*, 224.

93. Douglas, *Stand Your Ground*, 225.

government and judicial system, which defines our first challenge, not as creating public institutions, but as surfacing and defining the ways existing institutions do *not* serve equality and justice for all groups of people, most especially (but not exclusively) African Americans. Levels of violence in some urban areas domestically can approach the level of international war zones. At the same time, the commonalities in the kinds of responsive action required to meet this violence are striking and obvious. To reiterate briefly: *Nonviolent resistance works*, especially if it is unafraid of conflict and grows into a social movement. Black Lives Matter is a good example of nonviolent *resistance*, expressed partly through appropriate indignation and anger. The movement's courageous, confrontational, and black-affirming tactics and message have drawn public and media attention to the plight and political power of African Americans. Black Lives Matter is now moderately or strongly supported by the majority of Americans. What is still needed is action by white allies who take responsibility for personal and systemic racist bias, and who are more committed than in the past to surfacing and confronting the direct violence of the few and the complicit disengagement of the many. *Violent conflict leaves deep wounds*, as is evident in the impunity enjoyed by perpetrators, the continuing lack of public acknowledgement of rights violated, the "standing victory" of the perpetrators, the internalized racism of innocent children, and the grief and lament of parents sorrowing for their children. Not to be overlooked are the social and psychological wounds borne by white people whose distorted consciousness and fear prevent authentic human flourishing.

Peacebuilding is multidimensional, fallible, and involves moral dilemmas. The peace processes in North Carolina, Chicago, and Baltimore embody good-faith and comprehensive, yet fragile and fallible, processes of reform. Given the nature of racist violence in this country, the need for moral courage seems more salient than the reality of moral dilemmas. However, dilemmas will certainly arise in choices of resource allocation, and even more clearly in the political activism, negotiation, and compromise that will be a part of the consensus-building process toward more just laws, policies, and practices. Moral ambiguities are also part of the challenge to maintain compassionate connection among different constituencies (Republicans and Democrats, black and white Christians), even when there is pain, misunderstanding, unrecognized complicity in injustice, and the responsibility to prioritize the needs of the most vulnerable.

Women are essential peacebuilders, as we see in the creative, bold, and effective founders of the Black Lives Matter movement. Women in ecclesial settings are active peacebuilders too against American violence, both external and internal, as we have already seen in the ministry of Kimberly Lymore. The Academy of Catholic Hispanic Theologians of the United States (ACHTUS) has enjoyed both male and female leaders, and the top four officers in 2017–18 were women (María Teresa Dávila, Jaqueline Hidalgo, Neomi DeAnda, and Elsie Miranda). After the Charlottesville violence, ACHTUS released a statement of solidarity with the Black Catholic Theological symposium, on "the recent surge in racist violence."[94] Some women peacebuilders work in the just peace context and explicitly make the connection between the internal and external effects of violence in the United States, and between US actions and policy and violent situations globally. Marie Dennis is cochair (with Bishop Kevin Dowling of South Africa) of Pax Christi International, was a principal organizer of the 2016 Rome conference on nonviolence and just peace,[95] and for fifteen years worked with the Maryknoll missioners to bring their global experience into US public opinion and into the policies of the United States, United Nations, and international financial institutions.[96] In 2016, Pax Christi released a statement called "We Cry Out for Racial Justice in the United States," declaring "No Justice, No Peace," committing to racial justice education and activism.[97] Rose Berger is an editor at *Sojourners* magazine, a member of Pax Christi, and a founding member of the Catholic Nonviolence Initiative. In 2010, she published a book about a nine-year-old African American child who was shot and killed in front of his apartment building in her Columbia Heights neighborhood in Washington, DC.[98] Berger says that in the United States "few face ISIS or North Korea, but many deal with drug houses, crime and gun violence in neighborhoods. . . . If the church could make its nonviolence teaching a prominent part of daily life . . . it could help with such grassroots problems."[99] The sustaining role of

94. Academy of Catholic Hispanic Theologians of the United States, "CHTUS/BCTS Statement Regarding the Most Recent Surge in Racist Hate Crimes in the United States," September 4, 2017, accessed March 19, 2018, https://tinyurl.com/yamlj6m7.

95. For reflections and papers emerging from the conference, see Marie Dennis, ed., *Choosing Peace: The Catholic Church Returns to Gospel Nonviolence* (Maryknoll, NY: Orbis, 2018).

96. The *National Catholic Reporter* named Dennis Person of the Year in 2016. See NCR Editorial Staff, "Editorial: NCR'S Person of the Year for 2016," December 17, 2016, accessed March 15, 2018, https://tinyurl.com/ybwjg7d9.

97. Pax Christi USA, "We Cry Out for Racial Justice in the United States," November 15, 2016, accessed March 15, 2018, https://tinyurl.com/ya98un8j.

98. Rose Marie Berger, *Who Killed Donte Manning? The Story of an American Neighborhood* (Baltimore, MD: Apprentice House, 2010). See also Rose Marie Berger, "Who Killed Donte Manning?," *Sojourners*, January 2011, accessed March 15, 2018, https://tinyurl.com/ydy6l48m.

99. Ed Langlois, "She Yearns for a Church That Leads on Nonviolence," *Catholic Sentinel*, February 2, 2018.

women in churches' efforts to overcome violence and build community deserves more recognition, even in faith traditions reluctant to formalize women's equal leadership, like the Roman Catholic Church.

Re-formative social practices are key to sustainable peace. This criterion of peacebuilding runs into the huge challenge of knitting together transformative movements across identity divides that are also chasms of misunderstanding, ongoing grievances, and even enmity. That is why the leadership held up in this chapter is portrayed more in practical terms than in intellectual or strictly theological ones. William Barber, Blase Cupich, William Lori, Alicia Garza, Patrice Cullors, Opal Tometi, Marie Dennis, and Rose Berger—along with the grassroots and community movements that make their work possible—are all in different ways bringing adversaries together by attracting them at the practical level to shared ideals, common goals, and most importantly, opportunities to join together in forging new relationships of partnership and action.

Intercultural and interreligious cooperation is necessary for this process to be successful, as is well-attested in North Carolina, Chicago, and Baltimore. The "cultures" of blacks and whites, Democrats and Republicans, Christians and Muslims, Jews or other faiths, are different; in fact, this is one of the biggest factors in the polarization that US society and politics today experience. Alleviating this polarization will require confronting identity-based conflicts without minimizing or disparaging difference. The goal is what Daniel Philpott calls political reconciliation: the constitution or reconstitution of a society that is just in the sense that victims, perpetrators, citizens, institutions of government, civil society groups, and religious groups that have been involved in political injustices are now united going forward in shared understandings of, commitments to, and practices of human rights, democracy, and the rule of law.[100] Political reconciliation requires the social institutionalization of relations of respect, but not necessarily full personal understanding, forgiveness, or friendship—though these aspirations may eventually be realized.

PEACEBUILDING AND HOPE

Peacebuilders carry on despite profound obstacles and devastating losses. They carry on even when they do not meet with success, and even when their efforts risk death. How can they maintain hope when all the odds are stacked against them? There is a simple, even platitudinous, answer readily heard in Christian contexts: hope is a divine gift, transforming

100. Philpott, *Just and Unjust Peace*, 58.

our human reality.[101] Hope is humanly inexplicable, and does not depend on any real-world conditions; it is purely and simply a work of grace. I believe this answer is too facile and, in important ways, false. It is true that hope *is* a gift of God—but God's presence or "grace" is often if not always mediated through worldly realities and human relationships, such as women's peace demonstrations in Liberia, the Hormiguitas de la Paz in Colombia, and the black church in the United States. God's grace-filling presence is in the body of Christ, the actual community of solidarity in God's presence as Spirit and in resurrection life. The Christian virtue of "eschatological" hope not only bestows trust and courage from beyond ourselves but it is enhanced and increased by practical action for this-worldly goals.[102] Action for peace and justice in history intensifies our relation to God and makes real the presence of God's reign. Building peace increases in us the virtue of hope, of both a this-worldly and an eschatological kind.[103]

As religious peacebuilders are quick to testify, it is God's grace that enables them to work in solidarity with others, and relations of solidarity and compassion mediate grace. God's grace does not reach us apart from our social identities, or at least not only so. To Christians in Congo, Myanmar, or Colombia, in Berlin in 1943, New York in 1965, Memphis in 1968, or Charlottesville in 2017, authentic Christian identity requires political action for a just and peaceful world. Participation in collective action inspires and sustains a hopeful vision in which this world is really possible.

In the words of the Mexican American theologian Maria Pilar Aquino, for oppressed peoples, "hope is not a far-off ideal or a palliative. It is a deep spiritual force—because it comes from the Spirit—that encourages the poor in their struggles. It is an objective reality, an anticipation of God's justice and love as experienced in the life, death, and resurrection of Jesus," and in his ministry of the reign of God.[104] Kelly Brown Douglas reinforces this point in an especially powerful way, testifying that

---

101. On the interpretation of Christian hope as an infused virtue see Thomas Aquinas, *Summa theologiae*, II-II, qq. 17–21.

102. Dominic Doyle, "*Spe salvi* on Eschatological and Secular Hope," *Theological Studies* 71, no. 2 (2010): 350–79. See also Dominic Doyle, "Changing Hopes: The Theological Virtue of Hope in Thomas Aquinas, John of the Cross, and Karl Rahner," *Irish Theological Quarterly* 77, no. 1 (2012): 18–36. Laurie Johnston argues similarly, on the basis of *Pacem in terris*, that "peace is both divine gift and human task" and that "Humans can—at least sometimes—shift the dynamics of war and violence, and therefore we have a responsibility to try to do so." See Laurie Johnston, "*Pacem in terris* and Catholic Peacebuilding," *Journal of Catholic Social Thought* 11, no. 1 (2014): 94–95.

103. Doyle, "*Spe salvi*," 369–70.

104. Maria Pilar Aquino, *Our Cry for Life: Feminist Theology from Latin America* (Maryknoll, NY: Orbis, 1993), 107.

black faith took root "in the context of bondage." Black faith witnesses to the reality that God "is present even in the midst of the particular brutalities of 'living while black,' and that God wills people to be free.[105] The paradox of the cross is central because it enables faithful life to go on in the midst of contradictions. Even after the Trayvon Martin verdict, "no one lashed out at God. No one doubted God."[106] There is "an inherent absurdity in black faith," which is exactly why it is an indispensable witness to the possibility of faith and the character of God. This faith testifies to God's presence and promises as real, reliable, and existentially validated, even when they are not borne out by "the facts."[107] Privileged people who despair of changing longstanding injustices, or who see them as challenging the existence of a good God, might have something to learn from those who know the crucible of radical suffering and proclaim a living faith and hope.

From the instances cited in this chapter, it is obvious that peacebuilding starts with the desire, determination, and courage of people who are willing to take risks. Peacebuilders are driven by a passion to live in peace, but also by a faith and trust that people can make peace and build a life together. Peacebuilders empower individuals and communities to name and resist violence. They voice and magnify the agency of those who are targets and survivors of violence. They reach out in solidarity across religious, racial-ethnic, and cultural divides.

Peacebuilders go beyond personal acts and relationships, creating community and larger social institutions that encourage and support just peace. In the real world, peacemaking or peacebuilding must *usually* proceed in circumstances where it is precisely justice, equal respect, and human rights that are sorely lacking or entirely absent. To act when oppressive power makes action risky, or to take risks for those who have no power, is a hallmark of God's inbreaking reign. Taking the first step can break apart violent cycles and bring enemies to recognize one another's humanity.

It is important to stress that peacebuilding must issue in social practices that become broad and deep enough to resocialize former adversaries into coexistence, political reconciliation, and, in the ideal case, interpersonal empathy, respect, and forgiveness. Peacebuilding is a process that is always marred by incompleteness and moral ambiguity. The wounds of war and human rights violations are deep. It is difficult to reconcile

105. Douglas, *Stand Your Ground*, 164.
106. Douglas, *Stand Your Ground*, 168.
107. Douglas, *Stand Your Ground*, 170.

enemies, establish social trust, honestly face complicity and corruption, make reparations to victims, and overcome an ethos of impunity.[108]

Peacebuilding is thus a practical strategy of hope. Peacebuilding demonstrates the possibility of and way to hope in the face of over-whelming adversity. Peacebuilding is sustained by the actions of coura-geous individuals who resist the oppressive and violent activities and expectations in which everyone around them seems trapped. But peace-building also requires the action of groups like the Catholic Peacebuild-ing Network, black church initiatives, the World Council of Churches, and all those in worldwide religious traditions inspired by divine care, compassion, mercy, and righteousness. Peacebuilding consists most specifically in risky yet hopeful practices of solidarity and change. These practices engage not only the oppressed and the innocent, but also oppressors and sinners, who can come to imagine and embody reality differently. Practical peacebuilding strategies, by reaching out to victims and to adversaries within ongoing violence, already recognize human dignity, build social capital, and shape the building blocks of justice even if their short-term fate is defeat. Thus, even when there seem to be no rational or empirical justifications for the permanent cessation of violence, peacebuilding is a practical strategy of hope for conversion, transformation, and justice. And, though not guaranteed, peacebuilding is demonstrably and amply rewarded by concrete instances of success, when common humanity is recognized and solidarity renewed, when God's healing presence is among us, and peace with justice seen and touched.

---

108. Daniel Philpott, "A Catholic Ethic for Peacebuilding in the Political Order," in Schreiter, Appleby, and Powers, *Peacebuilding*, 92–124.

Index

O'Meara, Thomas F., 140n1
Omer, Atalia, 173n1, 25n2
Onaiyekan, John, 7
On Christian Doctrine (Augustine), 101n44, 106
On First Principles (Origen), 84, 87
On Idolatry (Tertullian), 76–77, 81
On Temporal Authority (Luther), 183, 185
On the Crown (Tertullian), 76
On the Freedom of a Christian (Luther), 212
On the Sermon on the Mount (Augustine), 107, 108
ontology, 189, 202
On War against the Turk (Luther), 198
Opongo, Elias Omondi, 20, 320, 338n41
Origen: and allegorical exegesis, 77, 84; and early Christian pacifism, 56, 74, 82–89, 249, 268; and importance of tradition, 86; on just war, 73; on legitimacy of government, 87; on piety, 87–88, 91; on violence of the military, 87
Origin of the Idea of Crusade (Erdmann), 215
Owens, xi–xii, 9n21

pacifism, 1–8, 31–36, 283–86; four kinds of, 248n2; and just war, 92–94; nuclear, 3, 248n2; as ongoing communal way of life, 17; in outline, 14–17; as perennially attractive and worthy, 5; as practice, 17; realistic, 3; typically derived from religious premises and commitments, 22. *See also* Anabaptists; Christian pacifism; humanism; just war; peacebuilding; Quakers
pacifists, 247–50, 280–82; belief in discipleship permitting no compromise with violence, 32; first Christians as, 5; and moral dilemma to use force, 33, 35; and moral responsibility to use force as power to deter, 35. *See also* Anabaptists; humanists; Quakers
paternalism, 200; violent, 114
patriarchy, 46n30, 86, 334, 343
Pax Christi International, x, 17, 321, 323, 328, 359
Pax Romana, 43, 71
peace: analysis of, 6; ethics of, 4; just, 18; liberal, 18; and politics, 275–80; possibility of, 37–39; Quakers testimony, 275–80; requires rebuilding of civil society, 7; requires transformation of attitudes and relationships, 7
peacebuilding, 1–8, 31–36, 167–68, 283–86; as alternative to more traditional forms of just war and pacifism, vii; belief in transforming conflicts nonviolently, 3; and biblical ministry of reconciliation, 36; can be either religious in inspiration or secular, 23; in Catholic social teaching, 312–24; and Christian discipleship, 8; consists of risky yet hopeful practices of solidarity and change, 363; defined, 7; diversity of, 21; global, 7, 36, 357–60; as on the ground efforts by people in communities, 5–6, 36; as newer

theology. *See* neoorthodox theology; scholastic theology
TPO Foundation, 344
Truce of God, 10, 220
Trump, Donald J., 319, 346–47, 350, 354
Tudor, Steven, 127
Tyconius, 107
Tyler, William R., 253n12

Union Theological Seminary, 295
United Church of Christ, 18, 292n34, 349
United Nations, 18, 20, 329
United States Institute for Peace (USIP), 18, 327n7
Urban II (pope), 219–21, 223–24
Urban VI (pope), 228
USIP. *See* United States Institute for Peace (USIP)

Vasko, Elizabeth, 350
Vatican Congregation for Justice and Peace, x
Vietnam War, x, 15, 24, 305, 310
Villa-Vicenzio, Charles, 331
vindictive violence, 66
violent conflict, ix, x, 34, 326, 329; in religion's defense, 118–21
Vitoria, Francisco de, 169–71

Waldron, Jeremy, 34
Walters, LeRoy, 170n99
Walzer, Michael, 125, 151, 154n52, 237, 294n41
war: analysis of, 6; bias against, 31; Christian justification of, 109–17; and Christian morality, 154–58; and common good, 32, 139–41, 145–54, 158, 169–72; conditions for, 3–4;

entails profound evil, 33; ethics of, 4, 34–35, 37, 87, 146, 291; fought in name of Christendom, 197; God of, 39–42; and gospel, 154–58; justification of, 28, 109–17, 145–54, 170, 172, 209–10, 312; as moral dilemma, 129, 160–66, 172; morality justification for, 152; morality of, 146, 158; political authority and, 191–99; as punishment, 111n100, 112–13; shared presumption against, 8n17, 26–31, 33, 171, 312–13; in some situations an unambiguous good, 33. *See also* civil wars; just war; nuclear war
Warning to His Dear German People (Luther), 196
Watt, Alan J., 117n130
weapons of mass destruction (WMDs), 11, 320
Weddle, Meredith, 278–79
Weiss, Johannes, 48–49
Weizsacker, Richard von, 130
white privilege, 347
Whitmore, Todd, 331, 339
Why Civil Resistance Works (Chenoweth and Stephan), 327
Wijze, Stephen de, 125
Williams, Bernard: on moral conflicts, 122–23; on moral dilemma, 124; on moral luck, 123; on remorse, 127
Williams, Dolores, 166
Williams, George Hunston, 256, 258n36
Winright, Tobias, 9n21, 12n28, 13, 115n122, 319n145, 321n153, 333n27
Wittenberg Church Order, 190

WMDs. *See* weapons of mass
    destruction (WMDs)
womanist theologians, 166
women, i, 10, 16n42, 41, 44n22,
    190, 206–7, 221, 225, 226,
    270–71, 274–75, 304n86, 329;
    as essential to peacebuilding,
    326, 328–29, 333–38, 340–41,
    343–45, 348–49; 358–60
World Council of Churches, 18,
    363
World Day of Peace Message, 321
World War I, 48, 284, 293, 306, 314

World War II, 17, 24, 30, 130, 132,
    283, 286, 293–94, 308–9, 314

xenophobia, 3

Yoder, John Howard, 16, 35, 67,
    249, 268–69, 285; abuse of
    women, 16n42; pacifism of, 25,
    32
Younan, Munib A., 211

Zwingli, Ulrich, 183, 198–99,
    257–58